GO!
Premium Media Site

Improve your grade with hands-on tools and resources!

- Master *Key Terms* to expand your vocabulary.
- Assess your knowledge with fun *Crossword Puzzles* and *Flipboards*, which let you flip through the definitions of the key terms and match them with the correct term.
- Prepare for exams by taking practice quizzes in the *Online Chapter Review*.
- Download *Student Data Files* for the application projects in each chapter.
- Answer matching and multiple choice questions to test what you learned in each chapter.

And for even more tools, you can access the following Premium Resources using your Access Code. Register now to get the most out of *GO!*.

- *Student Training Videos* for each Objective have been created by the author - a real instructor teaching the same types of courses that you take.*
- *GO! to Work* videos are short interviews with workers showing how they use Office in their job.*
- *GO! for Job Success* videos related to the projects in the chapter cover such important topics as Dressing for Success, Time Management, and Making Ethical Choices.*

*Access code required for these premium resources

Your Access Code is:

GMAB-SHELL-UMIAK-GONNA-HAUNT-OOSSE

Note: If there is no silver foil covering the access code, it may already have been redeemed, and therefore may no longer be valid. In that case, you can purchase online access using a major credit card or PayPal account. To do so, go to **www.pearsonhighered.com/go**, select your book cover, click on "Buy Access" and follow the on-screen instructions.

To Register:

- To start you will need a valid email address and this access code.
- Go to **www.pearsonhighered.com/go** and scroll to find your text book.
- Once you've selected your text, on the Home Page for the book, click the link to access the Student Premium Content.
- Click the Register button and follow the on-screen instructions.
- After you register, you can sign in any time via the log-in area on the same screen.

System Requirements

Windows 7 Ultimate Edition; IE 8
Windows Vista Ultimate Edition SP1; IE 8
Windows XP Professional SP3; IE 7
Windows XP Professional SP3; Firefox 3.6.4
Mac OS 10.5.7; Firefox 3.6.4
Mac OS 10.6; Safari 5

Technical Support

http://247pearsoned.custhelp.com

Photo credits: Goodluz/wrangler/Elena Elisseeva/Shutterstock

GO!

with Microsoft®

Access 2013

Brief

GO!

with Microsoft®

Access 2013

Brief

**Shelley Gaskin and
Carolyn McLellan**

PEARSON

Boston   Columbus   Indianapolis   New York   San Francisco   Upper Saddle River
Amsterdam   Cape Town   Dubai   London   Madrid   Milan   Munich   Paris   Montréal   Toronto
Delhi   Mexico City   São Paulo   Sydney   Hong Kong   Seoul   Singapore   Taipei   Tokyo

Editor in Chief: Michael Payne
Executive Acquisitions Editor: Jenifer Niles
Editorial Project Manager: Carly Prakapas
Product Development Manager: Laura Burgess
Development Editor: Ginny Munroe
Editorial Assistant: Andra Skaalrud
Director of Marketing: Maggie Leen
Marketing Manager: Brad Forrester
Marketing Coordinator: Susan Osterlitz
Marketing Assistant: Darshika Vyas
Managing Editor: Camille Trentacoste
Senior Production Project Manager: Rhonda Aversa

Operations Specialist: Maura Zaldivar-Garcia
Senior Art Director: Jonathan Boylan
Cover Photo: © photobar/Fotolia
Associate Director of Design: Blair Brown
Director of Media Development: Taylor Ragan
Media Project Manager, Production: Renata Butera
Full-Service Project Management: PreMediaGlobal
Composition: PreMediaGlobal
Printer/Binder: Webcrafters, Inc.
Cover Printer: Lehigh-Phoenix Color/Hagerstown
Text Font: MinionPro

Library of Congress data on file

10 9 8 7 6 5 4 3 2 1

ISBN 10: 0-13-341450-7
ISBN 13: 978-0-13-341450-9

Brief Contents

Table of Contents

Access Introduction to Microsoft Access 2013   49

Chapter 1   Getting Started with Microsoft Access 2013.................51

About the Authors

Shelley Gaskin, Series Editor, is a professor in the Business and Computer Technology Division at Pasadena City College in Pasadena, California. She holds a bachelor's degree in Business Administration from Robert Morris College (Pennsylvania), a master's degree in Business from Northern Illinois University, and a doctorate in Adult and Community Education from Ball State University (Indiana). Before joining Pasadena City College, she spent 12 years in the computer industry, where she was a systems analyst, sales representative, and director of Customer Education with Unisys Corporation. She also worked for Ernst & Young on the development of large systems applications for their clients. She has written and developed training materials for custom systems applications in both the public and private sector, and has also written and edited numerous computer application textbooks.

This book is dedicated to my students, who inspire me every day.

Carolyn McLellan is the dean of the Division of Information Technology and Business at Tidewater Community College in Virginia Beach, Virginia. She has a master's degree in Secondary Education from Regent University and a bachelor's degree in Business Education from Old Dominion University. She taught for Norfolk Public Schools for 17 years in Business Education and served as a faculty member at Tidewater Community College for eight years teaching networking, where she developed over 23 new courses and earned the Microsoft Certified Trainer and Microsoft Certified System Engineer industry certifications. In addition to teaching, Carolyn loves to play volleyball, boogie board at the beach, bicycle, crochet, cook, and read.

This book is dedicated to my daughters, Megan and Mandy, who have my eternal love;
to my mother, Jean, who always believes in me and encouraged me to become a teacher;
to my sister Debbie, who was my first student and who inspires me with her strength in
overcoming hardships; to my niece Jenna, for her bravery, composure, and beauty; to my
grandsons, Damon and Jordan, who bring me happiness and a renewed joie de vivre; and
to the students and IT faculty at Tidewater Community College.

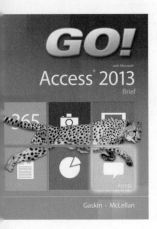

GO! with Access 2013 is the right solution for you and your students in today's fast-moving, mobile environment. The GO! Series content focuses on the real-world job skills students need to succeed in the workforce. They learn Office by working step-by-step through practical job-related projects that put the core functionality of Office in context. And as has always been true of the GO! Series, students learn the important concepts when they need them, and they never get lost in instruction, because the GO! Series uses Microsoft procedural syntax. Students learn how and learn why—at the teachable moment.

After completing the instructional projects, students are ready to apply the skills in a wide variety of progressively challenging projects that require them to solve problems, think critically, and create projects on their own. And, for those who want to go beyond the classroom and become certified, GO! provides clear MOS preparation guidelines so students know what is needed to ace the Core exam!

What's New

New Design reflects the look of Windows 8 and Office 2013 and enhances readability.

Enhanced Chapter Opener now includes a deeper introduction to the A and B instructional projects and more highly defined chapter Objectives and Learning Outcomes.

New Application Introductions provide a brief overview of the application and put the chapters in context for students.

Coverage of New Features of Office 2013 ensures that students are learning the skills they need to work in today's job market.

New Application Capstone Projects ensure that students are ready to move on to the next set of chapters. Each Application Capstone Project can be found on the Instructor Resource Center and is also a Grader project in MyITLab.

More Grader Projects based on the E, F, and G mastering-level projects, both homework and assessment versions! These projects are written by our GO! authors, who are all instructors in colleges like yours!

New Training and Assessment Simulations are now written by the authors to match the book one-to-one!

New MOS Map on the Instructor Resource Site and in the Annotated Instructor's Edition indicates clearly where each required MOS Objective is covered.

Three Types of Videos help students understand and succeed in the real world:

- *Student Training Videos* are broken down by Objective and created by the author—a real instructor teaching the same types of courses that you do. Real personal instruction.
- *GO! to Work* videos are short interviews with workers showing how they use Office in their jobs.
- *GO! for Job Success* videos relate to the projects in the chapter and cover important career topics such as *Dressing for Success*, *Time Management*, and *Making Ethical Choices*.

New GO! Learn It Online section at the end of the chapter indicates where various student learning activities can be found, including multiple choice and matching activities.

New Styles for In-Text Boxed Content: Another Way, Notes, More Knowledge, Alerts, and **new *By Touch* instructions** are included in line with the instruction and not in the margins so that the student is more likely to read this information.

Clearly Indicated Build from Scratch Projects: GO! has always had many projects that begin "from scratch," and now we have an icon to really call them out!

New Visual Summary focuses on the four key concepts to remember from each chapter.

New Review and Assessment Guide summarizes the end-of-chapter assessments for a quick overview of the different types and levels of assignments and assessments for each chapter.

New Skills and Procedures Summary Chart (online at the Instructor Resource Center) summarizes all of the shortcuts and commands covered in the chapter.

New End-of-Chapter Key Term Glossary with Definitions for each chapter, plus a comprehensive end-of-book glossary.

New Flipboards and Crossword Puzzles enable students to review the concepts and key terms learned in each chapter by completing online challenges.

Teach the Course You Want in Less Time

A Microsoft® Office textbook designed for student success!

- **Project-Based** – Students learn by creating projects that they will use in the real world.

- **Microsoft Procedural Syntax** – Steps are written to put students in the right place at the right time.

- **Teachable Moment** – Expository text is woven into the steps—at the moment students need to know it—not chunked together in a block of text that will go unread.

- **Sequential Pagination** – Students have actual page numbers instead of confusing letters and abbreviations.

New Feature

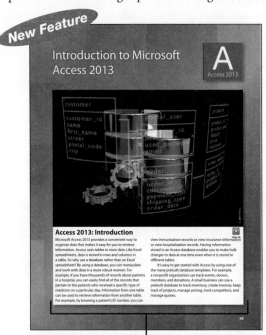

Student Outcomes and Learning Objectives – Objectives are clustered around projects that result in student outcomes.

New Design – Provides a more visually appealing and concise display of important content.

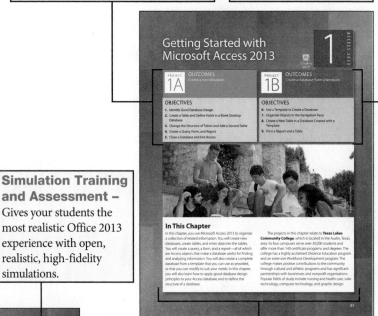

New Application Introductions – Provide an overview of the application to prepare students for the upcoming chapters.

Simulation Training and Assessment – Gives your students the most realistic Office 2013 experience with open, realistic, high-fidelity simulations.

Project Activities – A project summary stated clearly and quickly.

New Build from Scratch Icons – Enable you to easily see all the projects that the student builds from scratch.

Scenario – Each chapter opens with a job-related scenario that sets the stage for the projects the student will create.

Project Files – Clearly show students which files are needed for the project and the names they will use to save their documents.

Project Results – Show students what successful completion looks like.

In-Text Features
Another Way, Notes, *More* Knowledge, Alerts, and By Touch Instructions

Microsoft Procedural Syntax – Steps are written to put the student at the right place at the right time.

Color Coding – Each chapter has two instructional projects, which is less overwhelming for students than one large chapter project. The two projects are differentiated by different colored numbering and headings.

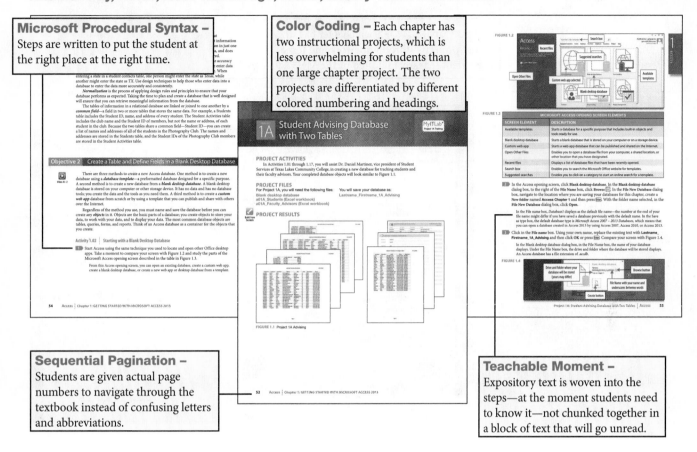

Sequential Pagination – Students are given actual page numbers to navigate through the textbook instead of confusing letters and abbreviations.

Teachable Moment – Expository text is woven into the steps—at the moment students need to know it—not chunked together in a block of text that will go unread.

End-of-Chapter
Content-Based Assessments – Assessments with defined solutions.

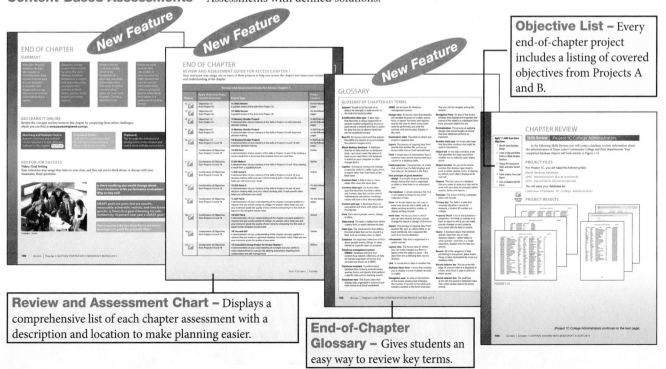

Review and Assessment Chart – Displays a comprehensive list of each chapter assessment with a description and location to make planning easier.

End-of-Chapter Glossary – Gives students an easy way to review key terms.

Objective List – Every end-of-chapter project includes a listing of covered objectives from Projects A and B.

End-of-Chapter

Content-Based Assessments – Assessments with defined solutions. (continued)

Grader projects – Each chapter has six MyITLab Grader projects—three homework and three assessment—clearly indicated by the MyITLab logo.

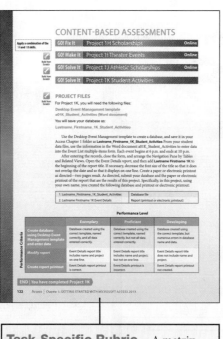

Task-Specific Rubric – A matrix specific to the GO! Solve It projects that states the criteria and standards for grading these defined-solution projects.

End-of-Chapter

Outcomes-Based Assessments – Assessments with open-ended solutions.

Outcomes Rubric – A matrix specific to the GO! Think projects that states the criteria and standards for grading these open-ended assessments.

GO! with Microsoft Office 365 – A collaboration project for each chapter teaches students how to use the cloud-based tools of Office 365 to communicate and collaborate from any device, anywhere.

Office Web Apps – For each instructional project, students can create the same or similar result in the corresponding Office Web Apps - 24 projects in all!

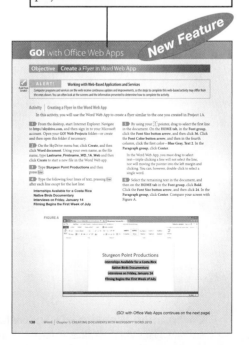

Student Materials

Student Data Files – All student data files are available to all on the companion website: www.pearsonhighered.com/go.

3 Types of Videos help students understand and succeed in the real world:

- **Student Training Videos** are by Objective and created by the author—a real instructor teaching the same types of courses that you teach.
- **GO! to Work** videos are short interviews with workers showing how they use Office in their job.
- **GO! for Job Success** videos related to the projects in the chapter cover important career topics such as *Dressing for Success*, *Time Management*, and *Making Ethical Choices*.

Flipboards and crossword puzzles provide a variety of review options for content in each chapter.
Available on the companion website using the access code included with your book.
pearsonhighered.com/go.

All Instructor and Student materials available at pearsonhighered .com/go

Instructor Materials

Annotated Instructor Edition – An instructor tool includes a full copy of the student textbook and a guide to implementing your course in three different ways, depending on the emphasis you want to place on digital engagement. Also included are teaching tips, discussion topics, and other useful pieces for teaching each chapter.

Student Assignment Tracker (previously called Assignment Sheets) – Lists all the assignments for the chapter. Just add the course information, due dates, and points. Providing these to students ensures they will know what is due and when.

Scripted Lectures – A script to guide your classroom lecture of each instructional project.

Annotated Solution Files – Coupled with the scorecards, these create a grading and scoring system that makes grading easy and efficient.

PowerPoint Lectures – PowerPoint presentations for each chapter.

Audio PowerPoints – Audio versions of the PowerPoint presentations for each chapter.

Scoring Rubrics – Can be used either by students to check their work or by you as a quick check-off for the items that need to be corrected.

Syllabus Templates – For 8-week, 12-week, and 16-week courses.

MOS Map – Provided at the Instructor Resource Center site and in the Annotated Instructor's Edition, showing where each required MOS Objective is covered either in the book or via additional instructional material provided.

Test Bank – Includes a variety of test questions for each chapter.

Companion Website – Online content such as the Online Chapter Review, Glossary, and Student Data Files are all at www.pearsonhighered.com/go.

Reviewers

GO! Focus Group Participants

Kenneth Mayer	Heald College
Carolyn Borne	Louisiana State University
Toribio Matamoros	Miami Dade College
Lynn Keane	University of South Carolina
Terri Hayes	Broward College
Michelle Carter	Paradise Valley Community College

GO! Reviewers

Abul Sheikh	Abraham Baldwin Agricultural College
John Percy	Atlantic Cape Community College
Janette Hicks	Binghamton University
Shannon Ogden	Black River Technical College
Karen May	Blinn College
Susan Fry	Boise State University
Chigurupati Rani	Borough of Manhattan Community College / CUNY
Ellen Glazer	Broward College
Kate LeGrand	Broward College
Mike Puopolo	Bunker Hill Community College
Nicole Lytle-Kosola	California State University, San Bernardino
Nisheeth Agrawal	Calhoun Community College
Pedro Diaz-Gomez	Cameron
Linda Friedel	Central Arizona College
Gregg Smith	Central Community College
Norm Cregger	Central Michigan University
Lisa LaCaria	Central Piedmont Community College
Steve Siedschlag	Chaffey College
Terri Helfand	Chaffey College
Susan Mills	Chambersburg
Mandy Reininger	Chemeketa Community College
Connie Crossley	Cincinnati State Technical and Community College
Marjorie Deutsch	City University of New York - Queensborough Community College
Mary Ann Zlotow	College of DuPage
Christine Bohnsak	College of Lake County
Gertrude Brier	College of Staten Island
Sharon Brown	College of The Albemarle
Terry Rigsby	Columbia College
Vicki Brooks	Columbia College
Donald Hames	Delgado Community College
Kristen King	Eastern Kentucky University
Kathie Richer	Edmonds Community College
Gary Smith	Elmhurst College
Wendi Kappersw	Embry-Riddle Aeronautical University
Nancy Woolridge	Fullerton College
Abigail Miller	Gateway Community & Technical College
Deep Ramanayake	Gateway Community & Technical College
Gwen White	Gateway Community & Technical College
Debbie Glinert	Gloria K School
Dana Smith	Golf Academy of America
Mary Locke	Greenville Technical College
Diane Marie Roselli	Harrisburg Area Community College
Linda Arnold	Harrisburg Area Community College - Lebanon
Daniel Schoedel	Harrisburg Area Community College - York Campus
Ken Mayer	Heald College
Xiaodong Qiao	Heald College
Donna Lamprecht	Hopkinsville Community College
Kristen Lancaster	Hopkinsville Community College
Johnny Hurley	Iowa Lakes Community College
Linda Halverson	Iowa Lakes Community College
Sarah Kilgo	Isothermal Community College
Chris DeGeare	Jefferson College
David McNair	Jefferson College
Diane Santurri	Johnson & Wales University
Roland Sparks	Johnson & Wales University
Ram Raghuraman	Joliet Junior College
Eduardo Suniga	Lansing Community College
Kenneth A. Hyatt	Lone Star College - Kingwood
Glenn Gray	Lone Star College - North Harris
Gene Carbonaro	Long Beach City College
Betty Pearman	Los Medanos College
Diane Kosharek	Madison College
Peter Meggison	Massasoit Community College
George Gabb	Miami Dade College
Lennie Alice Cooper	Miami Dade College
Richard Mabjish	Miami Dade College
Victor Giol	Miami Dade College
John Meir	Midlands Technical College
Greg Pauley	Moberly Area Community College
Catherine Glod	Mohawk Valley Community College
Robert Huyck	Mohawk Valley Community College
Kevin Engellant	Montana Western
Philip Lee	Nashville State Community College
Ruth Neal	Navarro College
Sharron Jordan	Navarro College
Richard Dale	New Mexico State University
Lori Townsend	Niagara County Community College
Judson Curry	North Park University
Mary Zegarski	Northampton Community College
Neal Stenlund	Northern Virginia Community College
Michael Goeken	Northwest Vista College
Mary Beth Tarver	Northwestern State University
Amy Rutledge	Oakland University
Marcia Braddock	Okefenokee Technical College
Richard Stocke	Oklahoma State University - OKC
Jane Stam	Onondaga Community College
Mike Michaelson	Palomar College
Kungwen (Dave) Chu	Purdue University Calumet
Wendy Ford	City University of New York - Queensborough Community College
Lewis Hall	Riverside City College
Karen Acree	San Juan College
Tim Ellis	Schoolcraft College
Dan Combellick	Scottsdale Community College
Pat Serrano	Scottsdale Community College
Rose Hendrickson	Sheridan College
Kit Carson	South Georgia College
Rebecca Futch	South Georgia State College
Brad Hagy	Southern Illinois University Carbondale
Mimi Spain	Southern Maine Community College
David Parker	Southern Oregon University
Madeline Baugher	Southwestern Oklahoma State University
Brian Holbert	St. Johns River State College
Bunny Howard	St. Johns River State College
Stephanie Cook	State College of Florida
Sharon Wavle	Tompkins Cortland Community College
George Fiori	Tri-County Technical College
Steve St. John	Tulsa Community College
Karen Thessing	University of Central Arkansas
Richard McMahon	University of Houston-Downtown
Shohreh Hashemi	University of Houston-Downtown
Donna Petty	Wallace Community College
Julia Bell	Walters State Community College
Ruby Kowaney	West Los Angeles College
Casey Thompson	Wiregrass Georgia Technical College
DeAnnia Clements	Wiregrass Georgia Technical College

Introduction to Microsoft Office 2013 Features

1

OFFICE 2013

PROJECT 1A

OUTCOMES
Create, save, and print a Microsoft Office 2013 document.

PROJECT 1B

OUTCOMES
Use the ribbon and dialog boxes to perform commands in Microsoft Office 2013.

OBJECTIVES

1. Use File Explorer to Download, Extract, and Locate Files and Folders
2. Use Start Search to Locate and Start a Microsoft Office 2013 Desktop App
3. Enter, Edit, and Check the Spelling of Text in an Office 2013 Program
4. Perform Commands from a Dialog Box
5. Create a Folder and Name and Save a File
6. Insert a Footer, Add Document Properties, Print a File, and Close a Desktop App

OBJECTIVES

7. Open an Existing File and Save It with a New Name
8. Sign In to Office and Explore Options for a Microsoft Office Desktop App
9. Perform Commands from the Ribbon and Quick Access Toolbar
10. Apply Formatting in Office Programs
11. Compress Files and Use the Microsoft Office 2013 Help System
12. Install Apps for Office and Create a Microsoft Account

etsa1112/Fotolia

In This Chapter

In this chapter, you will use File Explorer to navigate the Windows folder structure, create a folder, and save files in Microsoft Office 2013 programs. You will also practice using features in Microsoft Office 2013 that work similarly across Word, Excel, Access, and PowerPoint. These features include managing files, performing commands, adding document properties, signing in to Office, applying formatting, and using Help. You will also practice compressing files and installing Apps for Office from the Office Store. In this chapter, you will also learn how to set up a free Microsoft account so that you can use SkyDrive.

The projects in this chapter relate to **Skyline Metro Grill**, which is a chain of 25 casual, full-service restaurants based in Boston. The Skyline Metro Grill owners are planning an aggressive expansion program. To expand by 15 additional restaurants in Chicago, San Francisco, and Los Angeles by 2018, the company must attract new investors, develop new menus, develop new marketing strategies, and recruit new employees, all while adhering to the company's quality guidelines and maintaining its reputation for excellent service. To succeed, the company plans to build on its past success and maintain its quality elements.

PROJECT ACTIVITIES

In Activities 1.01 through 1.09, you will create a note form using Microsoft Word, save it in a folder that you create by using File Explorer, and then print the note form or submit it electronically as directed by your instructor. Your completed note form will look similar to Figure 1.1.

PROJECT FILES

For Project 1A, you will need the following file:

New blank Word document

You will save your file as:

Lastname_Firstname_1A_Note_Form

Build from Scratch

PROJECT RESULTS

Skyline Metro Grill, Chef's Notes
Executive Chef, Sarah Jackson

Lastname_Firstname_1A_Note_Form

FIGURE 1.1 Project 1A Note Form

Objective 1   Use File Explorer to Download, Extract, and Locate Files and Folders

Video OF1-1

A *file* is a collection of information stored on a computer under a single name, for example, a Word document or a PowerPoint presentation. A file is stored in a *folder*—a container in which you store files—or a *subfolder*, which is a folder within a folder. The Windows operating system stores and organizes your files and folders, which is a primary task of an operating system.

You *navigate*—explore within the organizing structure of Windows—to create, save, and find your files and folders by using the *File Explorer* program. File Explorer displays the files and folders on your computer and is at work anytime you are viewing the contents of files and folders in a *window*. A window is a rectangular area on a computer screen in which programs and content appear; a window can be moved, resized, minimized, or closed.

Activity 1.01 | Using File Explorer to Download, Extract, and Locate Files and Folders

> **A L E R T !**   **You Will Need a USB Flash Drive**
>
> You will need a USB flash drive for this activity to download the Student Data Files for this chapter. If your instructor is providing the files to you, for example by placing the files at your learning management system, be sure you have downloaded them to a location where you can access the files and then skip to Activity 1.02.

> **N O T E**   **Creating a Microsoft Account**
>
> Use a free Microsoft account to sign in to Windows 8 and Office 2013 so that you can work on different PCs and use your SkyDrive. You need not use the Microsoft account as your primary email address unless you want to do so. To create a Microsoft account, go to **www.outlook.com**.

1 Sign in to Windows 8 with your Microsoft account—or the account provided by your instructor—to display the Windows 8 **Start screen**, and then click the **Desktop** tile. Insert a **USB flash drive** in your computer; **Close** ☒ any messages or windows that display.

The *desktop* is the screen in Windows that simulates your work area. A *USB flash drive* is a small data storage device that plugs into a computer USB port.

2 On the taskbar, click **Internet Explorer** 🅴. Click in the **address bar** to select the existing text, type **www.pearsonhighered.com/go** and press Enter. Locate and click the name of this textbook, and then click the **STUDENT DATA FILES tab**.

The *taskbar* is the area along the lower edge of the desktop that displays buttons representing programs—also referred to as desktop apps. In the desktop version of Internet Explorer 10, the *address bar* is the area at the top of the Internet Explorer window that displays, and where you can type, a *URL—Uniform Resource Locator*—which is an address that uniquely identifies a location on the Internet.

3 On the list of files, move your mouse pointer over—*point* to—**Office Features Chapter 1** and then *click*—press the left button on your mouse pointing device one time.

4 In the **Windows Internet Explorer** dialog box, click **Save As**.

A *dialog box* is a small window that contains options for completing a task.

5 In the **Save As** dialog box, on the left, locate the **navigation pane**, and point to the vertical **scroll bar**.

The Save As dialog box is an example of a *common dialog box*; that is, this dialog box looks the same in Excel and in PowerPoint and in most other Windows-based desktop applications—also referred to as programs.

Use the *navigation pane* on the left side of the Save As dialog box to navigate to, open, and display favorites, libraries, folders, saved searches, and an expandable list of drives. A *pane* is a separate area of a window.

A *scroll bar* displays when a window, or a pane within a window, has information that is not in view. You can click the up or down scroll arrows—or the left and right scroll arrows in a horizontal scroll bar—to scroll the contents up and down or left and right in small increments.

You can also drag the *scroll box*—the box within the scroll bar—to scroll the window or pane in either direction.

This is a *compressed folder*—also called a *zipped folder*—which is a folder containing one or more files that have been reduced in size. A compressed folder takes up less storage space and can be transferred to other computers faster.

| **NOTE** | **Comparing Your Screen with the Figures in This Textbook** |

Your screen will match the figures shown in this textbook if you set your screen resolution to 1280 × 768. At other resolutions, your screen will closely resemble, but not match, the figures shown. To view your screen's resolution, on the desktop, right-click in a blank area, and then click Screen resolution.

---

6 In the **navigation pane**, if necessary, on the scroll bar click ☑ to scroll down. If necessary, to the left of **Computer**, click ▷ to expand the list. Then click the name of your **USB flash drive**.

7 With *Office_Features* displayed in the **File name** box, in the lower right corner click **Save**.

At the bottom of your screen, the *Notification bar* displays information about pending downloads, security issues, add-ons, and other issues related to the operation of your computer.

8 In the **Notification bar**, when the download is complete, click **Open folder** to display the folder window for your **USB flash drive**.

A *folder window* displays the contents of the current location—folder, library, or drive—and contains helpful parts so that you can navigate within the file organizing structure of Windows.

9 With the compressed **Office_Features** folder selected, on the ribbon, click the **Extract tab** to display the **Compressed Folder Tools**, and then click **Extract all**.

The *ribbon* is a user interface in both Office 2013 and Windows 8 that groups the commands for performing related tasks on tabs across the upper portion of a window.

In the dialog box, you can *extract*—decompress or pull out—files from a compressed folder.

You can navigate to some other location by clicking the Browse button and navigating within your storage locations.

10 In the **Extract Compressed (Zipped) Folders** dialog box, click to the right of the selected text, and then press [Backspace] until only the drive letter of your USB and the colon following it display—for example G:—and then click **Extract**. Notice that a progress bar indicates the progress of the extract process, and that when the extract is complete, the **Office_Features** folder displays on the file list of your **USB flash drive**.

In a dialog box or taskbar button, a **progress bar** indicates visually the progress of a task such as a download or file transfer.

The **address bar** in File Explorer displays your current location in the folder structure as a series of links separated by arrows, which is referred to as the **path**—a sequence of folders that leads to a specific file or folder.

By pressing [Backspace] in the Extract dialog box, you avoid creating an unneeded folder level.

11 Because you no longer need the compressed (zipped) version of the folder, be sure it is selected, click the **Home tab**, and then click **Delete**. In the upper right corner of the **USB drive** folder window, click **Close** ⊠. **Close** ⊠ the **Internet Explorer** window and in the Internet Explorer message, click **Close all tabs**.

Your desktop redisplays.

Objective 2 | Use Start Search to Locate and Start a Microsoft Office 2013 Desktop App

Video OF1-2

The term **desktop app** commonly refers to a computer program that is installed on your computer and requires a computer operating system such as Microsoft Windows or Apple OS to run. The programs in Microsoft Office 2013 are considered to be desktop apps. Apps that run from the **device software** on a smartphone or a tablet computer—for example, iOS, Android, or Windows Phone—or apps that run from **browser software** such as Internet Explorer, Safari, Firefox, or Chrome on a desktop PC or laptop PC are referred to simply as **apps**.

Activity 1.02 | Using Start Search to Locate and Start a Microsoft Office 2013 Desktop App

The easiest and fastest way to search for an app is to use the **Start search** feature—simply display the Windows 8 Start screen and start typing. By default, Windows 8 searches for apps; you can change it to search for files or settings.

1 With your desktop displayed, press ⊞ to display the Windows 8 **Start screen**, and then type **word 2013** With *word 2013* bordered in white in the search results, press [Enter] to return to the desktop and open Word. If you want to do so, in the upper right corner, sign in with your Microsoft account, and then compare your screen with Figure 1.2.

Documents that you have recently opened, if any, display on the left. On the right, you can select either a blank document or a **template**—a preformatted document that you can use as a starting point and then change to suit your needs.

 BY TOUCH   Swipe from the right edge of the screen to display the charms, and then tap Search. Tap in the Apps box, and then use the onscreen keyboard that displays to type *word 2013*. Tap the selected Word 2013 app name to open Word.

FIGURE 1.2

Recently opened documents, if any, display here

Start a blank document here

User signed in; this is optional

Templates to start different types of documents

2 Click **Blank document**. Compare your screen with Figure 1.3, and then take a moment to study the description of these screen elements in the table in Figure 1.4.

NOTE	Displaying the Full Ribbon

If your full ribbon does not display, click any tab, and then at the right end of the ribbon, click 📌 to pin the ribbon to keep it open while you work.

FIGURE 1.3

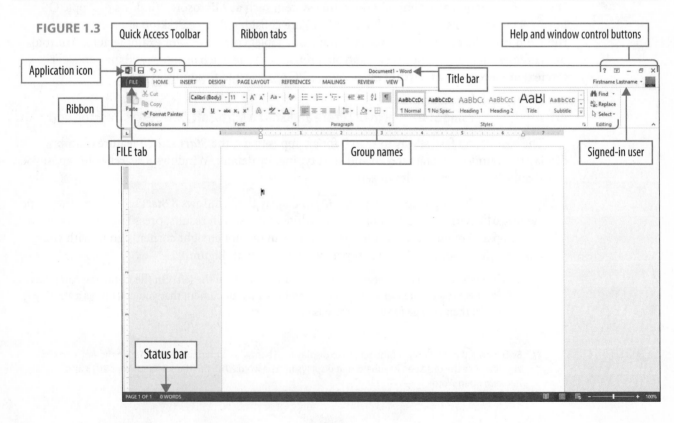

Quick Access Toolbar

Ribbon tabs

Help and window control buttons

Application icon

Title bar

Ribbon

FILE tab

Group names

Signed-in user

Status bar

FIGURE 1.4

MICROSOFT OFFICE SCREEN ELEMENTS	
SCREEN ELEMENT	**DESCRIPTION**
FILE tab	Displays Microsoft Office Backstage view, which is a centralized space for all of your file management tasks such as opening, saving, printing, publishing, or sharing a file—all the things you can do *with* a file.
Group names	Indicate the names of the groups of related commands on the displayed tab.
Help and window control buttons	Display Word Help and Full Screen Mode and enable you to Minimize, Restore Down, or Close the window.
Application icon	When clicked, displays a menu of window control commands including Restore, Minimize, and Close.
Quick Access Toolbar	Displays buttons to perform frequently used commands and use resources with a single click. The default commands include Save, Undo, and Redo. You can add and delete buttons to customize the Quick Access Toolbar for your convenience.
Ribbon	Displays a group of task-oriented tabs that contain the commands, styles, and resources you need to work in an Office 2013 desktop app. The look of your ribbon depends on your screen resolution. A high resolution will display more individual items and button names on the ribbon.
Ribbon tabs	Display the names of the task-oriented tabs relevant to the open program.
Status bar	Displays file information on the left; on the right displays buttons for Read Mode, Print Layout, and Web Layout views; on the far right displays Zoom controls.
Title bar	Displays the name of the file and the name of the program. The Help and window control buttons are grouped on the right side of the title bar.
Signed-in user	Name of the Windows 8 signed-in user.

Objective 3 | Enter, Edit, and Check the Spelling of Text in an Office 2013 Program

Video OF1-3

All of the programs in Office 2013 require some typed text. Your keyboard is still the primary method of entering information into your computer. Techniques to enter text and to *edit*—make changes to—text are similar among all of the Office 2013 programs.

Activity 1.03 | Entering and Editing Text in an Office 2013 Program

1 On the ribbon, on the HOME tab, in the Paragraph group, if necessary, click Show/Hide ¶ so that it is active—shaded. If necessary, on the VIEW tab, in the Show group, select the Ruler check box so that rulers display below the ribbon and on the left side of your window.

The *insertion point*—a blinking vertical line that indicates where text or graphics will be inserted—displays. In Office 2013 programs, the mouse *pointer*—any symbol that displays on your screen in response to moving your mouse device—displays in different shapes depending on the task you are performing and the area of the screen to which you are pointing.

When you press Enter, Spacebar, or Tab on your keyboard, characters display to represent these keystrokes. These screen characters do not print and are referred to as *formatting marks* or *nonprinting characters*.

NOTE | **Activating Show/Hide in Word Documents**

When Show/Hide is active—the button is shaded—formatting marks display. Because formatting marks guide your eye in a document—like a map and road signs guide you along a highway—these marks will display throughout this instruction. Many expert Word users keep these marks displayed while creating documents.

2 Type **Skyline Grille Info** and notice how the insertion point moves to the right as you type. Point slightly to the right of the letter *e* in *Grille* and click to place the insertion point there. Compare your screen with Figure 1.5.

> A *paragraph symbol* (¶) indicates the end of a paragraph and displays each time you press Enter. This is a type of formatting mark and does not print.

FIGURE 1.5

3 On your keyboard, locate and then press the Backspace key to delete the letter *e*.

> Pressing Backspace removes a character to the left of the insertion point.

4 Press → one time to place the insertion point to the left of the *I* in *Info*. Type **Chef's** and then press Spacebar one time.

> By *default*, when you type text in an Office program, existing text moves to the right to make space for new typing. Default refers to the current selection or setting that is automatically used by a program unless you specify otherwise.

5 Press Del four times to delete *Info* and then type **Notes**

> Pressing Del removes a character to the right of the insertion point.

6 With your insertion point blinking after the word *Notes*, on your keyboard, hold down the Ctrl key. While holding down Ctrl, press ← three times to move the insertion point to the beginning of the word *Grill*.

> This is a *keyboard shortcut*—a key or combination of keys that performs a task that would otherwise require a mouse. This keyboard shortcut moves the insertion point to the beginning of the previous word.

> A keyboard shortcut is commonly indicated as Ctrl + ← (or some other combination of keys) to indicate that you hold down the first key while pressing the second key. A keyboard shortcut can also include three keys, in which case you hold down the first two and then press the third. For example, Ctrl + Shift + ← selects one word to the left.

7 With the insertion point blinking at the beginning of the word *Grill*, type **Metro** and press Spacebar.

8 Press Ctrl + End to place the insertion point after the letter *s* in *Notes*, and then press Enter one time. With the insertion point blinking, type the following and include the spelling error:
Exective Chef, Madison Dunham

9 With your mouse, point slightly to the left of the *M* in *Madison*, hold down the left mouse button, and then **drag**—hold down the left mouse button while moving your mouse—to the right to select the text *Madison Dunham* but not the paragraph mark following it, and then release the mouse button. Compare your screen with Figure 1.6.

The **mini toolbar** displays commands that are commonly used with the selected object, which places common commands close to your pointer. When you move the pointer away from the mini toolbar, it fades from view.

Selecting refers to highlighting, by dragging or clicking with your mouse, areas of text or data or graphics so that the selection can be edited, formatted, copied, or moved. The action of dragging includes releasing the left mouse button at the end of the area you want to select.

The Office programs recognize a selected area as one unit to which you can make changes. Selecting text may require some practice. If you are not satisfied with your result, click anywhere outside of the selection, and then begin again.

⟳ BY TOUCH   Tap once on *Madison* to display the gripper—small circle that acts as a handle—directly below the word. This establishes the start gripper. If necessary, with your finger, drag the gripper to the beginning of the word. Then drag the gripper to the end of Dunham to select the text and display the end gripper.

FIGURE 1.6

10 With the text *Madison Dunham* selected, type **Sarah Jackson**

In any Windows-based program, such as the Microsoft Office 2013 programs, selected text is deleted and then replaced when you begin to type new text. You will save time by developing good techniques for selecting and then editing or replacing selected text, which is easier than pressing the Del key numerous times to delete text.

Activity 1.04 | Checking Spelling

Office 2013 has a dictionary of words against which all entered text is checked. In Word and PowerPoint, words that are not in the dictionary display a wavy red line, indicating a possible misspelled word or a proper name or an unusual word—none of which are in the Office 2013 dictionary.

In Excel and Access, you can initiate a check of the spelling, but red underlines do not display.

1 Notice that the misspelled word *Exective* displays with a wavy red underline.

2 Point to *Exective* and then **right-click**—click your right mouse button one time.

A **shortcut menu** displays, which displays commands and options relevant to the selected text or object. These are **context-sensitive commands** because they relate to the item you right-clicked. These types of menus are also referred to as **context menus**. Here, the shortcut menu displays commands related to the misspelled word.

⟳ BY TOUCH   Tap and hold a moment to select the misspelled word, then release your finger to display the shortcut menu.

3 Press (Esc) to cancel the shortcut menu, and then in the lower left corner of your screen, on the **status bar**, click the **Proofing** icon , which displays an *X* because some errors are detected. Compare your screen with Figure 1.7.

> The Spelling pane displays on the right. Here you have many more options for checking spelling than you have on the shortcut menu. The suggested correct word, *Executive*, is highlighted.
>
> You can click the speaker icon to hear the pronunciation of the selected word. You can also see some synonyms for *Executive*. Finally, if you have not already installed a dictionary, you can click *Get a Dictionary*—if you are signed in to Office with a Microsoft account—to find and install one from the online Office store; or if you have a dictionary app installed, it will display here and you can search it for more information.
>
> In the Spelling pane, you can ignore the word one time or in all occurrences, change the word to the suggested word, select a different suggestion, or add a word to the dictionary against which Word checks.

FIGURE 1.7

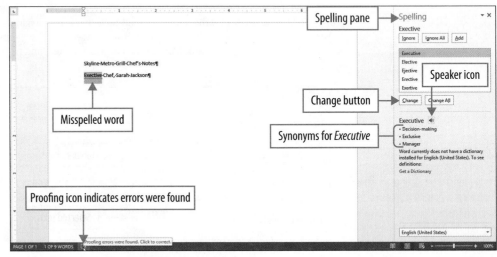

🔄 **ANOTHER WAY**   Press (F7) to display the Spelling pane; or, on the Review tab, in the Proofing group, click Spelling & Grammar.

4 In the **Spelling** pane, click **Change** to change the spelling to *Executive*. In the message box that displays, click **OK**.

Objective 4   Perform Commands from a Dialog Box

▶ Video OF1-4

In a dialog box, you make decisions about an individual object or topic. In some dialog boxes, you can make multiple decisions in one place.

Activity 1.05 │ Performing Commands from a Dialog Box

1 On the ribbon, click the **DESIGN tab**, and then in the **Page Background group**, click **Page Color**.

2 At the bottom of the menu, notice the command **Fill Effects** followed by an **ellipsis** (…). Compare your screen with Figure 1.8.

> An *ellipsis* is a set of three dots indicating incompleteness. An ellipsis following a command name indicates that a dialog box will display when you click the command.

FIGURE 1.8

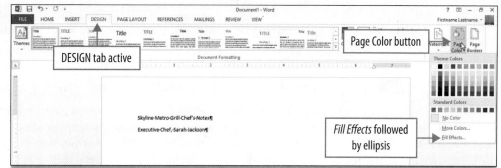

Page Color button

DESIGN tab active

Fill Effects followed by ellipsis

3 ▶ Click **Fill Effects** to display the **Fill Effects** dialog box. Compare your screen with Figure 1.9.

Fill is the inside color of a page or object. The Gradient tab is active. In a *gradient fill*, one color fades into another. Here, the dialog box displays a set of tabs across the top from which you can display different sets of options. Some dialog boxes display the option group names on the left.

FIGURE 1.9

Fill Effects dialog box

Tabs within a dialog box

4 ▶ Under **Colors**, click the **One color** option button.

The dialog box displays settings related to the One color option. An *option button* is a round button that enables you to make one choice among two or more options.

5 ▶ Click the **Color 1 arrow**—the arrow under the text *Color 1*—and then in the third column, point to the second color to display the ScreenTip *Gray-25%, Background 2, Darker 10%*.

A *ScreenTip* displays useful information about mouse actions, such as pointing to screen elements or dragging.

6 ▶ Click **Gray-25%, Background 2, Darker 10%**, and then notice that the fill color displays in the **Color 1** box. In the **Dark Light** bar, click the **Light arrow** as many times as necessary until the scroll box is all the way to right. Under **Shading styles**, click the **Diagonal down** option button. Under **Variants**, click the upper right variant. Compare your screen with Figure 1.10.

FIGURE 1.10

One color option button

Gray-25%, Background 2, Darker 10%

Scroll box at Light end

Upper right variant selected

Diagonal down option button

Sample box shows effects

7 At the bottom of the dialog box, click **OK**, and notice the subtle page color.

In Word, the gray shading page color will not print—even on a color printer—unless you set specific options to do so. However a subtle background page color is effective if people will be reading the document on a screen. Microsoft's research indicates that two-thirds of people who open Word documents never edit them; they only read them.

Activity 1.06 | Using Undo

1 Point to the *S* in *Skyline*, and then drag down and to the right to select both paragraphs of text and include the paragraph marks. On the mini toolbar, click **Styles,** and then *point to* but do not click **Title**. Compare your screen with Figure 1.11.

A **style** is a group of **formatting** commands, such as font, font size, font color, paragraph alignment, and line spacing that can be applied to a paragraph with one command. Formatting is the process of establishing the overall appearance of text, graphics, and pages in an Office file—for example, in a Word document.

Live Preview is a technology that shows the result of applying an editing or formatting change as you point to possible results—before you actually apply it.

FIGURE 1.11

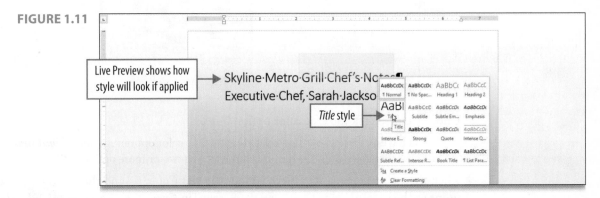

2 In the **Styles** gallery, click **Title**.

A **gallery** is an Office feature that displays a list of potential results.

3 On the ribbon, on the **HOME tab**, in the **Paragraph group**, click **Center** ☰ to center the two paragraphs.

Alignment refers to the placement of paragraph text relative to the left and right margins. **Center alignment** refers to text that is centered horizontally between the left and right margins. You can also align text at the left margin, which is the default alignment for text in Word, or at the right.

4 With the two paragraphs still selected, on the **HOME tab**, in the **Font Group**, click **Text Effects and Typography** Ⓐ ▾ to display a gallery.

5 In the second row, click the first effect—**Gradient Fill – Gray**. Click anywhere to *deselect*—cancel the selection—the text and notice the text effect.

6 Because this effect might be difficult to read, in the upper left corner of your screen, on the **Quick Access Toolbar**, click **Undo** 🔄.

The **Undo** command reverses your last action.

🔄 **ANOTHER WAY**   Press Ctrl + Z as the keyboard shortcut for the Undo command.

7 Display the **Text Effects and Typography** gallery again, and then in the second row, click the second effect—**Gradient Fill – Blue, Accent 1, Reflection**. Click anywhere to deselect the text and notice the text effect. Compare your screen with Figure 1.12.

As you progress in your study of Microsoft Office, you will practice using many dialog boxes and applying interesting effects such as this to your Word documents, Excel worksheets, Access database objects, and PowerPoint slides.

FIGURE 1.12

> Text formatted with blue reflective text effect → Skyline·Metro·Grill·Chef's·Notes¶ Executive·Chef,·Sarah·Jackson¶
>
> Gray page fill effects →

Objective 5   Create a Folder and Name and Save a File

Video OF1-5

A *location* is any disk drive, folder, or other place in which you can store files and folders. Where you store your files depends on how and where you use your data. For example, for your college classes, you might decide to store on a removable USB flash drive so that you can carry your files to different locations and access your files on different computers.

If you do most of your work on a single computer, for example your home desktop system or your laptop computer that you take with you to school or work, then you can store your files in one of the Libraries—Documents, Music, Pictures, or Videos—that the Windows 8 operating system creates on your hard drive.

The best place to store files if you want them to be available anytime, anywhere, from almost any device is on your *SkyDrive*, which is Microsoft's free *cloud storage* for anyone with a free Microsoft account. Cloud storage refers to online storage of data so that you can access your data from different places and devices. *Cloud computing* refers to applications and services that are accessed over the Internet, rather than to applications that are installed on your local computer.

Because many people now have multiple computing devices—desktop, laptop, tablet, smartphone—it is common to store data *in the cloud* so that it is always available. *Synchronization*, also called *syncing*—pronounced SINK-ing—is the process of updating computer files that are in two or more locations according to specific rules. So if you create and save a Word document on your SkyDrive using your laptop, you can open and edit that document on your tablet. And then when you close the document again, the file is properly updated to reflect your changes.

You need not be connected to the Internet to access documents stored on SkyDrive because an up-to-date version of your content is synched to your local system and available on SkyDrive. You must, however, be connected to the Internet for the syncing to occur. Saving to SkyDrive will keep the local copy on your computer and the copy in the cloud synchronized for as long as you need it. If you open and edit on a different computer, log into the SkyDrive website, and then edit using Office 2013, Office 2010, or the *Office Web Apps*, you can save any changes back to SkyDrive. Office Web Apps are the free online companions to Microsoft Word, Excel, PowerPoint, Access, and OneNote. These changes will be synchronized back to any of your computers that run the SkyDrive for Windows application, which you get for free simply by logging in with your Microsoft account at skydrive.com.

The Windows operating system helps you to create and maintain a logical folder structure, so always take the time to name your files and folders consistently.

Activity 1.07 | Creating a Folder and Naming and Saving a File

A Word document is an example of a file. In this activity, you will create a folder on your USB flash drive in which to store your files. If you prefer to store on your SkyDrive or in the Documents library on your hard drive, you can use similar steps.

1 If necessary, insert your **USB flash drive** into your computer.

As the first step in saving a file, determine where you want to save the file, and if necessary, insert a storage device.

2 At the top of your screen, in the title bar, notice that *Document1 – Word* displays.

The Blank option on the opening screen of an Office 2013 program displays a new unsaved file with a default name—*Document1, Presentation1*, and so on. As you create your file, your work is temporarily stored in the computer's memory until you initiate a Save command, at which time you must choose a file name and a location in which to save your file.

3 In the upper left corner of your screen, click the **FILE tab** to display **Backstage** view. Compare your screen with Figure 1.13.

Backstage view is a centralized space that groups commands related to *file* management; that is why the tab is labeled *FILE*. File management commands include opening, saving, printing, publishing, or sharing a file. The *Backstage tabs*—*Info, New, Open, Save, Save As, Print, Share, Export*, and *Close*—display along the left side. The tabs group file-related tasks together.

Here, the *Info tab* displays information—*info*—about the current file, and file management commands display under Info. For example, if you click the Protect Document button, a list of options that you can set for this file that relate to who can open or edit the document displays.

On the right, you can also examine the *document properties*. Document properties, also known as *metadata*, are details about a file that describe or identify it, such as the title, author name, subject, and keywords that identify the document's topic or contents. To close Backstage view and return to the document, you can click ⊕ in the upper left corner or press Esc.

FIGURE 1.13

4 On the left, click **Save As,** and notice that the default location for storing Office files is your **SkyDrive**—if you are signed in. Compare your screen with Figure 1.14.

> When you are saving something for the first time, for example a new Word document, the Save and Save As commands are identical. That is, the Save As commands will display if you click Save or if you click Save As.

FIGURE 1.14

NOTE   **Saving after Your File Is Named**

After you name and save a file, the Save command on the Quick Access Toolbar saves any changes you make to the file without displaying Backstage view. The Save As command enables you to name and save a *new* file based on the current one—in a location that you choose. After you name and save the new document, the original document closes, and the new document—based on the original one—displays.

---

5 To store your Word file on your **USB flash drive**—instead of your SkyDrive—click the **Browse** button to display the **Save As** dialog box. On the left, in the navigation pane, scroll down, and then under **Computer,** click the name of your **USB flash drive.** Compare your screen with Figure 1.15.

> In the Save As dialog box, you must indicate the name you want for the file and the location where you want to save the file. When working with your own data, it is good practice to pause at this point and determine the logical name and location for your file.

> In the Save As dialog box, a *toolbar* displays. This is a row, column, or block of buttons or icons, that usually displays across the top of a window and that contains commands for tasks you perform with a single click.

FIGURE 1.15

6 On the toolbar, click **New folder**.

In the file list, Word creates a new folder, and the text *New folder* is selected.

7 Type **Office Features Chapter 1** and press Enter. Compare your screen with Figure 1.16.

In Windows-based programs, the Enter key confirms an action.

FIGURE 1.16

8 In the **file list**, double-click the name of your new folder to open it and display its name in the **address bar**.

9 In the lower portion of the dialog box, click in the **File name** box to select the existing text. Notice that Office inserts the text at the beginning of the document as a suggested file name.

10 On your keyboard, locate the hyphen ⎼ key. Notice that the Shift of this key produces the underscore character. With the text still selected and using your own name, type **Lastname_Firstname_1A_Note_Form** and then compare your screen with Figure 1.17.

You can use spaces in file names, however, some people prefer not to use spaces. Some programs, especially when transferring files over the Internet, may insert the extra characters *%20* in place of a space. This can happen in **SharePoint**, so using underscores instead of spaces can be a good habit to adopt. SharePoint is Microsoft's collaboration software with which people in an organization can set up team sites to share information, manage documents, and publish reports for others to see. In general, however, unless you encounter a problem, it is OK to use spaces. In this textbook, underscores are used instead of spaces in file names.

FIGURE 1.17

11 In the lower right corner, click **Save** or press Enter. Compare your screen with Figure 1.18.

The Word window redisplays and your new file name displays in the title bar, indicating that the file has been saved to a location that you have specified.

FIGURE 1.18

12 ▶ In the first paragraph, click to place the insertion point after the word *Grill* and type , (a comma). In the upper left corner of your screen, on the **Quick Access Toolbar**, click **Save** ⊟.

> After a document is named and saved in a location, you can save any changes you have made since the last Save operation by using the Save command on the Quick Access Toolbar. When working on a document, it is good practice to save your changes from time to time.

Objective 6 | Insert a Footer, Add Document Properties, Print a File, and Close a Desktop App

Video OF1-6

For most of your files, especially in a workplace setting, it is useful to add identifying information to help in finding files later. You might also want to print your file on paper or create an electronic printout. The process of printing a file is similar in all of the Office applications.

Activity 1.08 | Inserting a Footer, Inserting Document Info, and Adding Document Properties

---

N O T E | **Are You Printing or Submitting Your Files Electronically?**

In this activity, you can either produce a paper printout or create an electronic file to submit to your instructor if required.

---

1 ▶ On the ribbon, click the **INSERT tab**, and then in the **Header & Footer group**, click **Footer**.

2 ▶ At the bottom of the list, click **Edit Footer**. On the ribbon, notice that the **HEADER & FOOTER TOOLS** display.

> The *Header & Footer Tools Design* tab displays on the ribbon. The ribbon adapts to your work and will display additional tabs like this one—referred to as ***contextual tabs***—when you need them.
>
> A ***footer*** is a reserved area for text or graphics that displays at the bottom of each page in a document. Likewise, a ***header*** is a reserved area for text or graphics that displays at the top of each page in a document. When the footer (or header) area is active, the document area is dimmed, indicating it is unavailable.

3 ▶ On the ribbon, under **HEADER & FOOTER TOOLS**, on the **DESIGN tab**, in the **Insert group**, click **Document Info**, and then click **File Name** to insert the name of your file in the footer, which is a common business practice. Compare your screen with Figure 1.19.

> Ribbon commands that display ▼ will, when clicked, display a list of options for the command.

· **FIGURE 1.19**

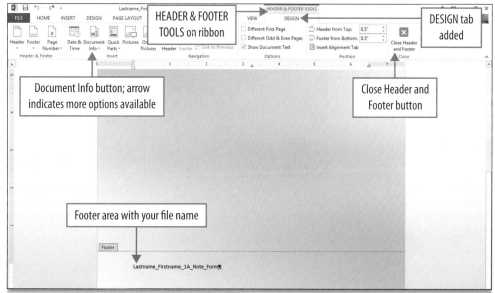

4 At the right end of the ribbon, click **Close Header and Footer**.

🔄 **ANOTHER WAY**   Double-click anywhere in the dimmed document to close the footer.

5 Click the **FILE tab** to display **Backstage** view. On the right, at the bottom of the **Properties** list, click **Show All Properties**.

🔄 **ANOTHER WAY**   Click the arrow to the right of Properties, and then click Show Document Panel to show and edit properties at the top of your document window.

6 On the list of **Properties**, click to the right of **Tags** to display an empty box, and then type **chef, notes, form**

> *Tags*, also referred to as *keywords*, are custom file properties in the form of words that you associate with a document to give an indication of the document's content. Adding tags to your documents makes it easier to search for and locate files in File Explorer and in systems such as Microsoft SharePoint document libraries.

🔄 **BY TOUCH**   Tap to the right of Tags to display the Tags box and the onscreen keyboard.

7 Click to the right of **Subject** to display an empty box, and then type your course name and section #; for example *CIS 10, #5543*.

8 Under **Related People**, be sure that your name displays as the author. If necessary, right-click the author name, click Edit Property, type your name, click outside of the Edit person dialog box, and then click OK. Compare your screen with Figure 1.20.

FIGURE 1.20

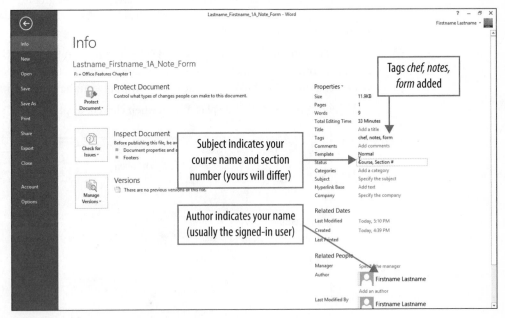

Activity 1.09 | Printing a File and Closing a Desktop App

1 ▶ On the left, click **Print**, and then compare your screen with Figure 1.21.

> Here you can select any printer connected to your system and adjust the settings related to how you want to print. On the right, the ***Print Preview*** displays, which is a view of a document as it will appear on paper when you print it.
>
> At the bottom of the Print Preview area, in the center, the number of pages and page navigation arrows with which you can move among the pages in Print Preview display. On the right, the Zoom slider enables you to shrink or enlarge the Print Preview. ***Zoom*** is the action of increasing or decreasing the viewing area of the screen.

↻ ANOTHER WAY   From the document screen, press ⌨Ctrl + ⌨P or ⌨Ctrl + ⌨F2 to display Print in Backstage view.

FIGURE 1.21

2 ▶ To submit your file electronically, skip this step and continue to Step 3. To print your document on paper using the default printer on your system, in the upper left portion of the screen, click the **Print** button.

> The document will print on your default printer; if you do not have a color printer, the blue text will print in shades of gray. The gray page color you applied to the document does not display in Print Preview nor does it print unless you specifically adjust some of Word's options. Backstage view closes and your file redisplays in the Word window.

3 ▶ To create an electronic file, on the left click **Export**. On the right, click the **Create PDF/XPS** button to display the **Publish as PDF or XPS** dialog box.

> ***PDF*** stands for ***Portable Document Format***, which is a technology that creates an image that preserves the look of your file. This is a popular format for sending documents electronically, because the document will display on most computers.
>
> ***XPS*** stands for ***XML Paper Specification***—a Microsoft file format that also creates an image of your document and that opens in the XPS viewer.

4 On the left in the **navigation pane**, if necessary expand ▷ Computer, and then navigate to your **Office Features Chapter 1** folder on your **USB flash drive**. Compare your screen with Figure 1.22.

FIGURE 1.22

Publish as PDF or XPS dialog box

Path to your Office Features Chapter 1 folder

Save as type indicates *PDF*

5 In the lower right corner of the dialog box, click **Publish**; if your Adobe Acrobat or Adobe Reader program displays your PDF, in the upper right corner, click Close ☒. Notice that your document redisplays in Word.

 ANOTHER WAY   In Backstage view, click Save As, navigate to the location of your Chapter folder, click the Save as type arrow, on the list click PDF, and then click Save.

6 Click the **FILE tab** to redisplay **Backstage** view. On the left, click **Close**, if necessary click Save, and then compare your screen with Figure 1.23.

FIGURE 1.23

Word window with all documents closed

Close button

7 In the upper right corner of the Word window, click **Close** ☒ . If directed by your instructor to do so, submit your paper or electronic file.

END | You have completed Project 1A

PROJECT ACTIVITIES

In Activities 1.10 through 1.21, you will open, edit, and then compress a Word file. You will also use the Office Help system and install an app for Office. Your completed document will look similar to Figure 1.24.

PROJECT FILES

For Project 1B, you will need the following file:

of01B_Rehearsal_Dinner

You will save your file as:

Lastname_Firstname_1B_Rehearsal_Dinner

PROJECT RESULTS

Skyline Metro Grill

TO:	Sarah Jackson, Executive Chef
FROM:	Laura Mabry Hernandez, General Manager
DATE:	February 17, 2016
SUBJECT:	Wedding Rehearsal Dinners

In the spring and summer months, wedding rehearsal dinners provide a new marketing opportunity for Skyline Metro Grill at all of our locations. A rehearsal dinner is an informal meal following a wedding rehearsal at which the bride and groom typically thank those who have helped them make their wedding a special event.

Our smaller private dining rooms with sweeping city views are an ideal location for a rehearsal dinner. At each of our locations, I have directed the Sales and Marketing Coordinator to partner with local wedding planners to promote Skyline Metro Grill as a relaxed yet sophisticated venue for rehearsal dinners. The typical rehearsal dinner includes the wedding party, the immediate family of the bride and groom, and out-of-town guests.

Please develop six menus—in varying price ranges—to present to local wedding planners so that they can easily promote Skyline Metro Grill to couples who are planning a rehearsal dinner. In addition to a traditional dinner, we should also include options for a buffet-style dinner and a family-style dinner.

This marketing effort will require extensive communication with our Sales and Marketing Coordinators and with local wedding planners. Let's meet to discuss the details and the marketing challenges, and to create a promotional piece that begins something like this:

Skyline Metro Grill for Your Rehearsal Dinner

Lastname_Firstname_1B_Rehearsal_Dinner

FIGURE 1.24 Project 1B Memo

Video OF1-7

In any Office program, you can display the **Open dialog box**, from which you can navigate to and then open an existing file that was created in that same program.

The Open dialog box, along with the Save and Save As dialog boxes, is a common dialog box. These dialog boxes, which are provided by the Windows programming interface, display in all Office programs in the same manner. So the Open, Save, and Save As dialog boxes will all look and perform the same regardless of the Office program in which you are working.

Activity 1.10 | Opening an Existing File and Saving It with a New Name

In this activity, you will display the Open dialog box, open an existing Word document, and then save it in your storage location with a new name.

1 Sign in to your computer, and then on the Windows 8 Start screen, type **word 2013** Press Enter to open Word on your desktop. If you want to do so, on the taskbar, right-click the **Word icon**, and then click **Pin this program to taskbar** to keep the Word program available from your desktop.

2 On Word's opening screen, on the left, click **Open Other Documents**. Under **Open**, click **Computer**, and then on the right click **Browse**.

3 In the **Open** dialog box, on the left in the **navigation pane**, scroll down, if necessary expand ▷ Computer, and then click the name of your **USB flash drive**. In the **file list**, double-click the **Office_Features** folder that you downloaded.

4 Double-click **of01B_Rehearsal_Dinner**. If **PROTECTED VIEW** displays at the top of your screen, in the center click **Enable Editing**.

In Office 2013, a file will open in **Protected View** if the file appears to be from a potentially risky location, such as the Internet. Protected View is a security feature in Office 2013 that protects your computer from malicious files by opening them in a restricted environment until you enable them. **Trusted Documents** is another security feature that remembers which files you have already enabled.

You might encounter these security features if you open a file from an email or download files from the Internet; for example, from your college's learning management system or from the Pearson website. So long as you trust the source of the file, click Enable Editing or Enable Content—depending on the type of file you receive—and then go ahead and work with the file.

5 With the document displayed in the Word window, be sure that **Show/Hide** is active; if necessary, on the HOME tab, in the Paragraph group, click Show/Hide to activate it. Compare your screen with Figure 1.25.

FIGURE 1.25

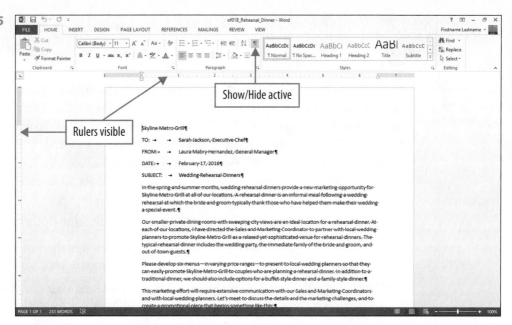

Show/Hide active

Rulers visible

Skyline·Metro·Grill¶

TO: → → Sarah·Jackson,·Executive·Chef¶

FROM:→ → Laura·Mabry·Hernandez,·General·Manager¶

DATE:→ February·17,·2016¶

SUBJECT:→ Wedding·Rehearsal·Dinners¶

In·the·spring·and·summer·months,·wedding·rehearsal·dinners·provide·a·new·marketing·opportunity·for·Skyline·Metro·Grill·at·all·of·our·locations.·A·rehearsal·dinner·is·an·informal·meal·following·a·wedding·rehearsal·at·which·the·bride·and·groom·typically·thank·those·who·have·helped·them·make·their·wedding·a·special·event.¶

Our·smaller·private·dining·rooms·with·sweeping·city·views·are·an·ideal·location·for·a·rehearsal·dinner.·At·each·of·our·locations,·I·have·directed·the·Sales·and·Marketing·Coordinator·to·partner·with·local·wedding·planners·to·promote·Skyline·Metro·Grill·as·a·relaxed·yet·sophisticated·venue·for·rehearsal·dinners.·The·typical·rehearsal·dinner·includes·the·wedding·party,·the·immediate·family·of·the·bride·and·groom,·and·out·of·town·guests.¶

Please·develop·six·menus—in·varying·price·ranges—to·present·to·local·wedding·planners·so·that·they·can·easily·promote·Skyline·Metro·Grill·to·couples·who·are·planning·a·rehearsal·dinner.·In·addition·to·a·traditional·dinner,·we·should·also·include·options·for·a·buffet·style·dinner·and·a·family·style·dinner.¶

This·marketing·effort·will·require·extensive·communication·with·our·Sales·and·Marketing·Coordinators·and·with·local·wedding·planners.·Let's·meet·to·discuss·the·details·and·the·marketing·challenges,·and·to·create·a·promotional·piece·that·begins·something·like·this:¶

6 Click the **FILE tab** to display **Backstage** view, and then on the left, click **Save As**. On the right, click the folder under **Current Folder** to open the **Save As** dialog box. Notice that the current folder is the **Office_Features** folder you downloaded.

ANOTHER WAY Press F12 to display the Save As dialog box.

7 In the upper left corner of the **Save As** dialog box, click the **Up** button ↑ to move up one level in the File Explorer hierarchy. In the **file list**, double-click your **Office Features Chapter 1** folder to open it.

8 Click in the **File name** box to select the existing text, and then, using your own name, type **Lastname_Firstname_1B_Rehearsal_Dinner** Compare your screen with Figure 1.26.

FIGURE 1.26

Save As dialog box

Up button

Path to your folder on your USB flash drive

File name (your own name displays)

9 Click **Save** or press Enter; notice that your new file name displays in the title bar.

The original document closes, and your new document, based on the original, displays with the name in the title bar.

More Knowledge **Read-Only**

Some files might display **Read-Only** in the title bar, which is a property assigned to a file that prevents the file from being modified or deleted; it indicates that you cannot save any changes to the displayed document unless you first save it with a new name.

Video OF1-8

If you sign in to Windows 8 with a Microsoft account, you may notice that you are also signed in to Office. This enables you to save files to and retrieve files from your SkyDrive and to *collaborate* with others on Office files when you want to do so. To collaborate means to work with others as a team in an intellectual endeavor to complete a shared task or to achieve a shared goal.

Within each Office application, an *Options dialog box* enables you to select program settings and other options and preferences. For example, you can set preferences for viewing and editing files.

Activity 1.11 | Signing In to Office and Viewing Application Options

1 In the upper right corner of your screen, if you are signed in with a Microsoft account, click the arrow to the right of your name, and then compare your screen with Figure 1.27.

Here you can change your photo, go to About me to edit your profile, examine your Account settings, or switch accounts to sign in with a different Microsoft account.

FIGURE 1.27

2 Click the **FILE tab** to display **Backstage** view. On the left, click the last tab—**Options**.

3 In the **Word Options** dialog box, on the left, click **Display**, and then on the right, locate the information under **Always show these formatting marks on the screen**.

4 Under **Always show these formatting marks on the screen**, be sure the last check box, **Show all formatting marks**, is selected—select it if necessary. Compare your screen with Figure 1.28.

FIGURE 1.28

5 In the lower right corner of the dialog box, click **OK**.

Video OF1-9

The ribbon that displays across the top of the program window groups commands in a manner that you would most logically use them. The ribbon in each Office program is slightly different, but all contain the same three elements: *tabs*, *groups*, and *commands*.

Tabs display across the top of the ribbon, and each tab relates to a type of activity; for example, laying out a page. Groups are sets of related commands for specific tasks. Commands—instructions to computer programs—are arranged in groups and might display as a button, a menu, or a box in which you type information.

You can also minimize the ribbon so only the tab names display, which is useful when working on a smaller screen such as a tablet computer where you want to maximize your screen viewing area.

Activity 1.12 | Performing Commands from and Customizing the Ribbon and the Quick Access Toolbar

1 ▶ Take a moment to examine the document on your screen. If necessary, on the ribbon, click the VIEW tab, and then in the Show group, click to place a check mark in the Ruler check box. Compare your screen with Figure 1.29.

This document is a memo from the General Manager to the Executive Chef regarding a new restaurant promotion for wedding rehearsal dinners.

When working in Word, display the rulers so that you can see how margin settings affect your document and how text and objects align. Additionally, if you set a tab stop or an indent, its location is visible on the ruler.

FIGURE 1.29

Ruler checkbox selected

VIEW tab active

Show group

Rulers display

2 ▶ In the upper left corner of your screen, above the ribbon, locate the **Quick Access Toolbar**.

Recall that the Quick Access Toolbar contains commands that you use frequently. By default, only the commands Save, Undo, and Redo display, but you can add and delete commands to suit your needs. Possibly the computer at which you are working already has additional commands added to the Quick Access Toolbar.

3 ▶ At the end of the **Quick Access Toolbar**, click the **Customize Quick Access Toolbar** button ⬚, and then compare your screen with Figure 1.30.

A list of commands that Office users commonly add to their Quick Access Toolbar displays, including New, Open, Email, Quick Print, and Print Preview and Print. Commands already on the Quick Access Toolbar display a check mark. Commands that you add to the Quick Access Toolbar are always just one click away.

Here you can also display the More Commands dialog box, from which you can select any command from any tab on the ribbon to add to the Quick Access Toolbar.

 BY TOUCH   Tap once on Quick Access Toolbar commands.

FIGURE 1.30

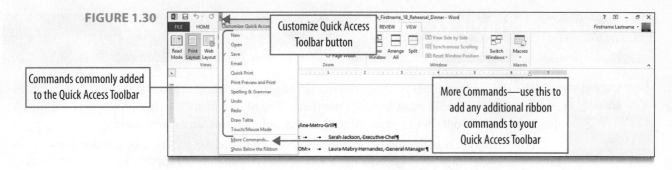

Commands commonly added to the Quick Access Toolbar

Customize Quick Access Toolbar button

More Commands—use this to add any additional ribbon commands to your Quick Access Toolbar

4 ▶ On the list, click **Print Preview and Print**, and then notice that the icon is added to the **Quick Access Toolbar**. Compare your screen with Figure 1.31.

The icon that represents the Print Preview command displays on the Quick Access Toolbar. Because this is a command that you will use frequently while building Office documents, you might decide to have this command remain on your Quick Access Toolbar.

↻ ANOTHER WAY   Right-click any command on the ribbon, and then on the shortcut menu, click Add to Quick Access Toolbar.

FIGURE 1.31

Icon for Print Preview and Print added to Quick Access Toolbar

5 ▶ In the first line of the document, if necessary, click to the left of the *S* in *Skyline* to position the insertion point there, and then press Enter one time to insert a blank paragraph. Press ↑ one time to position the insertion point in the new blank paragraph. Compare your screen with Figure 1.32.

FIGURE 1.32

Insertion point blinking in new blank paragraph

6 ▶ On the ribbon, click the **INSERT tab**. In the **Illustrations group**, *point* to the **Online Pictures** button to display its ScreenTip.

Many buttons on the ribbon have this type of *enhanced ScreenTip*, which displays useful descriptive information about the command.

7 ▶ Click **Online Pictures**, and then compare your screen with Figure 1.33.

In the Insert Pictures dialog box you can search for online pictures using Microsoft's Clip Art collection. *Clip art* refers to royalty-free photos and illustrations you can download from Microsoft's Office.com site.

Here you can also search for images using the Bing search engine, and if you are signed in with your Microsoft account, you can also find images on your SkyDrive or on your computer by clicking Browse. At the bottom, you can click the Flickr logo and download pictures from your Flickr account if you have one.

FIGURE 1.33

> Search Office.com

> Find pictures on your SkyDrive (if you are signed in with a Microsoft account)

> Search with Bing

> Browse your own files for pictures (if signed in)

> Find pictures on Flickr (if signed in with a Microsoft account)

8 Click **Office.com Clip Art** and in the box that displays to the right, type **salad in a bowl** and press Enter. As shown in Figure 1.34, point to the illustration of the salad bowl to display its keywords.

You can use various keywords to find clip art that is appropriate for your documents.

FIGURE 1.34

> ScreenTip displays keywords for this clip

> Insert button

9 Click the illustration of the salad to select it, and then in the lower right corner, click **Insert**. In the upper right corner of the picture, point to the **Layout Options** button to display its ScreenTip, and then compare your screen with Figure 1.35. If you cannot find the image, select a similar image, and then drag one of the corner sizing handles to match the approximate size shown in the figure.

Inserted pictures anchor—attach to—the paragraph at the insertion point location—as indicated by the anchor symbol. *Layout Options* enable you to choose how the *object*—in this instance an inserted picture—interacts with the surrounding text. An object is a picture or other graphic such as a chart or table that you can select and then move and resize.

When a picture is selected, the PICTURE TOOLS become available on the ribbon. Additionally, *sizing handles*—small squares that indicate an object is selected—surround the selected picture.

FIGURE 1.35

> PICTURE TOOLS available on the ribbon

> Layout Options button, ScreenTip displayed

> Sizing handles indicate object is selected

10 With the image selected, click **Layout Options** , and then under **With Text Wrapping**, in the second row, click the first layout—**Top and Bottom**.

11 Point to the image to display the ⇕ pointer, hold down the left mouse button to display a green line at the left margin, and then drag the image to the right and slightly upward until a green line displays in the center of the image and at the top of the image, as shown in Figure 1.36, and then release the left mouse button. If you are not satisfied with your result, on the Quick Access Toolbar, click Undo ↺ and begin again.

> *Alignment Guides* are green lines that display to help you align objects with margins or at the center of a page.

FIGURE 1.36

12 On the ribbon, in the **Picture Styles group**, point to the first style to display the ScreenTip *Simple Frame, White*, and notice that the image displays with a white frame.

13 Watch the image as you point to the second picture style, and then to the third, and then to the fourth.

> Recall that Live Preview shows the result of applying an editing or formatting change as you point to possible results—*before* you actually apply it.

14 In the **Picture Styles group**, click the second style—**Beveled Matte, White**—and then click anywhere outside of the image to deselect it. Notice that the *PICTURE TOOLS* no longer display on the ribbon. Compare your screen with Figure 1.37.

Contextual tabs on the ribbon display only when you need them.

FIGURE 1.37

15 On the **Quick Access Toolbar**, click **Save** 🔲 to save the changes you have made.

Activity 1.13 | Minimizing and Using the Keyboard to Control the Ribbon

Instead of a mouse, some individuals prefer to navigate the ribbon by using keys on the keyboard.

1 On your keyboard, press [Alt], and then on the ribbon, notice that small labels display. Press [N] to activate the commands on the **INSERT tab**, and then compare your screen with Figure 1.38.

Each label represents a *KeyTip*—an indication of the key that you can press to activate the command. For example, on the INSERT tab, you can press [F] to open the Online Pictures dialog box.

FIGURE 1.38

2 Press [Esc] to redisplay the KeyTips for the tabs. Then, press [Alt] or [Esc] again to turn off keyboard control of the ribbon.

3 Point to any tab on the ribbon and right-click to display a shortcut menu.

Here you can choose to display the Quick Access Toolbar below the ribbon or collapse the ribbon to maximize screen space. You can also customize the ribbon by adding, removing, renaming, or reordering tabs, groups, and commands, although this is not recommended until you become an expert Office user.

4 Click **Collapse the Ribbon**. Notice that only the ribbon tabs display. Click the **HOME tab** to display the commands. Click anywhere in the document, and notice that the ribbon goes back to the collapsed display.

5 Right-click any ribbon tab, and then click **Collapse the Ribbon** again to remove the check mark from this command.

Many expert Office users prefer the full ribbon display.

6 Point to any tab on the ribbon, and then on your mouse device, roll the mouse wheel. Notice that different tabs become active as you roll the mouse wheel.

You can make a tab active by using this technique instead of clicking the tab.

Objective 10 Apply Formatting in Office Programs

Video OF1-10

Activity 1.14 | Changing Page Orientation and Zoom Level

In this activity, you will practice common formatting techniques used in Office applications.

1 On the ribbon, click the **PAGE LAYOUT tab**. In the **Page Setup group**, click **Orientation**, and notice that two orientations display—*Portrait* and *Landscape*. Click **Landscape**.

In *portrait orientation*, the paper is taller than it is wide. In *landscape orientation*, the paper is wider than it is tall.

2 In the lower right corner of the screen, locate the **Zoom slider** .

Recall that to zoom means to increase or decrease the viewing area. You can zoom in to look closely at a section of a document, and then zoom out to see an entire page on the screen. You can also zoom to view multiple pages on the screen.

3 Drag the **Zoom slider** to the left until you have zoomed to approximately *60%*. Compare your screen with Figure 1.39.

FIGURE 1.39

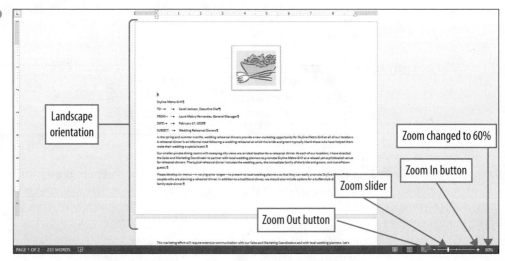

🔄 **BY TOUCH** Drag the Zoom slider with your finger.

4 Use the technique you just practiced to change the **Orientation** back to **Portrait**.

The default orientation in Word is Portrait, which is commonly used for business documents such as letters and memos.

5 In the lower right corner, click the **Zoom In** button ⊞ as many times as necessary to return to the **100%** zoom setting.

> Use the zoom feature to adjust the view of your document for editing and for your viewing comfort.

🔄 ANOTHER WAY   You can also control Zoom from the ribbon. On the VIEW tab, in the Zoom group, you can control the Zoom level and also zoom to view multiple pages.

6 On the **Quick Access Toolbar**, click **Save** 🖫.

More Knowledge   **Zooming to Page Width**

Some Office users prefer Page Width, which zooms the document so that the width of the page matches the width of the window. Find this command on the VIEW tab, in the Zoom group.

Activity 1.15 │ Formatting Text by Using Fonts, Alignment, Font Colors, and Font Styles

1 If necessary, on the right side of your screen, drag the vertical scroll box to the top of the scroll bar. To the left of *Skyline Metro Grill*, point in the margin area to display the 🔏 pointer and click one time to select the entire paragraph. Compare your screen with Figure 1.40.

> Use this technique to select complete paragraphs from the margin area—drag downward to select multiple-line paragraphs—which is faster and more efficient than dragging through text.

FIGURE 1.40

2 On the ribbon, click the **HOME tab**, and then in the **Paragraph group**, click **Center** 🗏 to center the paragraph.

3 On the **HOME tab**, in the **Font group**, click the **Font button arrow** [Calibri (Body) ▾]. On the alphabetical list of font names, scroll down and then locate and *point to* **Cambria**.

> A *font* is a set of characters with the same design and shape. The default font in a Word document is Calibri, which is a *sans serif* font—a font design with no lines or extensions on the ends of characters.
>
> The Cambria font is a *serif font*—a font design that includes small line extensions on the ends of the letters to guide the eye in reading from left to right.
>
> The list of fonts displays as a gallery showing potential results. For example, in the Font gallery, you can point to see the actual design and format of each font as it would look if applied to text.

4 Point to several other fonts and observe the effect on the selected text. Then, scroll back to the top of the **Font** gallery. Under **Theme Fonts**, click **Calibri Light**.

> A *theme* is a predesigned combination of colors, fonts, line, and fill effects that look good together and is applied to an entire document by a single selection. A theme combines two sets of fonts—one for text and one for headings. In the default Office theme, Calibri Light is the suggested font for headings.

5 With the paragraph *Skyline Metro Grill* still selected, on the **HOME tab**, in the **Font group**, click the **Font Size button arrow** , point to **36**, and then notice how Live Preview displays the text in the font size to which you are pointing. Compare your screen with Figure 1.41.

FIGURE 1.41

6 On the list of font sizes, click **20**.

Fonts are measured in *points*, with one point equal to 1/72 of an inch. A higher point size indicates a larger font size. Headings and titles are often formatted by using a larger font size. The word *point* is abbreviated as *pt*.

7 With *Skyline Metro Grill* still selected, on the **HOME tab**, in the **Font group**, click the **Font Color button arrow** . Under **Theme Colors**, in the last column, click the last color—**Green, Accent 6, Darker 50%**. Click anywhere to deselect the text.

8 To the left of *TO:*, point in the left margin area to display the ⟨pointer⟩ pointer, hold down the left mouse button, and then drag down to select the four memo headings. Compare your screen with Figure 1.42.

Use this technique to select complete paragraphs from the margin area—drag downward to select multiple paragraphs—which is faster and more efficient than dragging through text.

🔄 **BY TOUCH**   Tap once on TO: to display the gripper, then with your finger, drag to the right and down to select the four paragraphs.

FIGURE 1.42

9 With the four paragraphs selected, on the mini toolbar, click the **Font Color** button $\boxed{A \cdot}$, and notice that the text color of the four paragraphs changes.

> The font color button retains its most recently used color—Green, Accent 6, Darker 50%. As you progress in your study of Microsoft Office, you will use other buttons that behave in this manner; that is, they retain their most recently used format. This is commonly referred to as *MRU*—most recently used.

> Recall that the mini toolbar places commands that are commonly used for the selected text or object close by so that you reduce the distance that you must move your mouse to access a command. If you are using a touchscreen device, most commands that you need are close and easy to touch.

10 On the right, drag the vertical scroll box down slightly to position more of the text on the screen. Click anywhere in the paragraph that begins *In the spring*, and then *triple-click*—click the left mouse button three times—to select the entire paragraph. If the entire paragraph is not selected, click in the paragraph and begin again.

11 With the entire paragraph selected, on the mini toolbar, click the **Font Color button arrow** $\boxed{A \cdot}$, and then under **Theme Colors**, in the sixth column, click the last color— **Orange, Accent 2, Darker 50%**.

12 In the memo headings, select the guide word *TO:* and then on the mini toolbar, click **Bold** $\boxed{B}$ and **Italic** $\boxed{I}$.

> *Font styles* include bold, italic, and underline. Font styles emphasize text and are a visual cue to draw the reader's eye to important text.

13 On the mini toolbar, click **Italic** $\boxed{I}$ again to turn off the Italic formatting.

> A *toggle button* is a button that can be turned on by clicking it once, and then turned off by clicking it again.

Activity 1.16 │ Using Format Painter

Use the Format Painter to copy the formatting of specific text or of a paragraph and then apply it in other locations in your document.

1 With *TO:* still selected, on the mini toolbar, click **Format Painter** $\boxed{\cdot}$. Then, move your mouse under the word *Sarah*, and notice the $\boxed{\text{A}I}$ mouse pointer. Compare your screen with Figure 1.43.

> The pointer takes the shape of a paintbrush, and contains the formatting information from the paragraph where the insertion point is positioned. Information about the Format Painter and how to turn it off displays in the status bar.

FIGURE 1.43

2 With the pointer, drag to select the guide word *FROM:* and notice that Bold formatting is applied. Then, point to the selected text *FROM:* and on the mini toolbar, *double-click* **Format Painter** .

3 Select the guide word *DATE:* to copy the Bold formatting, and notice that the pointer retains the shape.

> When you *double-click* the Format Painter button, the Format Painter feature remains active until you either click the Format Painter button again, or press Esc to cancel it—as indicated on the status bar.

4 With Format Painter still active, select the guide word *SUBJECT:*, and then on the ribbon, on the **HOME tab**, in the **Clipboard group**, notice that **Format Painter** is selected, indicating that it is active. Compare your screen with Figure 1.44.

FIGURE 1.44

5 On the ribbon, click **Format Painter** to turn the command off.

🔄 **ANOTHER WAY**   Press Esc to turn off Format Painter.

---

6 ▶ In the paragraph that begins *In the spring*, triple-click again to select the entire paragraph. On the mini toolbar, click **Bold** [B] and *Italic* [I]. Click anywhere to deselect.

7 ▶ On the **Quick Access Toolbar**, click **Save** [🖫] to save the changes you have made to your document.

Activity 1.17 | Using Keyboard Shortcuts and Using the Clipboard to Copy, Cut, and Paste

The *Clipboard* is a temporary storage area that holds text or graphics that you select and then cut or copy. When you *copy* text or graphics, a copy is placed on the Clipboard and the original text or graphic remains in place. When you *cut* text or graphics, a copy is placed on the Clipboard, and the original text or graphic is removed—cut—from the document.

After copying or cutting, the contents of the Clipboard are available for you to *paste*—insert—in a new location in the current document, or into another Office file.

1 ▶ Hold down [Ctrl] and press [Home] to move to the beginning of your document, and then take a moment to study the table in Figure 1.45, which describes similar keyboard shortcuts with which you can navigate quickly in a document.

FIGURE 1.45

KEYBOARD SHORTCUTS TO NAVIGATE IN A DOCUMENT	
TO MOVE	**PRESS**
To the beginning of a document	[Ctrl] + [Home]
To the end of a document	[Ctrl] + [End]
To the beginning of a line	[Home]
To the end of a line	[End]
To the beginning of the previous word	[Ctrl] + [←]
To the beginning of the next word	[Ctrl] + [→]
To the beginning of the current word (if insertion point is in the middle of a word)	[Ctrl] + [←]
To the beginning of the previous paragraph	[Ctrl] + [↑]
To the beginning of the next paragraph	[Ctrl] + [↓]
To the beginning of the current paragraph (if insertion point is in the middle of a paragraph)	[Ctrl] + [↑]
Up one screen	[PgUp]
Down one screen	[PgDn]

2 ▶ To the left of *Skyline Metro Grill*, point in the left margin area to display the [⏶] pointer, and then click one time to select the entire paragraph. On the **HOME tab**, in the **Clipboard group**, click **Copy** [🗎].

Because anything that you select and then copy—or cut—is placed on the Clipboard, the Copy command and the Cut command display in the Clipboard group of commands on the ribbon. There is no visible indication that your copied selection has been placed on the Clipboard.

🔄 **ANOTHER WAY**   Right-click the selection, and then click Copy on the shortcut menu; or, use the keyboard shortcut [Ctrl] + [C].

3 On the **HOME tab**, in the **Clipboard group**, to the right of the group name *Clipboard*, click the **Dialog Box Launcher** button ⬚, and then compare your screen with Figure 1.46.

The Clipboard pane displays with your copied text. In any ribbon group, the ***Dialog Box Launcher*** displays either a dialog box or a pane related to the group of commands. It is not necessary to display the Clipboard in this manner, although sometimes it is useful to do so.

FIGURE 1.46

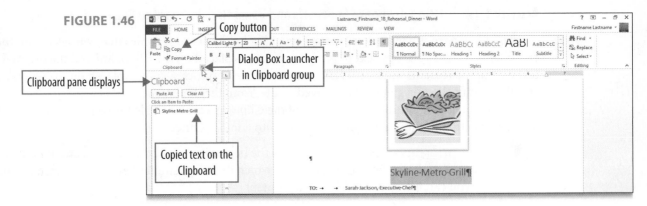

4 In the upper right corner of the **Clipboard** pane, click **Close** ✖.

5 Press Ctrl + End to move to the end of your document. Press Enter one time to create a new blank paragraph. On the **HOME tab**, in the **Clipboard group**, point to **Paste**, and then click the *upper* portion of this split button.

The Paste command pastes the most recently copied item on the Clipboard at the insertion point location. If you click the lower portion of the Paste button, a gallery of Paste Options displays. A ***split button*** is divided into two parts; clicking the main part of the button performs a command, and clicking the arrow displays a list or gallery with choices.

🔄 **ANOTHER WAY**   Right-click, on the shortcut menu under Paste Options, click the desired option button; or, press Ctrl + V.

6 Below the pasted text, click **Paste Options** 📋 as shown in Figure 1.47.

Here you can view and apply various formatting options for pasting your copied or cut text. Typically you will click Paste on the ribbon and paste the item in its original format. If you want some other format for the pasted item, you can choose another format from the ***Paste Options gallery***.

The Paste Options gallery provides a Live Preview of the various options for changing the format of the pasted item with a single click. The Paste Options gallery is available in three places: on the ribbon by clicking the lower portion of the Paste button—the Paste button arrow; from the Paste Options button that displays below the pasted item following the paste operation; or on the shortcut menu if you right-click the pasted item.

FIGURE 1.47

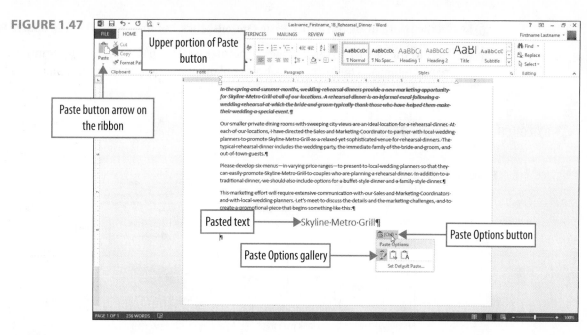

Upper portion of Paste button

Paste button arrow on the ribbon

Pasted text → Skyline·Metro·Grill¶

Paste Options button

Paste Options gallery

---

7 In the **Paste Options** gallery, *point* to each option to see the Live Preview of the format that would be applied if you clicked the button.

> The contents of the Paste Options gallery are contextual; that is, they change based on what you copied and where you are pasting.

8 Press Esc to close the gallery; the button will remain displayed until you take some other screen action.

9 Press Ctrl + Home to move to the top of the document, and then click the **salad image** one time to select it. While pointing to the selected image, right-click, and then on the shortcut menu, click **Cut**.

> Recall that the Cut command cuts—removes—the selection from the document and places it on the Clipboard.

🔁 **ANOTHER WAY**   On the HOME tab, in the Clipboard group, click the Cut button; or, use the keyboard shortcut Ctrl + X.

10 Press Del one time to remove the blank paragraph from the top of the document, and then press Ctrl + End to move to the end of the document.

11 With the insertion point blinking in the blank paragraph at the end of the document, right-click, and notice that the **Paste Options** gallery displays on the shortcut menu. Compare your screen with Figure 1.48.

FIGURE 1.48

Paste Options on the shortcut menu

12 On the shortcut menu, under **Paste Options**, click the first button—**Keep Source Formatting**.

13 Point to the picture to display the pointer, and then drag to the right until the center green **Alignment Guide** displays and the blank paragraph is above the picture, as shown in Figure 1.49. Release the left mouse button.

🔁 **BY TOUCH**   Drag the picture with your finger to display the Alignment Guide.

FIGURE 1.49

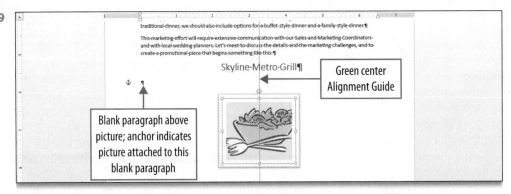

14 Above the picture, click to position the insertion point at the end of the word *Grill*, press Spacebar one time, type **for Your Rehearsal Dinner** and then **Save** 💾 your document. Compare your screen with Figure 1.50.

FIGURE 1.50

15 On the **INSERT tab**, in the **Header & Footer group**, click **Footer**. At the bottom of the list, click **Edit Footer**, and then with the **HEADER & FOOTER Design tab** active, in the **Insert group**, click **Document Info**. Click **File Name** to add the file name to the footer.

16 On the right end of the ribbon, click **Close Header and Footer**.

17 On the **Quick Access Toolbar**, point to the **Print Preview and Print icon** 🔍 you placed there, right-click, and then click **Remove from Quick Access Toolbar**.

   If you are working on your own computer and you want to do so, you can leave the icon on the toolbar; in a lab setting, you should return the software to its original settings.

18 Click **Save** 💾 and then click the **FILE tab** to display **Backstage** view. With the **Info tab** active, in the lower right corner click **Show All Properties**. As **Tags**, type **weddings, rehearsal dinners, marketing**

19 As the **Subject**, type your course name and number—for example *CIS 10, #5543*. Under **Related People**, be sure your name displays as the author (edit it if necessary), and then on the left, click **Print** to display the Print Preview. Compare your screen with Figure 1.51.

FIGURE 1.51

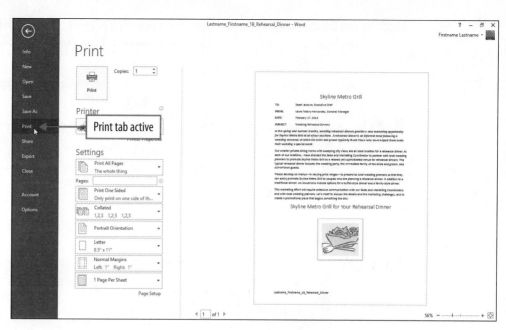

20 ▶ On the left side of **Backstage** view, click **Save**. As directed by your instructor, print or submit your file electronically as described in Project 1A, and then in the upper right corner of the Word window, click **Close** | ✕ |.

21 ▶ If a message indicates *Would you like to keep the last item you copied?* click **No**.

This message displays if you have copied some type of image to the Clipboard. If you click Yes, the items on the Clipboard will remain for you to use in another program or document.

Objective 11 | Compress Files and Use the Microsoft Office 2013 Help System

Video OF1-11

A *compressed file* is a file that has been reduced in size. Compressed files take up less storage space and can be transferred to other computers faster than uncompressed files. You can also combine a group of files into one compressed folder, which makes it easier to share a group of files.

Within each Office program, the Help feature provides information about all of the program's features and displays step-by-step instructions for performing many tasks.

Activity 1.18 | Compressing Files

In this activity, you will combine the two files you created in this chapter into one compressed file.

1 ▶ On the Windows taskbar, click **File Explorer** [icon]. On the left, in the **navigation pane**, navigate to your **USB flash drive**, and then open your **Office Features Chapter 1** folder. Compare your screen with Figure 1.52.

FIGURE 1.52

2 In the **file list**, click your **Lastname_Firstname_1A_Note_Form** Word file one time to select it. Then, hold down Ctrl, and click your **Lastname_Firstname_1B_Rehearsal_Dinner** file to select the files in the list.

In any Windows-based program, holding down Ctrl while selecting enables you to select multiple items.

3 On the **File Explorer** ribbon, click **Share**, and then in the **Send group**, click **Zip**. Compare your screen with Figure 1.53.

Windows creates a compressed folder containing a *copy* of each of the selected files. The folder name is selected—highlighted in blue—so that you can rename it.

⟳ BY TOUCH   Tap the ribbon commands.

FIGURE 1.53

⟳ ANOTHER WAY   Point to the selected files in the File List, right-click, point to Send to, and then click Compressed (zipped) folder.

4 Using your own name, type **Lastname_Firstname_Office_Features_Chapter_1** and press Enter.

The compressed folder is ready to attach to an email or share in some other format.

5 In the upper right corner of the folder window, click **Close** ⊠.

Activity 1.19 | Using the Microsoft Office 2013 Help System in Excel

In this activity, you will use the Microsoft Help feature to find information about formatting numbers in Excel.

1 Press ⊞ to display the Windows 8 **Start screen**, and then type **excel 2013** Press Enter to open the Excel desktop app.

2 On Excel's opening screen, click **Blank workbook**, and then in the upper right corner, click **Microsoft Excel Help** ⊙.

⟳ ANOTHER WAY   Press F1 to display Help in any Office program.

3 In the **Excel Help** window, click in the **Search online help** box, type **formatting numbers** and then press Enter.

4 On the list of results, click **Format numbers as currency**. Compare your screen with Figure 1.54.

FIGURE 1.54

> 5 ▶ If you want to do so, at the top of the **Excel Help** window, click Print 🖶 to print a copy of this information for your reference.

> 6 ▶ In the upper right corner of the Help window, click **Close** ×.

> 7 ▶ Leave Excel open for the next activity.

Objective 12 | Install Apps for Office and Create a Microsoft Account

A L E R T !   **Working with Web-Based Applications and Services**

Computer programs and services on the web receive continuous updates and improvements. Thus, the steps to complete the following web-based activities may differ from the ones shown. You can often look at the screens and the information presented to determine how to complete the activity.

Video OF1-12

Apps for Office 2013 and SharePoint 2013 are a collection of downloadable apps that enable you to create and view information within your familiar Office programs. Some of these apps are developed by Microsoft, but many more are developed by specialists in different fields. As new apps are developed, they will be available from the online Office Store.

An ***app for Office*** is a webpage that works within one of the Office applications, such as Excel, that you download from the Office Store. Office apps combine cloud services and web technologies within the user interface of Office and SharePoint. For example, in Excel, you can use an app to look up and gather search results for a new apartment by placing the information in an Excel worksheet, and then use maps to determine the distance of each apartment to work and to family members.

Activity 1.20 | Installing Apps for Office

A L E R T !   **You Must Be Signed In to Office with a Microsoft Account to Complete This Activity**

To download an Office app, you must be signed in to Office with a free Microsoft account. If you do not have a Microsoft account, refer to the next activity to create one by using Microsoft's outlook.com email service, which includes free SkyDrive cloud storage.

> 1 ▶ On the Excel ribbon, click the **INSERT tab**. In the **Apps group**, click the **Apps for Office** arrow, and then click **See All**.

> 2 ▶ Click **FEATURED APPS**, and then on the right, click in the **Search for apps on the Office Store** box, type **Bing Maps** and press Enter.

> 3 ▶ Click the **Bing logo**, and then click the **Add** button, and then if necessary, click Continue.

> 4 ▶ **Close** ⊠ Internet Explorer, and then **Close** ⊠ the **Apps for Office** box.

5 On the **INSERT tab**, in the **Apps group**, click **Apps for Office**, click **See All**, click **MY APPS**, click the **Bing Map**s app, and then in the lower right corner, click **Insert**.

6 On the Welcome message, click **Insert Sample Data**.

Here, the Bing map displays information related to the sample data. Each state in the sample data displays a small pie chart that represents the two sets of data. Compare your screen with Figure 1.55.

This is just one example of many apps downloadable from the Office store.

FIGURE 1.55

7 **Close** ☒ Excel without saving.

Activity 1.21 | Creating a Microsoft Account

ALERT! **This Is an Optional Activity**

You will find both Windows 8 and Office 2013 to be much more useful if you sign in with a Microsoft account. If you already have an email account from msn.com, hotmail.com, live.com, or outlook.com, then you already have a Microsoft account. If you do not, you can create a free Microsoft account by following the steps in this activity.

In Windows 8, you can create a Microsoft account, and then use that account to sign in to *any* Windows 8 PC. Signing in with a Microsoft account is recommended because you can:

- Download Windows 8 apps from the Windows Store.
- Get your online content—email, social network updates, updated news—automatically displayed in an app on the Windows 8 Start screen when you sign in.
- Synch settings online to make every Windows 8 computer you use look and feel the same.
- Sign in to Office so that you can store documents on your SkyDrive and download Office apps.

1 Open Internet Explorer 🅴, and then go to **www.outlook.com**

2 Locate and click **Sign up now** to display a screen similar to Figure 1.56. Complete the form to create your account.

FIGURE 1.56

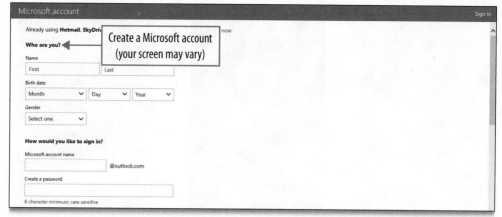

3 Close ⊠ Internet Explorer.

END | You have completed Project 1B

END OF CHAPTER

SUMMARY

Many Office features and commands, such as the Open and Save As dialog boxes, performing commands from the ribbon and from dialog boxes, and using the Clipboard are the same in all Office desktop apps.

A desktop app is installed on your computer and requires a computer operating system such as Microsoft Windows or Apple OS to run. The programs in Microsoft Office 2013 are considered to be desktop apps.

Apps that run on a smartphone or tablet computer—for example, iOS, Android, or Windows Phone—or apps that run from browser software such as Internet Explorer or Chrome on a PC, are referred to as apps.

Within each Office app, you can install additional Apps for Office from the Office Store. You must have a Microsoft account, which includes free SkyDrive storage, to download Windows 8 or Office apps.

GO! LEARN IT ONLINE

Review the concepts and key terms in this chapter by completing these online challenges, which you can find at **www.pearsonhighered.com/go**.

Matching and Multiple Choice:
Answer matching and multiple choice questions to test what you learned in this chapter. MyITLab®

Crossword Puzzle:
Spell out the words that match the numbered clues, and put them in the puzzle squares.

Flipboard:
Flip through the definitions of the key terms in this chapter and match them with the correct term.

GLOSSARY

GLOSSARY OF CHAPTER KEY TERMS

Address bar (Internet Explorer) The area at the top of the Internet Explorer window that displays, and where you can type, a URL—Uniform Resource Locator—which is an address that uniquely identifies a location on the Internet.

Address bar (Windows) The bar at the top of a folder window with which you can navigate to a different folder or library, or go back to a previous one.

Alignment The placement of text or objects relative to the left and right margins.

Alignment guides Green lines that display when you move an object to assist in alignment.

App The term that commonly refers to computer programs that run from the device software on a smartphone or a tablet computer—for example, iOS, Android, or Windows Phone—or computer programs that run from the browser software on a desktop PC or laptop PC—for example Internet Explorer, Safari, Firefox, or Chrome.

App for Office A webpage that works within one of the Office applications, such as Excel, and that you download from the Office Store.

Apps for Office 2013 and SharePoint 2013 A collection of downloadable apps that enable you to create and view information within your familiar Office programs.

Backstage tabs The area along the left side of Backstage view with tabs to display screens with related groups of commands.

Backstage view A centralized space for file management tasks; for example, opening, saving, printing, publishing, or sharing a file. A navigation pane displays along the left side with tabs that group file-related tasks together.

Center alignment The alignment of text or objects that is centered horizontally between the left and right margins.

Click The action of pressing and releasing the left button on a mouse pointing device one time.

Clip art Downloadable predefined graphics available online from Office.com and other sites.

Clipboard A temporary storage area that holds text or graphics that you select and then cut or copy.

Cloud computing Refers to applications and services that are accessed over the Internet, rather than to applications that are installed on your local computer.

Cloud storage Online storage of data so that you can access your data from different places and devices.

Collaborate To work with others as a team in an intellectual endeavor to complete a shared task or to achieve a shared goal.

Commands An instruction to a computer program that causes an action to be carried out.

Common dialog boxes The set of dialog boxes that includes Open, Save, and Save As, which are provided by the Windows programming interface, and which display and operate in all of the Office programs in the same manner.

Compressed file A file that has been reduced in size and thus takes up less storage space and can be transferred to other computers quickly.

Compressed folder A folder that has been reduced in size and thus takes up less storage space and can be transferred to other computers quickly; also called a *zipped* folder.

Context menus Menus that display commands and options relevant to the selected text or object; also called *shortcut menus*.

Context-sensitive commands Commands that display on a shortcut menu that relate to the object or text that you right-clicked.

Contextual tabs Tabs that are added to the ribbon automatically when a specific object, such as a picture, is selected, and that contain commands relevant to the selected object.

Copy A command that duplicates a selection and places it on the Clipboard.

Cut A command that removes a selection and places it on the Clipboard.

Default The term that refers to the current selection or setting that is automatically used by a computer program unless you specify otherwise.

Deselect The action of canceling the selection of an object or block of text by clicking outside of the selection.

Desktop In Windows, the screen that simulates your work area.

Desktop app The term that commonly refers to a computer program that is installed on your computer and requires a computer operating system like Microsoft Windows or Apple OS to run.

Dialog box A small window that contains options for completing a task.

Dialog Box Launcher A small icon that displays to the right of some group names on the ribbon, and which opens a related dialog box or pane providing additional options and commands related to that group.

Document properties Details about a file that describe or identify it, including the title, author name, subject, and keywords that identify the document's topic or contents; also known as *metadata*.

Drag The action of holding down the left mouse button while moving your mouse.

Edit The process of making changes to text or graphics in an Office file.

Ellipsis A set of three dots indicating incompleteness; an ellipsis following a command name indicates that a dialog box will display if you click the command.

Enhanced ScreenTip A ScreenTip that displays more descriptive text than a normal ScreenTip.

Extract To decompress, or pull out, files from a compressed form.

File A collection of information stored on a computer under a single name, for example, a Word document or a PowerPoint presentation.

File Explorer The program that displays the files and folders on your computer, and which is at work anytime you are viewing the contents of files and folders in a window.

Fill The inside color of an object.

Folder A container in which you store files.

Folder window In Windows, a window that displays the contents of the current folder, library, or device, and contains helpful parts so that you can navigate the Windows file structure.

Font A set of characters with the same design and shape.

Font styles Formatting emphasis such as bold, italic, and underline.

Footer A reserved area for text or graphics that displays at the bottom of each page in a document.

Formatting The process of establishing the overall appearance of text, graphics, and pages in an Office file—for example, in a Word document.

Formatting marks Characters that display on the screen, but do not print, indicating where the Enter key, the Spacebar, and the Tab key were pressed; also called *nonprinting characters*.

Gallery An Office feature that displays a list of potential results instead of just the command name.

Gradient fill A fill effect in which one color fades into another.

Groups On the Office ribbon, the sets of related commands that you might need for a specific type of task.

Header A reserved area for text or graphics that displays at the top of each page in a document.

Info tab The tab in Backstage view that displays information about the current file.

Insertion point A blinking vertical line that indicates where text or graphics will be inserted.

Keyboard shortcut A combination of two or more keyboard keys, used to perform a task that would otherwise require a mouse.

KeyTip The letter that displays on a command in the ribbon and that indicates the key you can press to activate the command when keyboard control of the ribbon is activated.

Keywords Custom file properties in the form of words that you associate with a document to give an indication of the document's content; used to help find and organize files. Also called *tags*.

Landscape orientation A page orientation in which the paper is wider than it is tall.

Layout Options A button that displays when an object is selected and that has commands to choose how the object interacts with surrounding text.

Live Preview A technology that shows the result of applying an editing or formatting change as you point to possible results—*before* you actually apply it.

Location Any disk drive, folder, or other place in which you can store files and folders.

Metadata Details about a file that describe or identify it, including the title, author name, subject, and keywords that identify the document's topic or contents; also known as *document properties*.

Mini toolbar A small toolbar containing frequently used formatting commands that displays as a result of selecting text or objects.

MRU Acronym for *most recently used*, which refers to the state of some commands that retain the characteristic most recently applied; for example, the Font Color button retains the most recently used color until a new color is chosen.

Navigate The process of exploring within the organizing structure of Windows.

Navigation pane In a folder window, the area on the left in which you can navigate to, open, and display favorites, libraries, folders, saved searches, and an expandable list of drives.

Nonprinting characters Characters that display on the screen, but do not print, indicating where the Enter key, the Spacebar, and the Tab key were pressed; also called *formatting marks*.

Notification bar An area at the bottom of an Internet Explorer window that displays information about pending downloads, security issues, add-ons, and other issues related to the operation of your computer.

Object A text box, picture, table, or shape that you can select and then move and resize.

Office Web Apps The free online companions to Microsoft Word, Excel, PowerPoint, Access, and OneNote.

Open dialog box A dialog box from which you can navigate to, and then open on your screen, an existing file that was created in that same program.

Option button In a dialog box, a round button that enables you to make one choice among two or more options.

Options dialog box A dialog box within each Office application where you can select program settings and other options and preferences.

Pane A separate area of a window.

Paragraph symbol The symbol ¶ that represents the end of a paragraph.

Paste The action of placing text or objects that have been copied or cut from one location to another location.

Paste Options gallery A gallery of buttons that provides a Live Preview of all the Paste options available in the current context.

Path A sequence of folders that leads to a specific file or folder.

PDF The acronym for Portable Document Format, which is a file format that creates an image that preserves the look of your file; this is a popular format for sending documents electronically because the document will display on most computers.

Point The action of moving your mouse pointer over something on your screen.

Pointer Any symbol that displays on your screen in response to moving your mouse.

Points A measurement of the size of a font; there are 72 points in an inch.

Portable Document Format A file format that creates an image that preserves the look of your file, but that cannot be easily changed; a popular format for sending documents electronically, because the document will display on most computers.

Portrait orientation A page orientation in which the paper is taller than it is wide.

Print Preview A view of a document as it will appear when you print it.

Progress bar In a dialog box or taskbar button, a bar that indicates visually the progress of a task such as a download or file transfer.

Protected View A security feature in Office 2013 that protects your computer from malicious files by opening them in a restricted environment until you enable them; you might encounter this feature if you open a file from an email or download files from the Internet.

pt The abbreviation for *point*; for example, when referring to a font size.

Quick Access Toolbar In an Office program window, the small row of buttons in the upper left corner of the screen from which you can perform frequently used commands.

Read-Only A property assigned to a file that prevents the file from being modified or deleted; it indicates that you cannot save any changes to the displayed document unless you first save it with a new name.

Ribbon A user interface in both Office 2013 and File Explorer that groups the commands for performing related tasks on tabs across the upper portion of the program window.

Right-click The action of clicking the right mouse button one time.

Sans serif font A font design with no lines or extensions on the ends of characters.

ScreenTip A small box that that displays useful information when you perform various mouse actions such as pointing to screen elements or dragging.

Scroll bar A vertical or horizontal bar in a window or a pane to assist in bringing an area into view, and which contains a scroll box and scroll arrows.

Scroll box The box in the vertical and horizontal scroll bars that can be dragged to reposition the contents of a window or pane on the screen.

Selecting Highlighting, by dragging with your mouse, areas of text or data or graphics, so that the selection can be edited, formatted, copied, or moved.

Serif font A font design that includes small line extensions on the ends of the letters to guide the eye in reading from left to right.

SharePoint Collaboration software with which people in an organization can set up team sites to share information, manage documents, and publish reports for others to see.

Shortcut menu A menu that displays commands and options relevant to the selected text or object; also called a *context menu*.

Sizing handles Small squares that indicate a picture or object is selected.

SkyDrive Microsoft's free cloud storage for anyone with a free Microsoft account.

Split button A button divided into two parts and in which clicking the main part of the button performs a command and clicking the arrow opens a menu with choices.

Start search The search feature in Windows 8 in which, from the Start screen, you can begin to type and by default, Windows 8 searches for apps; you can adjust the search to search for files or settings.

Status bar The area along the lower edge of an Office program window that displays file information on the left and buttons to control how the window looks on the right.

Style A group of formatting commands, such as font, font size, font color, paragraph alignment, and line spacing that can be applied to a paragraph with one command.

Subfolder A folder within a folder.

Synchronization The process of updating computer files that are in two or more locations according to specific rules—also called *syncing*.

Syncing The process of updating computer files that are in two or more locations according to specific rules—also called *synchronization*.

Tabs (ribbon) On the Office ribbon, the name of each activity area.

Tags Custom file properties in the form of words that you associate with a document to give an indication of the document's content; used to help find and organize files. Also called *keywords*.

Taskbar The area along the lower edge of the desktop that displays buttons representing programs.

Template A preformatted document that you can use as a starting point and then change to suit your needs.

Theme A predesigned combination of colors, fonts, and effects that look good together and is applied to an entire document by a single selection.

Title bar The bar at the top edge of the program window that indicates the name of the current file and the program name.

Toggle button A button that can be turned on by clicking it once, and then turned off by clicking it again.

Toolbar In a folder window, a row of buttons with which you can perform common tasks, such as changing the view of your files and folders or burning files to a CD.

Triple-click The action of clicking the left mouse button three times in rapid succession.

Trusted Documents A security feature in Office that remembers which files you have already enabled; you might encounter this feature if you open a file from an email or download files from the Internet.

Uniform Resource Locator An address that uniquely identifies a location on the Internet.

URL The acronym for Uniform Resource Locator, which is an address that uniquely identifies a location on the Internet.

USB flash drive A small data storage device that plugs into a computer USB port.

Window A rectangular area on a computer screen in which programs and content appear, and which can be moved, resized, minimized, or closed.

XML Paper Specification A Microsoft file format that creates an image of your document and that opens in the XPS viewer.

XPS The acronym for XML Paper Specification—a Microsoft file format that creates an image of your document and that opens in the XPS viewer.

Zipped folder A folder that has been reduced in size and thus takes up less storage space and can be transferred to other computers quickly; also called a *compressed* folder.

Zoom The action of increasing or decreasing the size of the viewing area on the screen.

Introduction to Microsoft Access 2013

A

Access 2013

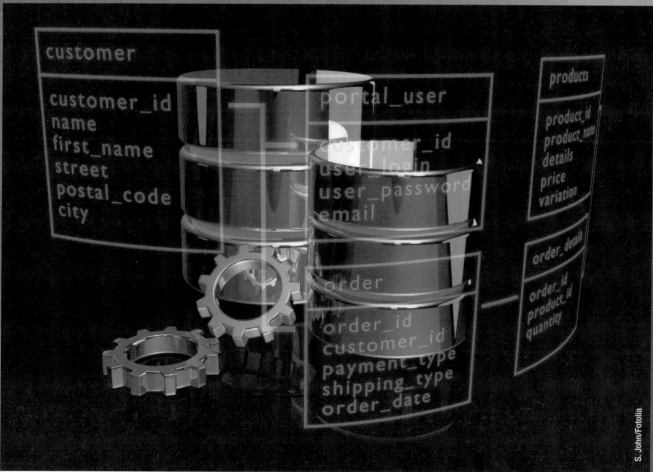

S. John/Fotolia

Access 2013: Introduction

Video AA

Microsoft Access 2013 provides a convenient way to organize data that makes it easy for you to retrieve information. Access uses tables to store data. Like Excel spreadsheets, data is stored in rows and columns in a table. So why use a database rather than an Excel spreadsheet? By using a database, you can manipulate and work with data in a more robust manner. For example, if you have thousands of records about patients in a hospital, you can easily find all of the records that pertain to the patients who received a specific type of medicine on a particular day. Information from one table can be used to retrieve information from another table. For example, by knowing a patient's ID number, you can

view immunization records or view insurance information or view hospitalization records. Having information stored in an Access database enables you to make bulk changes to data at one time even when it is stored in different tables.

It's easy to get started with Access by using one of the many prebuilt database templates. For example, a nonprofit organization can track events, donors, members, and donations. A small business can use a prebuilt database to track inventory, create invoices, keep track of projects, manage pricing, track competitors, and manage quotes.

Getting Started with Microsoft Access 2013

GO! to Work
Video A1

PROJECT 1A	OUTCOMES
	Create a new database.

OBJECTIVES

1. Identify Good Database Design
2. Create a Table and Define Fields in a Blank Desktop Database
3. Change the Structure of Tables and Add a Second Table
4. Create a Query, Form, and Report
5. Close a Database and Exit Access

PROJECT 1B	OUTCOMES
	Create a database from a template.

OBJECTIVES

6. Use a Template to Create a Database
7. Organize Objects in the Navigation Pane
8. Create a New Table in a Database Created with a Template
9. Print a Report and a Table

Riccardo Piccinini/Fotolia

In This Chapter

In this chapter, you use Microsoft Access 2013 to organize a collection of related information. You will create new databases, create tables, and enter data into the tables. You will create a query, a form, and a report—all of which are Access objects that make a database useful for finding and analyzing information. You will also create a complete database from a template that you can use as provided, or that you can modify to suit your needs. In this chapter, you will also learn how to apply good database design principles to your Access database and to define the structure of a database.

The projects in this chapter relate to **Texas Lakes Community College**, which is located in the Austin, Texas, area. Its four campuses serve over 30,000 students and offer more than 140 certificate programs and degrees. The college has a highly acclaimed Distance Education program and an extensive Workforce Development program. The college makes positive contributions to the community through cultural and athletic programs and has significant partnerships with businesses and nonprofit organizations. Popular fields of study include nursing and health care, solar technology, computer technology, and graphic design.

Student Advising Database with Two Tables

PROJECT ACTIVITIES

In Activities 1.01 through 1.17, you will assist Dr. Daniel Martinez, vice president of Student Services at Texas Lakes Community College, in creating a new database for tracking students and their faculty advisors. Your completed database objects will look similar to Figure 1.1.

PROJECT FILES

For Project 1A, you will need the following files:

Blank desktop database
a01A_Students (Excel workbook)
a01A_Faculty_Advisors (Excel workbook)

You will save your database as:

Lastname_Firstname_1A_Advising

Build from
Scratch

PROJECT RESULTS

FIGURE 1.1 Project 1A Advising

- Tap an item to click it.
- Press and hold for a few seconds to right-click; release when the information or commands display.
- Touch the screen with two or more fingers and then pinch together to zoom in or stretch your fingers apart to zoom out.
- Slide your finger on the screen to scroll—slide left to scroll right and slide right to scroll left.
- Slide to rearrange—similar to dragging with a mouse.
- Swipe from edge: from right to display charms; from left to expose open apps, snap apps, or close apps; from top or bottom to show commands or close an app.
- Swipe to select—slide an item a short distance with a quick movement—to select an item and bring up commands, if any.

Objective 1 | Identify Good Database Design

Video A1-1

A *database* is an organized collection of *data*—facts about people, events, things, or ideas—related to a specific topic or purpose. *Information* is data that is organized in a useful manner. Your contact list is a type of database because it is a collection of data about one topic—the people with whom you communicate. A simple database of this type is called a *flat database* because it is not related or linked to any other collection of data. Another example of a simple database is a list of your music collection. You do not keep information about your music collection in your contact list because the data is not related to the people in your contact list.

A more sophisticated type of database is a *relational database*, so-called because multiple collections of data in the database are related to one another; for example, data about the students, the courses, and the faculty members at a college. Microsoft Access 2013 is a relational *database management system*—also referred to as a *DBMS*—which is software that controls how related collections of data are stored, organized, retrieved, and secured.

Activity 1.01 | Using Good Design Techniques to Plan a Database

Before creating a new database, the first step is to determine the information you want to keep track of by asking yourself, *What questions should this database be able to answer?* The purpose of a database is to store the data in a manner that makes it easy to get the information you need by asking questions. For example, in a student database for Texas Lakes Community College, the questions to be answered might include:

- How many students are enrolled at the college?
- How many students have not yet been assigned a faculty advisor?
- Which students live in Austin, Texas?
- Which students owe money for tuition?
- Which students are majoring in Information Systems Technology?

Tables are the foundation of an Access database because all of the data is stored in one or more tables. A table is similar in structure to an Excel worksheet because data is organized into rows and columns. Each table row is a *record*—all of the categories of data pertaining to one person, place, event, thing, or idea. Each table column is a *field*—a single piece of information for every record. For example, in a table storing student contact information, each row forms a record for only one student. Each column forms a field for every record; for example, the student ID number or the student last name.

When organizing the fields of information in your table, break each piece of information into its smallest, most useful part. For example, create three fields for the name of a student—one field for the last name, one field for the first name, and one field for the middle name or initial.

The *first principle of good database design* is to organize data in the tables so that *redundant*—duplicate—data does not occur. For example, record the student contact information in only *one* table, so that if a student's address changes, you can change the information in just one place. This conserves space, reduces the likelihood of errors when recording new data, and does not require remembering all of the different places where the student's address is stored.

The *second principle of good database design* is to use techniques that ensure the accuracy and consistency of data as it is entered into the table. Typically, many different people enter data into a database—think of all the people who enter data about students at your college. When entering a state in a student contacts table, one person might enter the state as *Texas*, while another might enter the state as *TX*. Use design techniques to help those who enter data into a database to enter the data more accurately and consistently.

Normalization is the process of applying design rules and principles to ensure that your database performs as expected. Taking the time to plan and create a database that is well designed will ensure that you can retrieve meaningful information from the database.

The tables of information in a relational database are linked or joined to one another by a *common field*—a field in two or more tables that stores the same data. For example, a Students table includes the Student ID, name, and address of every student. The Student Activities table includes the club name and the Student ID of members, but not the name or address, of each student in the club. Because the two tables share a common field—Student ID—you can create a list of names and addresses of all of the students in the Photography Club. The names and addresses are stored in the Students table, and the Student IDs of the Photography Club members are stored in the Student Activities table.

Objective 2 | Create a Table and Define Fields in a Blank Desktop Database

Video A1-2

There are three methods to create a new Access database. One method is to create a new database using a *database template*—a preformatted database designed for a specific purpose. A second method is to create a new database from a *blank desktop database*. A blank desktop database is stored on your computer or other storage device. It has no data and has no database tools; you create the data and the tools as you need them. A third method is to create a *custom web app* database from scratch or by using a template that you can publish and share with others over the Internet.

Regardless of the method you use, you must name and save the database before you can create any *objects* in it. Objects are the basic parts of a database; you create objects to store your data, to work with your data, and to display your data. The most common database objects are tables, queries, forms, and reports. Think of an Access database as a container for the objects that you create.

Activity 1.02 | Starting with a Blank Desktop Database

1 Start Access using the same technique you used to locate and open other Office desktop apps. Take a moment to compare your screen with Figure 1.2 and study the parts of the Microsoft Access opening screen described in the table in Figure 1.3.

From this Access opening screen, you can open an existing database, create a custom web app, create a blank desktop database, or create a new web app or desktop database from a template.

FIGURE 1.2

FIGURE 1.3

MICROSOFT ACCESS OPENING SCREEN ELEMENTS	
SCREEN ELEMENT	**DESCRIPTION**
Available templates	Starts a database for a specific purpose that includes built-in objects and tools ready for use.
Blank desktop database	Starts a blank database that is stored on your computer or on a storage device.
Custom web app	Starts a web app database that can be published and shared on the Internet.
Open Other Files	Enables you to open a database file from your computer, a shared location, or other location that you have designated.
Recent files	Displays a list of database files that have been recently opened.
Search box	Enables you to search the Microsoft Office website for templates.
Suggested searches	Enables you to click on a category to start an online search for a template.

2 ▶ In the Access opening screen, click **Blank desktop database**. In the **Blank desktop database** dialog box, to the right of the **File Name** box, click **Browse** ▭. In the **File New Database** dialog box, navigate to the location where you are saving your databases for this chapter, create a **New folder** named **Access Chapter 1** and then press Enter. With the folder name selected, in the **File New Database** dialog box, click **Open**.

In the File name box, *Database1* displays as the default file name—the number at the end of your file name might differ if you have saved a database previously with the default name. In the Save as type box, the default database type is *Microsoft Access 2007 – 2013 Databases*, which means that you can open a database created in Access 2013 by using Access 2007, Access 2010, or Access 2013.

3 ▶ Click in the **File name** box. Using your own name, replace the existing text with **Lastname_ Firstname_1A_Advising** and then click **OK** or press Enter. Compare your screen with Figure 1.4.

In the Blank desktop database dialog box, in the File Name box, the name of your database displays. Under the File Name box, the drive and folder where the database will be stored displays. An Access database has a file extension of *.accdb*.

FIGURE 1.4

4 In the **Blank desktop database** dialog box, click **Create**. Compare your screen with Figure 1.5, and then take a moment to study the screen elements described in the table in Figure 1.6.

Access creates the new database and opens *Table1*. Recall that a table is an Access object that stores data in columns and rows, similar to the format of an Excel worksheet. Table objects are the foundation of a database because tables store the data that is used by other database objects.

FIGURE 1.5

FIGURE 1.6

MICROSOFT ACCESS DATABASE WINDOW ELEMENTS	
ACCESS WINDOW ELEMENT	**DESCRIPTION**
Navigation Pane	Displays the database objects that you can open in the object window.
Object tab	Identifies and enables you to work with the open object.
Object window	Displays the active or open object (table, query, or other object).
Close button for object	Closes the active object (table, query, or other object).
Ribbon with command groups arranged in tabs	Groups the commands for performing related database tasks on tabs.
Status bar	Indicates the active view and the status of action occurring within the database on the left; provides buttons on the right to switch between Datasheet view and Design view.
Table Tools	Provides tools for working with a table object—only available when a table object is active.
Title bar	Displays the database name.

Activity 1.03 | Assigning the Data Type and Name to Fields

After you have named and saved your database, the next step is to consult your database design plan and then create the tables for your data. Limit the data in each table to *one* subject. For example, in this project, your database will have two tables—one for student information and one for faculty advisor information.

Recall that each column in a table is a field; field names display at the top of each column of the table. Recall also that each row in a table is a record—all of the data pertaining to one person, place, thing, event, or idea. Each record is broken up into its smallest usable parts—the fields. Use meaningful names for fields; for example, *Last Name*.

> **1** Notice the new blank table that displays in **Datasheet** view, and then take a moment to study the elements of the table's object window. Compare your screen with Figure 1.7.
>
> The table displays in *Datasheet view*, which displays the data in columns and rows similar to the format of an Excel worksheet. Another way to view a table is in *Design view*, which displays the underlying design—the *structure*—of the table's fields. The *object window* displays the open object—in this instance, the table object.
>
> In a new blank database, there is only one object—a new blank table. Because you have not yet named this table, the object tab displays a default name of *Table1*. Access creates the first field and names it *ID*. In the ID field, Access assigns a unique sequential number—each number incremented by one—to each record as it is entered into the table.

FIGURE 1.7

> **2** In the **Navigation Pane**, click **Shutter Bar Open/Close Button** « to collapse the **Navigation Pane** to a narrow bar on the left.
>
> The *Navigation Pane* displays and organizes the names of the objects in a database. From the Navigation Pane, you can open objects. Collapse or close the Navigation Pane to display more of the object—in this case, the table.

↻ **ANOTHER WAY**   Press F11 to close or open the Navigation Pane.

> **3** In the field names row, click anywhere in the text *Click to Add* to display a list of data types. Compare your screen with Figure 1.8.
>
> A *data type* defines the kind of data that you can store in a field, such as numbers, text, or dates. A field in a table can have only one data type. The data type of each field should be included in your database design. After selecting the data type, you can name the field.

↻ **ANOTHER WAY**   To the right of *Click to Add*, click the arrow.

FIGURE 1.8

Navigation Pane closed

When clicked, displays list of data types

List of data types

4 ▶ On the list of data types, click **Short Text**, and notice that in the second column, *Click to Add* changes to *Field1*, which is selected. Type **Last Name** and then press Enter.

The second column displays *Last Name* as the field name, and, in the third column, the data type list displays. The ***Short Text data type*** describes text, a combination of text and numbers, or numbers that are not used in calculations, such as the Postal Code. This data type enables you to enter up to 255 characters in the field.

🔄 **ANOTHER WAY**   With the list of data types displayed, type the character that is underscored to select the data type. For example, type *t* to select Short Text or type *u* to select Currency.

5 ▶ In the third field name box, type **t** to select *Short Text*, type **First Name** and then press Enter.

6 ▶ In the fourth field name box, click **Short Text**, type **Middle Initial** and then press Enter.

7 ▶ Create the remaining fields from the table given by first selecting the data type, typing the field name, and then pressing Enter. The field names in the table will display on one line—do not be concerned if the field names do not completely display in the column; you will adjust the column widths later.

Data Type		Short Text	Short Text	Short Text	Short Text	Short Text	Short Text	Short Text	Short Text	Short Text	Short Text	Currency
Field Name	ID	Last Name	First Name	Middle Initial	Address	City	State	Postal Code	Phone	Email	Faculty Advisor ID	Amount Owed

The Postal Code and Phone fields are assigned a data type of Short Text because the numbers are never used in calculations. The Amount Owed field is assigned the ***Currency data type***, which describes monetary values and numeric data that can be used in calculations and that have one to four decimal places. A U.S. dollar sign ($) and two decimal places are automatically included for all of the numbers in a field with the Currency data type.

8 ▶ If necessary, scroll to bring the first column—**ID**—into view, and then compare your screen with Figure 1.9.

Access automatically created the ID field, and you created 11 additional fields in the table.

FIGURE 1.9

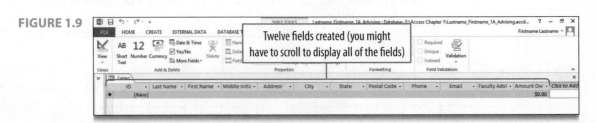

Twelve fields created (you might have to scroll to display all of the fields)

Activity 1.04 | Renaming Fields and Changing Data Types in a Table

1 ▶ In the first column, click anywhere in the text *ID*. On the ribbon, under **TABLE TOOLS**, on the **FIELDS tab**, in the **Properties group**, click **Name & Caption**. In the **Enter Field Properties** dialog box, in the **Name** box, change *ID* to **Student ID**

The field name *Student ID* is a clearer and more precise description of this field's data. In the Enter Field Properties dialog box, you have the option to change the **Caption** to display a name for a field other than the name that displays in the Name box. Many database designers do not use spaces in field names; instead, they might name a field *LastName* or *LName* and then create a caption for the field so it displays as *Last Name* in tables, forms, or reports. In the Enter Field Properties dialog box, you can also provide a description for the field.

ANOTHER WAY   Right-click the field name to display the shortcut menu, and then click Rename Field; or, double-click the field name to select the existing text, and then type the new field name.

2 ▶ Click **OK** to close the **Enter Field Properties** dialog box. On the ribbon, in the **Formatting group**, notice that the **Data Type** for the **Student ID** field is *AutoNumber*. Click the **Data Type arrow**, click **Short Text**, and then compare your screen with Figure 1.10.

In the new record row, the Student ID field is selected. By default, Access creates an ID field for all new tables and sets the data type for the field to AutoNumber. The **AutoNumber data type** describes a unique sequential or random number assigned by Access as each record is entered. Changing the data type of this field to Short Text enables you to enter a custom student ID number.

When records in a database have *no* unique value, such as a book ISBN or a license plate number, the AutoNumber data type is a useful way to automatically create a unique number. In this manner, you are sure that every record is different from the others.

FIGURE 1.10

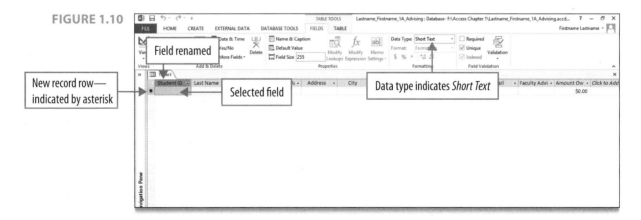

New record row— indicated by asterisk

Field renamed

Selected field

Data type indicates *Short Text*

Activity 1.05 | Adding a Record to a Table

A new contact list is not useful until you fill it with names and phone numbers. Likewise, a new database is not useful until you **populate** it by filling one or more tables with data. You can populate a table with records by typing data directly into the table.

1 In the new record row, click in the **Student ID** field to display the insertion point, type **1023045** and then press Enter. Compare your screen with Figure 1.11.

> The pencil icon [✎] in the ***record selector box*** indicates that a record is being entered or edited. The record selector box is the small box at the left of a record in Datasheet view. When clicked, the entire record is selected.

↻ ANOTHER WAY   Press Tab to move the insertion point to the next field.

FIGURE 1.11

First Student ID is 1023045

Pencil icon in record selector box indicates record being entered or edited

Insertion point in Last Name field

2 With the insertion point positioned in the **Last Name** field, type **Fresch** and then press Enter.

NOTE   **Correcting Typing Errors**

Correct any typing errors you make by using the techniques you have practiced in other Office applications. For example, use Backspace to remove characters to the left of the insertion point. Use Del to remove characters to the right of the insertion point. Or select the text you want to replace and type the correct information. Press Esc to exit out of a record that has not been completely entered.

---

3 In the **First Name** field, type **Jenna** and then press Enter.

4 In the **Middle Initial** field, type **A** and then press Enter.

5 In the **Address** field, type **7550 Douglas Ln** and then press Enter.

> Do not be concerned if the data does not completely display in the column. As you progress in your study of Access, you will adjust column widths so that you can view all of the data.

6 Continue entering data in the fields as indicated in the table given, pressing Enter to move to the next field.

City	State	Postal Code	Phone	Email	Faculty Advisor ID
Austin	**TX**	**78749**	**(512) 555-0857**	**jfresch@tlcc.edu**	**FAC-2289**

NOTE   **Format for Typing Telephone Numbers in Access**

Access does not require a specific format for typing telephone numbers in a record. The examples in this textbook use the format of Microsoft Outlook. Using such a format facilitates easy transfer of Outlook information to and from Access.

---

7 In the **Amount Owed** field, type **250** and then press Enter. Compare your screen with Figure 1.12.

> Pressing Enter or Tab in the last field moves the insertion point to the next row to begin a new record. Access automatically saves the record as soon as you move to the next row; you do not have to take any specific action to save a record.

FIGURE 1.12

First record entered
and saved

Insertion point blinking
in first field of new
record row

8 To give your table a meaningful name, on the **Quick Access Toolbar**, click **Save** 🖫. In the **Save As** dialog box, in the **Table Name** box, using your own name, replace the selected text by typing **Lastname Firstname 1A Students**

Save each database object with a name that identifies the data that it contains. When you save objects within a database, it is not necessary to use underscores in place of the spaces between words. Your name is included as part of the object name so that you and your instructor can identify your printouts or electronic files easily.

9 In the **Save As** dialog box, click **OK**. Notice that the object tab—located directly above the **Student ID** field name—displays the new table name that you just entered.

More Knowledge | **Renaming or Deleting a Table**

To change the name of a table, close the table, display the Navigation Pane, right-click the table name, and then click Rename. Type the new name or edit as you would any selected text. To delete a table, close the table, display the Navigation Pane, right-click the table name, and then click Delete.

Activity 1.06 | Adding Additional Records to a Table

1 In the new record row, click in the **Student ID** field, and then enter the data for two additional students as shown in the table given. Press Enter or Tab to move from field to field. The data in each field will display on one line in the table.

Student ID	Last Name	First Name	Middle Initial	Address	City	State	Postal Code	Phone	Email	Faculty Advisor ID	Amount Owed
2345677	Ingram	Joey	S	621 Hilltop Dr	Leander	TX	78646	(512) 555-0717	jingram@tlcc.edu	FAC-2377	378.5
3456689	Snyder	Amanda	J	4786 Bluff St	Buda	TX	78610	(512) 555-9120	asnyder@tlcc.edu	FAC-9005	0

2 Compare your screen with Figure 1.13.

FIGURE 1.13

Some fields may be out
of view on your screen

Records for three students entered

Activity 1.07 | Importing Data from an Excel Workbook into an Existing Access Table

You can type records directly into a table. You can also *import* data from a variety of sources. Importing is the process of copying data from one source or application to another application. For example, you can import data from a Word table or an Excel spreadsheet into an Access database because the data is arranged in columns and rows, similar to a table in Datasheet view.

In this activity, you will **append**—add on—data from an Excel spreadsheet to your *1A Students* table. To append data, the table must already be created, and it must be closed.

1 In the upper right corner of the table, below the ribbon, click **Object Close** ⊠ to close your **1A Students** table. Notice that no objects are open.

2 On the ribbon, click the **EXTERNAL DATA tab**. In the **Import & Link group**, click **Excel**. In the **Get External Data – Excel Spreadsheet** dialog box, click **Browse**.

3 In the **File Open** dialog box, navigate to your student files, double-click the Excel file **a01A_Students**, and then compare your screen with Figure 1.14.

The path to the *source file*—the file being imported—displays in the File name box. There are three options for importing data from an Excel spreadsheet: import the data into a *new* table in the current database, append a copy of the records to an existing table, or link the data from the spreadsheet to a linked table in the database. A *link* is a connection to data in another file. When linking, Access creates a table that maintains a link to the source data, so that changes to the data in one file are automatically made in the other—linked—file.

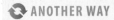 **ANOTHER WAY**   Click the file name, and then in the File Open dialog box, click Open.

FIGURE 1.14

4 Click the **Append a copy of the records to the table** option button, and then, in the box to the right, click the **arrow**.

Currently, your database has only one table, so no other tables display on the list. However, when a database has multiple tables, click the arrow to select the table to which you want to append records. The table into which you import or append data is referred to as the *destination table*.

5 Press Esc to cancel the list, and in the dialog box, click **OK**. Compare your screen with Figure 1.15.

The first screen of the Import Spreadsheet Wizard displays, and the presence of scroll bars indicates that records and fields are out of view in this window. To append records from an Excel workbook to an existing database table, the column headings in the Excel worksheet or spreadsheet must be identical to the field names in the table. The *wizard* identifies the first row of the spreadsheet as column headings, which are equivalent to field names. A wizard is a feature in a Microsoft Office program that walks you step by step through a process.

FIGURE 1.15

First row identified as column headings, which are equivalent to field names

Field names in Excel Spreadsheet exactly match the field names in the Access table

Scroll bars indicate more data

6 ▸ In the lower right corner of the wizard, click **Next**. Notice that the name of your table displays under **Import to Table**. In the lower right corner of the wizard, click **Finish**.

7 ▸ In the **Get External Data – Excel Spreadsheet** dialog box, click **Close**. Open [»] the **Navigation Pane**.

8 ▸ Point to the right edge of the **Navigation Pane** to display the [↔] pointer. Drag to the right to increase the width of the **Navigation Pane** so that the entire table name displays, and then compare your screen with Figure 1.16.

FIGURE 1.16

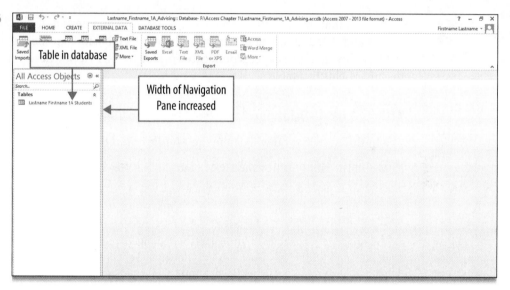

Table in database

Width of Navigation Pane increased

9 ▸ In the **Navigation Pane**, double-click your **1A Students** table to open the table in **Datasheet** view, and then **Close** [«] the **Navigation Pane**.

🔄 ANOTHER WAY   To open an object from the Navigation Pane, right-click the object name, and then click Open.

10 ▸ In the lower left corner of your screen, locate the navigation area, and notice that there are a total of **25** records in the table—you entered three records and imported 22 additional records. Compare your screen with Figure 1.17.

The records that you entered and the records you imported from the Excel spreadsheet display in your table; the first record in the table is selected. The *navigation area* indicates the number of records in the table and has controls in the form of arrows that you click in order to navigate among the records.

FIGURE 1.17

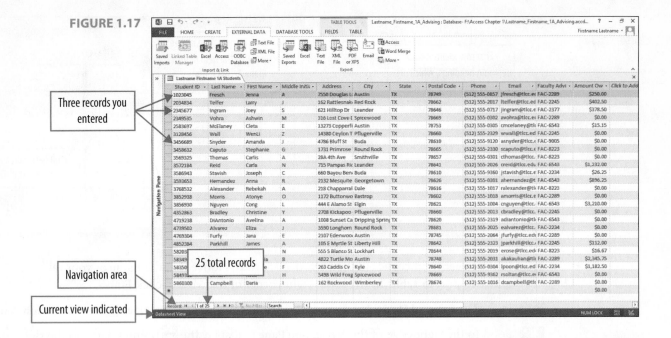

Three records you
entered

25 total records

Navigation area

Current view indicated

Objective 3 | Change the Structure of Tables and Add a Second Table

Video A1-3

Recall that the structure of a table is the underlying design of the table and includes field names and data types. You can create or modify a table in Datasheet view. To define and modify fields, many database experts prefer to work in Design view, where you have more options for defining fields in a table.

Activity 1.08 | Deleting a Table Field in Design View

In this activity, you will delete the *Middle Initial* field from the table.

1 On the ribbon, click the **HOME tab**. In the **Views group**, click the **View arrow** to display a list of views.

There are two views for tables: Datasheet view and Design view. Other objects have different views. On the list, Design view is represented by a picture of a pencil, a ruler, and an angle. Datasheet view is represented by a picture of a table arranged in columns and rows. In the Views group, if the View button displays the pencil, ruler, and angle, clicking View will switch your view to Design view. Likewise, clicking the View button that displays as a datasheet will switch your view to Datasheet view.

2 On the list, click **Design View**, and then compare your screen with Figure 1.18.

Design view displays the underlying design—the structure—of the table and its fields. In Design view, the records with the data in the table do not display. You can only view the information about each field's characteristics. Each field name is listed, along with its data type. You can add more descriptive information about a field in the Description column.

You can decide how each field should look and behave in the Field Properties area. For example, you can set a specific field size in the Field Properties area. In the lower right corner, information displays about the active selection—in this case, the Field Name.

FIGURE 1.18

3 ▶ In the **Field Name** column, to the left of **Middle Initial**, point to the row selector box to display the [→] pointer, and then click one time to select the entire row.

4 ▶ Under **TABLE TOOLS**, on the **DESIGN tab**, in the **Tools group**, click **Delete Rows**. Read the message in the message box, and then click **Yes**.

Deleting a field deletes both the field and its data. After you save the changes, you cannot undo this action, so Access prompts you to be sure you want to proceed. If you change your mind after deleting a field and saving the changes, you must add the field back into the table and then reenter the data for that field for every record.

🔄 **ANOTHER WAY** In Design view, right-click the selected row, and then click Delete Rows; or, in Datasheet view, select the field—column—and on the HOME tab, in the Records group, click Delete.

Activity 1.09 | Changing a Field Size and Adding a Description

Typically, many different individuals in an organization have the ability to enter data into a table. For example, at your college, many registration assistants enter and modify student and course information daily. Two ways to help reduce errors are to restrict what can be typed in a field and to add descriptive information to help the individuals when entering the data.

1 ▶ With your table still displayed in **Design** view, in the **Field Name** column, click anywhere in the **Student ID** field name.

2 ▶ In the lower area of the screen, under **Field Properties**, click **Field Size** to select *255*, type **7** and then press [Enter].

This action limits the size of the Student ID field to no more than seven characters. *Field properties* control how the field displays and how data can be entered into the field. You can define properties for each field in the Field Properties area by first clicking on the field name.

The default field size for a Short Text field is 255. Limiting the Field Size property to seven ensures that no more than seven characters can be entered for each Student ID. However, this does not prevent someone from entering seven characters that are incorrect or entering fewer than seven characters. Setting the proper data type for the field and limiting the field size are two ways to *help* reduce errors during data entry.

🔄 **ANOTHER WAY** In Datasheet view, click in the field. On the FIELDS tab, in the Properties group, click in the Field Size box, and then type the number that represents the maximum number of characters for that field.

3 In the **Student ID** row, click in the **Description** box, type **Seven-digit Student ID number** and then press Enter. Compare your screen with Figure 1.19.

> Descriptions for fields in a table are optional. Include a description if the field name does not provide an obvious explanation of the type of data to be entered. If a description is provided for a field, when data is entered in that field in Datasheet view, the text in the Description displays on the left side of the status bar to provide additional information for the individuals who are entering the data.

> When you enter a description for a field, a Property Update Options button displays below the text you typed, which enables you to copy the description for the field to all other database objects that use this table as an underlying source.

FIGURE 1.19

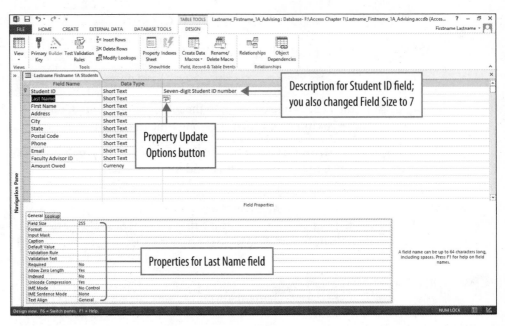

4 Click in the **State** field name box. In the **Field Properties** area, change the **Field Size** to **2** and in the **Description** box for this field, type **Two-character state abbreviation** and then press Enter.

5 Click in the **Faculty Advisor ID** field name box. In the **Field Properties** area, change the **Field Size** to **8** and in the **Description** box for this field, type **Eight-character ID of instructor assigned as advisor** and then press Enter.

6 On the **Quick Access Toolbar**, click **Save** 🖫 to save the design changes to your table, and then notice the message.

> The message indicates that the field size property of one or more fields has changed to a shorter size. If more characters are currently present in the Student ID, State, or Faculty Advisor ID fields than you have set as the field size, the data will be *truncated*—cut off or shortened—because the fields were not previously restricted to these specific number of characters.

7 In the message box, click **Yes**.

Activity 1.10 | Viewing the Primary Key in Design View

Primary key refers to the field in the table that uniquely identifies a record. For example, in a college registration database, your Student ID number uniquely identifies you—no other student at the college has your exact student number. In the 1A Students table, the Student ID uniquely identifies each student.

When you create a table using the blank desktop database template, Access designates the first field as the primary key field and names the field ID. It is good database design practice to establish a primary key for every table, because doing so ensures that you do not enter the same record more than once. You can imagine the confusion if another student at your college had the same Student ID number as your own.

1 With your table still displayed in **Design** view, in the **Field Name** column, click in the **Student ID** field name box. To the left of the box, notice the small icon of a key, as shown in Figure 1.20.

Access automatically designates the first field as the primary key field, but you can set any field as the primary key by clicking the field name, and then in the Tools group, clicking Primary Key.

FIGURE 1.20

2 On the **DESIGN tab**, in the **Views group**, notice that the **View** button displays a picture of a datasheet, indicating that clicking **View** will switch the view to **Datasheet** view. Click the top of the **View** button.

If you make design changes to a table and switch views without first saving the table, Access prompts you to save the table before changing views.

Activity 1.11 | Adding a Second Table to a Database by Importing an Excel Spreadsheet

Many Microsoft Office users track data in an Excel spreadsheet. The sorting and filtering capabilities of Excel are useful for a simple database where all of the information resides in one large Excel spreadsheet. However, Excel is limited as a database management tool because it cannot *relate* the information in multiple spreadsheets in a way that you can ask a question and get a meaningful result. Because data in an Excel spreadsheet is arranged in columns and rows, the spreadsheet can easily become an Access table by importing the spreadsheet.

1 On the ribbon, click the **EXTERNAL DATA tab**, and then in the **Import & Link group**, click **Excel**. In the **Get External Data – Excel Spreadsheet** dialog box, click **Browse**.

2 In the **File Open** dialog box, navigate to the location where your student data files are stored, and then double-click **a01A_Faculty_Advisors**. Compare your screen with Figure 1.21.

FIGURE 1.21

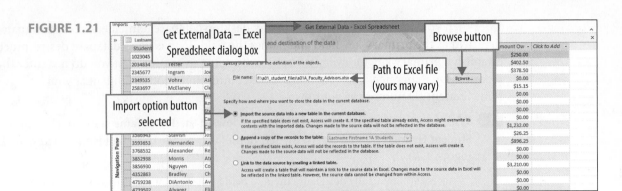

3 Be sure that the **Import the source data into a new table in the current database** option button is selected, click **OK**, and then click **Next**.

The Import Spreadsheet Wizard displays the spreadsheet data.

4 In the upper left corner of the wizard, select the **First Row Contains Column Headings** check box.

The Excel data is framed, indicating that the first row of Excel column titles will become the Access table field names, and the remaining rows will become the individual records in the new Access table.

5 Click **Next**. Notice that the first column—**Faculty ID**—is selected, and in the upper area of the wizard, the **Field Name** and the **Data Type** display. Compare your screen with Figure 1.22.

Here, under Field Options, you can review and change the name or the data type of each selected field. You can also identify fields in the spreadsheet that you do not want to import into the Access table by selecting the Do not import field (Skip) check box.

FIGURE 1.22

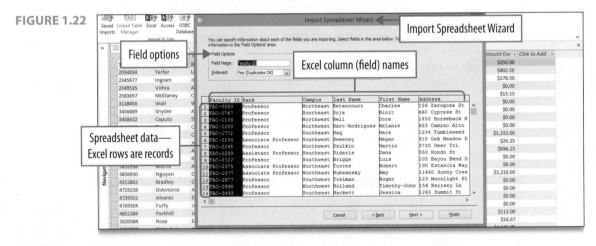

6 Click **Next**. In the upper area of the wizard, click the **Choose my own primary key** option button, and then be sure that **Faculty ID** displays in the box to the right.

In the new table, Faculty ID will be the primary key. No two faculty members have the same Faculty ID. By default, Access selects the first field as the primary key, but you can click the arrow to select a different field.

7 Click **Next**. In the **Import to Table** box, using your own name, type **Lastname Firstname 1A Faculty Advisors** and then click **Finish**.

8 In the **Get External Data – Excel Spreadsheet** dialog box, click **Close**. **Open** ⟩⟩ the **Navigation Pane**.

9 ▶ In the **Navigation Pane**, double-click your **1A Faculty Advisors** table to open it in **Datasheet** view, and then **Close** 〈«〉 the **Navigation Pane**.

Two tables that are identified by their object tabs are open in the object window. Your 1A Faculty Advisors table is the active table and displays the 29 records that you imported from the Excel spreadsheet.

10 ▶ In your **1A Faculty Advisors** table, click in the **Postal Code** field in the first record. On the ribbon, under **TABLE TOOLS**, click the **FIELDS tab**. In the **Formatting group**, click the **Data Type arrow**, and then click **Short Text**. Compare your screen with Figure 1.23.

When you import data from an Excel spreadsheet, check the data types of all fields to ensure they are correct. Recall that if a field, such as the Postal Code, contains numbers that are not used in calculations, the data type should be set to Short Text. To change the data type of a field, click in the field in any record.

FIGURE 1.23

Activity 1.12 | Adjusting Column Widths

You can adjust the column widths in a table displayed in Datasheet view by using techniques similar to those you use for Excel spreadsheets.

1 ▶ In the object window, click the **object tab** for your **1A Students** table to make it the active object and to display it in the object window.

Clicking the object tabs along the top of the object window enables you to display open objects and make them active so that you can work with them. All of the columns in the datasheet are the same width, regardless of the length of the data in the field, the length of the field name, or the field size that was set. If you print the table as currently displayed, some of the data or field names will not print fully, so you will want to adjust the column widths.

2 ▶ In the field names row, point to the right edge of the **Address** field to display the ⊞ pointer, and then compare your screen with Figure 1.24.

FIGURE 1.24

3 ▶ With the ⊞ pointer positioned as shown in Figure 1.24, double-click the right edge of the **Address** field.

The column width of the Address field widens to display fully the longest entry in the field. In this manner, the width of a column can be increased or decreased to fit its contents in the same manner as a column in an Excel spreadsheet. In Access, adjusting the column width to fit the contents is referred to as *Best Fit*.

4 Point to the **City** field name to display the ⬇ pointer, right-click to select the entire column, and then click **Field Width**. In the **Column Width** dialog box, click **Best Fit**.

This is a second way to adjust column widths.

5 If necessary, scroll to the right to view the last three fields. Point to the **Email** field name to display the ⬇ pointer, hold down the left mouse button, and then drag to the right to select this column, the **Faculty Advisor ID** column, and the **Amount Owed** column. Point to the right edge of any of the selected columns to display the ➕ pointer, and then double-click to apply **Best Fit** to all three columns.

You can select multiple columns and adjust the widths of all of them at one time by using this technique or by right-clicking any of the selected columns, clicking Field Width, and clicking Best Fit in the Column Width dialog box.

6 If necessary, scroll to the left to view the **Student ID** field. To the left of the **Student ID** field name, click **Select All** ⬜. Notice that all of the fields are selected.

7 On the ribbon, click the **HOME tab**. In the **Records group**, click **More**, and then click **Field Width**. In the **Column Width** dialog box, click **Best Fit**. Click anywhere in the **Student ID** field, and then compare your screen with Figure 1.25.

Using the More command is a third way to adjust column widths. By using Select All, you can adjust the widths of all of the columns at one time. Adjusting the width of columns does not change the data in the table's records; it only changes the *display* of the data.

FIGURE 1.25

NOTE **Adjusting Column Widths**

After adjusting column widths, scroll horizontally and vertically to be sure that all of the data displays in all of the fields. Access adjusts column widths to fit the screen size based on the displayed data. If data is not displayed on the screen when you adjust column widths—even if you use Select All—the column width might not be adjusted adequately to display all of the data in the field. After adjusting column widths, save the table before performing other tasks. The column width adjustments might not save with the table. When you reopen a table, be sure to readjust the column widths if you plan to print the table or work with the data in the table.

---

8 On the **Quick Access Toolbar**, click **Save** 🖫 to save the table design changes—changing the column widths.

If you do not save the table after making design changes, Access prompts you to save when you close the table.

Activity 1.13 | Printing a Table

There are times when you will want to print a table, even though a report may look more professional. For example, you may need a quick reference, or you may want to proofread the data that has been entered. Before printing a table, be sure to apply Best Fit to all of the columns in the table.

1 On the ribbon, click the **FILE tab**, click **Print**, and then click **Print Preview**. Compare your screen with Figure 1.26.

> The table displays in Print Preview with the default zoom setting of Fit to Window, a view that enables you to see how your table will print on the page. It is a good idea to view any object in Print Preview before printing so that you can make changes to the object if needed before actually printing it. In the navigation area, the Next Page button is darker (available), an indication that more than one page will print.

FIGURE 1.26

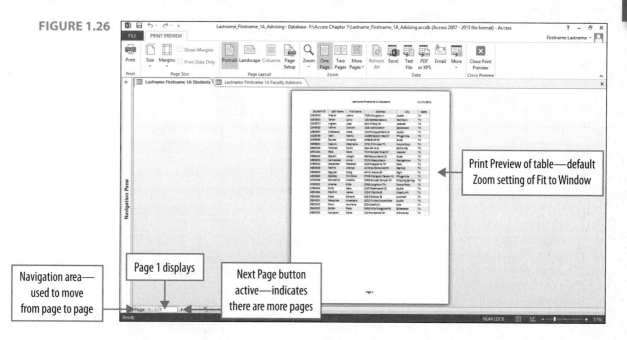

Print Preview of table—default Zoom setting of Fit to Window

Page 1 displays

Next Page button active—indicates there are more pages

Navigation area— used to move from page to page

2 In the navigation area, click **Next Page** ▶ to display Page 2. Point to the top of the page to display the 🔍 pointer, click one time to zoom in, and then compare your screen with Figure 1.27.

> The Print Preview display enlarges, and the Zoom Out pointer displays. The second page of the table displays the last five fields. The Next Page button is dimmed, indicating that the button is unavailable because there are no more pages after Page 2. The Previous Page button is available, indicating that a page exists before this page.

FIGURE 1.27

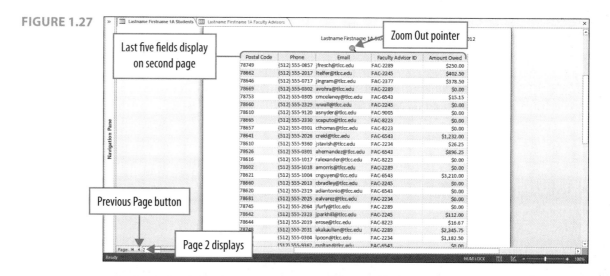

Last five fields display on second page

Zoom Out pointer

Previous Page button

Page 2 displays

3 On the ribbon, on the **PRINT PREVIEW tab**, in the **Zoom group**, click the top portion of the **Zoom** button to change the zoom setting back to the default setting of Fit to Window.

4 In the **Page Layout group**, click **Landscape**, and notice that there are only three fields on Page 2. In the navigation area, click **Previous Page** ◀ to display Page 1, and then compare your screen with Figure 1.28.

The orientation of the page to be printed changes. Included on the page are the table name and current date at the top of the page and the page number at the bottom of the page. The change in orientation from portrait to landscape is not saved with the table. Each time you print, you must check the page orientation, the margins, and any other print parameters so that the object prints as you intend. You should also be sure that Best Fit is applied to each column or to the entire table.

FIGURE 1.28

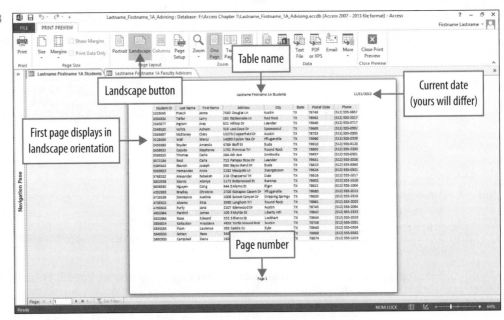

5 On the **PRINT PREVIEW tab**, in the **Print group**, click **Print**. In the **Print** dialog box, under **Print Range**, verify that **All** is selected. Under **Copies**, verify that the **Number of Copies** is **1**. Compare your screen with Figure 1.29.

FIGURE 1.29

6 Determine whether your instructor wants you to submit your work for this project on paper or electronically. If submitting electronically, determine whether, in addition to submitting your Access database, your instructor wants you to create and submit electronic printouts of individual database objects.

7 To print on paper, in the **Print** dialog box, click **OK**; and then on the ribbon, in the **Close Preview group**, click **Close Print Preview**. If you are required to create and submit electronic printouts, in the **Print** dialog box, click **Cancel**, and then follow the steps in the following Note—or follow the specific directions provided by your instructor.

NOTE   **Creating a PDF Electronic Printout of an Access Object**

Display the object (table, query, form, report, and so on) in Print Preview and adjust margins and orientation as needed. On the PRINT PREVIEW tab, in the Data group, click PDF or XPS. In the Publish as PDF or XPS dialog box, navigate to your chapter folder. Use the default file name, or follow your instructor's directions to name the object. If wish to view the PDF file, in the dialog box, select the Open file after publishing check box. In the Publish as PDF or XPS dialog box, click Publish. If necessary, close the Windows 8 Reader, Adobe Reader, or Adobe Acrobat window and the Export – PDF dialog box. On the ribbon, click Close Print Preview; your electronic printout is saved.

---

8 In the upper right corner of the object window, click **Close Object** ⊠ to close your **1A Students** table. Notice that the **1A Faculty Advisors** table is the active object in the object window.

⟳ ANOTHER WAY   In the object window, right-click your 1A Students object tab, and then click Close.

---

9 In your **1A Faculty Advisors** table, to the left of the **Faculty ID** field name, click **Select All** ⬜ to select all of the columns. On the **HOME tab**, in the **Records group**, click **More**, and then click **Field Width**. In the **Column Width** dialog box, click **Best Fit** to adjust the widths of all of the columns so that all of the data display. Scroll horizontally and vertically to be sure that all of the data display in each field; if necessary, use the techniques you practiced to apply **Best Fit** to individual columns. **Save** 🖫 the changes you made to the table's column widths, and then click in any record to cancel the selection.

10 On the ribbon, click the **FILE tab**, click **Print**, and then click **Print Preview**. On the **PRINT PREVIEW tab**, in the **Page Layout group**, click **Landscape**. Notice that the table will print on more than one page. In the **Page Size group**, click **Margins**, click **Normal**, and then notice that one more column moved to the first page—your results may differ depending upon your printer's capabilities.

> In addition to changing the page orientation to Landscape, you can change the margins to Normal to see if all of the fields will print on one page. In this instance, there are still too many fields to print on one page, although the Postal Code field moved from Page 2 to Page 1.

11 If directed to do so by your instructor, create a paper or electronic printout of your **1A Faculty Advisors** table, and then click **Close Print Preview**.

12 In the object window, **Close** ⊠ your **1A Faculty Advisors** table.

> All of your database objects—your *1A Students* table and your *1A Faculty Advisors* table—are closed; the object window is empty.

Video A1-4

Recall that tables are the foundation of an Access database because all of the data is stored in one or more tables. You can display the data stored in tables in other database objects such as queries, forms, and reports.

Activity 1.14 | Creating a Query by Using the Simple Query Wizard

A *query* is a database object that retrieves specific data from one or more database objects—either tables or other queries—and then, in a single datasheet, displays only the data that you specify when you design the query. Because the word *query* means *to ask a question*, think of a query as a question formed in a manner that Access can answer.

A *select query* is one type of Access query. A select query, also called a *simple select query*, retrieves (selects) data from one or more tables or queries and then displays the selected data in a datasheet. A select query creates a subset of the data to answer specific questions; for example, *Which students live in Austin, TX?*

The objects from which a query selects the data are referred to as the query's *data source*. In this activity, you will create a simple select query using a wizard that walks you step by step through the process. The process involves selecting the data source and indicating the fields that you want to include in the query results. The query—the question you want to ask—is *What is the last name, first name, email address, phone number, and Student ID of every student?*

1 ▸ On the ribbon, click the **CREATE tab**, and then in the **Queries group**, click **Query Wizard**. In the **New Query** dialog box, be sure **Simple Query Wizard** is selected, and then click **OK**. Compare your screen with Figure 1.30.

FIGURE 1.30

2 ▸ In the wizard, click the **Tables/Queries arrow**, and then click **Table: Lastname Firstname 1A Students**.

In the wizard, the displayed table or query name is the object that was last selected on the Navigation Pane. The last object you worked with was your 1A Faculty Advisors table, so that object name displayed in the wizard.

To create a query, first select the data source—the object from which the query is to select the data. The information you need to answer the question is stored in your 1A Students table, so this table is your data source.

3 ▸ Under **Available Fields**, click **Last Name**, and then click **Add Field** > to move the field to the **Selected Fields** list on the right. Double-click the **First Name** field to add the field to the **Selected Fields** list.

Use either method to add fields to the Selected Fields list—you can add fields in any order.

4 By using **Add Field** `>` or by double-clicking the field name, add the following fields to the **Selected Fields** list in the order specified: **Email**, **Phone**, and **Student ID**. Compare your screen with Figure 1.31.

Selecting these five fields will answer the question, *What is the last name, first name, email address, phone number, and Student ID of every student?*

FIGURE 1.31

5 In the wizard, click **Next**. Click in the **What title do you want for your query?** box. Using your own name, edit as necessary so that the query name is **Lastname Firstname 1A All Students Query** and then compare your screen with Figure 1.32.

FIGURE 1.32

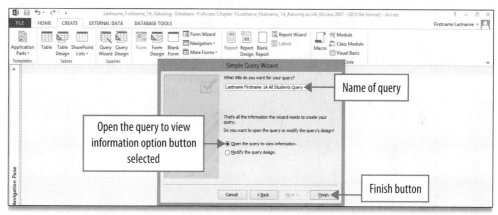

6 In the wizard, click **Finish**. Select all of the columns, apply **Best Fit**, and then **Save** 🖫 the query. In the first record, click in the **Last Name** field to cancel the selection. Compare your screen with Figure 1.33.

Access *runs* the query—performs the actions indicated in your query design—by searching the records in the specified data source, and then finds the records that match specified criteria. The records that match the criteria display in a datasheet. A select query *selects*—finds and displays—*only* the information from the data source that you request, including the specified fields.

In the object window, Access displays every student from your 1A Students table—the data source—but displays *only* the five fields that you moved to the Selected Fields list in the Simple Query Wizard.

FIGURE 1.33

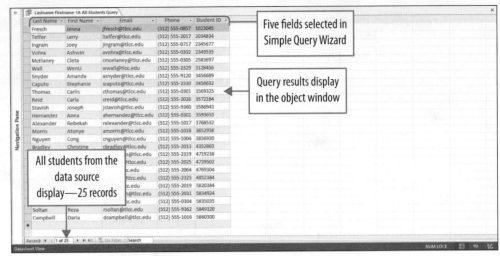

Five fields selected in Simple Query Wizard

Query results display in the object window

All students from the data source display—25 records

7 ▶ On the ribbon, click the **FILE tab**, click **Print**, and then click **Print Preview**. Notice that the query results will print on one page. As directed by your instructor, create a paper or electronic printout. Click **Close Print Preview**.

8 ▶ In the object window, **Close** ✕ the query.

Activity 1.15 | Creating and Printing a Form

A **form** is an Access object with which you can enter data, edit data, or display data from a table or query. In a form, the fields are laid out in an attractive format on the screen, which makes working with the database easier for those who must enter and look up data.

One type of form displays only one record at a time. Such a form is useful not only to the individual who performs the data entry—typing in the records—but also to anyone who has the job of viewing information in the database. For example, when you visit the Records office at your college to obtain a transcript, someone displays your record on the screen. For the viewer, it is much easier to look at one record at a time, using a form, than to look at all of the student records in the database table.

1 ▶ Open ⏵ the **Navigation Pane**. Drag the right edge of the **Navigation Pane** to the right to increase the width of the pane so that all object names display fully. Notice that a table name displays with a datasheet icon, and a query name displays an icon of two overlapping datasheets. Right-click your **1A Students** table, and then compare your screen with Figure 1.34.

FIGURE 1.34

Navigation Pane Close button

Table icon

Shortcut menu for your 1A Students table

Query icon

2 ▶ On the shortcut menu, click **Open** to display the table in the object window, and then **Close** « the **Navigation Pane** to maximize your object window space.

ANOTHER WAY On the Navigation Pane, double-click the object name to open it.

3 Notice that there are 11 fields in the table. On the **CREATE tab**, in the **Forms group**, click **Form**, and then compare your screen with Figure 1.35.

The Form tool creates a form based on the active object—your 1A Students table. The form displays all of the fields from the underlying data source—one record at a time—in a simple top-to-bottom format with all 11 fields lined up in a single column. You can use this new form immediately, or you can modify it. Records that you create or edit in a form are automatically added to or updated in the underlying table or data source.

The new form displays in *Layout view*—the Access view in which you can make changes to an object while the object is open and displaying the data from the data source. Each field in the form displayed in Figure 1.35 displays the data for the first student record—*Jenna Fresch*—from your 1A Students table.

FIGURE 1.35

Form object icon

First record for *Jenna Fresch* displays

Total number of records is 25

Navigation buttons to move among records

Next record button

Design View button

Layout View button active

Form View button

4 At the right side of the status bar, notice the three buttons. Point to each button to display its ScreenTip, and notice that **Layout View** is active, indicating that the form is displayed in Layout view.

5 In the status bar, click **Form View**.

In *Form view*, you can view the records, create a new record, edit a record, and delete a record. You cannot change the layout or design of the form. Form view is useful for individuals who *access records* in your database. Layout view is useful for individuals who *design* the form.

ANOTHER WAY On the DESIGN tab, or on the HOME tab, in the Views group, click the top portion of the View button when it displays an icon of a form.

6 In the navigation area, click **Next record** two times to display the third record—the record for *Joey Ingram*.

Use the navigation buttons to scroll among the records and to display any single record.

7 Using your own name, **Save** the form as **Lastname Firstname 1A Student Form**

8 ▸ Be sure that Record 3 displays. On the ribbon, click the **FILE tab**, click **Print**, and then on the right, click **Print**—do *not* click **Print Preview** because you are going to print a *single* record—not all of the records.

9 ▸ In the **Print** dialog box, under **Print Range**, click the **Selected Record(s)** option button, and then click **Setup**.

10 ▸ In the **Page Setup** dialog box, click the **Columns tab**. Under **Column Size**, double-click in the **Width** box to select the existing value, type **7.5** and then click **OK**.

> Forms are usually not printed, so the default width for a form created with the Form command is larger than most printers can handle to print on one page. If you do not change the width, the form will print on two pages because the last column flows over the margins allowed by the printer. If, after changing the Width to 7.5, your form still prints on two pages, try entering a different Width; for example, 7 or 6.5.

11 ▸ If instructed to print your objects, in the **Print** dialog box, click **OK** to print the record for *Joey Ingram* on one page; otherwise, click **Cancel**. If instructed to print an electronic copy, follow the steps in the following Note or the directions provided by your instructor.

> After printing, along the left edge of the record, the narrow bar—the ***record selector bar***—displays in black, indicating that the record is selected.

NOTE   **Printing a Single Form in PDF**

On the FILE tab, click Print, and then on the right, click Print. In the Print dialog box, click Setup. In the Page Setup dialog box, click the Columns tab. Under Column Size, double-click in the Width box, type 7.5 and then click OK. In the Print dialog box, click Cancel. On the left edge of the form, click the record selector bar so that it is black—selected.

On the ribbon, click the EXTERNAL DATA tab. In the Export group, click PDF or XPS. In the Publish as PDF or XPS dialog box, navigate to your chapter folder, and at the lower right corner of the dialog box, click Options. In the Options dialog box, under Range, click the Selected records option button, and then click OK. In the Publish as PDF or XPS dialog box, click Publish. If necessary, close the Window 8 Reader, Adobe Reader, or Adobe Acrobat window.

---

12 ▸ **Close** ☒ your **1A Student Form** object; leave your **1A Students** table open.

Activity 1.16 │ Creating, Modifying, and Printing a Report

A ***report*** is a database object that displays the fields and records from a table or query in an easy-to-read format suitable for printing. Create professional-looking reports to summarize database information.

1 ▸ **Open** ⏵ the **Navigation Pane**, and then open your **1A Faculty Advisors** table by double-clicking the table name or by right-clicking the table name and clicking **Open. Close** ⏴ the **Navigation Pane**.

2 ▸ On the ribbon, click the **CREATE tab**. In the **Reports group**, click **Report**.

> The Report tool creates a report in Layout view and includes all of the fields and all of the records in the data source—your 1A Faculty Advisors table. Dotted lines indicate how the report will break across pages if you print it now. In Layout view, you can make quick changes to the report layout while viewing the data from the table.

3 ▸ In the report, click the **Faculty ID** field name, and then on the ribbon, under **REPORT LAYOUT TOOLS**, click the **ARRANGE tab**. In the **Rows & Columns group**, click **Select Column**, and then press Del. Using the same technique, delete the **Rank** field.

> The Faculty ID and Rank fields, along with the data, are deleted from the report. The fields readjust by moving to the left. Deleting the fields from the report does *not* delete the fields and data from the data source—your 1A Faculty Advisors table.

ANOTHER WAY   Right-click the field name, click Select Entire Column, and then press Del.

4 Click the **Address** field name, and then by using the scroll bar at the bottom of the screen, scroll to the right to display the **Cell Phone** field; be careful not to click in the report.

5 Hold down Shift, and then click the **Cell Phone** field name to select all of the fields from *Address* through *Cell Phone*. With the six field names selected—surrounded by a colored border—in the **Rows & Columns group**, click **Select Column**, and then press Del.

Use this method to select and delete multiple columns in Layout view.

6 Scroll to the left, and notice that the four remaining fields display within the dotted lines—they are within the margins of the report. Click the **Campus** field name. Hold down Shift, and then click the **First Name** field name to select the first three fields.

7 On the ribbon, under **REPORT LAYOUT TOOLS**, click the **DESIGN tab**. In the **Tools group**, click **Property Sheet**.

The *Property Sheet* for the selected columns displays on the right side of the screen. Every object and every item in an object has an associated Property Sheet where you can make precise changes to the properties—characteristics—of selected items.

8 In the **Property Sheet**, if necessary, click the **Format tab**. Click **Width**, type **1.5** and then press Enter. Compare your screen with Figure 1.36.

The width of the three selected field names and the columns changes to 1.5", and the fields readjust by moving to the left. When you change the Width property, you do not need to select the entire column. Change the Width property if you need to move columns within the margins of a report. In this report, the fields already displayed within the margins, but some reports may need this minor adjustment to print on one page.

 ANOTHER WAY   Select the column, and then drag the right edge of the column to the left to decrease the width of the field, or drag to the right to increase the width of the field.

FIGURE 1.36

9 Close ☒ the **Property Sheet**. Click the **Last Name** field name. On the ribbon, click the **HOME tab**, and then in the **Sort & Filter group**, click **Ascending**.

Access sorts the report in ascending alphabetical order by the Last Name field. By default, tables are sorted in ascending order by the primary key field—in this instance, the Faculty ID field. Changing the sort order in the report does *not* change the sort order in the underlying table.

10 At the top of the report, to the right of the green report icon, click anywhere in the title of the report to select the title. On the **HOME tab**, in the **Text Formatting group**, click the **Font Size arrow**, and then click **14**. **Save** 🖫 the report. In the **Save As** dialog box, in the **Report Name** box, add **Report** to the end of *Lastname Firstname 1A Faculty Advisors*, and then click **OK**.

11 ▸ On the **FILE tab**, click **Print**, and then click **Print Preview**. On the **PRINT PREVIEW tab**, in the **Zoom group**, click **Two Pages**, and then compare your screen with Figure 1.37.

As currently formatted, the report will print on two pages because the page number at the bottom of the report is positioned beyond the right margin of the report.

FIGURE 1.37

12 ▸ In the **Close Preview group**, click **Close Print Preview**. Scroll down to display the bottom of the report, and then, if necessary, scroll to the right to display the page number. Click the page number—**Page 1 of 1**—and then press (Del).

Because all of the data will print on one page, the page number is not necessary for this report. If you want the page number to display, you can drag it within the margins of the report.

13 ▸ Display the report in **Print Preview**, and notice that the report will now print on one page. In the **Zoom group**, click **One Page**. Click **Save** 🖫 to save the changes to the design of the report, and then create a paper or electronic printout as directed. Click **Close Print Preview**.

When you create a report by using the Report tool, the default margins are 0.25 inch. Some printers require a greater margin, so your printed report may result in two pages. As you progress in your study of Access, you will practice making these adjustments. Also, if a printer is not installed on your system, the electronic PDF printout may result in a two-page report.

14 ▸ In the object window, right-click any **object tab**, and then click **Close All** to close all of the open objects. Notice that the object window is empty.

Objective 5 | Close a Database and Exit Access

Video A1-5

When you close a table, any changes made to the records are saved automatically. If you make changes to the structure or adjust column widths, you are prompted to save the table when you close the table or when you switch views. Likewise, you are prompted to save queries, forms, and reports if you make changes to the layout or design. If the Navigation Pane is open when you exit Access, it will display when you reopen the database. When you are finished using your database, close the database, and then exit Access.

Activity 1.17 | Closing a Database and Exiting Access

> **1** **Open** » the **Navigation Pane**. If necessary, increase the width of the **Navigation Pane** so that all object names display fully. Notice that your report object displays with a green report icon. Compare your screen with Figure 1.38.

FIGURE 1.38

> **2** On the ribbon, click the **FILE tab**. Click **Close** to close the database but leave Access open. This action enables you to continue working in Access with another database if you want to do so. In the Access opening screen, in the upper right corner, click **Close** ☒ to exit Access. As directed by your instructor, submit your database and the paper or electronic printouts of the five objects—two tables, one query, one form, and one report—that are the results of this project. Specifically, in this project, using your own name, you created the following database and printouts or electronic printouts:

1. Lastname_Firstname_1A_Advising	Database file
2. Lastname Firstname 1A Students	Table (printout or electronic printout – two pages)
3. Lastname Firstname 1A Faculty Advisors	Table (printout or electronic printout – two pages)
4. Lastname Firstname 1A All Students Query	Query (printout or electronic printout)
5. Lastname Firstname 1A Student Form	Form (printout or electronic printout – Record 3)
6. Lastname Firstname 1A Faculty Advisors Report	Report (printout or electronic printout)

ANOTHER WAY On the left side of the title bar, click 🗗 and then click Close, or on the right side of the title bar, click ☒ to close the database and to exit Access.

END | You have completed Project 1A

GO! with Office Web Apps

Objective	Export an Access Table to an Excel Spreadsheet, Save to SkyDrive, Edit a Record, and Save to Your Computer

Access web apps are designed to work with Microsoft's **SharePoint**, an application for setting up websites to share and manage documents. Your college may not have SharePoint installed, so you will use other tools to share objects from your database so that you can work collaboratively with others. Recall that Window's SkyDrive is a free file storage and file sharing service. For Access, you can export a database object to an Excel worksheet, a PDF file, or a text file, and then save the file to SkyDrive.

> **ALERT!** **Working with Web-Based Applications and Services**
>
> Computer programs and services on the web receive continuous updates and improvements. Therefore, the steps to complete this web-based activity may differ from the ones shown. You can often look at the screens and the information presented to determine how to complete the activity.

Activity | **Exporting an Access Table to an Excel Spreadsheet, Saving the Spreadsheet to SkyDrive, Editing a Record in SkyDrive, and Saving to Your Computer**

In this activity, you will *export*—copy data from one file into another file—your 1A Students table to an Excel spreadsheet, upload your Excel file to SkyDrive, edit a record in SkyDrive, and then download a copy of the edited spreadsheet to your computer.

1 Start Access, navigate to your **Access Chapter 1** folder, and then open your **1A_Advising** database file. If necessary, on the Message Bar, click Enable Content. In the **Navigation Pane**, click your **1A Students** table to select it—do not open it.

2 On the ribbon, click the **EXTERNAL DATA tab**, and then in the **Export group**, click **Excel**. In the **Export – Excel Spreadsheet** dialog box, click **Browse**, and then navigate to your **Access Chapter 1** folder. In the **File Save** dialog box, click in the **File name** box, type **Lastname_ Firstname_AC_1A_Web** and then click **Save**.

3 In the **Export – Excel Spreadsheet** dialog box, under **Specify export options**, select the first two check boxes—**Export data with formatting and layout** and **Open the destination file after the export operation is complete**—and then click **OK**. In the **Microsoft Excel**

window, in the column headings row, to the left of column **A**, click **Select All**. On the **HOME tab**, in the **Cells group**, click **Format**, and then click **AutoFit Column Width**. Click in cell **A1** to cancel the selection, and then compare your screen with Figure A.

4 **Save** the spreadsheet, and then **Close** Excel. In the **Export – Excel Spreadsheet** dialog box, click **Close**, and then **Close** Access.

5 From the desktop, start Internet Explorer. Navigate to **http://skydrive.com**, and then sign in to your Microsoft account. Open your **GO! Web Projects** folder—or create and then open this folder if necessary.

6 On the menu bar, click **Upload**. In the **Choose File to Upload** dialog box, navigate to your **Access Chapter 1** folder, and then double-click your **AC_1A_Web** Excel file to upload it to SkyDrive.

FIGURE A

1A Students table exported to Excel spreadsheet

(GO! with Office Web Apps continues on the next page)

7 When the upload is completed, in your **GO! Web Projects** folder, click your **AC_1A_Web** file to open it in Microsoft Excel Web App.

On the ribbon, notice that you can open this worksheet in Excel instead of using the web app. If you are working on a computer that does not have Microsoft Excel installed, you can still create and modify workbooks in your web browser by using the Microsoft Excel Web app.

8 In the first record, click in the **Last Name** field. Using your own last name, type **Lastname** and then press Tab to replace *Fresch* with your last name. In the **First Name** field, using your own first name, type **Firstname** to replace *Jenna* with your own first name, and then press ↓ to save the record. Compare your screen with Figure B.

9 On the ribbon, click the **FILE tab**, click **Save As**, and then click **Download**. In the message box—usually displays at the bottom of your screen—click the **Save arrow**, and then click **Save as**. In the **Save As** dialog box, navigate to your **Access Chapter 1** folder, and then click in the **File name** box. Type **Lastname_Firstname_AC_1A_Web_Download** and then click **Save**. **Close** the message box.

10 In SkyDrive, on the title bar, click **SkyDrive** to return to your home page. At the top right corner of your screen, click your SkyDrive name, and then click **Sign out**. **Close** your browser window.

11 Start Excel. In the Excel opening screen, click **Open Other Workbooks**. Under **Open**, click **Computer**. Under **Computer**, click **Browse**. Navigate to your **Access Chapter 1** folder, and then double-click your **AC_1A_Web** Excel file. Notice that this file is the original file—the first record is not changed. If you are required to print your documents, use one of the methods in the Note box given. **Close** your Excel file, saving the changes to your worksheet, and then **Open** and print your **AC_1A_Web_Download** file by using one of the methods in the following Note. **Close** Excel, saving the changes to your worksheet. As directed by your instructor, submit your two workbooks and the two paper or electronic printouts that are the results of this project.

NOTE   **Adding the File Name to the Footer and Printing or Creating an Electronic Printout of an Excel Spreadsheet on One Page**

Click the FILE tab, click Print, and then click Page Setup. In the Page Setup dialog box, on the Page tab, under Orientation, click Landscape. Under Scaling, click the Fit to option button. In the Page Setup dialog box, click the Header/Footer tab, and then click Custom Footer. With the insertion point blinking in the Left section box, click the Insert File Name button, and then click OK. In the Page Setup dialog box, click OK.

To print on paper, click Print. To create an electronic file of your printout, on the left side of your screen, click Export. Under Export, be sure Create PDF/XPS Document is selected, and then, on the right, click Create PDF/XPS. Navigate to your Access Chapter 1 folder, and then click Publish to save the file with the default name and an extension of pdf.

FIGURE B

Student Workshops Database

PROJECT ACTIVITIES

In Activities 1.18 through 1.25, you will assist Dr. Miriam Yong, director of student activities, in creating a database to store information about student workshops held at Texas Lakes Community College campuses. You will use a database template that tracks event information, add workshop information to the database, and then print the results. Your completed report and table will look similar to Figure 1.39.

PROJECT FILES

For Project 1B, you will need the following files:

**Desktop Event Management template
a01B_Workshops (Excel workbook)**

You will save your database as:

Lastname_Firstname_1B_Student_Workshops

PROJECT RESULTS

Build from
Scratch

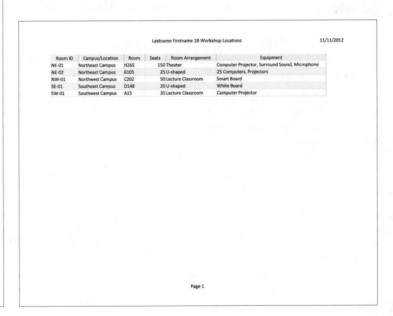

FIGURE 1.39 Project 1B Student Workshops

Video A1-6

A **database template** contains prebuilt tables, queries, forms, and reports that perform a specific task, such as tracking a large number of events. For example, your college may hold events such as athletic contests, plays, lectures, concerts, and club meetings. Using a predefined template, your college's activities director can quickly create a database to manage these events. The advantage of using a template to start a new database is that you do not have to create the objects—all you need to do is enter the data and modify the prebuilt objects to suit your needs.

The purpose of the database in this project is to track the student workshops that are held by Texas Lakes Community College. The questions to be answered might include:

- What workshops will be offered, and when will they be offered?
- In what rooms and on what campuses will the workshops be held?
- Which workshop locations have a computer projector for PowerPoint presentations?

Activity 1.18 │ Using a Template to Create a Database

There are two types of database templates—those that will be stored on your desktop and those that are designed to share with others over the Internet. In this activity, you will use a desktop template to create your database.

1 Start Access. In the Access opening screen, scroll down until the last templates display. Notice that there is a **Task management** template and a **Desktop task management** template. Compare your screen with Figure 1.40.

These templates are included with the Access program. To store a database to manage tasks on your desktop, select the *Desktop task management* template. To publish a database to manage tasks and share it with others, select the *Task management* template—the one that displays a globe image. The names of templates designed to create databases stored on your computer start with the word *Desktop*.

You can search the Microsoft Office website for more templates. You can also click on a category under the search box, where templates will be suggested.

FIGURE 1.40

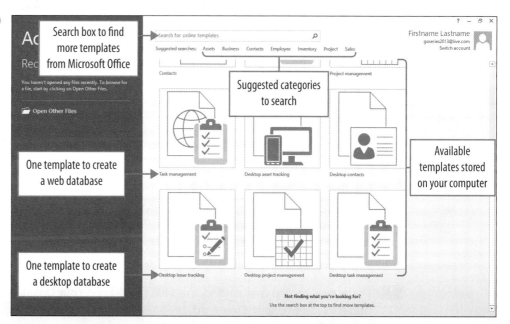

2 At the top of the window, click in the **Search for online templates** box, type **event** and then press Enter. Compare your screen with Figure 1.41.

You must have an Internet connection to search for online templates. Access displays several templates, including the Desktop Event Management template.

FIGURE 1.41

3 Click the **Desktop Event Management** template. In the dialog box, to the right of the **File Name** box, click **Browse** 📁, and then navigate to your **Access Chapter 1** folder.

4 In the **File New Database** dialog box, click in the **File name** box to select the existing text. Using your own name, type **Lastname_Firstname_1B_Student_Workshops** and then press Enter.

5 In the **Desktop Event Management** dialog box, click **Create** to download the template and to save the database.

Access creates the *1B_Student_Workshops* database, and the database name displays in the title bar. A predesigned *form*—Event List—automatically displays in the object window. Although you can enter events for any date, when you open the database in the future, the Event List form will display only those events for the current date and future dates.

6 Under the ribbon, on the **Message Bar**, a *SECURITY WARNING* displays. On the **Message Bar**, click **Enable Content**.

Databases provided by Microsoft are safe to use on your computer.

Activity 1.19 | Building a Table by Entering Records in a Multiple-Items Form and a Single-Record Form

One purpose of a form is to simplify the entry of data into a table—either for you or for others who enter data. In Project 1A, you created a simple form that enabled you to display or enter records in a table, one record at a time. The Desktop Event Management template contains a ***multiple-items form*** that enables you to display or enter *multiple* records in a table, but with an easier and simplified layout rather than typing directly into the table itself.

1 In the new record row, click in the **Title** field. Type **Your Online Reputation** and then press Tab. In the **Start Time** field, type **3/9/18 7p** and then press Tab.

Access formats the date and time. As you enter dates and times, a small calendar displays to the right of the field. You can use the calendar to select a date instead of typing it.

2 In the **End Time** field, type **3/9/18 9p** and then press (Tab). In the **Description** field, type **Internet Safety** and then press (Tab). In the **Location** field, type **Northeast Campus** and then press (Tab) three times to move to the **Title** field in the new record row. Compare your screen with Figure 1.42.

> Because the workshops have no unique value, Access uses the AutoNumber data type in the ID field to assign a unique, sequential number to each record.

FIGURE 1.42

3 In the form, directly above the field names row, click **New Event**.

> A *single-record form* with the name *Event Details* displays, similar to the simple form you created in Project 1A. A single-record form enables you to display or enter one record at a time into a table.

4 Using (Tab) to move from field to field, enter the following record in the **Event Details** form—press (Tab) three times to move from the **End Time** field to the **Description** field. Then compare your screen with Figure 1.43.

Title	Location	Start Time	End Time	Description
Writing a Research Paper	Southwest Campus	3/10/18 4p	3/10/18 6p	Computer Skills

FIGURE 1.43

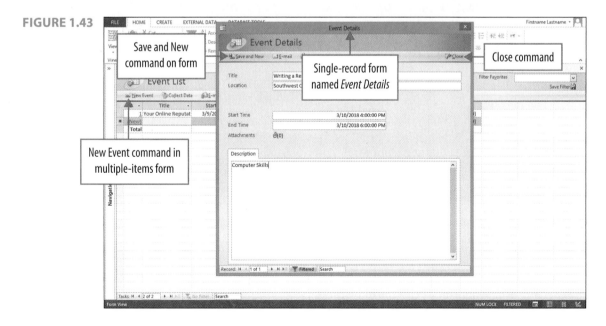

5 In the **Event Details** single-record form, in the upper right corner, click **Close**, and notice that the new record displays in the multiple-items form—*Event List*.

6 Enter the following records by using either the **Event List** form—the multiple-items form—or the **Event Details** form—the single-record form that is accessed by clicking the *New Event* command on the **Event List** form. The data in the table given is arranged in the same order as the **Event List** form. Be sure the multiple-items form displays, and then compare your screen with Figure 1.44.

ID	Title	Start Time	End Time	Description	Location
3	**Resume Writing**	3/18/18 2p	3/18/18 4p	**Job Skills**	**Northwest Campus**
4	**Careers in the Legal Profession**	3/19/18 2p	3/19/18 4p	**Careers**	**Southeast Campus**

ALERT!   **Does a Single-Record Form—*Event Details*–Open?**

In the multiple-items form, pressing Enter three times at the end of the row to begin a new record will display the single-record form—*Event Details*. If you prefer to use the multiple-items form—Event List—close the single-record form and continue entering records, using the Tab key to move from field to field.

FIGURE 1.44

Four records entered

7 In the object window, click **Close** ⊠ to close the **Event List** form.

Activity 1.20 | Appending Records by Importing from an Excel Spreadsheet

In this activity, you will append records to the table that stores the data that displays in the Events List form. You will import the records from an Excel spreadsheet.

1 On the ribbon, click the **EXTERNAL DATA tab**. In the **Import & Link group**, click **Excel**.

2 In the **Get External Data – Excel Spreadsheet** dialog box, click **Browse**. Navigate to the location where your student data files are stored, and then double-click **a01B_Workshops**.

3 Click the second option button—**Append a copy of the records to the table**—and then click **OK**.

The table that stores the data is named *Events*. Recall that other objects, such as forms, queries, and reports, display data from tables; so the Event Details form displays data that is stored in the Events table.

4 In the **Import Spreadsheet Wizard**, click **Next**, and then click **Finish**. In the **Get External Data – Excel Spreadsheet** dialog box, click **Close**.

5 Open ⊠ the **Navigation Pane**. Double-click **Event List** to open the form that displays data from the **Events** table, and then **Close** ⊠ the **Navigation Pane**. Compare your screen with Figure 1.45.

A total of 12 records display; you entered four records, and you appended eight records from the a01B_Workshops Excel workbook. The data is truncated in several fields because the columns are not wide enough to display all of the data.

FIGURE 1.45

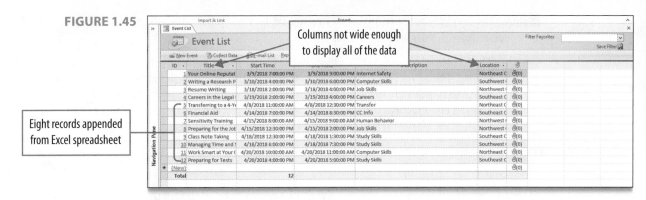

Eight records appended from Excel spreadsheet

6 ▶ To the left of the **ID** field name, click **Select All** ☐ to select all of the columns and rows.

7 ▶ In the field names row, point to the right edge of any of the selected columns to display the ⊹ pointer, and then double-click to apply **Best Fit** to all of the columns. **Save** 🖫 the form, and then click in any field to cancel the selection.

Objective 7 Organize Objects in the Navigation Pane

Video A1-7

Use the Navigation Pane to open objects, organize database objects, and perform common tasks, such as renaming an object or deleting an object.

Activity 1.21 | Grouping Database Objects in the Navigation Pane

The Navigation Pane groups and displays your database objects and can do so in predefined arrangements. In this activity, you will group your database objects using the ***Tables and Related Views*** category, which groups objects by the table to which the objects are related. This grouping is useful because you can determine easily the table that is the data source of queries, forms, and reports.

1 ▶ **Open** » the **Navigation Pane**. At the top right side of the **Navigation Pane**, click 🔽. On the list, under **Navigate To Category**, click **Tables and Related Views**. Compare your screen with Figure 1.46.

In the Navigation Pane, you can see the number of objects that are included in the Desktop Event Management template, including the table named *Events*. Other objects in the database that display data from the Events table include one query, two forms, and five reports. In the Navigation Pane, the Event List form is selected because it is open in the object window and is the active object. Other objects might display on the Navigation Pane; for example, Filters and Unrelated Objects. These filters are objects created for use by the Desktop Event Management template.

FIGURE 1.46

One table—data source for all other objects

Two forms

Five reports

Filters included with the template

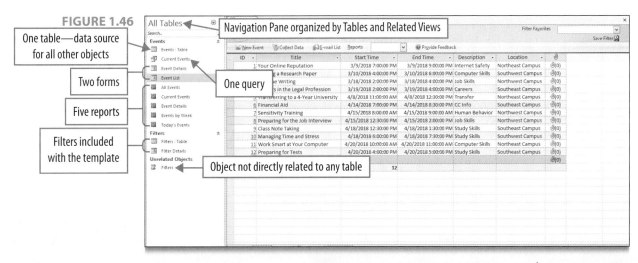

Navigation Pane organized by Tables and Related Views

One query

Object not directly related to any table

2 In the **Navigation Pane**, point to **Events: Table**, right-click, and then click **Open** to display the records in the underlying table.

> The Events table is the active object in the object window. Use the Navigation Pane to open objects for use. The 12 records that display in the Event List multiple-items form are stored in this table. Recall that tables are the foundation of your database because your data must be stored in a table. You can enter records directly into a table or you can use a form to enter records.

🔄 **ANOTHER WAY**   Double-click the table name to open it in the object window.

3 In the object window, click the **Event List tab** to display the form as the active object in the object window.

> Recall that a form presents a more user-friendly screen for entering records into a table.

4 In the **Navigation Pane**, double-click the **Current Events** *report* (green icon) to open the report. Compare your screen with Figure 1.47.

> An advantage of using a template to create a database is that many objects, such as reports, are already designed for you.

FIGURE 1.47

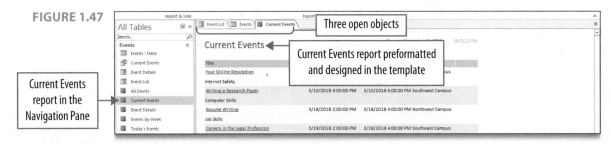

5 In the object window, **Close** ☒ the **Current Events** report.

6 By double-clicking or right-clicking, from the **Navigation Pane**, open the **Events by Week** report.

> In this predesigned report, the events are displayed by week. After entering records in the form or table, the preformatted reports are updated with the records from the table.

7 In the object window, right-click any one of the **object tabs**, and then click **Close All** to close all of the objects. **Close** ☒ the **Navigation Pane**.

Objective 8   Create a New Table in a Database Created with a Template

Video A1-8

The Desktop Event Management template included only one table—the *Events* table. It is easy to start a database with a template, and then you can add additional objects as needed.

Activity 1.22 | Using the Table Tool to Create a New Table

Dr. Yong has information about the various locations where workshops are held. For example, on the Northeast Campus, she has information about the room, seating arrangements, number of seats, and multimedia equipment. In the Events table, workshops are scheduled in rooms at each of the four campuses. It would not make sense to store information about the campus rooms multiple times in the same table. It is *not* considered good database design to have duplicate information in a table.

When data becomes redundant, it is usually an indication that you need a new table to store that information. In this activity, you will create a table to track the workshop locations, the equipment, and the seating arrangements in each location.

1 On the ribbon, click the **CREATE tab**, and then in the **Tables group**, click **Table**.

2 In the field names row, click **Click to Add**, click **Short Text**, type **Campus/Location** and then press Enter.

3 In the third column, click **Short Text**, type **Room** and then press Enter. In the fourth column, click **Number**, type **Seats** and then press Enter.

> The *Number data type* describes numbers that may be used in calculations. For the Seats field, you may need to determine the number of seats remaining after reservations are booked for a room. In the new record row, a *0* displays in the field.

4 In the fifth column, type **t** to select *Short Text*, type **Room Arrangement** and then press Enter. In the sixth column, type **t** and then type **Equipment** On your keyboard, press ↓.

> With the data type list displayed, you can select the data type by either clicking it or typing the letter that is underscored for the data type.

> This table has six fields. Access automatically creates the first field in the table—the ID field—to ensure that every record has a unique value. Before naming each field, you must define the data type for the field.

5 Right-click the **ID** field name, and then click **Rename Field**. Type **Room ID** and then press Enter. On the ribbon, under **TABLE TOOLS**, on the **FIELDS tab**, in the **Formatting group**, click the **Data Type arrow**, and then click **Short Text**. On the ribbon, in the **Field Validation group**, notice that **Unique** is selected.

> Recall that, by default, Access creates the ID field with the AutoNumber data type so that the field can be used as the primary key. Here, this field will store a unique room ID that is a combination of letters, symbols, and numbers; therefore, it is appropriate to change the data type to Short Text. In Datasheet view, the primary key field is identified by the selection of the Unique check box.

Activity 1.23 | Entering Records into a New Table

1 If necessary, in the new record row, click in the **Room ID** field. Enter the following record, pressing Enter or Tab to move from one field to the next. Do not be concerned that all of your text does not display; you will adjust the column widths later. After entering the record, compare your screen with Figure 1.48.

> Recall that Access saves a record when you move to another row within the table. You can press either Enter or Tab to move between fields in a table.

Room ID	Campus/Location	Room	Seats	Room Arrangement	Equipment
NE-01	Northeast Campus	H265	150	Theater	Computer Projector, Surround Sound, Microphone

FIGURE 1.48

- New table
- Field renamed
- Selected field—*Room ID*—assigned the data type of *Short Text*
- First record entered
- Selected field—*Room ID*—designated as the primary key field

2 In the **Views group**, click the top of the **View** button to switch to **Design** view. In the **Save As** dialog box, in the **Table Name** box, using your own name, type **Lastname Firstname 1B Workshop Locations** and then click **OK**.

Recall that when you switch views or when you close a table, Access prompts you to save the table if you have not previously saved it.

ANOTHER WAY On the right side of the status bar, click Design View 🔲 to switch to Design view.

3 In the **Field Name** column, to the left of **Room ID**, notice the key icon.

In Design view, the key icon indicates that the field—Room ID—is the primary key field.

4 In the **Views group**, click the top of the **View** button to switch back to **Datasheet** view.

ANOTHER WAY On the right side of the status bar, click Datasheet View 🔲 to switch to Datasheet view.

5 In the new record row, click in the **Room ID** field. Enter the following records, pressing Enter or Tab to move from one field to the next.

Room ID	Campus/Location	Room	Seats	Room Arrangement	Equipment
SW-01	Southwest Campus	A15	35	Lecture Classroom	Computer Projector
NW-01	Northwest Campus	C202	50	Lecture Classroom	Smart Board
SE-01	Southeast Campus	D148	20	U-shaped	White Board
NE-02	Northeast Campus	B105	25	U-shaped	25 Computers, Projector

6 To the left of the **Room ID** field name, click **Select All** ☐ to select all of the columns and rows in the table. On the **HOME tab**, in the **Records group**, click **More**, and then click **Field Width**. In the **Column Width** dialog box, click **Best Fit** to display all of the data in each column. **Save** 🔲 the changes to the table, and then click in any field to cancel the selection. In the object window, **Close** ☒ your **1B Workshop Locations** table.

7 **Open** ☒ the **Navigation Pane**, and notice that your new table name displays in its own group. Point to the right edge of the **Navigation Pane** to display the ⟷ pointer. Drag to the right to increase the width of the **Navigation Pane** so that your entire table name displays. Compare your screen with Figure 1.49.

Recall that by organizing the Navigation Pane by Tables and Related Views, the Navigation Pane groups the objects by each table and displays the related objects under each table name.

FIGURE 1.49

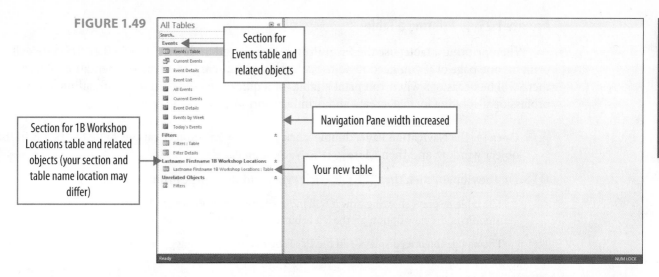

Section for Events table and related objects

Navigation Pane width increased

Section for 1B Workshop Locations table and related objects (your section and table name location may differ)

Your new table

Objective 9 | Print a Report and a Table

Video A1-9

Recall that one advantage to starting a new database with a template, instead of from a blank database, is that many report objects are already created for you.

Activity 1.24 | Viewing Reports and Printing a Report

1 In the **Navigation Pane**, double-click the report (not the form) named **Event Details** to open it in the object window.

This prebuilt Event Details report displays in an attractively arranged format.

2 Close ☒ the **Event Details** report. Open the **All Events** report, and then **Close** ☒ the **Navigation Pane**. On the **HOME** tab, in the **Views group**, click the top of the **View** button to switch to **Layout** view.

Recall that Layout view enables you to make changes to an object while viewing the data in the fields. Each prebuilt report displays the records in the table in different useful formats.

ANOTHER WAY On the right side of the status bar, click Layout View ▣ to switch to Layout view.

3 At the top of the report, click the title—*All Events*—to display a colored border around the title. Click to the left of the letter *A* to place the insertion point there. Using your own name, type **Lastname Firstname 1B** and then press Spacebar. Press Enter, and then **Save** 🖫 the report.

Including your name in the title will help you and your instructor identify any submitted work.

4 On the right side of the status bar, click **Print Preview** 🔍. In the navigation area, notice that the navigation arrows are unavailable, an indication that this report will print on one page.

ANOTHER WAY On the HOME tab, in the Views group, click the View arrow, and then click Print Preview. Or, on the FILE tab, click Print, and then click Print Preview. Or, right-click the object tab, and then click Print Preview.

5 Create a paper or electronic printout as instructed. Click **Close Print Preview**, and then **Close** ☒ the report.

Activity 1.25 | Printing a Table

When printing a table, use the Print Preview command to determine whether the table will print on one page or if you need to adjust column widths, margins, or page orientation. Recall that there will be occasions when you print a table for a quick reference or for proofreading. For a more professional-looking format, create and print a report.

1 Open ☐»☐ the **Navigation Pane**, double-click your **1B Workshop Locations** table to open it in the object window, and then **Close** ☐«☐ the **Navigation Pane**.

2 On the ribbon, click the **FILE tab**, click **Print**, and then click **Print Preview**.

The table displays showing how it will look when printed. Generally, tables are not printed, so there is no Print Preview option on the View button or on the status bar.

The navigation area displays *1* in the Pages box, and the navigation arrows to the right of the box are active, an indication that the table will print on more than one page.

3 In the navigation area, click **Next Page** ☐▶☐.

The second page of the table displays the last field. Whenever possible, try to print all of the fields horizontally on one page. Of course, if there are many records, more than one page may be needed to print all of the records and all of the fields.

4 On the **PRINT PREVIEW tab**, in the **Page Layout group**, click **Landscape**, and then compare your screen with Figure 1.50. In landscape orientation, notice that the entire table will print on one page—all of the navigation buttons are unavailable.

FIGURE 1.50

5 Create a paper or electronic printout as instructed, and then click **Close Print Preview**.

6 **Close** ☐×☐ your **1B Workshop Locations** table. For the convenience of the next individual opening the database, **Open** ☐»☐ the **Navigation Pane**.

7 On the right side of the title bar, click **Close** ☒ to close the database and to exit Access. As directed by your instructor, submit your database and the paper or electronic printouts of the two objects—one report and one table—that are the results of this project. Specifically, in this project, using your own name, you created the following database and printouts or electronic printouts:

1. Lastname_Firstname_1B_Student_Workshops	Database file
2. All Events	Report (printout or electronic printout)
3. Lastname Firstname 1B Workshop Locations	Table (printout or electronic printout)

END | You have completed Project 1B

GO! with Office Web Apps

Objective	Export an Access Table to an Excel Spreadsheet, Save to Google Drive, Add a Record, and Save to Your Computer

Access web apps are designed to work with Microsoft's SharePoint, a service for setting up websites to share and manage documents. Your college may not have SharePoint installed, so you will use other tools to share objects from your database so that you can work collaboratively with others. Recall that Google Docs is Google's free, web-based word processor, spreadsheet, slide show, form, and data storage service. Google Drive is Google's free file storage and sharing service. For Access, you can export a database object to an Excel worksheet, a PDF file, or a text file, and then save the file to Google Drive.

ALERT!	Working with Web-Based Applications and Services

Computer programs and services on the web receive continuous updates and improvements. Therefore, the steps to complete this web-based activity may differ from the ones shown. You can often look at the screens and the information presented to determine how to complete the activity.

Activity | **Exporting an Access Table to an Excel Spreadsheet, Saving the Spreadsheet to Google Drive, Editing a Record in Google Drive, and Saving to Your Computer**

In this activity, you will export your 1B Workshop Locations table to an Excel spreadsheet, upload your Excel file to Google Drive as a Google Doc, add a record in Google Drive, and then download a copy of the edited spreadsheet to your computer.

1 Start Access, navigate to your **Access Chapter 1** folder, and then **Open** your **1B_Student_Workshops** database file. If necessary, on the Message Bar, click Enable Content, and then **Close** the **Event List** form. In the **Navigation Pane**, click your **1B Workshop Locations** table to select it—do not open it.

2 On the ribbon, click the **EXTERNAL DATA tab**, and then in the **Export group**, click **Excel**. In the **Export – Excel Spreadsheet** dialog box, click **Browse**, and then navigate to your **Access Chapter 1** folder. In the **File Save** dialog box, click in the **File name** box, type **Lastname_Firstname_AC_1B_Web** and then click **Save**.

3 In the **Export – Excel Spreadsheet** dialog box, under **Specify export options**, select the first two check boxes—**Export data with formatting and layout** and **Open the destination file after the export operation is complete**—and then click **OK**. Take a moment to examine the data in the file, and then **Close** Excel. In the **Export – Excel Spreadsheet** dialog box, click **Close**, and then **Close** Access.

4 From the desktop, start Internet Explorer, navigate to **http://drive.google.com**, and sign in to your Google account; if necessary, create a new Google account and then sign in. On the right side of the screen, click the **Settings arrow** ⚙, and then point to **Upload settings**. Be sure that **Convert uploaded files to Google Docs format** is selected.

If this setting is not selected, your document will upload as a pdf file and cannot be edited without further action.

5 Open your **GO! Web Projects** folder—or create and then open this folder by clicking **New folder** 📁. Under **Drive**, to the right of **Create**, click **Upload** ⬆, and then click **Files**. In the **Choose File to Upload** dialog box, navigate to your **Access Chapter 1** folder, and then double-click your **AC_1B_Web** Excel file to upload it to Google Drive. When the title bar of the message box indicates *Upload complete*, **Close** the message box. Compare your screen with Figure A.

FIGURE A

(GO! with Office Web Apps continues on the next page)

6 Click your **AC_1B_Web** file to open the file in Google Drive. If necessary, maximize the window.

The worksheet displays column letters, row numbers, and data.

7 Click in cell **A7**, type **SW-02** and then press Tab. In cell **B7**, type **Southwest Campus** and then press Tab. In cell **C7**, type **B101** and then press Tab. In cell **D7**, type **25** and then press ↓ to save the record.

The new record might display with a different font than the other records.

8 Above row **1** and to the left of column **A**, click **Select All** ⬜. On the menu bar, click **Format**, and then click **Clear formatting** so that the font is the same for all data. Click in cell **A8**, and then compare your screen with Figure B.

9 On the menu, click **File**, point to **Download as**, and then click **Microsoft Excel (.xlsx)**. In the message box—usually displays at the bottom of your screen—click the **Save arrow**, and then click **Save as**. In the **Save As** dialog box, navigate to your **Access Chapter 1** folder, click in the **File name** box, type **Lastname_Firstname_ AC_1B_Web_Download** and then click **Save**. **Close** the message box.

10 In Google Drive, at the top right corner of your screen, click your user name, and then click **Sign out**. **Close** your browser window.

11 Start Excel. In the Excel opening screen, click **Open Other Workbooks**. Under **Open**, click **Computer**. On the right, under **Computer**, click **Browse**. Navigate to your **Access Chapter 1** folder, and then double-click your **AC_1B_Web** Excel file. Notice that this file is the original file—the new record is not entered. If you are required to print your documents, use one of the methods in following Note. **Close** your Excel file; and, if prompted, save the changes to your worksheet. Then **Open** and print your **AC_1B_Web_Download** Excel file using one of the methods in the following Note. **Close** Excel; and, if prompted, save the changes to your worksheet. As directed by your instructor, submit your two workbooks and the two paper or electronic printouts that are the results of this project.

NOTE — Adding the File Name to the Footer and Printing or Creating an Electronic Printout of an Excel Spreadsheet on One Page

Click the FILE tab, click Print, and then click Page Setup. In the Page Setup dialog box, on the Page tab, under Orientation, click Landscape. Under Scaling, click the Fit to option button. In the Page Setup dialog box, click the Header/Footer tab, and then click Custom Footer. With the insertion point blinking in the Left section box, click the Insert File Name button, and then click OK. In the Page Setup dialog box, click OK.

To print on paper, click Print. To create an electronic file of your printout, on the left side of your screen, click Export. Under Export, be sure Create PDF/XPS Document is selected, and then, on the right, click Create PDF/XPS. Navigate to your Access Chapter 1 folder, and then click Publish to save the file with the default name and an extension of pdf.

FIGURE B

Andrew Rodriguez / Fotolia; FotolEdhar/ Fotolia; apops/ Fotolia; Yuri Arcurs/ Fotolia

Office 365 includes business-class security and is backed by Microsoft. For an organization, what does that mean?

When you and a few classmates work together on a class project, you are not concerned about the security of your data. You probably use free personal email services such as Hotmail, Gmail, or Yahoo Mail to exchange documents, or perhaps you post your documents to free services such as Google Docs.

Organizations, on the other hand—even small ones with only two or three employees—must be concerned with the privacy and security of their data. Organizations cannot entrust their data and confidential communications to free services that may change frequently or that have no legal responsibility for the security of the data.

Organizations must provide each employee with a company email address rather than having each employee use his or her own personal free email address for business communications. Organizations must provide a central storage location for its data rather than having employees store data on flash drives or local hard drives with no control or oversight.

An organization must have a *secure environment*, which is a system that uses controlled *servers*—computers that provide services on a network such as an email server or a file server—to ensure the security and privacy of email, to control the storage and use of information, and to protect against the loss of confidential data.

Most small organizations cannot afford to hire the people with the skills necessary to install and maintain servers. So to establish and maintain a secure environment, many small organizations contract with and rely on small IT—the acronym for *Information Technology*—hosting companies to host their email communications and to provide secure storage.

Activity | **Using the Exchange Online Outlook Meeting Tool to Collaborate**

This group project relates to the **Bell Orchid Hotels**. If your instructor assigns this project to your class, you can expect to use the **Outlook Meeting tool** in **Office 365 Exchange Online** to collaborate on the following tasks for this chapter:

- If you are in the **Accounting Group**, you and your teammates will meet virtually to create a Stockholders Database to track individuals who have purchased stock in the hotel.

- If you are in the **Engineering Group**, you and your teammates will meet virtually to create a Subcontractors Database to track companies used by the Hotel for maintenance and renovation projects.

- If you are in the **Food and Beverage Group**, you and your teammates will meet virtually to create a Banquet Clients Database to track the types of functions taking place in the Hotel's banquet rooms.

- If you are in the **Human Resources Group**, you and your teammates will meet virtually to create an Employee Database for salaried employees.

- If you are in the **Operations Group**, you and your teammates will meet virtually to create a Guests Database to track guest information, as well as room rates and availability.

- If you are in the **Sales and Marketing Group**, you and your teammates will meet virtually to create an Associations Database to track industry and trade associations that book conventions for large groups.

FIGURE A

END OF CHAPTER

SUMMARY

Principles of good database design, also known as normalization, help ensure that the data in your database is accurate and organized in a way that you can retrieve information that is useful.

Databases can be created from scratch by using the blank desktop database template or a custom web app or by using a template that contains prebuilt tables, queries, forms, reports, and other objects.

Before entering records in a table, which is the foundation of a database, you must define data types and name the fields. Common data types are Short Text, Number, Currency, and Date/Time.

Forms are used to enter data into a table or view the data in a table. Queries are used to retrieve information from tables, and reports display information from tables in a professional-looking format.

GO! LEARN IT ONLINE

Review the concepts and key terms in this chapter by completing these online challenges, which you can find at **www.pearsonhighered.com/go.**

Matching and Multiple Choice: Answer matching and multiple choice questions to test what you learned in this chapter. MyITLab®

Crossword Puzzle: Spell out the words that match the numbered clues, and put them in the puzzle squares.

Flipboard: Flip through the definitions of the key terms in this chapter and match them with the correct term.

GO! FOR JOB SUCCESS

Video: Goal Setting

Your instructor may assign this video to your class, and then ask you to think about, or discuss with your classmates, these questions:

FotolEdhar / Fotolia

Is there anything you would change about Theo's behavior at his performance evaluation? Why or why not?

SMART goals are goals that are specific, measurable, achievable, realistic, and time-frame specific. Is Theo's first goal of beating his sales numbers by 10 percent next year a SMART goal?

How important do you think it is to set career development goals for yourself? Why?

END OF CHAPTER

REVIEW AND ASSESSMENT GUIDE FOR ACCESS CHAPTER 1

Your instructor may assign one or more of these projects to help you review the chapter and assess your mastery and understanding of the chapter.

	Review and Assessment Guide for Access Chapter 1		
Project	**Apply Skills from These Chapter Objectives**	**Project Type**	**Project Location**
1C	Objectives 1-5 from Project 1A	**1C Skills Review** A guided review of the skills from Project 1A.	On the following pages
1D	Objectives 6-9 from Project 1B	**1D Skills Review** A guided review of the skills from Project 1B.	On the following pages
1E	Objectives 1-5 from Project 1A	**1E Mastery (Grader Project)** A demonstration of your mastery of the skills in Project 1A with extensive decision making.	In MyITLab and on the following pages
1F	Objectives 6-9 from Project 1B	**1F Mastery (Grader Project)** A demonstration of your mastery of the skills in Project 1B with extensive decision making.	In MyITLab and on the following pages
1G	Objectives 1-9 from Projects 1A and 1B	**1G Mastery (Grader Project)** A demonstration of your mastery of the skills in Projects 1A and 1B with extensive decision making.	In MyITLab and on the following pages
1H	Combination of Objectives from Projects 1A and 1B	**1H GO! Fix It** A demonstration of your mastery of the skills in Projects 1A and 1B by creating a correct result from a document that contains errors you must find.	Online
1I	Combination of Objectives from Projects 1A and 1B	**1I GO! Make It** A demonstration of your mastery of the skills in Projects 1A and 1B by creating a result from a supplied picture.	Online
1J	Combination of Objectives from Projects 1A and 1B	**1J GO! Solve It** A demonstration of your mastery of the skills in Projects 1A and 1B, your decision-making skills, and your critical thinking skills. A task-specific rubric helps you self-assess your result.	Online
1K	Combination of Objectives from Projects 1A and 1B	**1K GO! Solve It** A demonstration of your mastery of the skills in Projects 1A and 1B, your decision-making skills, and your critical thinking skills. A task-specific rubric helps you self-assess your result.	On the following pages
1L	Combination of Objectives from Projects 1A and 1B	**1L GO! Think** A demonstration of your understanding of the chapter concepts applied in a manner that you would outside of college. An analytic rubric helps you and your instructor grade the quality of your work by comparing it to the work an expert in the discipline would create.	On the following pages
1M	Combination of Objectives from Projects 1A and 1B	**1M GO! Think** A demonstration of your understanding of the chapter concepts applied in a manner that you would outside of college. An analytic rubric helps you and your instructor grade the quality of your work by comparing it to the work an expert in the discipline would create.	Online
1N	Combination of Objectives from Projects 1A and 1B	**1N You and GO!** A demonstration of your understanding of the chapter concepts applied in a manner that you would in a personal situation. An analytic rubric helps you and your instructor grade the quality of your work.	Online
1O	Combination of Objectives from Projects 1A and 1B	**1O Cumulative Group Project for Access Chapter 1** A demonstration of your understanding of concepts and your ability to work collaboratively in a group role-playing assessment, requiring both collaboration and self-management.	Online

GLOSSARY

GLOSSARY OF CHAPTER KEY TERMS

Append To add on to the end of an object; for example, to add records to the end of an existing table.

AutoNumber data type A data type that describes a unique sequential or random number assigned by Access as each record is entered and that is useful for data that has no distinct field that can be considered unique.

Best Fit An Access command that adjusts the width of a column to accommodate the column's longest entry.

Blank desktop database A database that has no data and has no database tools—you must create the data and tools as you need them; the database is stored on your computer or other storage device.

Caption A property setting that displays a name for a field in a table, query, form, or report other than that listed as the field name.

Common field A field in two or more tables that stores the same data.

Currency data type An Access data type that describes monetary values and numeric data that can be used in mathematical calculations involving values with one to four decimal places.

Custom web app A database that you can publish and share with others over the Internet.

Data Facts about people, events, things, or ideas.

Data source The table or tables from which a query, form, or report retrieves its data.

Data type The characteristic that defines the kind of data that can be stored in a field, such as numbers, text, or dates.

Database An organized collection of facts about people, events, things, or ideas related to a specific topic or purpose.

Database management system (DBMS) Database software that controls how related collections of data are stored, organized, retrieved, and secured; also known as a DBMS.

Database template A preformatted database that contains prebuilt tables, queries, forms, and reports that perform a specific task, such as tracking events.

Datasheet view The Access view that displays data organized in columns and rows similar to an Excel worksheet.

DBMS An acronym for database management system.

Design view An Access view that displays the detailed structure of a table, query, form, or report. For forms and reports, may be the view in which some tasks must be performed, and only the controls, and not the data, display in this view.

Destination table The table to which you import or append data.

Export The process of copying data from one file into another file, such as an Access table into an Excel spreadsheet.

Field A single piece of information that is stored in every record; represented by a column in a database table.

Field properties Characteristics of a field that control how the field displays and how data can be entered in the field.

First principle of good database design A principle of good database design stating that data is organized in tables so that there is no redundant data.

Flat database A simple database file that is not related or linked to any other collection of data.

Form An Access object you can use to enter new records into a table, edit or delete existing records in a table, or display existing records.

Form view The Access view in which you can view records, but you cannot change the layout or design of the form.

Import The process of copying data from another file, such as a Word table or an Excel workbook, into a separate file, such as an Access database.

Information Data that is organized in a useful manner.

Layout view The Access view in which you can make changes to a form or report while the object is open—the data from the underlying data source displays.

Link A connection to data in another file.

Multiple-items form A form that enables you to display or enter multiple records in a table.

Navigation area An area at the bottom of the Access window that indicates the number of records in the table and contains controls in the form of arrows

that you click to navigate among the records.

Navigation Pane An area of the Access window that displays and organizes the names of the objects in a database; from here, you open objects for use.

Normalization The process of applying design rules and principles to ensure that your database performs as expected.

Number data type An Access data type that describes numbers that might be used in calculations.

Object tab In the object window, a tab that identifies the object and which enables you to make the open object active.

Object window An area of the Access window that displays open objects, such as tables, queries, forms, or reports; by default, each object displays on its own tab.

Objects The basic parts of a database that you create to store your data and to work with your data; for example, tables, queries, forms, and reports.

Populate The action of filling a database table with records.

Primary key The field in a table that uniquely identifies a record; for example, a Student ID number at a college.

Property Sheet A list of characteristics—properties—for fields or controls on a form or report in which you can make precise changes to each property associated with the field or control.

Query A database object that retrieves specific data from one or more database objects—either tables or other queries—and then, in a single datasheet, displays only the data you specify.

Record All of the categories of data pertaining to one person, place, event, thing, or idea; represented by a row in a database table.

Record selector bar The bar at the left edge of a record when it is displayed in a form, and which is used to select an entire record.

Record selector box The small box at the left of a record in Datasheet view that, when clicked, selects the entire record.

Redundant In a database, information that is duplicated in a manner that indicates poor database design.

Relational database A sophisticated type of database that has multiple collections of data within the file that are related to one another.

Report A database object that summarizes the fields and records from a table or query in an easy-to-read format suitable for printing.

Run The process in which Access searches the records in the table(s) included in the query design, finds the records that match the specified criteria, and then displays the records in a datasheet; only the fields that have been included in the query design display.

Second principle of good database design A principle stating that appropriate database techniques are used to ensure the accuracy and consistency of data as it is entered into the table.

Secure environment A system that uses controlled servers to ensure the security and privacy of email, to control the storage and use of information and to protect against the loss of confidential data.

Select query A type of Access query that retrieves (selects) data from one or more tables or queries, displaying the selected data in a datasheet; also known as a simple select query.

Server A computer that provides services on a network such as an email server or a file server.

SharePoint A Microsoft application used for setting up websites to share and manage documents.

Short Text data type An Access data type that describes text, a combination of text and numbers, or numbers that are not used in calculations, such as a Postal Code.

Simple select query Another name for a select query.

Single-record form A form that enables you to display or enter one record at a time in a table.

Source file When importing a file, refers to the file being imported.

Structure In Access, the underlying design of a table, including field names, data types, descriptions, and field properties.

Table A format for information that organizes and presents text and data in columns and rows; the foundation of a database.

Tables and Related Views An arrangement in the Navigation Pane that groups objects by the table to which they are related.

Truncated Refers to data that is cut off or shortened because the field or column is not wide enough to display all of the data or the field size is too small to contain all of the data.

Wizard A feature in Microsoft Office that walks you step by step through a process.

CHAPTER REVIEW

Apply 1A skills from these Objectives:

1 Identify Good Database Design

2 Create a Table and Define Fields in a Blank Desktop Database

3 Change the Structure of Tables and Add a Second Table

4 Create a Query, Form, and Report

5 Close a Database and Exit Access

In the following Skills Review, you will create a database to store information about the administrators of Texas Lakes Community College and their departments. Your completed database objects will look similar to Figure 1.51.

PROJECT FILES

For Project 1C, you will need the following files:

Blank desktop database

a01C_Administrators (Excel workbook)

a01C_Departments (Excel workbook)

You will save your database as:

Lastname_Firstname_1C_College_Administrators

Build from Scratch

PROJECT RESULTS

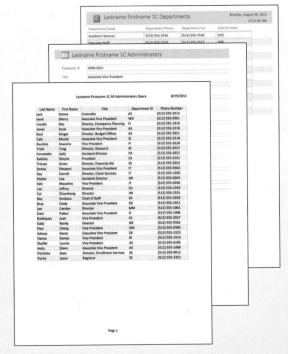

FIGURE 1.51

(Project 1C College Administrators continues on the next page)

Skills Review   Project 1C College Administrators (continued)

1 Start Access. In the Access opening screen, click **Blank desktop database**. In the **Blank desktop database** dialog box, to the right of the **File Name** box, click **Browse**. In the **File New Database** dialog box, navigate to your **Access Chapter 1** folder. In the **File New Database** dialog box, click in the **File name** box, type **Lastname_Firstname_1C_College_Administrators** and then press Enter. In the **Blank desktop database** dialog box, click **Create**.

a. **Close** the **Navigation Pane**. In the field names row, click in the text *Click to Add*, and then click **Short Text**. Type **Title** and then press Enter.

b. In the third field name box, click **Short Text**, type **Last Name** and then press Enter. In the fourth field name box, click **Short Text**, type **First Name** and then press Enter. Create the remaining fields shown in **Table 1**, pressing Enter after the last field name. All of the data is typed on one line.

c. If necessary, scroll to bring the first column into view, and then click the **ID** field name. Under **TABLE TOOLS**, on the **FIELDS tab**, in the **Properties group**, click **Name & Caption**. In the **Name** box, change *ID* to **Employee ID** and then click **OK**. On the ribbon, in the **Formatting group**, click the **Data Type arrow**, and then click **Short Text**.

d. In the new record row, click in the **Employee ID** field, type, **ADM-9200** and press Enter. In the **Title** field, type **Vice President** and press Enter. Continue entering data in the fields shown in **Table 2**, pressing Enter or Tab to move to the next field and to the next row.

e. On the **Quick Access Toolbar**, click **Save**. In the **Save As** dialog box, in the **Table Name** box, using your own name, replace the selected text by typing **Lastname Firstname 1C Administrators** and then click **OK**.

f. In the new record row, enter the data for two college administrators shown in **Table 3**, pressing Enter or Tab to move from field to field and to the next row.

TABLE 1

Data Type		Short Text	Short Text	Short Text	Short Text	Short Text	Short Text	Short Text	Short Text	Short Text	Short Text	Currency
Field Name	ID	Title	Last Name	First Name	Middle Initial	Address	City	State	Postal Code	Phone Number	Department ID	Salary

(Return to Step 1c)

TABLE 2

Last Name	First Name	Middle Initial	Address	City	State	Postal Code	Phone Number	Department ID	Salary
Shaffer	Lonnie	J	489 Ben Ave	Austin	TX	78734	(512) 555-6185	AS	123500

(Return to Step 1e)

TABLE 3

Employee ID	Title	Last Name	First Name	Middle Initial	Address	City	State	Postal Code	Phone Number	Department ID	Salary
ADM-9201	Associate Vice President	Holtz	Diann	S	8416 Spencer Ln	Georgetown	TX	78627	(512) 555-1069	AS	101524
ADM-9202	Director, Enrollment Services	Fitchette	Sean	H	3245 Deer Trl	Spicewood	TX	78669	(512) 555-9012	SS	45070

(Return to Step 1g)

(Project 1C College Administrators continues on the next page)

CHAPTER REVIEW

g. **Close** your **1C Administrators** table. On the ribbon, click the **EXTERNAL DATA tab**, in the **Import & Link group**, click **Excel**. In the **Get External Data – Excel Spreadsheet** dialog box, click **Browse**. In the **File Open** dialog box, navigate to your student data files, and then double-click the **a01C_Administrators** Excel file.

h. Click the **Append a copy of the records to the table** option button, and then click **OK**. In the **Import Spreadsheet Wizard**, click **Next**, and then click **Finish**. In the **Get External Data – Excel Spreadsheet** dialog box, click **Close**.

i. **Open** the **Navigation Pane**. Point to the right edge of the **Navigation Pane** to display the ⟷ pointer, and then drag to the right so that the entire table name displays. In the **Navigation Pane**, double-click your **1C Administrators** table to open it, and then **Close** the **Navigation Pane**—there are 30 records in this table.

2 ▶ Click the **HOME tab**, and then in the **Views group**, click the top of the **View** button to switch to **Design** view. In the **Field Name** column, to the left of **Middle Initial**, click the row selector box to select the entire row. Under **TABLE TOOLS, o**n the **DESIGN tab**, in the **Tools group**, click **Delete Rows**. In the message box, click **Yes**.

a. Click in the **Employee ID** field name box. Under **Field Properties**, click **Field Size** to select the existing text. Type **8** and then in the **Employee ID** field row, click in the **Description** box. Type **Eight-character Employee ID** and then press Enter.

b. Click in the **State** field name box. In the **Field Properties** area, click **Field Size**, and then type **2** In the **State Description** box, type **Two-character state abbreviation** and then press Enter.

c. **Save** the design changes to your table, and in the message box, click **Yes**. On the **DESIGN tab**, in the **Views group**, click the top of the **View** button to switch to **Datasheet** view.

d. On the ribbon, click the **EXTERNAL DATA tab**, and then in the **Import & Link group**, click **Excel**. In the **Get External Data – Excel Spreadsheet** dialog box, to the right of the **File name** box, click **Browse**. In the

File Open dialog box, navigate to your student data files, and then double-click **a01C_Departments**. Be sure that the **Import the source data into a new table in the current database** option button is selected, and then click **OK**.

e. In the upper left corner of the wizard, select the **First Row Contains Column Headings** check box, and then click **Next**. Click **Next** again. Click the **Choose my own primary key** option button, be sure that **Department ID** displays, and then click **Next**. In the **Import to Table** box, type **Lastname Firstname 1C Departments** and then click **Finish**. In the **Get External Data – Excel Spreadsheet** dialog box, click **Close**.

f. **Open** the **Navigation Pane**, double-click your **1C Departments** table, and then **Close** the **Navigation Pane**. There are 12 records in your **1C Departments** table.

g. To the left of the **Department** field name, click **Select All**. On the ribbon, click the **HOME tab**. In the **Records group**, click **More**, and then click **Field Width**. In the **Column Width** dialog box, click **Best Fit**. **Save** the table, and then click in any field to cancel the selection. In the object window, click the **object tab** for your **1C Administrators** table. Using the techniques you just practiced, apply **Best Fit** to the columns, **Save** the table, and then cancel the selection.

h. With your **1C Administrators** table displayed, on the ribbon, click the **FILE tab**, click **Print**, and then click **Print Preview**. On the **PRINT PREVIEW tab**, in the **Page Layout group**, click **Landscape**. Create a paper or electronic printout as directed by your instructor—two pages result. On the ribbon, click **Close Print Preview**, and then **Close** your **1C Administrators** table.

i. With your **1C Departments** table displayed, view the table in **Print Preview**. Change the orientation to **Landscape**, and then create a paper or electronic printout as directed by your instructor—one page results. Click **Close Print Preview**, and then **Close** your **1C Departments** table.

(Project 1C College Administrators continues on the next page)

CHAPTER REVIEW

3 On the ribbon, click the **CREATE tab**, and then in the **Queries group**, click **Query Wizard**. In the **New Query** dialog box, be sure **Simple Query Wizard** is selected, and then click **OK**. In the wizard, click the **Tables/Queries arrow**, and then, if necessary, click **Table: Lastname Firstname 1C Administrators**.

a. Under **Available Fields**, click **Last Name**, and then click **Add Field** to move the field to the **Selected Fields** list on the right. Double-click the **First Name** field to move it to the **Selected Fields** list. By using **Add Field** or by double-clicking the field name, add the following fields to the **Selected Fields** list in the order specified: **Title**, **Department ID**, and **Phone Number**. This query will answer the question, *What is the last name, first name, title, Department ID, and phone number of every administrator?*

b. In the wizard, click **Next**. Click in the **What title do you want for your query?** box. Using your own name, edit as necessary so that the query name is **Lastname Firstname 1C All Administrators Query** and then click **Finish**. If necessary, apply **Best Fit** to the columns, and then **Save** the query. Display the query in **Print Preview**, and then create a paper or electronic printout as directed—one page results. Click **Close Print Preview**, and then **Close** the query.

c. **Open** the Navigation Pane, right-click your **1C Administrators** table, and then click **Open** to display the table in the object window. **Close** the **Navigation Pane**. Notice that the table has 11 fields. On the ribbon, click the **CREATE tab**, and in the **Forms group**, click **Form**. On the **Quick Access Toolbar**, click **Save**. In the **Save As** dialog box, click in the **Form Name** box, edit to name the form **Lastname Firstname 1C Administrator Form** and then click **OK**.

d. In the navigation area, click **Last record**, and then click **Previous record** two times to display the record for *Diann Holtz*. Using the instructions in Activity 1.15, print or create an electronic printout of only this record on one page. **Close** the form object, saving it if prompted. Your **1C Administrators** table object remains open.

e. **Open** the Navigation Pane, open your **1C Departments** table by double-clicking the table name or by right-clicking the table name and clicking **Open**. **Close** the **Navigation Pane**. On the **CREATE tab**, in the **Reports group**, click **Report**.

f. Click the **Department ID** field name, and then on the ribbon, click the **ARRANGE tab**. In the **Rows & Columns group**, click **Select Column**, and then press **Del**. Using the same technique, delete the **Department Email** field.

g. Click the **Department Phone** field name. Hold down **Shift**, and then click the **Suite Number** field name to select the last three field names. On the ribbon, click the **DESIGN tab**, and then in the **Tools group**, click **Property Sheet**. In the **Property Sheet**, on the **Format tab**, click **Width**, type **1.5** and then press **Enter**. **Close** the **Property Sheet**.

h. Click the **Department Name** field name. On the ribbon, click the **HOME tab**. In the **Sort & Filter group**, click **Ascending** to sort the report in alphabetic order by *Department Name*. At the bottom of the report, on the right side, click **Page 1 of 1**, and then press **Del**.

i. **Save** the report as **Lastname Firstname 1C Departments Report** and then click **OK**. Display the report in **Print Preview**, and then create a paper or electronic printout of the report as directed. Click **Close Print Preview**. In the object window, right-click any **object tab**, and then click **Close All** to close all open objects, leaving the object window empty.

(Project 1C College Administrators continues on the next page)

CHAPTER REVIEW

4 ▸ **Open** the **Navigation Pane**. If necessary, increase the width of the **Navigation Pane** so that all object names display fully. On the right side of the title bar, click **Close** to close the database and to exit Access. As directed by your instructor, submit your database and the paper or electronic printouts of the five objects—two tables, one query, one form, and one report—that are the results of this project. Specifically, in this project, using your own name, you created the following database and printouts or electronic printouts:

1. Lastname_Firstname_1C_College_Administrators	Database file
2. Lastname Firstname 1C Administrators	Table (printout or electronic printout – two pages)
3. Lastname Firstname 1C Departments	Table (printout or electronic printout)
4. Lastname Firstname 1C All Administrators Query	Query (printout or electronic printout)
5. Lastname Firstname 1C Administrator Form	Form (printout or electronic printout – Record 28)
6. Lastname Firstname 1C Departments Report	Report (printout or electronic printout)

END | You have completed Project 1C

CHAPTER REVIEW

Apply 1B skills from these Objectives:

6 Use a Template to Create a Database

7 Organize Objects in the Navigation Pane

8 Create a New Table in a Database Created with a Template

9 Print a Report and a Table

Skills Review Project 1D Certification Events

In the following Skills Review, you will create a database to store information about certification test preparation events at Texas Lakes Community College. Your completed report and table will look similar to Figure 1.52.

PROJECT FILES

For Project 1D, you will need the following files:

Desktop Event Management template
a01D_Certification_Events (Excel workbook)

You will save your database as:

Lastname_Firstname_1D_Certification_Events

Build from Scratch

PROJECT RESULTS

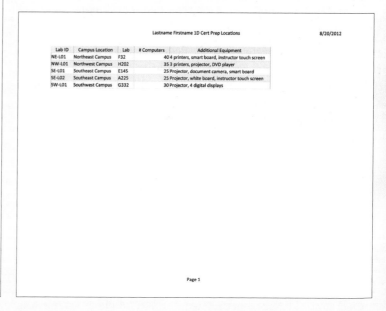

FIGURE 1.52

(Project 1D Certification Events continues on the next page)

CHAPTER REVIEW

1 Start Access. In the Access opening screen, click in the **Search** box, type **event** and then press Enter to search for a template to manage events. Click the **Desktop Event Management** template. In the **Desktop Event Management** dialog box, to the right of the **File Name** box, click **Browse**, and then navigate to your **Access Chapter 1** folder. In the **File New Database** dialog box, click in the **File name** box to select the existing text. Using your own name, type **Lastname_Firstname_1D_ Certification_Events** and then press Enter. In the **Desktop Event Management** dialog box, click **Create** to download the template and to save the database. Under the ribbon, on the **Message Bar**, click **Enable Content**.

a. In the first row, click in the **Title** field, type **Word 2013** and then press Tab. In the **Start Time** field, type **7/9/18 9a** and then press Tab. In the **End Time** field, type **7/9/18 3p** and then press Tab. In the **Description** field, type **Office 2013** and then press Tab. In the **Location** field, type **Southwest Campus** and then press Tab three times to move to the **Title** field in the new record row.

b. In the form, directly above the field names row, click **New Event** to open the **Event Details** single-record form. Using Tab to move from field to field, enter the record shown in **Table 1**. Press Tab three times to move from the **End Time** field to the **Description** field.

c. In the **Events Detail** form, click **Close**. Using either the **Event List** multiple-items form or the **Event Details** single-record form, enter the records shown in **Table 2**. If you use the **Events Detail** form, be sure to close it after entering records to display the records in the **Event List** form.

d. **Close** the **Event List** form. On the ribbon, click the **EXTERNAL DATA tab**, and in the **Import & Link group**, click **Excel**. In the **Get External Data – Excel Spreadsheet** dialog box, click **Browse**. Navigate to your student data files, and then double-click **a01D_Certification_Events**. Click the second option button—**Append a copy of the records to the table**—and then click **OK**.

e. In the **Import Spreadsheet Wizard**, click **Next**, and then click **Finish**. In the **Get External Data – Excel Spreadsheet** dialog box, click **Close**. **Open** the **Navigation Pane**, and then double-click **Event List** to open the form that displays data stored in the **Events** table—12 total records display. **Close** the **Navigation Pane**.

f. To the left of the **ID** field name, click **Select All**. In the field names row, point to the right edge of any of the selected columns to display the ⊞ pointer, and then double-click to apply **Best Fit** to all of the columns. **Save** the form, and then click in any field to cancel the selection.

2 **Open** the **Navigation Pane**. At the top of the **Navigation Pane**, click the arrow. On the list, under **Navigate To Category**, click **Tables and Related Views**.

a. In the **Navigation Pane**, point to **Events: Table**, right-click, and then click **Open** to display the records in the underlying table. In the **Navigation Pane**, double-click the **Current Events** *report* (green icon) to view this predesigned report. From the **Navigation Pane**, open the **Events by Week** report to view this predesigned report.

TABLE 1

Title	Location	Start Time	End Time	Description
Excel 2013	**Northeast Campus**	**7/16/18 10a**	**7/16/18 4p**	**Office 2013**

- - - → (Return to Step 1c)

TABLE 2

ID	Title	Start Time	End Time	Description	Location
3	**Access 2013**	**7/23/18 12p**	**7/23/18 6p**	**Office 2013**	**Southeast Campus**
4	**PowerPoint 2013**	**7/30/18 9a**	**7/30/18 3p**	**Office 2013**	**Northwest Campus**

- - - → (Return to Step 1d)

(Project 1D Certification Events continues on the next page)

CHAPTER REVIEW

b. In the object window, right-click any of the **object tabs**, and then click **Close All**. **Close** the **Navigation Pane**.

3 On the ribbon, click the **CREATE tab**, and in the **Tables group**, click **Table**.

a. In the field names row, click **Click to Add**, click **Short Text**, type **Campus Location** and then press Enter. In the third column, click **Short Text**, type **Lab** and then press Enter. In the fourth column, click **Number**, type **# Computers** and then press Enter. In the fifth column, click **Short Text**, type **Additional Equipment** and then press ↓.

b. Right-click the **ID** field name, and then click **Rename Field**. Type **Lab ID** and then press Enter. On the **FIELDS tab**, in the **Formatting group**, click the **Data Type arrow**, and then click **Short Text**.

c. In the new record row, click in the **Lab ID** field, and then enter the records shown in **Table 3**, pressing Enter or Tab to move from one field to the next.

d. In the **Views group**, click the top of the **View** button to switch to **Design** view. In the **Save As** dialog box, in the **Table Name** box, using your own name, type **Lastname Firstname 1D Cert Prep Locations** and then click **OK**. Notice that the **Lab ID** field is the **Primary Key**. On the **DESIGN tab**, in the **Views group**, click the top of the **View** button to switch to **Datasheet** view.

e. To the left of the **Lab ID** field name, click **Select All** to select all of the columns and rows in the table. On the **HOME tab**, in the **Records group**, click **More**, and then click **Field Width**. In the **Column Width** dialog box, click **Best Fit**. **Save** the changes to the table, and then click in any field to cancel the selection. **Close** the table, and then **Open** the Navigation Pane. Increase the width of the **Navigation Pane** so that your entire table name displays.

4 In the **Navigation Pane**, double-click the **All Events** report to open it in the object window. **Close** the **Navigation Pane**. On the **HOME tab**, in the **Views group**, click the top of the **View** button to switch to **Layout** view. At the top of the report, click the title—*All Events*—to display a colored border around the title. Click to the left of the letter *A* to place the insertion point there. Using your own name, type **Lastname Firstname 1D** and then press Spacebar. Press Enter, and then **Save** the report.

a. On the right side of the status bar, click **Print Preview**, and notice that the report will print on one page. Create a paper or electronic printout as instructed. Click **Close Print Preview**, and then **Close** the report.

b. **Open** the Navigation Pane, double-click your **1D Cert Prep Locations** table, and then **Close** the Navigation Pane. On the ribbon, click the **FILE tab**, click **Print**, and then click **Print Preview**. On the **PRINT PREVIEW tab**, in the **Page Layout group**, click **Landscape**. Create a paper or electronic printout as directed, and then click **Close Print Preview**. Close your **1D Cert Prep Locations** table.

TABLE 3

Lab ID	Campus Location	Lab	# Computers	Additional Equipment
NW-L01	Northwest Campus	H202	35	3 printers, projector, DVD player
SE-L01	Southeast Campus	E145	25	Projector, document camera, smart board
NE-L01	Northeast Campus	F32	40	4 printers, smart board, instructor touch screen
SW-L01	Southwest Campus	G332	30	Projector, 4 digital displays
SE-L02	Southeast Campus	A225	25	Projector, white board, instructor touch screen

(Return to Step 3d)

(Project 1D Certification Events continues on the next page)

CHAPTER REVIEW

c. **Open** the **Navigation Pane**. On the right side of the title bar, click **Close** to close the database and to exit Access. As directed by your instructor, submit your database and the paper or electronic printouts of the two objects—one report and one table—that are the results of this project. Specifically, in this project, using your own name, you created the following database and printouts or electronic printouts:

1. Lastname_Firstname_1D_Certification_Events	Database file
2. Lastname Firstname 1D Cert Prep Locations	Table (printout or electronic printout)
3. All Events	Report (printout or electronic printout)

END | You have completed Project 1D

CONTENT-BASED ASSESSMENTS

Mastering Access Project 1E Kiosk Inventory

In the following Mastering Access project, you will create a database to track information about the inventory of items for sale in the kiosk located in the snack bar at the Southeast Campus of Texas Lakes Community College. Your completed database objects will look similar to Figure 1.53.

Apply 1A skills from these Objectives:

1 Identify Good Database Design

2 Create a Table and Define Fields in a Blank Desktop Database

3 Change the Structure of Tables and Add a Second Table

4 Create a Query, Form, and Report

5 Close a Database and Exit Access

PROJECT FILES

For Project 1E, you will need the following files:

Blank desktop database

a01E_Inventory (Excel workbook)

a01E_Inventory_Storage (Excel workbook)

You will save your database as:

Lastname_Firstname_1E_Kiosk_Inventory

PROJECT RESULTS

Build from Scratch

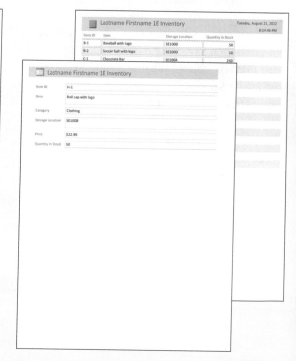

FIGURE 1.53

(Project 1E Kiosk Inventory continues on the next page)

1 Start Access. Create a **Blank desktop database** in your **Access Chapter 1** folder. Name the database **Lastname_Firstname_1E_Kiosk_Inventory** and then **Close** the **Navigation Pane**. Create the fields shown in **Table 1**.

2 For the **ID** field, change the **Data Type** to **Short Text**, rename the field to **Item ID** and then enter the records shown in **Table 2**.

3 **Save** the table as **Lastname Firstname 1E Inventory** and then **Close** the table. From your student data files, import and then **Append** the data in the Excel file **a01E_Inventory** to your **1E Inventory** table. After importing, open your **1E Inventory** table—17 records display.

4 In **Design** view, delete the **Campus** field, which is redundant data. For the **Category** field, change the **Field Size** to **25** and enter a **Description** of **Enter the category of the item** For the **Item ID** field, change the **Field Size** to **10** and then **Save** the changes to your table. Switch to **Datasheet** view, apply **Best Fit** to all of the fields in the table, and then **Save** your changes. Display the table in **Print Preview**, change the orientation to **Landscape**, and then create a paper or electronic printout as directed by your instructor. **Close Print Preview**, and then **Close** the table.

5 From your student data files, import the **Excel** file **a01E_Inventory_Storage** into the database as a new table; designate the first row as column headings and the **Category** field as the primary key. In the wizard, name the table **Lastname Firstname 1E Inventory Storage** and then open your **1E Inventory Storage** table—five records display. In **Design** view, for the **Location Detail** field, change the **Field Size** to **30** and enter a **Description** of **Room and bin number or alternate location of inventory item Save** the design changes, switch to **Datasheet** view, apply **Best Fit** to all of the fields, and then **Save** your changes. Display the table in **Print Preview**, create a paper or electronic printout as directed, **Close Print Preview**, and then **Close** the table.

6 Use the **Query Wizard** to create a simple query based on your **1E Inventory** table. Include only the three fields that will answer the question, *For all item names, what is the storage location and quantity in stock?* In the wizard, accept the default name for the query. Display the query in **Print Preview**, create a paper or electronic printout as directed, **Close Print Preview**, and then **Close** the query.

TABLE 1

Data Type		Short Text	Short Text	Short Text	Short Text	Currency	Number
Field Name	ID	Item	Category	Campus	Storage Location	Price	Quantity in Stock

(Return to Step 2)

TABLE 2

Item ID	Item	Category	Campus	Storage Location	Price	Quantity in Stock
C-1	Chocolate Bar	Candy	Southeast	SE100A	.89	250
C-2	Lollipop	Candy	Southeast	SE100A	.5	500
T-1	T-shirt, S	Clothing	Southeast	SE100B	17.5	100

(Return to Step 3)

(Project 1E Kiosk Inventory continues on the next page)

CONTENT-BASED ASSESSMENTS

7 Open your **1E Inventory** table, and then create a **Form** for this table. **Save** the form as **Lastname Firstname 1E Inventory Form** and then display and select the fifth record. By using the instructions in Activity 1.15, create a paper or electronic printout of only this record on one page, as directed by your instructor. **Close** the form object, saving changes if prompted.

8 With your **1E Inventory** table open, create a **Report**. Delete the **Category** and **Price** fields, and then sort the **Item ID** field in **Ascending** order. Using the **Property Sheet**, for the **Item ID** field, change the **Width** to **0.75** and then for the **Storage Location** field, change the **Width** to **1.5** Scroll to display the bottom of the report, and then

delete the page number—**Page 1 of 1**. **Save** the report as **Lastname Firstname 1E Inventory Report** and then display the report in **Print Preview**. Create a paper or electronic printout as directed. Click **Close Print Preview**.

9 **Close All** open objects. **Open** the **Navigation Pane** and be sure that all object names display fully. **Close** the database, and then **Close** Access. As directed by your instructor, submit your database and the paper or electronic printouts of the five objects—two tables, one query, one form, and one report—that are the results of this project. Specifically, in this project, using your own name, you created the following database and printouts or electronic printouts:

1. Lastname_Firstname_1E_Kiosk_Inventory	Database file
2. Lastname Firstname 1E Inventory	Table (printout or electronic printout)
3. Lastname Firstname 1E Inventory Storage	Table (printout or electronic printout)
4. Lastname Firstname 1E Inventory Query	Query (printout or electronic printout)
5. Lastname Firstname 1E Inventory Form	Form (printout or electronic printout – Record 5)
6. Lastname Firstname 1E Inventory Report	Report (printout or electronic printout)

END | You have completed Project 1E

CONTENT-BASED ASSESSMENTS

Mastering Access   Project 1F Recruiting Events

MyITLab®
grader

Apply 1B skills from these Objectives:

6 Use a Template to Create a Database

7 Organize Objects in the Navigation Pane

8 Create a New Table in a Database Created with a Template

9 Print a Report and a Table

Build from Scratch

In the following Mastering Access project, you will create a database to store information about the recruiting events that are scheduled to attract new students to Texas Lakes Community College. Your completed report and tables will look similar to Figure 1.54.

PROJECT FILES

For Project 1F, you will need the following files:

Desktop Event Management template
a01F_Recruiting_Events (Excel workbook)

You will save your database as:

Lastname_Firstname_1F_Recruiting_Events

PROJECT RESULTS

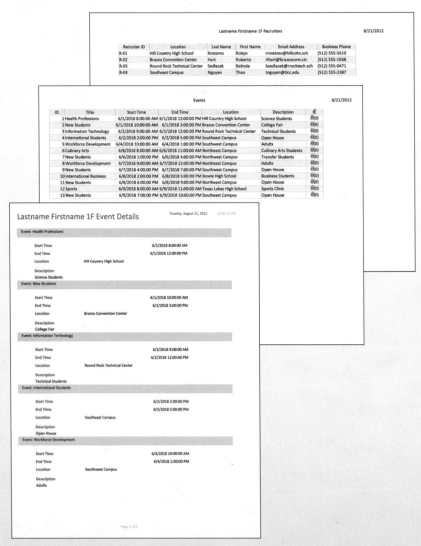

FIGURE 1.54

(Project 1F Recruiting Events continues on the next page)

CONTENT-BASED ASSESSMENTS

1 Start Access. In the Access opening screen, search for **event** and then click the **Desktop Event Management** template. Save the database in your **Access Chapter 1** folder as **Lastname_Firstname_1F_Recruiting_Events** and on the **Message Bar**, click **Enable Content**.

2 In the **Event List** multiple-items form or the **Event Details** single-record form—open by clicking **New Event** on the **Event List** form—enter the records shown in **Table 1**.

3 **Close** the **Event List** form. From your student data files, import and append the data from the **Excel** file **a01F_Recruiting_Events** to the **Events** table. **Open** the **Navigation Pane**, organize the objects by **Tables and Related Views**, and then open the **Events** table to display 13 records. **Close** the table, and then **Close** the **Navigation Pane**.

4 Create a new **Table** defining the new fields shown in **Table 2**.

5 For the **ID** field, change the **Data Type** to **Short Text**, rename the field to **Recruiter ID** and then enter the records shown in **Table 3**.

TABLE 1

ID	Title	Start Time	End Time	Description	Location
1	Health Professions	6/1/18 8a	6/1/18 12p	Science Students	Hill Country High School
2	New Students	6/1/18 10a	6/1/18 3p	College Fair	Brazos Convention Center
3	Information Technology	6/2/18 9a	6/2/18 12p	Technical Students	Round Rock Technical Center
4	International Students	6/2/18 2p	6/2/18 5p	Open House	Southeast Campus

Return to Step 3

TABLE 2

Data Type		Short Text	Short Text	Short Text	Short Text	Short Text
Field Name	ID	Location	Last Name	First Name	Email Address	Business Phone

Return to Step 5

TABLE 3

Recruiter ID	Location	Last Name	First Name	Email Address	Business Phone
R-01	Hill Country High School	Rostamo	Robyn	rrostamo@hillcohs.sch	(512) 555-3410
R-02	Brazos Convention Center	Hart	Roberto	rlhart@brazosconv.ctr	(512) 555-1938
R-03	Round Rock Technical Center	Sedlacek	Belinda	bsedlacek@rrocktech.sch	(512) 555-0471
R-04	Southeast Campus	Nguyen	Thao	tnguyen@tlcc.edu	(512) 555-2387

Return to Step 6

(Project 1F Recruiting Events continues on the next page)

CONTENT-BASED ASSESSMENTS

6 Apply **Best Fit** to all of the columns. **Save** the table as **Lastname Firstname 1F Recruiters** and then **Close** the table.

7 From the **Navigation Pane**, open the **Event Details** *report* (green icon). Switch to **Layout** view. In the report, click in the title—*Event Details*—and then click to position the insertion point to the left of the word *Event*. Using your own name, type **Lastname Firstname 1F** and then press Spacebar and Enter. If necessary, decrease the font size of the title so that the title does not overlap the date on the right side or does not extend to two lines.

    Save the report, and then display it in **Print Preview**. If directed to create a paper printout, in the **Print group**, click **Print**. In the **Print** dialog box, under **Print Range**, to the right of **Pages**, click in the **From** box, type **1** and then click in the **To** box and type **1** and then click **OK** to print only the first page. If directed to create an electronic printout, in the **Publish as PDF or XPS** dialog box, click **Options**, and then under **Range**, click the **Pages** option button, and then click **OK**. **Close Print Preview**, and then **Close** the report.

8 From the **Navigation Pane**, open the **Events** table, select all of the columns, and then apply **Best Fit** to all of the columns by double-clicking the right edge of any one of the selected columns. **Save** the table, and then cancel the selection. Display the table in **Print Preview**, change the orientation to **Landscape**, change the **Margins** to **Normal**, and then create a paper or electronic printout as directed. **Close Print Preview**, and then **Close** the table.

9 From the **Navigation Pane**, open your **1F Recruiters** table. Display the table in **Print Preview**, change the orientation to **Landscape**, and then create a paper or electronic printout as directed. **Close Print Preview**, and then **Close** the table.

10 Open the **Navigation Pane**, and be sure that all object names display fully. **Close** Access. As directed by your instructor, submit your database and the paper or electronic printouts of the three objects—one report and two tables—that are the results of this project. Specifically, in this project, using your own name, you created the following database and printouts or electronic printouts:

1. Lastname_Firstname_1F_Recruiting_Events	Database file
2. Event Details	Report (printout or electronic printout – Page 1)
3. Events	Table (printout or electronic printout)
4. Lastname Firstname 1F Recruiters	Table (printout or electronic printout)

END | You have completed Project 1F

CONTENT-BASED ASSESSMENTS

Mastering Access | Project 1G College Construction

In the following Mastering Access project, you will create one database to store information about construction projects for Texas Lakes Community College and a second database to store information about the public events related to the construction projects. Your completed database objects will look similar to Figure 1.55.

Apply 1A and 1B skills from these Objectives:

1 Identify Good Database Design
2 Create a Table and Define Fields in a Blank Desktop Database
3 Change the Structure of Tables and Add a Second Table
4 Create a Query, Form, and Report
5 Close a Database and Exit Access
6 Use a Template to Create a Database
7 Organize Objects in the Navigation Pane
8 Create a New Table in a Database Created with a Template
9 Print a Report and a Table

PROJECT FILES

For Project 1G, you will need the following files:

Blank desktop database
a01G_Projects (Excel workbook)
a01G_Contractors (Excel workbook)
Desktop Event Management template

You will save your databases as:

Lastname_Firstname_1G_College_Construction
Lastname_Firstname_1G_Public_Events

PROJECT RESULTS

Build from Scratch

FIGURE 1.55

(Project 1G College Construction continues on the next page)

CONTENT-BASED ASSESSMENTS

1 Start Access. Create a **Blank desktop database** in your **Access Chapter 1** folder. Name the database **Lastname_ Firstname_1G_College_Construction** and then **Close** the Navigation Pane. Create the fields shown in **Table 1**.

2 For the **ID** field, change the **Data Type** to **Short Text**, rename the field to **Project ID** and then enter the three records shown in **Table 2**.

3 Save the table as **Lastname Firstname 1G Projects** and then **Close** the table. From your student data files, import and then append the data in the **Excel** file **a01G_ Projects** to your **1G Projects** table. After importing, open your **1G Projects** table—eight records display.

4 In **Design** view, for the **Project ID** field, change the **Field Size** to **5** and then enter a **Description** of **Enter the Project ID using the format P-###** Save the changes to your table. Switch to **Datasheet** view, apply **Best Fit** to all of the fields in the table, and then **Save** your changes. Display the table in **Print Preview**, change the orientation to **Landscape**, and then create a paper or electronic printout as directed by your instructor. **Close Print Preview**, and then **Close** the table.

5 From your student data files, import the **Excel** file **a01G_Contractors** into the database as a new table; designate the first row as column headings and the **ID** field as the primary key. In the wizard, name the table **Lastname Firstname 1G Contractors** and then open your **1G Contractors** table—four records display. Apply **Best Fit** to all of the fields, and then **Save** your changes. Display the table in **Print Preview**, change the orientation to **Landscape**, and then create a paper or electronic printout as directed. **Close Print Preview**, and then **Close** the table.

6 Use the **Query Wizard** to create a simple query based on your **1G Projects** table. Include only the three fields that will answer the question, *For every site, what is the building project and the budget amount?* In the wizard, accept the default name for the query. Display the query in **Print Preview**, create a paper or electronic printout as directed, **Close Print Preview**, and then **Close** the query.

7 Open your **1G Projects** table, and then create a **Form** for this table. **Save** the form as **Lastname Firstname 1G Project Form** and then display and select the seventh record. By using the instructions in Activity 1.15, create a paper or electronic printout of only this record on one page as directed by your instructor. **Close** the form object, saving changes if prompted.

8 With your **1G Projects** table open, create a **Report**. Delete the **Budget Amount** field, and then sort the **Building Project** field in **Ascending** order. For the **Building Project**, **Site**, and **Contractor** fields, using the **Property Sheet**, change the **Width** of all three fields to **2** At the bottom of the report, delete the page number—**Page 1 of 1**. Save the report as **Lastname Firstname 1G Projects Report** and then display the report in **Print Preview**. Create a paper or electronic printout as directed. **Close Print Preview**.

9 **Close All** open objects. **Open** the **Navigation Pane**, arrange the objects by **Tables and Related Views**, and be sure that all object names display fully. **Close** the database, but do *not* close Access.

TABLE 1

Data Type		Short Text	Short Text	Short Text	Currency
Field Name	ID	Building Project	Site	Contractor	Budget Amount

Return to Step 2

TABLE 2

Project ID	Building Project	Site	Contractor	Budget Amount
P-356	Student Center, 3-story	Northeast Campus	RR Construction	61450000
P-823	Student Center, 2-story	Southeast Campus	RR Construction	41960000
P-157	Health Professions Center	Northwest Campus	Marshall Ellis Construction	42630000

Return to Step 3

(Project 1G College Construction continues on the next page)

CONTENT-BASED ASSESSMENTS

Mastering Access **Project 1G College Construction** (continued)

10 In the Access opening screen, search for **event** and then click the **Desktop Event Management** template. Save the database in your **Access Chapter 1** folder as **Lastname_Firstname_1G_Public_Events** and on the **Message Bar**, click **Enable Content**.

11 In the **Event List** multiple-items form or the **Event Details** single-record form—open by clicking **New Event** on the **Event List** form—enter the three records shown in **Table 3**.

12 **Close** the **Event List** form. **Open** the **Navigation Pane**, organize the objects by **Tables and Related Views**, and then open the **Current Events** *report* (green icon). Switch to **Layout** view. In the report, click in the title—*Current Events*—and then click to position the insertion point to the left of the letter *C*. Using your own name, type **Lastname Firstname 1G** and then press

Spacebar and Enter. If necessary, decrease the font size of the title so that the title does not overlap the date on the right side or does not extend to two lines. **Save** the report, display it in **Print Preview**, and then create a paper or electronic printout as directed. **Close Print Preview**, and then **Close** the report.

13 Open the **Navigation Pane**, and be sure that all object names display fully. **Close** Access. As directed by your instructor, submit your database and the paper or electronic printouts of the six objects—two tables, one query, one form, and two reports—that are the results of this project. Specifically, in this project, using your own name, you created the following database and printouts or electronic printouts:

1. Lastname_Firstname_1G_College_Construction	Database file
2. Lastname_Firstname_1G_Public_Events	Database file
3. Lastname Firstname 1G Projects	Table (printout or electronic printout)
4. Lastname Firstname 1G Contractors	Table (printout or electronic printout)
5. Lastname Firstname 1G Projects Query	Query (printout or electronic printout)
6. Lastname Firstname 1G Project Form	Form (printout or electronic printout - Record 7)
7. Lastname Firstname 1G Projects Report	Report (printout or electronic printout)
8. Current Events	Report (printout or electronic printout)

TABLE 3

ID	Title	Start Time	End Time	Description	Location
1	Groundbreaking	6/13/18 10a	6/13/18 11a	Student Center groundbreaking	Northeast Campus
2	Dedication	8/26/18 12:30 p	8/26/18 2p	Gymnasium building dedication	Southwest Campus
3	Community Arts Expo	10/5/18 6p	10/5/18 9p	Book and Art Expo at Library	Southeast Campus

(Return to Step 12)

END | You have completed Project 1G

221

CONTENT-BASED ASSESSMENTS

Build from Scratch

GO! Fix It	Project 1H Scholarships	Online

GO! Make It	Project 1I Theater Events	Online

Build from Scratch

GO! Solve It	Project 1J Athletic Scholarships	Online

GO! Solve It	Project 1K Student Activities	

Build from Scratch

PROJECT FILES

For Project 1K, you will need the following files:

Desktop Event Management template
a01K_Student_Activities (Word document)

You will save your database as:

Lastname_Firstname_1K_Student_Activities

Use the Desktop Event Management template to create a database, and save it in your Access Chapter 1 folder as **Lastname_Firstname_1K_Student_Activities** From your student data files, use the information in the Word document a01K_Student_Activities to enter data into the Event List multiple-items form. Each event begins at 6 p.m. and ends at 10 p.m.

After entering the records, close the form, and arrange the Navigation Pane by Tables and Related Views. Open the Event Details *report*, and then add **Lastname Firstname 1K** to the beginning of the report title. If necessary, decrease the font size of the title so that it does not overlap the date and so that it displays on one line. Create a paper or electronic printout as directed—two pages result. As directed, submit your database and the paper or electronic printout of the report that are the results of this project. Specifically, in this project, using your own name, you created the following database and printout or electronic printout:

1. Lastname_Firstname_1K_Student_Activities	Database file
2. Lastname Firstname 1K Event Details	Report (printout or electronic printout)

Performance Level

		Exemplary	Proficient	Developing
Performance Criteria	**Create database using Desktop Event Management template and enter data**	Database created using the correct template, named correctly, and all data entered correctly.	Database created using the correct template, named correctly, but not all data entered correctly.	Database created using the correct template, but numerous errors in database name and data.
	Modify report	Event Details report title includes name and project on one line.	Event Details report title includes name and project, but not on one line.	Event Details report title does not include name and project.
	Create report printout	Event Details report printout is correct.	Event Details printout is incorrect.	Event Details report printout not created.

END | You have completed Project 1K

OUTCOMES-BASED ASSESSMENTS

RUBRIC

The following outcomes-based assessments are *open-ended assessments*. That is, there is no specific correct result; your result will depend on your approach to the information provided. Make *Professional Quality* your goal. Use the following scoring rubric to guide you in *how* to approach the problem and then to evaluate *how well* your approach solves the problem.

The *criteria*—Software Mastery, Content, Format & Layout, and Process—represent the knowledge and skills you have gained that you can apply to solving the problem. The *levels of performance*—Professional Quality, Approaching Professional Quality, or Needs Quality Improvements—help you and your instructor evaluate your result.

	Your completed project is of Professional Quality if you:	Your completed project is Approaching Professional Quality if you:	Your completed project Needs Quality Improvements if you:
1-Software Mastery	Choose and apply the most appropriate skills, tools, and features and identify efficient methods to solve the problem.	Choose and apply some appropriate skills, tools, and features, but not in the most efficient manner.	Choose inappropriate skills, tools, or features, or are inefficient in solving the problem.
2-Content	Construct a solution that is clear and well organized, contains content that is accurate, appropriate to the audience and purpose, and is complete. Provide a solution that contains no errors in spelling, grammar, or style.	Construct a solution in which some components are unclear, poorly organized, inconsistent, or incomplete. Misjudge the needs of the audience. Have some errors in spelling, grammar, or style, but the errors do not detract from comprehension.	Construct a solution that is unclear, incomplete, or poorly organized; contains some inaccurate or inappropriate content; and contains many errors in spelling, grammar, or style. Do not solve the problem.
3-Format & Layout	Format and arrange all elements to communicate information and ideas, clarify function, illustrate relationships, and indicate relative importance.	Apply appropriate format and layout features to some elements, but not others. Overuse features, causing minor distraction.	Apply format and layout that does not communicate information or ideas clearly. Do not use format and layout features to clarify function, illustrate relationships, or indicate relative importance. Use available features excessively, causing distraction.
4-Process	Use an organized approach that integrates planning, development, self-assessment, revision, and reflection.	Demonstrate an organized approach in some areas, but not others; or, use an insufficient process of organization throughout.	Do not use an organized approach to solve the problem.

Build from
Scratch

OUTCOMES-BASED ASSESSMENTS

GO! Think   Project 1L Student Clubs

PROJECT FILES

For Project 1L, you will need the following files:

Blank desktop database
a01L_Clubs (Word document)
a01L_Student_Clubs (Excel workbook)
a01L_Club_Presidents (Excel workbook)

You will save your database as

Lastname_Firstname_1L_Student_Clubs

Dr. Daniel Martinez, vice president of Student Services, needs a database that tracks information about student clubs. The database should contain two tables—one for club information and one for contact information for the club presidents.

Create a desktop database, and save the database in your Access Chapter 1 folder as **Lastname_Firstname_1L_Student_Clubs** From your student data files, use the information in the Word document a01L_Clubs to create the first table and to enter two records. Name the table appropriately to include your name and 1L, and then append the 23 records from the Excel workbook a01L_Student_Clubs to your table. For the Club ID and President ID fields, add a description and change the field size.

Create a second table in the database by importing 25 records from the Excel workbook a01L_Club_Presidents, and name the table appropriately to include your name and 1L. For the State and Postal Code fields, add a description and change the field size. Be sure that the field data types are correct—recall that numbers that are not used in calculations should have a data type of Short Text. Be sure all of the data and field names display in each table.

Create a simple query based on the Clubs table that answers the question, *What is the club name, meeting day, meeting time, campus, and Room ID for all of the clubs?* Create a form based on the Clubs table, saving it with an appropriate name that includes your name and 1L. Create a report based on the Presidents table, saving it with an appropriate name that includes your name and 1L, that displays the president's last name (in ascending order), the president's first name, and the phone number of every president. Change the width of the three fields so that there is less space between them, but being sure that each record prints on a single line. Delete the page number from the report.

Create paper or electronic printouts of the two tables, the query, only Record 21 of the form, and the report as directed and being sure that each object prints on one page. Organize the objects on the Navigation Pane by Tables and Related Views, and be sure that all object names display fully. As directed, submit your database and the paper or electronic printouts of the five objects—two tables, one query, one form, and one report—that are the results of this project.

END | You have completed Project 1L

Build from
Scratch

GO! Think   Project 1M Faculty Training   **Online**

Build from
Scratch

You and GO!   Project 1N Personal Contacts   **Online**

Build from
Scratch

GO! Cumulative Group Project   Project 1O Bell Orchid Hotels
                                                             Online

Sort and Query a Database

PROJECT 2A

OUTCOMES
Sort and query a database.

PROJECT 2B

OUTCOMES
Create complex queries.

OBJECTIVES

1. Open and Save an Existing Database
2. Create Table Relationships
3. Sort Records in a Table
4. Create a Query in Design View
5. Create a New Query from an Existing Query
6. Sort Query Results
7. Specify Criteria in a Query

OBJECTIVES

8. Specify Numeric Criteria in a Query
9. Use Compound Criteria in a Query
10. Create a Query Based on More Than One Table
11. Use Wildcards in a Query
12. Create Calculated Fields in a Query
13. Calculate Statistics and Group Data in a Query
14. Create a Crosstab Query
15. Create a Parameter Query

Robert Kneschke/Fotolia

In This Chapter

In this chapter, you will sort Access database tables and create and modify queries. To convert data into meaningful information, you must manipulate your data in a way that you can answer questions. One question might be: *Which students have a grade point average of 3.0 or higher?* By having this list of students, you could send information about scholarships or internships to those who meet the grade point average criteria. Queries are one of the most powerful tools in an Access database—a query not only answers questions, but it also provides data for meaningful reports.

The projects in this chapter relate to **Texas Lakes Community College**, which is located in the Austin, Texas, area. Its four campuses serve more than 30,000 students and offer more than 140 certificate programs and degrees. The college has a highly acclaimed Distance Education program and an extensive Workforce Development program. The college makes positive contributions to the community through cultural and athletic programs and has significant partnerships with businesses and nonprofit organizations. Popular fields of study include nursing and health care, solar technology, computer technology, and graphic design.

Instructors and Courses Database

PROJECT ACTIVITIES

In Activities 2.01 through 2.17, you will assist Dr. Carolyn Judkins, dean of the Business Division at the Northeast Campus of Texas Lakes Community College, in locating information about instructors and courses in the division. Your completed database objects will look similar to Figure 2.1.

PROJECT FILES

For Project 2A, you will need the following file:

a02A_Instructors_Courses

You will save your database as:

Lastname_Firstname_2A_Instructors_Courses

PROJECT RESULTS

FIGURE 2.1 Project 2A Instructors and Courses

NOTE **If You Are Using a Touchscreen**

- Tap an item to click it.
- Press and hold for a few seconds to right-click; release when the information or command displays.
- Touch the screen with two or more fingers and then pinch together to zoom in or stretch your fingers apart to zoom out.
- Slide your finger on the screen to scroll—slide left to scroll right and slide right to scroll left.
- Slide to rearrange—similar to dragging with a mouse.
- Swipe from edge: from right to display charms; from left to expose open apps, snap apps, or close apps; from top or bottom to show commands or close an app.
- Swipe to select—slide an item a short distance with a quick movement—to select an item and bring up commands, if any.

Objective 1 Open and Save an Existing Database

Video A2-1

There will be instances when you need to work with a database and still keep the original, unaltered version of the database. Like the other Microsoft Office 2013 applications, you can open a database file and save it with another name.

Activity 2.01 | Opening and Saving an Existing Database

1 **Start** Access. In the Access opening screen, click **Open Other Files**. Under **Open**, click **Computer**, and then on the right, click **Browse**. In the **Open** dialog box, navigate to the location where your student data files for this chapter are stored, and then double-click **a02A_Instructors_Courses** to open the database.

2 On the ribbon, click the **FILE tab**, and then click **Save As**. Under **File Types**, be sure **Save Database As** is selected. On the right, under **Database File Types**, be sure **Access Database** is selected, and then at the bottom of the screen, click **Save As**.

The Access Database file type saves your database in a format that enables the database to be opened with Access 2007, Access 2010, or Access 2013. If you are sharing your database with individuals who have an earlier version of Access, you can save the database in a version that is compatible with that application, although some functionality might be lost if an earlier version of Access does not have the same feature as the later version of Access.

3 In the **Save As** dialog box, navigate to the location where you are saving your databases. Create a **New folder** named **Access Chapter 2**, and then **Open** the folder. Click in the **File name** box, drag to select the existing text, and using your own name, type **Lastname_ Firstname_2A_Instructors_Courses** and then click **Save** or press Enter.

Use this technique when you need to keep a copy of the original database file.

4 On the **Message Bar**, notice the **SECURITY WARNING**. In the **Navigation Pane**, notice that this database contains two table objects. Compare your screen with Figure 2.2.

FIGURE 2.2

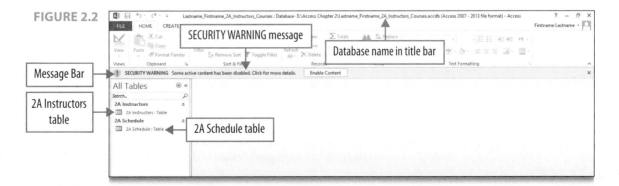

Activity 2.02 | Resolving Security Alerts and Renaming Tables

The *Message Bar* is the area directly below the ribbon that displays information such as security alerts when there is potentially unsafe, active content in an Office document that you open. Settings that determine the alerts that display on your Message Bar are set in the Access *Trust Center*, an area in Access where you can view the security and privacy settings for your Access installation.

You may not be able to change the settings in the Trust Center, depending upon decisions made by your organization. To display the Trust Center, click the FILE tab, click Options, and then click Trust Center.

1 On the **Message Bar**, click **Enable Content**.

> When working with the student data files that accompany this textbook, repeat this action each time you see the security warning. Databases for this textbook are safe to use on your computer.

2 In the **Navigation Pane**, right-click the **2A Instructors** table, and then click **Rename**. With the table name selected and using your own name, type **Lastname Firstname 2A Instructors** and then press Enter to rename the table. Use the same technique to **Rename** the **2A Schedule** table to **Lastname Firstname 2A Schedule**

> Including your name in the table enables you and your instructor to easily identify your work, because Access includes the table name in the header of your paper or electronic printouts.

3 Point to the right edge of the **Navigation Pane** to display the ↔ pointer. Drag to the right to increase the width of the pane until both table names display fully.

Objective 2 Create Table Relationships

Video A2-2

Access databases are relational databases because the tables in the database can relate—actually connect—to other tables through common fields. Recall that common fields are fields in two or more tables that store the same data; for example, a Student ID number may be stored in two tables in the same database.

After you have a table for each subject in your database, you must provide a way to connect the data in the tables when you need to obtain meaningful information from the stored data. To do this, create common fields in the related tables, and then define table *relationships*. A relationship is an association that you establish between two tables based on common fields. After the relationship is established, you can create a query, form, or report that displays information from more than one table.

Activity 2.03 | Selecting the Tables and Common Field to Establish the Table Relationship

In this activity, you will select the two tables in the database that you will use to establish the table relationship and identify the common field that will connect the tables.

1 In the **Navigation Pane**, double-click your **2A Instructors** table to open it in the object window. Examine the fields in the table. Double-click your **2A Schedule** table, and examine the fields in the table.

> In the 2A Instructors table, *Instructor ID* is the primary key field, which ensures that each instructor has only one record in the table. No two instructors have the same Instructor ID.

> In the 2A Schedule table, *Schedule ID* is the primary key field. Every scheduled course section during an academic term has a unique Schedule ID. Some colleges refer to this as the *Section Number*.

2 In the **2A Schedule** table, scroll to display the **Instructor ID** field—third from last column—and then compare your screen with Figure 2.3.

> Both the 2A Instructors table and the 2A Schedule table include the *Instructor ID* field, which is the common field of the two tables. Because *one* instructor can teach *many* different courses, *one* Instructor ID can be present *many* times in the 2A Schedule table. When the relationship is established, it will be a **one-to-many relationship**, which is the most common type of relationship in a relational database.

FIGURE 2.3

3 In the object window, right-click the **2A Schedule object tab**, and then click **Close All** to close both tables. On the ribbon, click the **DATABASE TOOLS tab**, and then in the **Relationships group**, click **Relationships**. Compare your screen with Figure 2.4.

> You can close all of the open objects by right-clicking any object tab. The Show Table dialog box displays in the Relationships window. In the Show Table dialog box, the Tables tab displays the two tables that are in this database.

FIGURE 2.4

4 Point to the title bar of the **Show Table** dialog box, and then drag downward and to the right to move the dialog box away from the top of the **Relationships** window.

> Moving the Show Table dialog box enables you to see the tables as they are added to the Relationships window.

5 In the **Show Table** dialog box, if necessary, click your **2A Instructors** table, and then click **Add**. In the **Show Table** dialog box, double-click your **2A Schedule** table to add it to the **Relationships** window. In the **Show Table** dialog box, click **Close**, and then compare your screen with Figure 2.5.

> You can use either technique to add a table to the Relationships window. A *field list*—a list of the field names in a table—for each of the two table objects displays, and each table's primary key is identified by the key icon. Although this database has only two tables, larger databases have many tables. Scroll bars in a field list indicate that there are fields that are not currently in view.

FIGURE 2.5

ALERT!   **Are There More Than Two Field Lists in the Relationships Window?**

In the Show Table dialog box, if you double-click a table name more than one time, a duplicate field list displays in the Relationships window. To remove a field list from the Relationships window, right-click the title bar of the field list, and then click Hide Table. Alternatively, click anywhere in the field list, and then on the DESIGN tab, in the Relationships group, click Hide Table.

6 ▶ In the **2A Schedule** field list—the field list on the right—point to the title bar to display the ▯ pointer. Drag the field list to the right until there are about two inches of space between the field lists.

7 ▶ In the **2A Instructors** field list—the field list on the left—point to the lower right corner of the field list to display the ▯ pointer, and then drag downward and to the right to increase the height and width of the field list until the entire name of the table in the title bar displays and all of the field names display.

This action enables you to see all of the available fields and removes the vertical scroll bar.

8 ▶ Use the same technique to resize the **2A Schedule** field list so that the table name and all of the field names display as shown in Figure 2.6.

Recall that *one* instructor can teach *many* scheduled courses. The arrangement of field lists in the Relationships window displays the *one table* on the left side and the *many table* on the right side. Recall also that the primary key in each table is the field that contains the data that uniquely identifies each record in the table. In the 2A Instructors table, each instructor is uniquely identified by the Instructor ID. In the 2A Schedule table, each scheduled course section is uniquely identified by the Schedule ID.

FIGURE 2.6

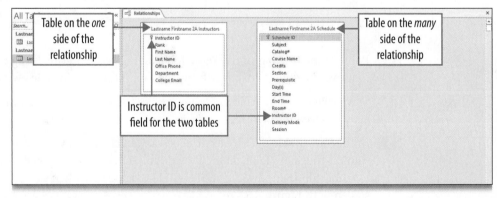

NOTE   **The Field That Is Highlighted Does Not Matter**

After you rearrange the field lists in the Relationships window, the highlighted field name indicates the active field list, which is the list that you moved or resized last. This is of no consequence for this activity.

9 In the **2A Instructors** field list, point to **Instructor ID**, and then drag the field name downward and to the right into the **2A Schedule** field list until the ▨ pointer's arrow is on top of **Instructor ID**. Release the mouse button to display the **Edit Relationships** dialog box.

As you drag, a small graphic displays to indicate that you are dragging a field name from one field list to another. A table relationship works by matching data in two fields—the common field. In these two tables, the common field has the same name—*Instructor ID*. Common fields are not required to have the same name; however, they must have the same data type and field size.

⟳ ANOTHER WAY   On the DESIGN tab, in the Tools group, click Edit Relationships. In the Edit Relationships dialog box, click Create New. In the Create New dialog box, designate the tables and fields that will create the relationship and click OK.

10 Point to the title bar of the **Edit Relationships** dialog box, and then drag the dialog box downward and to the right below the two field lists as shown in Figure 2.7.

By dragging the common field, you create the *one-to-many* relationship. In the 2A Instructors table, Instructor ID is the primary key. In the 2A Schedule table, Instructor ID is the *foreign key* field. The foreign key is the field in the related table used to connect to the primary key in another table. The field on the *one* side of the relationship is typically the primary key.

FIGURE 2.7

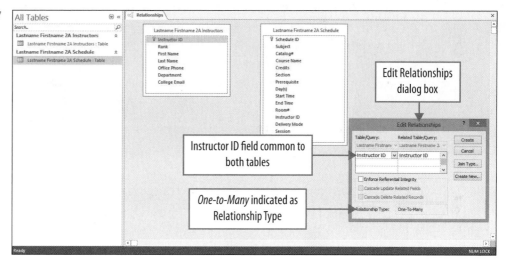

Activity 2.04 | Setting Relationship Options

In this activity, you will set relationship options that enable you to work with records in the two related tables.

1 In the **Edit Relationships** dialog box, click to select the **Enforce Referential Integrity** check box. Notice that the two options under **Enforce Referential Integrity** are now available.

Referential integrity is a set of rules that Access uses to ensure that the data between related tables is valid. Enforcing referential integrity ensures that an Instructor ID cannot be added to a course in the 2A Schedule table if the Instructor ID is *not* included in the 2A Instructors table. Similarly, enforcing referential integrity without selecting a cascade option below ensures that you cannot delete an instructor from the 2A Instructors table if there is a course that has been assigned to that instructor in the 2A Schedule table.

After selecting Enforce Referential Integrity, *cascade options*—relationship options that enable you to update records in related tables when referential integrity is enforced—become available for use.

2 In the **Edit Relationships** dialog box, click to select the **Cascade Update Related Fields** check box.

> The *Cascade Update Related Fields* option enables you to change the data in the primary key field for the table on the *one* side of the relationship, and updates that change to any fields in the related table that store the same data. For example, in the 2A Instructors table, if you change the data in the Instructor ID field for one instructor, Access automatically finds every scheduled course assigned to that instructor in the 2A Schedule table and changes the data in the common field, in this case, the Instructor ID field. Without this option, if you try to change the Instructor ID number for an instructor, an error message displays if there is a related record in the related table on the *many* side of the relationship.

3 In the **Edit Relationships** dialog box, click to select the **Cascade Delete Related Records** check box, and then compare your screen with Figure 2.8.

> The *Cascade Delete Related Records* option enables you to delete a record in the table on the *one* side of the relationship and also delete all of the related records in related tables. For example, if an instructor retires or leaves the college and the courses that the instructor teaches must be canceled because no other instructor can be found, you can delete the instructor's record from the 2A Instructors table, and then all of the courses that are assigned to that instructor in the 2A Schedule table are also deleted. Without this option, an error message displays if you try to delete the instructor's record from the 2A Instructors table.

FIGURE 2.8

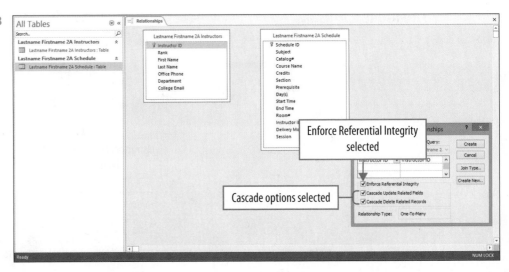

4 In the **Edit Relationships** dialog box, click **Create**, and then compare your screen with Figure 2.9.

> The Edit Relationships dialog box closes and a *join line*—the line connecting or joining the two tables—displays between the two field lists. The join line connects the primary key field—Instructor ID—in the 2A Instructors field list to the common field—Instructor ID—in the 2A Schedule field list. On the join line, *1* indicates the *one* side of the relationship, and the infinity symbol (∞) indicates the *many* side of the relationship. These symbols display when referential integrity is enforced.

FIGURE 2.9

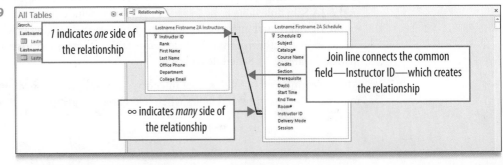

Activity 2.05 | Printing and Saving a Relationship Report

The Relationships window provides a map of how your database tables are related, and you can print and save this information as a report.

1 Under **RELATIONSHIP TOOLS**, on the **DESIGN tab**, in the **Tools group**, click **Relationship Report**.

The report is created and displays in the object window in Print Preview.

2 On the **PRINT PREVIEW tab**, in the **Page Size group**, click **Margins**, and then click **Normal** to increase the margins slightly—some printers cannot print with narrow margins. Compare your screen with Figure 2.10. Create a paper or electronic printout of the relationship report as directed.

FIGURE 2.10

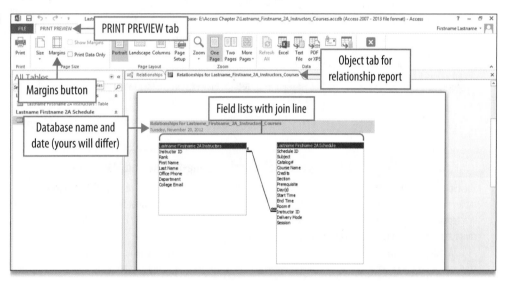

3 On the **Quick Access Toolbar**, click **Save** 🔲. In the **Save As** dialog box, click **OK** to accept the default report name.

The report name displays in the Navigation Pane under *Unrelated Objects*. Because the report is just a map of the relationship between the tables, and not a report containing records from a table, it is not associated with or related to any tables.

4 In the object window, click **Close** ☒ to close the report, and then **Close** ☒ the **Relationships** window.

> **NOTE** | **Close Print Preview and the Relationship Report**
>
> If you click Close Print Preview when the report is displayed in Print Preview, the Relationship Report displays in Design view in the object window. If this happens, you can Close the object while it is displayed in this view.

Activity 2.06 | Displaying Subdatasheet Records

When you open the table on the *one* side of the relationship, the related records from the table on the *many* side are available for you to view and to modify.

1 In the **Navigation Pane**, double-click your **2A Instructors** table to open it in the object window, and then **Close** ☒ the **Navigation Pane**.

2 On the left side of the first record—*Instructor ID* of *1224567*—click ⊞, and then compare your screen with Figure 2.11.

The ⊞ symbol to the left of a record in a table indicates that *related* records may exist in another table. Click ⊞ to display the related records in a **subdatasheet**. In the first record for *Craig Fresch*, you can see that related records exist in the 2A Schedule table—he is scheduled to teach five LGL (Legal) courses. The ⊞ symbol to the left of each record displays because you created a relationship between the two tables using the Instructor ID field—the common field.

When you click ⊞ to display the subdatasheet, the symbol changes to ⊟, an indication that the subdatasheet is expanded. Click ⊟ to collapse the subdatasheet.

FIGURE 2.11

Course sections from your 2A Schedule table for *Associate Professor Craig Fresch*

⊟ indicates subdatasheet is expanded, displaying related records from another table

⊞ indicates that related records may exist in another table

More Knowledge | **Other Types of Relationships: One-to-One and Many-to-Many**

The type of relationship is determined by the placement of the primary key field. A one-to-one relationship exists between two tables when a record in one table is related to only one record in a second table. In this case, both tables use the same field as the primary key. This is most often used when data is placed in a separate table because access to that information is restricted; for example, using an Employee ID field as the primary key field, there is one table for contact information and a second table with payroll information.

A many-to-many relationship between tables exists when many records in one table are related to many records in another table. For example, many students can enroll in many courses. To create a many-to-many relationship, you must create a third table that contains the primary key fields from both tables. In the Relationships window, you create a join line from this table to the other two tables. In effect, you create multiple one-to-many relationships.

Activity 2.07 | Testing Cascade Options

Recall that cascade options enable you to make changes to records on the *one* side table of the relationship and update or delete records in the table on the *many* side of the relationship. In this activity, you will change the data in the Instructor ID field—the primary key field—for one instructor, and then delete all of the records associated with another instructor from both tables.

1 In the subdatasheet for the first record—*Instructor ID* of *1224567*—notice that the first course that this instructor is scheduled to teach has a *Schedule ID* of *51113—LGL 216*. In the **2A Instructors** table, to the left of the first record, click ⊟ to collapse the subdatasheet.

2 If necessary, in the first record, in the **Instructor ID** field, select the data—**1224567**. Type **8224567** and then press ↓ to save the record.

Because you enabled Cascade Update Related Fields in the Edit Relationships dialog box, you can change the data in the Instructor ID field—the primary key field—and all records in the 2A Schedule table that store that Instructor ID number are automatically updated. If this option is not enabled, an error message displays.

3 Open » the **Navigation Pane**. In the **Navigation Pane**, double-click your **2A Schedule** table to open it, and then **Close** « the **Navigation Pane**.

 ANOTHER WAY | Press F11 to open or close the Navigation Pane.

---

4 Scroll to locate the record with a **Schedule ID** of **51113**—*LGL 216*. If necessary, scroll to the right to display the **Instructor ID** field, and notice that for this record, the **Instructor ID** is **8224567**. Compare your screen with Figure 2.12.

> The Cascade Update Related Fields option enables you to change the data in the primary key field in your 2A Instructors table, and the five related records for *Craig Fresch* in the 2A Schedule table were updated to store his new Instructor ID of *8224567*.

FIGURE 2.12

Course assigned to *Craig Fresch*

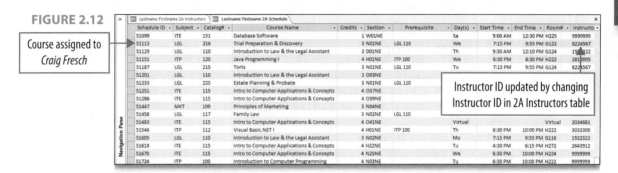

Instructor ID updated by changing Instructor ID in 2A Instructors table

5 Close your **2A Schedule** table. In your **2A Instructors** table, scroll to display the last few records. On the left side of the record for **Instructor ID** of **6145288**—*Professor Ivey Clarke*—click to display the subdatasheet. Notice that this instructor is scheduled to teach two courses—*Schedule IDs* of *42837* and *42930*.

6 Click to collapse the subdatasheet. For the same record—*Instructor ID* of *6145288*—point to the record selector box to display the pointer, and then click to select the record. On the **HOME tab**, in the **Records group**, click **Delete**.

> A message displays warning you that this record and related records in related tables will be deleted. The record you selected does not display in the table, and the next record is selected. Because you enabled Cascade Delete Related Records, you are able to delete the record for Professor Ivey Clarke and delete the two courses she is scheduled to teach from the 2A Schedule table—with no error message.

🔄 **ANOTHER WAY** With the record selected, press Del ; or with the record selected, right-click within the record, and then click Delete Record.

7 In the message box, click **Yes**.

> The record for *Instructor ID* of *6145288* is deleted, and the two courses she was scheduled to teach are deleted from the 2A Schedule table. On the Quick Access Toolbar, Undo is unavailable—if you mistakenly delete a record and its related records, you must enter them again in both tables.

8 Open the **Navigation Pane**, open your **2A Schedule** table, and then **Close** the **Navigation Pane**. Scroll through the records and notice that the records for a **Schedule ID** of **42837** and **42930** have been deleted from the table.

> The Cascade Delete Related Records option in the Edit Relationships dialog box enables you to delete a record in the table on the *one* side of the relationship—2A Instructors—and simultaneously delete the records in the table on the *many* side of the relationship—2A Schedule—that are related to the deleted record.

9 In the object window, right-click either **object tab**, and then click **Close All** to close both tables.

Video A2-3

Sorting is the process of arranging data in a specific order based on the value in a field. For example, you can sort the names in your contact list alphabetically by each person's last name, or you can sort your music collection by the artist. Initially, records in an Access table display in the order they are entered into the table. After you close the table and reopen it, the records display in order by the primary key field.

Activity 2.08 | Sorting Records in a Table in Ascending or Descending Order

In this activity, you will determine the departments of the faculty in the Business Division by sorting the data. Data can be sorted in either ***ascending order*** or ***descending order***. Ascending order sorts text alphabetically (A to Z) and sorts numbers from the lowest number to the highest number. Descending order sorts text in reverse alphabetical order (Z to A) and sorts numbers from the highest number to the lowest number.

1 **Open** » the **Navigation Pane**, open your **2A Instructors** table, and then **Close** « the **Navigation Pane**. Notice that the records in the table are sorted in ascending order by the **Instructor ID** field, which is the primary key field.

2 In the field names row, click the **Department arrow**, click **Sort A to Z**, and then compare your screen with Figure 2.13.

> To sort records in a table, click the arrow to the right of the field name in the column on which you want to sort, and then click the sort order. After a field is sorted, a small arrow in the field name box indicates the sort order. For the Department field, the small arrow points upward, indicating an ascending sort; on the ribbon, Ascending is selected.

> The records display in alphabetical order by the Department field. Because the department names are now grouped together, you can quickly scroll through the table to see the instructors for each department. The first record in the table has no data in the Department field because the *Instructor ID* of 9999999 is reserved for *Staff*, a designation that is used until a scheduled course has been assigned to a specific instructor.

 ANOTHER WAY Click in the field in any record, and then on the HOME tab, in the Sort & Filter group, click Ascending; or right-click in the field in any record, and then click Sort A to Z.

FIGURE 2.13

> **3** On the **HOME tab**, in the **Sort & Filter group**, click **Remove Sort** to clear the sort and to return the records to the default sort order, which is by the primary key field—**Instructor ID**.

> **4** Click the **Last Name arrow**, and then click **Sort Z to A**.

> The records in the table are sorted by the Last Name field in reverse alphabetical order. The small arrow in the field name box points downward, indicating a descending sort. On the ribbon, Descending is selected.

> **5** In the **Sort & Filter group**, click **Remove Sort** to clear the sort.

Activity 2.09 | Sorting Records in a Table on Multiple Fields

To sort a table on two or more fields, first identify the fields that will act as the ***outermost sort field*** and the ***innermost sort field***. The outermost sort field is the first level of sorting, and the innermost sort field is the second level of sorting. To alphabetize a table by Last Name and then First Name—also called First Name within Last Name—the Last Name field is identified as the outermost sort field. If there are duplicate last names, the records should be further sorted by the First Name field—the innermost sort field. For tables, you sort the *innermost* field *first* and then sort the outermost field.

In this activity, you will sort the records by Last Name—innermost sort field—within the Department—outermost sort field.

> **1** In the **Last Name** field, click in any record. On the ribbon, on the **HOME tab**, in the **Sort & Filter group**, click **Ascending**.

> The records are sorted in ascending order by Last Name—the innermost sort field.

> **2** In any record, point in the **Department** field, right-click, and then click **Sort Z to A**. Compare your screen with Figure 2.14.

> The records are sorted in descending order first by Department—the outermost sort field. Within each Department grouping, the records are sorted in ascending order by Last Name—the innermost sort field. Records can be sorted on multiple fields using both ascending and descending order.

FIGURE 2.14

> **3** On the ribbon, click the **FILE tab**, click **Print**, and then click **Print Preview**. On the **PRINT PREVIEW tab**, in the **Page Layout group**, click **Landscape**. In the **Zoom group**, click **Two Pages**, and notice that the table will print on two pages.

4 ▶ In the **Print group**, click **Print**. In the **Print** dialog box, under **Print Range**, click in the **From** box, type **1** and then click in the **To** box. Type **1** to print only the first page. If directed to submit a paper printout, click **OK**. If directed to create an electronic printout, in the **Print** dialog box, click **Cancel**. On the **PRINT PREVIEW tab**, in the **Data group**, click **PDF or XPS**, click **Options**, and then under **Range**, click the **Pages** option button, click **OK**, and then click **Publish**.

5 ▶ In the object window, **Close** ⊠ the table. In the message box, click **Yes** to save the changes to the sort order.

6 ▶ **Open** ⧉ the **Navigation Pane**, double-click your **2A Instructors** table to open it, and then **Close** ⧏ the **Navigation Pane**. Notice that the table displays the sort order you specified.

7 ▶ On the **HOME tab**, in the **Sort & Filter group**, click **Remove Sort**. **Close** ⊠ the table, and in the message box, click **Yes** to save the table with the sort removed.

> Generally, tables are not stored with the data sorted. Instead, queries are created that sort the data, and then reports are created to display the sorted data.

Objective 4   Create a Query in Design View

Video A2-4

Recall that a select query is a database object that retrieves (selects) specific data from one or more tables and then displays the specified data in a table in Datasheet view. A query answers a question, such as *Which instructors teach courses in the IST department?* Unless a query has already been designed to ask this question, you must create a new query.

Database users rarely need to see all of the records in all of the tables. That is why a query is so useful; it creates a ***subset*** of records—a portion of the total records—according to your specifications and then displays only those records.

Activity 2.10 │ Creating a New Select Query in Design View

Previously, you created a query using the Query Wizard. To create more complex queries, use Query Design view. The table (or tables) from which a query selects its data is referred to as the ***data source***.

1 ▶ On the ribbon, click the **CREATE tab**, and then in the **Queries group**, click **Query Design**. Compare your screen with Figure 2.15.

> A new query opens in Design view, and the Show Table dialog box displays, which lists both tables in the database.

FIGURE 2.15

2 In the **Show Table** dialog box, double-click **2A Instructors**, and then, in the dialog box, click **Close**.

A field list for your 2A Instructors table displays in the upper area of the query window. Instructor ID is the primary key field in this table.

The query window has two parts: the upper area called the *table area* that displays the field lists for tables that are used in the query, and the lower area called the *design grid* that displays the design of the query.

ALERT! **Is There More Than One Field List in the Table Area?**

If you double-click a table more than one time, a duplicate field list displays in the table area of the query window. To remove a field list from the query window, right-click the title bar of the field list, and then click Remove Table.

---

3 Point to the lower right corner of the field list to display the pointer, and then drag downward and to the right to resize the field list, displaying all of the field names and the entire table name. In the **2A Instructors** field list, double-click **Rank**, and then look at the design grid.

The Rank field name displays in the design grid in the Field row. You limit the fields that display in the query results by placing only the desired field names in the design grid.

4 In the **2A Instructors** field list, point to **First Name**, drag the field name down into the design grid until the pointer displays in the **Field** row in the second column, and then release the mouse button. Compare your screen with Figure 2.16.

This is a second way to add field names to the design grid. As you drag the field, a small rectangular shape attaches to the mouse pointer. When you release the mouse button, the field name displays in the Field row.

FIGURE 2.16

2A Instructors field list resized in table area of query window

Two field names added to the Field row in the design grid of query window

5 In the design grid, in the **Field** row, click in the third column, and then click the **arrow** that displays. From the list, click **Last Name** to add the field to the design grid.

This is a third way to add field names to the design grid.

6 Using one of the three techniques you just practiced, add the **Office Phone** field to the fourth column and the **Department** field to the fifth column in the design grid.

ALERT! **Is There a Duplicate Field Name or an Incorrect Field Name in the Design Grid?**

If you double-click a field name more than one time, a duplicate field name displays in the design grid. To remove a duplicate field name, in the design grid, in the Field row, right-click the duplicate field name, and then click Cut. Use this same method to delete a field name that you placed in the design grid by mistake. As you progress in your study of query design, you will learn alternate ways to delete field names from the design grid.

Activity 2.11 | Running, Saving, Printing, and Closing a Query

After you design a query, you **run** the query to display the results. When you run a query, Access looks at the records in the table (or tables) you have included in the query, finds the records that match the specified conditions (if any), and displays only those records in a datasheet. Only the fields that you have added to the design grid display in the query results. The query always runs using the current table or tables, presenting the most up-to-date information.

> **1** Under **QUERY TOOLS**, on the **DESIGN tab**, in the **Results group**, click **Run**, and then compare your screen with Figure 2.17.

This query answers the question, *What is the rank, first name, last name, office phone number, and department of all of the instructors in the 2A Instructors table?* A query is a subset of the records in the table, arranged in Datasheet view, using the fields and conditions that you specify in the design grid. The five fields you specified in the design grid display in columns, and the records from the 2A Instructors table display in rows.

ANOTHER WAY   On the DESIGN tab, in the Results group, click the top portion of the View button, which runs the query by switching to Datasheet view.

FIGURE 2.17

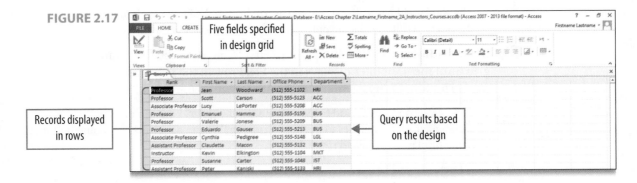

> **2** On the **Quick Access Toolbar**, click **Save** 🖫. In the **Save As** dialog box, type **Lastname Firstname 2A Instructors Query** and then click **OK**.

The query name displays on the object tab in the object window. Save your queries if you are likely to ask the same question again; doing so will save you the effort of creating the query again to answer the same question.

ALERT!   **Does a Message Display After Entering a Query Name?**

Query names are limited to 64 characters. For all projects, if you have a long last name or first name that results in your query name exceeding the 64-character limit, use your first initial instead of your first name.

> **3** On the ribbon, click the **FILE tab**, click **Print**, and then click **Print Preview**. Create a paper or electronic printout as directed, and then click **Close Print Preview**.

Queries answer questions and gather information from the data in tables. Typically, queries are created as a basis for a report, but query results can be printed just like any table of data.

> **4** Close ⊠ the query. Open ⊠ the **Navigation Pane**, and then notice that your **2A Instructors Query** object displays under your **2A Instructors** table object.

The new query name displays in the Navigation Pane under the table with which it is related—the 2A Instructors table, which is the data source. Only the design of the query is saved; the records reside in the table object. Each time you open a query, Access runs it again and displays the results based on the data stored in the data source. Thus, the results of the query always reflect the most up-to-date information.

Video A2-5

You can create a new query from scratch, or you can copy an existing query and modify the design to answer another question. Using an existing query saves you time if your new query uses all or some of the same fields and conditions in an existing query.

Activity 2.12 | Copying an Existing Query

1 In the **Navigation Pane**, right-click your **2A Instructors Query**, and then click **Copy**.

ANOTHER WAY   To create a copy of the query, in the Navigation Pane, click the query name to select it. On the HOME tab, in the Clipboard group, click Copy.

2 In the **Navigation Pane**, point to a blank area, right-click, and then click **Paste**.

The Paste As dialog box displays, which enables you to name the copied query.

ANOTHER WAY   On the HOME tab, in the Clipboard group, click Paste.

3 In the **Paste As** dialog box, type **Lastname Firstname 2A Instructor IDs Query** and then click **OK**.

A new query, based on a copy of your 2A Instructors Query is created and displays in the Navigation Pane under its data source—your 2A Instructors table object.

4 In the **Navigation Pane**, double-click your **2A Instructor IDs Query** to run the query and open the query results in **Datasheet** view. **Close** « the **Navigation Pane**.

Activity 2.13 | Modifying the Design of a Query

1 On the **HOME tab**, in the **Views group**, click the top portion of the **View** button to switch to **Design** view.

ANOTHER WAY   On the HOME tab, in the Views group, click the View arrow, and then click Design View; or on the right side of the status bar, click Design View. If the query is not open, in the Navigation Pane, right-click the query name, and then click Design View.

2 In the design grid, point to the thin gray selection bar above the **Office Phone** field name to display the ⬇ pointer, and then compare your screen with Figure 2.18.

FIGURE 2.18

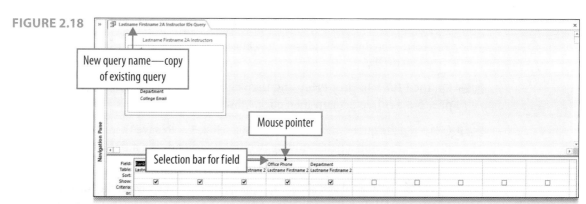

3 With the ⬇ pointer displayed in the selection bar above the **Office Phone** field name, click to select the column, and then press ⌈Del⌋.

> This action deletes the field from the query design only—it has no effect on the field in the data source—2A Instructors table. The Department field moves to the left. Similarly, by using the selection bar, you can drag to select multiple fields and delete them at one time.

🔄 **ANOTHER WAY**   In the design grid, click in the field name. On the DESIGN tab, in the Query Setup group, click Delete Columns; or right-click the field name, and then click Cut; or select the column, and on the HOME tab, in the Records group, click Delete.

4 Point to the selection bar above the **First Name** column, and then click to select the column. In the selected column, point to the selection bar, hold down the left mouse button to display the 🖱 pointer, and then drag to the right until a dark vertical line displays on the right side of the **Last Name** column. Release the mouse button to position the **First Name** field in the third column.

> To rearrange fields in a query, first select the field to move, and then drag it to a new position in the design grid.

5 Using the technique you just practiced, move the **Department** field to the left of the **Rank** field.

6 From the field list, drag the **Instructor ID** field down to the first column in the design grid until the 🖱 pointer displays, and then release the mouse button. Compare your screen with Figure 2.19.

> The Instructor ID field displays in the first column, and the remaining four fields move to the right. Use this method to insert a field to the left of a field already displayed in the design grid.

FIGURE 2.19

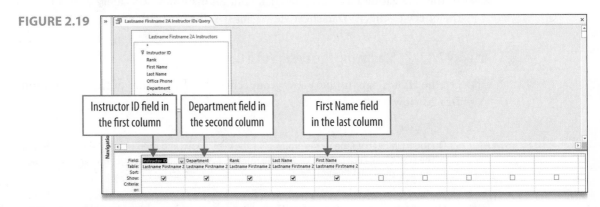

> Instructor ID field in the first column

> Department field in the second column

> First Name field in the last column

7 On the **DESIGN tab**, in the **Results group**, click **Run**.

> This query answers the question, *What is the instructor ID, department, rank, last name, and first name of every instructor in the 2A Instructors table?* The results of the query are a subset of the records stored in the 2A Instructors table. The records are sorted by the table's primary key field—Instructor ID.

8 On the **FILE tab**, click **Print**, and then click **Print Preview**. Create a paper or electronic printout as directed, and then click **Close Print Preview**.

9 Close ⌈×⌋ the query. In the message box, click **Yes** to save the changes to the query design—deleting a field, moving two fields, and adding a field. **Open** ⌈»⌋ the **Navigation Pane**.

> The query is saved and closed, and the query name displays in the Navigation Pane under the related table. Recall that only the *design* of the query is saved; the records reside in the related table.

Video A2-6

You can sort the results of a query in ascending or descending order in either Datasheet view or Design view. Use Design view if your query results should always display in a specified sort order or if you intend to use the sorted results in a report.

Activity 2.14 | Sorting Query Results

In this activity, you will copy an existing query and then sort the query results by using the Sort row in Design view.

1 In the **Navigation Pane**, right-click your **2A Instructor IDs Query**, and then click **Copy**. In the **Navigation Pane**, point to a blank area, right-click, and then click **Paste**.

2 In the **Paste As** dialog box, type **Lastname Firstname 2A Department Sort Query** and then click **OK**. Increase the width of the **Navigation Pane** so that the names of all of the objects display fully.

> A new query is created based on a copy of your 2A Instructor IDs Query; that is, the new query includes the same fields in the same order as the query that you copied.

3 In the **Navigation Pane**, right-click your **2A Department Sort Query**, and then click **Design View. Close** ⟪ the **Navigation Pane**.

> Use this technique to display the query in Design view if you are redesigning the query. Recall that if you double-click a query name in the Navigation Pane, Access runs the query and displays the query results.

4 In the design grid, in the **Sort** row, under **Last Name**, click to display the insertion point and an arrow. Click the **arrow**, click **Ascending**, and then compare your screen with Figure 2.20.

FIGURE 2.20

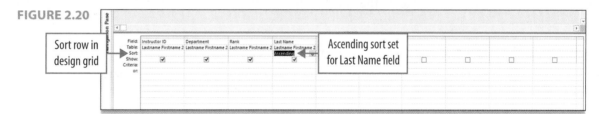

5 On the **DESIGN tab**, in the **Results group**, click **Run**.

> In the query results, the records are sorted in ascending order by the Last Name field, and two instructors have the same last name of *Carter—Susanne* and *Lisle*.

6 On the **HOME tab**, in the **Views group**, click the top of the **View** button to switch to **Design** view.

7 In the design grid, click in the **Sort** row under **First Name**, click the **arrow**, and then click **Ascending. Run** the query.

> In the query results, the records are sorted first by the Last Name field. If two instructors have the same last name, then those records are sorted by the First Name field. The two instructors with the same last name of *Carter* are sorted by their first names, and the two records with the same last name of *Fresch* are sorted by their first names.

8 ▸ Switch to **Design** view. In the design grid, click in the **Sort** row under **Department**, click the **arrow**, and then click **Descending**. **Run** the query, and then compare your screen with Figure 2.21.

> In Design view, fields with a Sort setting are sorted from left to right. That is, the sorted field on the left becomes the outermost sort field, and the sorted field on the right becomes the innermost sort field. Thus, the records in this query are sorted first in descending order by the Department field—the leftmost sort field. Then, within each department, the records are sorted in ascending order by the Last Name field. And, finally, within each duplicate last name, the records are sorted in ascending order by the First Name field.

> If you run a query and the sorted results are not what you intended, be sure the fields are displayed from left to right according to the groupings that you desire.

FIGURE 2.21

9 ▸ Display the query results in **Print Preview**. Create a paper or electronic printout as directed, and then click **Close Print Preview**. **Close** ⊗ the query. In the message box, click **Yes** to save the changes to the query design.

More Knowledge **Sorting in Design View or Datasheet View**

If you add a sort order to the *design* of a query, it remains as a permanent part of the query design. If you use the sort buttons in Datasheet view, the sort order will override the sort order of the query design and can be saved as part of the query. A sort order designated in Datasheet view does not display in the Sort row of the query design grid. As with sorting tables, in Datasheet view, a small arrow displays to the right of the field name to indicate the sort order of the field.

Objective 7 Specify Criteria in a Query

Video A2-7

Queries locate information in a table based on **criteria** that you specify as part of the query design. Criteria are conditions that identify the specific records that you are looking for. Criteria enable you to ask a more specific question; therefore, you will get a more specific result. For example, to find out how many instructors are in the IST department, limit the results to display only that specific department by entering criteria in the design grid.

Activity 2.15 │ Specifying Text Criteria in a Query

In this activity, you will assist Dean Judkins by creating a query to answer the question, *How many instructors are in the IST Department?*

1 ▸ On the ribbon, click the **CREATE tab**, and then in the **Queries group**, click **Query Design**.

2 ▸ In the **Show Table** dialog box, double-click your **2A Instructors** table to add it to the table area, and then **Close** the **Show Table** dialog box.

3 By dragging the lower right corner downward and to the right, resize the field list to display all of the field names and the table name. Add the following fields to the design grid in the order given: **Department, Instructor ID, Rank, Last Name,** and **First Name**.

4 In the design grid, click in the **Criteria** row under **Department**, type **IST** and then press [Enter]. Compare your screen with Figure 2.22.

Access places quotation marks around the criteria to indicate that this is a ***text string***—a sequence of characters. Use the Criteria row to specify the criteria that will limit the results of the query to your exact specifications. The criteria is not case sensitive; you can type *ist* instead of *IST*.

FIGURE 2.22

NOTE Pressing Enter After Adding Criteria

After adding criteria, when you press [Enter] or click in another column or row in the query design grid, you can see how Access alters the criteria so it can interpret what you have typed. Sometimes there is no change, such as when you add criteria to a field that stores a numeric or currency value. Other times, Access capitalizes a letter or adds quotation marks, words, or other symbols to clarify the criteria. Pressing [Enter] after adding criteria has no effect on the query results; it is used here to help you see how the program behaves.

5 In the design grid, click in the **Sort** row under **Last Name**, click the **arrow**, and then click **Ascending**. Click in the **Sort** row under **First Name**, click the **arrow**, and then click **Ascending**.

6 **Run** the query, and then compare your screen with Figure 2.23.

Thirteen records display. There are 13 instructors in the IST Department; or, more specifically, there are 13 records that have *IST* in the Department field. The records are sorted in ascending order, first by the Last Name field and then by the First Name field.

FIGURE 2.23

ALERT! Do Your Query Results Differ?

If you mistype the criteria, or enter it under the wrong field, or make some other error, the query results will display no records. This indicates that there are no records in the table that match the criteria as you entered it. If this occurs, return to Design view and examine the query design. Verify that the criteria is entered in the Criteria row, under the correct field, and without typing errors. Then, run the query again.

7 **Save** 💾 the query as **Lastname Firstname 2A IST Query** and then display the query results in **Print Preview**. Create a paper or electronic printout as directed, and then click **Close Print Preview**.

8 Close ☒ the query, **Open** » the **Navigation Pane**, and then notice that your **2A IST Query** object name displays under your **2A Instructors** table—its data source.

> Recall that in the Navigation Pane, queries display an icon of two overlapping datasheets.

Activity 2.16 | Specifying Criteria and Hiding the Field in the Query Results

So far, all of the fields that you included in the query design have also been included in the query results. There are times when you need to use the field in the query design, but you do not need to display that field in the results, usually, when the data in the field is the same for all of the records. In this activity, you will create a query to answer the question, *Which instructors have a rank of professor?*

1 Close « the **Navigation Pane**. On the ribbon, click the **CREATE tab**, and then in the **Queries group**, click **Query Design**.

2 In the **Show Table** dialog box, double-click your **2A Instructors** table to add it to the table area, and then **Close** the **Show Table** dialog box.

3 Resize the field list, and then add the following fields to the design grid in the order given: **Instructor ID**, **Last Name**, **First Name**, and **Rank**.

4 Click in the **Sort** row under **Last Name**, click the **arrow**, and then click **Ascending**. Click in the **Sort** row under **First Name**, click the **arrow**, and then click **Ascending**.

5 Click in the **Criteria** row under **Rank**, type **professor** and then press Enter. Compare your screen with Figure 2.24.

> Recall that criteria is not case sensitive. As you start typing *professor*, a list of functions displays, from which you can select if a function is included in your criteria. After pressing Enter, the insertion point moves to the next criteria box, and quotation marks are added around the text string that you entered.

FIGURE 2.24

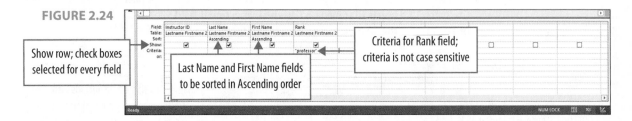

Show row; check boxes selected for every field

Last Name and First Name fields to be sorted in Ascending order

Criteria for Rank field; criteria is not case sensitive

6 In the design grid, in the **Show** row, notice that a check box is selected for every field. **Run** the query.

> Eighteen records meet the criteria—*professor* in the *Rank* field. In the Rank column, every record displays *Professor*, and the records are sorted in ascending order by the First Name field within the Last Name field.

7 Switch to **Design** view. In the design grid, in the **Show** row under **Rank**, click to clear the check box.

> Because it is repetitive and not particularly useful to display *Professor* for every record in the query results, clear the Show check box so that the field is hidden and does not display. It is good practice, however, to run the query first before clearing the Show check box to be sure that the correct records display.

8 ▶ **Run** the query, and then notice that the *Rank* field does not display even though it is used to specify criteria in the query.

> The same 18 records display, but the *Rank* field is hidden from the query results. Although the Rank field is included in the query design so that you can specify the criteria of *professor*, it is not necessary to display the field in the results. When appropriate, clear the Show check box to avoid cluttering the query results with data that is not useful.

9 ▶ **Save** 🖫 the query as **Lastname Firstname 2A Professor Query** and then display the query results in **Print Preview**. Create a paper or electronic printout as directed, and then click **Close Print Preview**. **Close** ✕ the query.

Activity 2.17 | Using *Is Null* Criteria to Find Empty Fields

Sometimes you must locate records where data is missing. You can locate such records by using *Is Null* as the criteria in a field. *Is Null* is used to find empty fields. Additionally, you can display only the records where data has been entered in the field by using the criteria of *Is Not Null*, which excludes records where the specified field is empty. In this activity, you will design a query to answer the question, *Which scheduled courses have no credits listed?*

1 ▶ On the ribbon, click the **CREATE tab**, and then in the **Queries group**, click **Query Design**. In the **Show Table** dialog box, double-click your **2A Schedule** table to add it to the table area, and then **Close** the **Show Table** dialog box.

2 ▶ Resize the field list, and then add the following fields to the design grid in the order given: **Subject**, **Catalog#**, **Section**, **Course Name**, and **Credits**.

3 ▶ Click in the **Criteria** row under **Credits**, type **is null** and then press [Enter].

> Access capitalizes *is null*. The criteria *Is Null* examines the Credits field and locates records that do *not* have any data entered in the field.

4 ▶ Click in the **Sort** row under **Subject**, click the **arrow**, and then click **Ascending**. **Sort** the **Catalog#** field in **Ascending** order, and then **Sort** the **Section** field in **Ascending** order. Compare your screen with Figure 2.25.

FIGURE 2.25

Three fields sorted in Ascending order

Is Null criteria for Credits field

5 ▶ **Run** the query, and then compare your screen with Figure 2.26.

> Four scheduled courses do not have credits listed—the Credits field is empty. The records are sorted in ascending order first by the Subject field. Within the Subject field, the records are sorted in ascending order by the Catalog# field. Within the Catalog# field, the records are sorted in ascending order by the Section field. Using the information displayed in the query results, a course scheduler can more easily locate the records in the table and enter the credits for these courses.

FIGURE 2.26

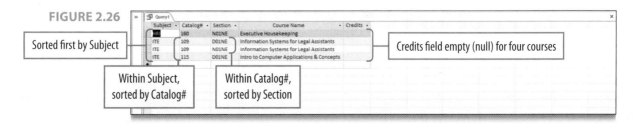

Sorted first by Subject

Credits field empty (null) for four courses

Within Subject, sorted by Catalog#

Within Catalog#, sorted by Section

6 Save 🔲 the query as **Lastname Firstname 2A No Credits Query**, and then display the query results in **Print Preview**. Create a paper or electronic printout as instructed, click **Close Print Preview**, and then **Close** ☒ the query.

7 **Open** 》 the **Navigation Pane**, and then notice that your **2A No Credits Query** object displays under your **2A Schedule** table object, its data source.

8 On the right side of the title bar, click **Close** ☒ to close the database and to exit Access. As directed by your instructor, submit your database and the paper or electronic printouts of the eight objects—relationship report, sorted table, and six queries—that are the results of this project. Specifically, in this project, using your own name, you created the following database and printouts or electronic printouts:

1. Lastname_Firstname_2A_Instructors_Courses	Database file
2. Relationships for Lastname_Firstname_2A_Instructors_Courses	Relationships Report (printout or electronic printout)
3. Lastname Firstname 2A Instructors table sorted (not saved)	Table sorted (printout or electronic printout - Page 1)
4. Lastname Firstname 2A Instructors Query	Query (printout or electronic printout)
5. Lastname Firstname 2A Instructor IDs Query	Query (printout or electronic printout)
6. Lastname Firstname 2A Department Sort Query	Query (printout or electronic printout)
7. Lastname Firstname 2A IST Query	Query (printout or electronic printout)
8. Lastname Firstname 2A Professor Query	Query (printout or electronic printout)
9. Lastname Firstname 2A No Credits Query	Query (printout or electronic printout)

END | You have completed Project 2A

GO! with Office Web Apps

Objective | Export an Access Query to a PDF File, Save to SkyDrive, and Add a Description to the PDF File

Access web apps are designed to work with Microsoft's SharePoint, an application for setting up websites to share and manage documents. Your college may not have SharePoint installed, so you will use other tools to share objects from your database so that you can work collaboratively with others. When you have information that you want to share with others, you can upload files to SkyDrive. Some files can be opened in SkyDrive; some can only be downloaded. Because database files are typically large in size, and free storage space on SkyDrive is limited, you can export database objects to different formats and then upload those files to SkyDrive.

> **ALERT!** Working with Web-Based Applications and Services
>
> Computer programs and services on the web receive continuous updates and improvements. Thus, the steps to complete this web-based activity may differ from the ones shown. You can often look at the screens and the information presented to determine how to complete the activity.

Activity | Exporting an Access Query to a PDF File, Uploading a PDF File to SkyDrive, and Adding a Description to a PDF File

In this activity, you will export your 2A No Credits Query object to a PDF file, upload your PDF file to SkyDrive, and then add a description to the PDF File. Recall that PDF stands for Portable Document Format—a file format that creates an image that preserves the look of your file, but that cannot be easily changed. The results of the query will be available for individuals with whom you have shared your SkyDrive files or folders.

1 Start Access, navigate to your **Access Chapter 2** folder, and then **Open** your **2A_Instructors_Courses** database file. If necessary, on the Message Bar, click Enable Content. In the **Navigation Pane**, click your **2A No Credits Query** object to select it—do not open it.

2 On the ribbon, click the **EXTERNAL DATA tab**, and then in the **Export group**, click **PDF or XPS**. In the **Publish as PDF or XPS** dialog box, navigate to your **Access Chapter 2** folder. Click in the **File name** box, type **Lastname_Firstname_AC_2A_Web** and then be sure the **Open file after publishing** check box is selected, and the **Minimum size (publishing online)** option button is

selected. Click **Publish**, and then compare your screen with Figure A.

The PDF file is created and opens in the Windows 8 Reader, Adobe Reader, or Adobe Acrobat, depending on the software that is installed on your computer.

3 Close your **AC_2A_Web** file. In the **Export – PDF** dialog box, click **Close**, and then **Close** Access.

4 From the desktop, start Internet Explorer, navigate to **http://skydrive.com**, and then sign in to your Microsoft account. Open your **GO! Web Projects** folder—or create and then open this folder if necessary.

FIGURE A

Your 2A No Credits Query exported as a PDF file and opened in Adobe Reader (yours may open in Windows 8 Reader or Adobe Acrobat)

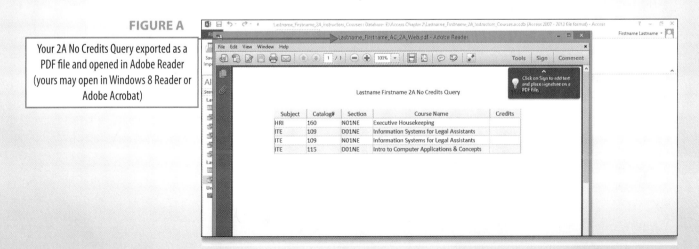

(GO! with Office Web Apps continues on the next page)

5 On the menu bar, click **Upload**. In the **Choose File to Upload** dialog box, navigate to your **Access Chapter 2** folder, and then double-click your **AC_2A_Web** file to upload it to SkyDrive.

6 In your **GO! Web Projects** folder, right-click your **AC_2A_Web** file, and then click **Properties**.

A properties panel displays on the right side of the window.

7 In the properties panel, click **Add a description**. In the box, type **This query displays courses in the schedule that do not have credits assigned to them.** and then press Enter. Compare your screen with Figure B.

8 On your keyboard, press the ⊞ key, type **snip**, and then click **Snipping Tool**. In the **Snipping Tool** dialog box, click the **New arrow**, and then click **Full-screen snip**.

9 On the **Snipping Tool** toolbar, click **Save Snip** 🖫. In the **Save As** dialog box, navigate to your **Access Chapter 2** folder. Click in the **File name** box, type **Lastname_Firstname_AC_2A_Web_Snip** and then click the **Save as type arrow**. Click **JPEG file**, and then click **Save**. **Close** ⊠ the **Snipping Tool** window.

10 In SkyDrive, on the title bar, click **SkyDrive** to return to your home page. At the top right corner of your screen, click your SkyDrive name, and then click **Sign out**. **Close** your browser window.

11 If directed to submit a paper printout of your pdf and snip file, follow the directions given in the Note. As directed by your instructor, submit your pdf file and your snip file that are the results of this project.

N O T E   **Printing Your PDF and Snip .jpeg File**

Using Windows Explorer, navigate to your Access Chapter 2 folder. Locate and double-click your AC_2A_Web file. On the toolbar, click the Print file button. Then Close the Windows 8 Reader, Adobe Reader, or Adobe Acrobat window. In your Access Chapter 2 folder, locate and double-click your AC_2A_Web_Snip file. If this is the first time you have tried to open a .jpeg file, you will be asked to identify a program. If you are not sure which program to use, select Windows Photo Viewer. From the ribbon, menu bar, or toolbar, click the Print command, and then Close the program window.

FIGURE B

Athletic Scholarships Database

MyITLab®
Project 2B Training

PROJECT ACTIVITIES

In Activities 2.18 through 2.33, you will assist Roberto Garza, athletic director for Texas Lakes Community College, in creating queries to locate information about athletic scholarships that are awarded to students. Your completed database objects will look similar to Figure 2.27.

PROJECT FILES

For Project 2B, you will need the following files:

a02B_Athletes_Scholarships
a02B_Athletes (Excel workbook)

You will save your database as:

Lastname_Firstname_2B_Athletes_Scholarships

PROJECT RESULTS

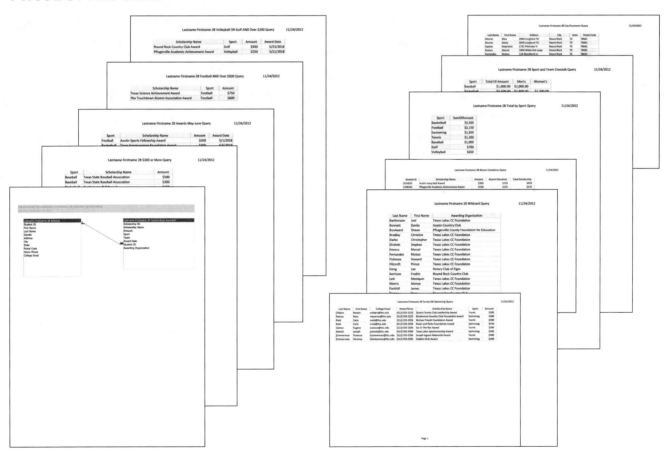

FIGURE 2.27 Project 2B Athletic Scholarships

Video A2-8

Criteria can be set for fields containing numeric data. When you design your table, set the appropriate data type for fields that will contain numbers, currency, or dates so that mathematical calculations can be performed.

Activity 2.18 | Opening, Renaming, and Saving an Existing Database and Importing a Spreadsheet as a New Table

In this activity, you will open, rename, and save an existing database, and then import an Excel spreadsheet as a new table in the database.

1 **Start** Access. In the Access opening screen, click **Open Other Files**. Under **Open**, click **Computer**. Under **Recent Folders**, if displayed, click the location where your student data files are stored; otherwise, click **Browse** and then navigate to the location where your student data files are stored. Double-click **a02B_Athletes_Scholarships** to open the database.

2 Click the **FILE tab**, click **Save As**, and then under **File Types**, be sure **Save Database As** is selected. On the right, under **Database File Types**, be sure **Access Database** is selected, and then click **Save As**. In the **Save As** dialog box, navigate to your **Access Chapter 2** folder, click in the **File name** box, type **Lastname_Firstname_2B_Athletes_Scholarships** and then press Enter.

3 On the **Message Bar**, click **Enable Content**. In the **Navigation Pane**, right-click **2B Scholarships Awarded**, and then click **Rename**. Using your own name, type **Lastname Firstname 2B Scholarships Awarded** and then press Enter. In the **Navigation Pane**, double-click the table name to open it in **Datasheet** view. **Close** « the **Navigation Pane**, and then examine the data in the table. Compare your screen with Figure 2.28.

In this table, Mr. Garza tracks the names and amounts of scholarships awarded to student athletes. Students are identified only by their Student ID numbers, and the primary key is the Scholarship ID field.

FIGURE 2.28

4 **Close** × the table. On the ribbon, click the **EXTERNAL DATA tab**, and then in the **Import & Link group**, click **Excel**. In the **Get External Data – Excel Spreadsheet** dialog box, to the right of the **File name** box, click **Browse**.

5 In the **File Open** dialog box, navigate to your student data files, and then double-click **a02B_Athletes**. Be sure that the **Import the source data into a new table in the current database** option button is selected, and then click **OK**.

The Import Spreadsheet Wizard opens and displays the spreadsheet data.

6 In the wizard, click **Next**. In the upper left area of the wizard, select the **First Row Contains Column Headings** check box, click **Next**, and then click **Next** again.

7 ▶ In the wizard, click the **Choose my own primary key** option button, and then be sure that **Student ID** displays in the box.

> In the new table, Student ID will be designated as the primary key. No two students have the same Student ID.

8 ▶ Click **Next**. With the text selected in the **Import to Table** box, type **Lastname Firstname 2B Athletes** and then click **Finish**. In the **Get External Data – Excel Spreadsheet** dialog box, click **Close**.

9 ▶ Open ⟩⟩ the **Navigation Pane**, and increase the width of the pane so that the two table names display fully. In the **Navigation Pane**, right-click your **2B Athletes** table, and then click **Design View**. Close ⟨⟨ the **Navigation Pane**.

10 ▶ To the right of **Student ID**, click in the **Data Type** box, click the **arrow**, and then click **Short Text**. For the **Postal Code** field, change the **Data Type** to **Short Text**, and in the **Field Properties** area, click **Field Size**, type **5** and then press Enter. In the **Field Name** column, click **State**, set the **Field Size** to **2** and then press Enter. Compare your screen with Figure 2.29.

> Recall that numeric data that is not used in a calculation, such as the Student ID and Postal Code, should be assigned a data type of Short Text.

FIGURE 2.29

11 ▶ On the **DESIGN tab**, in the **Views group**, click the top of the **View** button to switch to **Datasheet** view. In the message box, click **Yes** to save the table. In the second message box, click **Yes**—no data will be lost. Take a moment to examine the data in the imported table.

12 ▶ In the datasheet, to the left of the **Student ID** field name, click **Select All** ▢. On the **HOME** tab, in the **Records group**, click **More**, and then click **Field Width**. In the **Column Width** dialog box, click **Best Fit**. Save ▢ the table, click in any record to cancel the selection, and then **Close** ✕ the table.

Activity 2.19 | Creating a One-to-Many Table Relationship

In this activity, you will create a one-to-many relationship between your 2B Athletes table and your 2B Scholarships Awarded table by using the common field—*Student ID*.

1 ▶ On the ribbon, click the **DATABASE TOOLS tab**, and then in the **Relationships group**, click **Relationships**.

2 ▶ In the **Show Table** dialog box, double-click your **2B Athletes** table, and then double-click your **2B Scholarships Awarded** table to add both tables to the **Relationships** window. **Close** the **Show Table** dialog box.

3 ▶ Point to the title bar of the field list on the right, and drag the field list to the right until there are approximately three inches of space between the field lists. By dragging the lower right corner of the field list downward and to the right, resize each field list to display all of the field names and the entire table name.

Repositioning and resizing the field lists are not required, but doing so makes it easier for you to view the field names and the join line when creating relationships.

4 ▶ In the **2B Athletes** field list, point to **Student ID**, and then drag the field name into the **2B Scholarships Awarded** field list on top of **Student ID**. Release the mouse button to display the **Edit Relationships** dialog box.

5 ▶ Point to the title bar of the **Edit Relationships** dialog box, and then drag it downward below the two field lists. In the **Edit Relationships** dialog box, be sure that **Student ID** displays as the common field for both tables.

Repositioning the Edit Relationships dialog is not required, but doing so enables you to see the field lists. The Relationship Type is *One-To-Many*—*one* athlete can have *many* scholarships. The common field in both tables is the *Student ID* field. In the 2B Athletes table, Student ID is the primary key. In the 2B Scholarships Awarded table, Student ID is the foreign key.

6 ▶ In the **Edit Relationships** dialog box, click to select the **Enforce Referential Integrity** check box, the **Cascade Update Related Fields** check box, and the **Cascade Delete Related Records** check box. Click **Create**, and then compare your screen with Figure 2.30.

The one-to-many relationship is established. The *1* and ∞ symbols indicate that referential integrity is enforced, which ensures that a scholarship cannot be awarded to a student whose Student ID is not included in the 2B Athletes table. Recall that the Cascade options enable you to update and delete records automatically on the *many* side of the relationship when changes are made in the table on the *one* side of the relationship.

FIGURE 2.30

7 ▶ Under **RELATIONSHIP TOOLS**, on the **DESIGN tab**, in the **Tools group**, click **Relationship Report**. On the **PRINT PREVIEW tab**, in the **Page Size group**, click **Margins**, and then click **Normal. Save** 🖫 the report as **Lastname Firstname 2B Relationships** and then create a paper or electronic printout as directed.

8 ▶ In the object window, right-click either **object tab**, and then click **Close All** to close the **Relationship Report** and the **Relationships** window.

9 ▶ **Open** ⟫ the **Navigation Pane**, double-click your **2B Athletes** table to open it, and then **Close** ⟪ the **Navigation Pane**. On the left side of the first record, click ⊞ to display the subdatasheet for the record.

In the first record, for *Joel Barthmaier*, one related record exists in the 2B Scholarships Awarded table. Joel has been awarded the *Austin Jump Ball Award* in the amount of *$300*. The subdatasheet displays because you created a relationship between the two tables using Student ID as the common field.

10 Close ✕ the **2B Athletes** table.

When you close the table, the subdatasheet collapses—you do not need to click ☐ before closing a table.

Activity 2.20 | Specifying Numeric Criteria in a Query

In this activity, you will create a query to answer the question, *Which scholarships are in the amount of $300, and for which sports?*

1 On the ribbon, click the **CREATE tab**. In the **Queries group**, click **Query Design**.

2 In the **Show Table** dialog box, double-click your **2B Scholarships Awarded** table to add it to the table area, and then **Close** the **Show Table** dialog box. Resize the field list to display all of the fields and the entire table name.

3 Add the following fields to the design grid in the order given: **Sport**, **Scholarship Name**, and **Amount**.

4 Click in the **Sort** row under **Sport**, click the **arrow**, and then click **Ascending**. Click in the **Sort** row under **Scholarship Name**, click the **arrow**, and then click **Ascending**.

The records will be sorted in ascending order by the Scholarship Name field within the Sport field.

5 Click in the **Criteria** row under **Amount**, type **300** and then press Enter. Compare your screen with Figure 2.31.

When you enter currency values as criteria, do not type the dollar sign. Include a decimal point only if you are looking for a specific amount that includes cents; for example, 300.49. Access does not insert quotation marks around the criteria because the data type of the field is Currency, which is a numeric format.

FIGURE 2.31

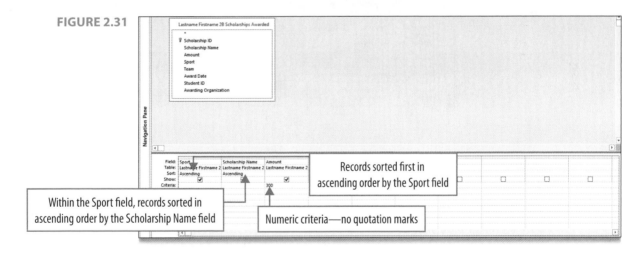

6 Under **QUERY TOOLS**, on the **DESIGN tab**, in the **Results group**, click **Run** to display the query results.

Five scholarships in the exact amount of $300 were awarded to student athletes. In the navigation area, *1 of 5* displays—1 represents the first record that is selected, and 5 represents the total number of records that meet the criteria.

7 On the **HOME tab**, in the **Views group**, click the top of the **View** button to switch to **Design** view.

Activity 2.21 | Using Comparison Operators in Criteria

Comparison operators are symbols you can use to evaluate data in the field to determine if it is the same (=), greater than (>), less than (<), or in between a range of values as specified by the criteria. If no comparison operator is specified, equal (=) is assumed. For example, in the previous activity, you created a query to display only those records where the *Amount* is *300*. The comparison operator of = was assumed, and the query results displayed only those records that had values in the Amount field equal to 300.

1 In the design grid, in the **Criteria** row under **Amount**, select the existing criteria of *300*. Type **>300** and then press Enter. **Run** the query.

Fourteen records display, and each has a value *greater than* $300 in the Amount field; there are no records for which the Amount is *equal to* $300.

2 Switch to **Design** view. In the **Criteria** row under **Amount**, select the existing criteria of *>300*. Type **<300** and then press Enter. **Run** the query.

Eleven records display, and each has a value *less than* $300 in the Amount field; there are no records for which the Amount is *equal to* $300.

3 Switch to **Design** view. In the **Criteria** row under **Amount**, select the existing criteria of *<300*. Type **>=300** and then press Enter. **Run** the query, and then compare your screen with Figure 2.32.

Nineteen records display, including the records for scholarships in the exact amount of $300. The records include scholarships *greater than* or *equal to* $300. In this manner, comparison operators can be combined. This query answers the question, *Which scholarships have been awarded in the amount of $300 or more, and for which sports, arranged alphabetically by sport?*

FIGURE 2.32

4 Save the query as **Lastname Firstname 2B $300 or More Query** and then display the query results in **Print Preview**. Create a paper or electronic printout as directed, and then click **Close Print Preview**.

5 Close ☒ the query. Open ☒ the **Navigation Pane**, and notice that this new query displays under *2B Scholarships Awarded*, its data source.

Activity 2.22 | Using the Between … And Comparison Operator

The **Between … And operator** is a comparison operator that looks for values within a range. It is useful when you need to locate records that are within a range of dates; for example, scholarships awarded between May 1 and June 30.

In this activity, you will create a new query from an existing query, and then add criteria to look for values within a range of dates. The query will answer the question, *Which scholarships were awarded between May 1 and June 30?*

1 ▸ In the **Navigation Pane**, right-click your **2B $300 or More Query** object, and then click **Copy**. In the **Navigation Pane**, point to a blank area, right-click, and then click **Paste**.

2 ▸ In the **Paste As** dialog box, type **Lastname Firstname 2B Awards May-June Query** and then click **OK**.

> A new query, based on a copy of your 2B $300 or More Query is created and displays in the Navigation Pane under its data source—your 2B Scholarships Awarded table.

3 ▸ In the **Navigation Pane**, right-click your **2B Awards May-June Query** object, click **Design View**, and then **Close** the **Navigation Pane**.

4 ▸ In the **2B Scholarships Awarded** field list, double-click **Award Date** to add it as the fourth column in the design grid.

5 ▸ In the **Criteria** row under **Amount**, select the existing criteria of *>=300*, and then press Del so that the query is not restricted by a monetary value.

6 ▸ Click in the **Criteria** row under **Award Date**, type **between 5/1/18 and 6/30/18** and then press Enter.

7 ▸ Click in the **Sort** row under **Sport**, click the **arrow**, and then click (**not sorted**) to remove the sort from this field. Click in the **Sort** row under **Scholarship Name**, click the **arrow**, and then click (**not sorted**) to remove the sort from this field. Click in the **Sort** row under **Award Date**, click the **arrow**, and then click **Ascending**.

8 ▸ In the selection bar of the design grid, point to the right edge of the **Award Date** column to display the ⊞ pointer, and then double-click to apply Best Fit to this column. Compare your screen with Figure 2.33.

> The width of the Award Date column is increased to fit the longest entry in the column, which enables you to see all of the criteria. Access places pound signs (#) around the dates and capitalizes *between* and *and*. This criteria instructs Access to look for values in the Award Date field that begin with 5/1/18 and end with 6/30/18. Both the beginning and ending dates will be included in the query results.

FIGURE 2.33

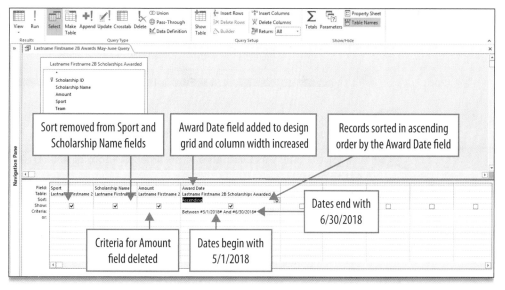

9 ▸ **Run** the query, and notice that eight scholarships were awarded between 5/1/2018 and 6/30/2018.

10 ▸ Display the query results in **Print Preview**, create a paper or electronic printout as directed, and then click **Close Print Preview**. **Close** ✕ the query, and in the message box, click **Yes** to save the changes to the query design.

Video A2-9

You can specify more than one condition—criteria—in a query; this is called **compound criteria**. Compound criteria use **logical operators** such as AND and OR. Logical operators evaluate data to determine if a condition is met (true) or not met (false). The AND and OR logical operators enable you to enter multiple criteria for the same field or for different fields.

Activity 2.23 | Using AND Criteria in a Query

The **AND condition** is an example of a compound criteria you can use to display records that match all parts of the specified criteria. In this activity, you will design a query to answer the question, *Which scholarships over $500 were awarded for football?*

1   On the ribbon, click the **CREATE tab**, and in the **Queries group**, click **Query Design**. In the **Show Table** dialog box, double-click your **2B Scholarships Awarded** table to add it to the table area, and then **Close** the **Show Table** dialog box. Resize the field list to display all of the fields and the entire table name.

2   Add the following fields to the design grid in the order given: **Scholarship Name**, **Sport**, and **Amount**.

3   Click in the **Criteria** row under **Sport**, type **football** and then press Enter.

4   In the **Criteria** row under **Amount**, type **>500** and then press Enter. Compare your screen with Figure 2.34.

> You create the AND condition by placing the criteria for both fields on the same line in the Criteria row. The criteria indicates that records should be located that contain *Football* in the Sport field AND a value greater than *500* in the Amount field. Both conditions must exist or be true for the records to display in the query results.

FIGURE 2.34

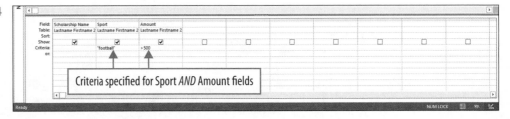

Criteria specified for Sport *AND* Amount fields

5   **Run** the query, and notice that two records display that match both conditions—*Football* in the **Sport** field AND a value greater than *$500* in the **Amount** field.

6   **Save** 🖫 the query as **Lastname Firstname 2B Football AND Over $500 Query** and then **Close** ☒ the query.

7   **Open** 》 the **Navigation Pane**, and then click to select your **2B Football AND Over $500 Query** object. On the ribbon, click the **FILE tab**, click **Print**, and then click **Print Preview**.

> You can view an object in Print Preview or print any selected object in the Navigation Pane—the object does not need to be open in the object window to print it.

8   Create a paper or electronic printout as directed, and then click **Close Print Preview**. **Close** 《 the **Navigation Pane**.

Activity 2.24 | Using OR Criteria in a Query

The **OR condition** is an example of a compound criteria you can use to display records that meet one or more parts of the specified criteria. The OR condition can specify criteria in a single field or in different fields. In this activity, you will help Mr. Garza answer the question, *Which scholarships over $200 were awarded for volleyball or golf, and what is the award date of each?*

1 On the ribbon, click the **CREATE tab**. In the **Queries group**, click **Query Design**.

2 In the **Show Table** dialog box, double-click your **2B Scholarships Awarded** table to add it to the table area, and then **Close** the **Show Table** dialog box. Resize the field list, and then add the following fields to the design grid in the order given: **Scholarship Name**, **Sport**, **Amount**, and **Award Date**.

3 In the design grid, click in the **Criteria** row under **Sport**, type **volleyball** and then press ⬇.

The insertion point is blinking in the *or* row under Sport.

4 In the **or** row under **Sport**, type **golf** and then press [Enter]. **Run** the query.

Six records were located in the 2B Scholarships Awarded table that have either *volleyball* OR *golf* stored in the Sport field. This is an example of using the OR condition to locate records that meet one or more parts of the specified criteria in a single field—*Sport*.

5 Switch to **Design** view. In the **or** row under **Sport**, select *"golf"* and then press [Del]. In the **Criteria** row under **Sport**, select and delete *"volleyball"*. Type **volleyball or golf** and then press [Enter].

6 In the **Criteria** row under **Amount**, type **>200** and then press [Enter]. Compare your screen with Figure 2.35.

This is an alternative way to enter the OR condition in the Sport field and is a good method to use when you add an AND condition to the criteria. Access will locate records where the Sport field contains *volleyball* OR *golf* AND where the Amount field contains a value greater than *200*.

If you enter *volleyball* in the Criteria row, and *golf* in the or row for the Sport field, then you must enter *>200* in both the Criteria row and the or row for the Amount field so that the correct records are located when you run the query.

FIGURE 2.35

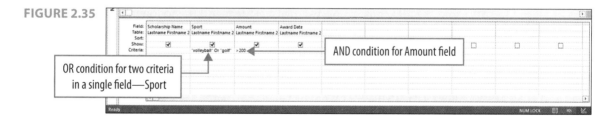

7 Run the query.

Two records were located in the 2B Scholarships Awarded table that have either *Volleyball* OR *Golf* stored in the Sport field AND a value greater than $200 stored in the Amount field. This is an example of using the OR condition in combination with an AND condition.

8 Save 🖫 the query as **Lastname Firstname 2B Volleyball OR Golf AND Over $200 Query** and then display the query results in **Print Preview**. Create a paper or electronic printout as directed, click **Close Print Preview**, and then **Close** ⊠ the query.

Objective 10 | Create a Query Based on More Than One Table

Video A2-10

In a relational database, you can retrieve information from more than one table. Recall that a table in a relational database contains all of the records about a single topic. Tables are joined to one another by relating the primary key in one table to the foreign key in another table. This common field is used to create the relationship and is used to find records from multiple tables when the query is created and run.

For example, the Athletes table stores all of the data about the student athletes—name, address, and so on. The Scholarships Awarded table stores data about the scholarship name, the amount, and so on. When an athlete receives a scholarship, only the Student ID of the athlete is used to identify the athlete in the Scholarships Awarded table. It is not necessary to include any other data about the athlete in the Scholarships Awarded table; doing so would result in redundant data.

Activity 2.25 | Creating a Query Based on More Than One Table

In this activity, you will create a query that selects records from two tables. This is possible because you created a relationship between the two tables in the database. The query will answer the questions, *What is the name, email address, and phone number of athletes who have received a scholarship for tennis or swimming, and what is the name and amount of the scholarship?*

1 On the ribbon, click the **CREATE tab**, and then in the **Queries group**, click **Query Design**. In the **Show Table** dialog box, double-click your **2B Athletes** table, and then double-click your **2B Scholarships Awarded** table to add both tables to the table area. In the **Show Table** dialog box, click **Close**. Drag the **2B Scholarships Awarded** field list—the field list on the right—to the right so that there are approximately three inches of space between the two field lists, and then resize each field list to display all of the field names and the table names.

> The join line displays because you created a one-to-many relationship between the two tables using the common field of Student ID; *one* athlete can receive *many* scholarships.

2 From the **2B Athletes** field list, add the following fields to the design grid in the order given: **Last Name**, **First Name**, **College Email**, and **Home Phone**.

3 From the **2B Scholarships Awarded** field list, add the following fields to the design grid in the order given: **Scholarship Name**, **Sport**, and **Amount**.

4 Click in the **Sort** row under **Last Name**, click the **arrow**, and then click **Ascending**. Click in the **Sort** row under **First Name**, click the **arrow**, and then click **Ascending**.

5 Click in the **Criteria** row under **Sport**, type **tennis or swimming** and then press Enter.

6 In the selection bar of the design grid, point to the right edge of the **Home Phone** column to display the ⊞ pointer, and then double-click to increase the width of the column and to display the entire table name on the **Table** row. Using the same technique, increase the width of the **Scholarship Name** column. If necessary, scroll to the right to display both of these columns in the design grid, and then compare your screen with Figure 2.36.

> When locating data from multiple tables, the information in the Table row is helpful, especially when different tables include the same field name, such as Address. Although the field name is the same, the data may be different; for example, you might have an athlete's address or a coach's address from two different related tables.

FIGURE 2.36

Table row indicates data source

Sorted in ascending order by Last Name and First Name fields

Criteria entered for Sport field

7 **Run** the query, and then compare your screen with Figure 2.37.

Eight records display for athletes who received either a Tennis *or* Swimming scholarship, and the records are sorted in ascending order by the Last Name field, and then the First Name field. Because the common field of Student ID is included in both tables, Access can locate the specified fields in both tables by using one query. Two students—*Carla Reid* and *Florence Zimmerman*—received two scholarships, one for tennis and one for swimming. Recall that *one* student athlete can receive *many* scholarships.

FIGURE 2.37

Students with scholarships in both sports

Records sorted by First Name field within the Last Name field

Sport of *Tennis* OR *Swimming*

Records sorted first by Last Name field

8 **Save** 🖫 the query as **Lastname Firstname 2B Tennis OR Swimming Query** and then display the query results in **Print Preview**. Change the orientation to **Landscape**, and the **Margins** to **Normal**. Create a paper or electronic printout as directed, and then click **Close Print Preview**.

9 **Close** × the query, **Open** » the **Navigation Pane**, increase the width of the **Navigation Pane** to display all object names fully, and then compare your screen with Figure 2.38.

Your *2B Tennis OR Swimming Query* object name displays under both tables from which it selected records.

FIGURE 2.38

Query displays under both of its data sources

10 **Close** « the **Navigation Pane**.

Video A2-11

Wildcard characters serve as a placeholder for one or more unknown characters in criteria. When you are unsure of the specific character or set of characters to include in the criteria, use a wildcard character in place of the character.

Activity 2.26 | Using a Wildcard in a Query

Use the asterisk (*) wildcard character to represent one or more unknown characters. For example, entering Fo* as the criteria in a last name field will result in displaying records containing last names of Foster, Forrester, Fossil, or any other last name that begins with *Fo*. In this activity, you will use the asterisk (*) wildcard character in criteria to answer the question, *Which athletes received scholarships from local rotary clubs, country clubs, or foundations?*

1 On the ribbon, click the **CREATE tab**, and then in the **Queries group**, click **Query Design**. In the **Show Table** dialog box, double-click your **2B Athletes** table, and then double-click your **2B Scholarships Awarded** table to add both tables to the table area. In the **Show Table** dialog box, click **Close**. Drag the **2B Scholarships Awarded** field list to the right so that there are approximately three inches of space between the two field lists, and then resize each field list to display all of the field names and the table names.

2 From the **2B Athletes** field list, add the following fields to the design grid in the order given: **Last Name** and **First Name**. From the **2B Scholarships Awarded** field list, add the **Awarding Organization** field to the design grid.

3 Click in the **Sort** row under **Last Name**, click the **arrow**, and then click **Ascending**. Click in the **Sort** row under **First Name**, click the **arrow**, and then click **Ascending**.

4 Click in the **Criteria** row under **Awarding Organization**, type **rotary*** and then press Enter.

The * wildcard character is a placeholder you can use to match one or more unknown characters. After pressing Enter, Access adds *Like* to the beginning of the criteria and places quotation marks around *rotary**.

5 **Run** the query, and then compare your screen with Figure 2.39.

Three athletes received scholarships from a rotary club from different cities. The results are sorted alphabetically by the Last Name field. If there were two athletes with the same Last Name, the records would be sorted by the First Name field.

FIGURE 2.39

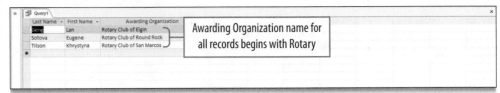

6 Switch to **Design** view. Click in the **or** row under **Awarding Organization**, type ***country club** and then press Enter.

You can use the * wildcard character at the beginning, middle, or end of the criteria. The position of the * determines the location of the unknown characters. By entering **country club*, Access will locate records with an Awarding Organization name that ends in *Country Club*.

7 **Run** the query.

Six records display for students receiving scholarships; three from organizations with a name that begins with *Rotary*, and three from organizations with a name that ends with *Country Club*.

8 ▶ Switch to **Design** view. In the design grid under **Awarding Organization** and under **Like "*country club"**, type ***foundation*** and then press Enter. Compare your screen with Figure 2.40.

This query will also display records where the Awarding Organization has *Foundation* anywhere in its name—at the beginning, in the middle, or at the end of the organization name. Three *OR* criteria have been entered for the Awarding Organization field. When run, this query will locate records where the Awarding Organization has a name that begins with *Rotary*, OR ends with *Country Club*, OR has *Foundation* anywhere in its name.

FIGURE 2.40

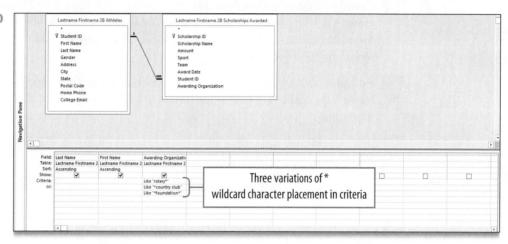

9 ▶ **Run** the query.

Twenty-eight scholarships were awarded from organizations where the name of the organization begins with *Rotary*, ends with *Country Club*, or has *Foundation* anywhere in its name. The records are sorted alphabetically by the Last Name field and then by the First Name field.

10 ▶ **Save** 🖫 the query as **Lastname Firstname 2B Wildcard Query** and then display the query results in **Print Preview**. Create a paper or electronic printout as directed, and then click **Close Print Preview**.

11 ▶ **Close** ✕ the query, and then **Open** » the **Navigation Pane**. Notice that your **2B Wildcard Query** displays under both tables because the query selected data from both tables—the data sources.

> **More Knowledge** **Using the ? Wildcard Character to Search for a Single Unknown Character**
>
> You can use the question mark (?) wildcard character to search for a single unknown character. For each question mark included in the criteria, the query results can display any character. For example, entering *b?d* as the criteria will result in the display of words such as *bed*, *bid*, or *bud*, or any three-character word that begins with *b* and ends with *d*. Entering *b??d* as the criteria will result in the display of words such as *bard*, *bend*, or *bind*, or any four-character word that begins with *b* and ends with *d*.

Objective 12 Create Calculated Fields in a Query

Video A2-12

Queries can create calculated values that are stored in a ***calculated field***. A calculated field stores the value of a mathematical operation. For example, you can multiply the value stored in a field named Total Hours Worked by the value stored in a field named Hourly Pay to display the Gross Pay value for each work study student.

There are two steps to create a calculated field in a query. First, name the field that will store the results of the calculation. Second, enter the ***expression***—the formula—that will perform the calculation. When entering the information for the calculated field in the query, the new field name must be followed by a colon (:), and each field name used in the expression must be enclosed within its own pair of brackets.

Activity 2.27 | Creating a Calculated Field in a Query

For each scholarship received by student athletes, the Texas Lakes Community College Alumni Association will donate an amount equal to 50 percent of each scholarship amount. In this activity, you will create a calculated field to determine the amount that the Alumni Association will donate for each scholarship. The query will answer the question, *How much money will the Alumni Association donate for each student athlete who is awarded a scholarship?*

1 Close « the **Navigation Pane**. On the ribbon, click the **CREATE tab**, and then in the **Queries group**, click **Query Design**. In the **Show Table** dialog box, double-click your **2B Scholarships Awarded** table to add the table to the table area, **Close** the **Show Table** dialog box, and then resize the field list.

2 Add the following fields to the design grid in the order given: **Student ID**, **Scholarship Name**, and **Amount**. Click in the **Sort** row under **Student ID**, click the **arrow**, and then click **Ascending**.

3 In the **Field** row, right-click in the first empty column to display a shortcut menu, and then click **Zoom**.

> Although the calculation can be typed directly in the empty Field box, the Zoom dialog box gives you more working space and enables you to see the entire calculation as you enter it.

4 In the **Zoom** dialog box, type **Alumni Donation:[Amount]*0.5** and then compare your screen with Figure 2.41.

> The first element, *Alumni Donation*, is the new field name that will display the result of the calculation when the query is run. The new field name is followed by a colon (:), which separates the new field name from the expression. *Amount* is enclosed in brackets because it is an existing field name in your 2B Scholarships Awarded table; it contains the numeric data on which the calculation is performed. Following the right square bracket is the asterisk (*), the mathematical operator for multiplication. Finally, the percentage expressed as a decimal—*0.5*—displays.

FIGURE 2.41

5 In the **Zoom** dialog box, click **OK**, **Run** the query, and then compare your screen with Figure 2.42.

> The query results display three fields from your 2B Scholarships Awarded table and a fourth field—*Alumni Donation*—that displays a calculated value. Each calculated value equals the value in the Amount field multiplied by 0.5 or 50%.

FIGURE 2.42

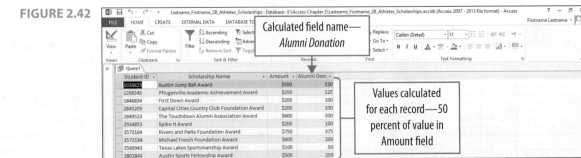

6 Notice the formatting of the values in the **Alumni Donation** field—there are no dollar signs to match the formatting in the **Amount** field; you will adjust the formatting of this field later.

When using a number, such as 0.5, in an expression, the values that display in the calculated field might not be formatted the same as the existing field that was part of the calculation.

Activity 2.28 | Creating a Second Calculated Field in a Query

In this activity, you will create a calculated field to determine the total value of each scholarship after the Alumni Association donates an additional 50% based on the amount awarded by various organizations. The query will answer the question, *What is the total value of each scholarship after the Alumni Association donates an additional 50%?*

1 Switch to **Design** view. In the **Field** row, right-click in the first empty column to display a shortcut menu, and then click **Zoom**.

2 In the **Zoom** dialog box, type **Total Scholarship:[Amount]+[Alumni Donation]** and then compare your screen with Figure 2.43.

Each existing field name—*Amount* and *Alumni Donation*—must be enclosed in separate pairs of brackets.

FIGURE 2.43

3 In the **Zoom** dialog box, click **OK**, and then **Run** the query.

The value in the *Total Scholarship* field is calculated by adding together the values in the Amount field and the Alumni Donation field. The values in the Total Scholarship field are formatted with dollar signs, commas, and decimal points, which is carried over from the Currency format in the Amount field.

Activity 2.29 | Formatting Calculated Fields

In this activity, you will format the calculated fields so that the values display in a consistent manner.

1 Switch to **Design** view. In the **Field** row, click in the **Alumni Donation** field name box.

2 Under **QUERY TOOLS**, on the **DESIGN tab**, in the **Show/Hide group**, click **Property Sheet**.

The Property Sheet displays on the right. Recall that a Property Sheet enables you to make precise changes to the properties—characteristics—of selected items, in this case, a field.

 ANOTHER WAY   In the design grid, on the Field row, right-click in the Alumni Donation field name box, and then click Properties.

3 In the **Property Sheet**, on the **General tab**, click **Format**. In the property setting box, click the **arrow**, and then compare your screen with Figure 2.44.

A list of available formats for the Alumni Donation field displays.

FIGURE 2.44

4 On the list, click **Currency**. In the **Property Sheet**, click **Decimal Places**. In the property setting box, click the **arrow**, and then click **0**.

5 In the design grid, in the **Field** row, click in the **Total Scholarship** field name. In the **Property Sheet**, set the **Decimal Places** property setting to **0**.

You do not need to set the Format setting to Currency as the field already displays with the currency symbol.

6 Close ☒ the **Property Sheet**, and then **Run** the query.

The Alumni Donation and Total Scholarship fields are formatted as Currency with 0 decimal places.

7 To the left of the **Student ID** field name, click **Select All** ☐. On the **HOME tab**, in the **Records group**, click **More**, and then click **Field Width**. In the **Column Width** dialog box, click **Best Fit**. Save 🖫 the query as **Lastname Firstname 2B Alumni Donations Query** and then click in any field to cancel the selection.

The field widths adjust to display fully the calculated field names.

8 Display the query results in **Print Preview**. On the **PRINT PREVIEW tab**, in the **Page Layout group**, click **Landscape**. Create a paper or electronic printout as directed, and then click **Close Print Preview**. Close ☒ the query.

Objective 13 | Calculate Statistics and Group Data in a Query

Video A2-13

You can use queries to perform statistical calculations known as *aggregate functions* on a group of records. For example, you can find the total or average amount for a group of records, or you can find the lowest or highest number in a group of records.

Activity 2.30 | Using the Min, Max, Avg, and Sum Functions in a Query

In this activity, you will use aggregate functions to find the lowest and highest scholarship amounts and the average and total scholarship amounts. The last query in this activity will answer the question, *What is the total dollar amount of all scholarships awarded?*

1 On the ribbon, click the **CREATE tab**, and then in the **Queries group**, click **Query Design**. In the **Show Table** dialog box, double-click your **2B Scholarships Awarded** table to add the table to the table area, **Close** the **Show Table** dialog box, and then resize the field list.

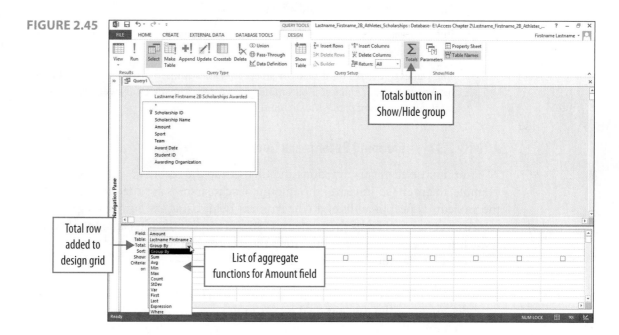

2 ▶ Add the **Amount** field to the design grid.

Include only the field to summarize in the design grid, so that the aggregate function is applied only to that field.

3 ▶ Under **QUERY TOOLS**, on the **DESIGN tab**, in the **Show/Hide group**, click **Totals** to add a **Total** row as the third row in the design grid. Notice that in the design grid, on the **Total** row under **Amount**, *Group By* displays.

Use the Total row to select an aggregate function for the selected field.

4 ▶ In the **Total** row under **Amount**, click in the box that displays *Group By*, and then click the **arrow** to display a list of aggregate functions. Compare your screen with Figure 2.45, and then take a moment to review the available aggregate functions and the purpose of each function as shown in Table 2.46.

FIGURE 2.45

FIGURE 2.46

AGGREGATE FUNCTIONS	
FUNCTION NAME	**PURPOSE**
Group By	Groups the records alphabetically, for example, groups by Sport.
Sum	Totals the values in a field.
Avg	Averages the values in a field.
Min	Locates the smallest value in a field.
Max	Locates the largest value in a field.
Count	Displays the number of records based on a field.
StDev	Calculates the standard deviation for the values in a field.
Var	Calculates the variance for the values in a field.
First	Displays the first value in a field or column.
Last	Displays the last value in a field or column.
Expression	Creates a calculated field that includes an aggregate function.
Where	Limits the records to those that match a condition specified in the Criteria row of a field.

5 ▶ In the list of functions, click **Min**, and then **Run** the query. Point to the right edge of the first column to display the pointer, and then double-click to apply Best Fit to the field.

> Access locates the minimum (smallest) value—*$100*—in the Amount field for all of the records in the 2B Scholarships Awarded table. The field name *MinOfAmount* is automatically created. This query answers the question, *What is the minimum (smallest) scholarship amount awarded to athletes?*

6 ▶ Switch to **Design** view. In the **Total** row under **Amount**, click the **arrow**, and then click **Max**. **Run** the query.

> The maximum (largest) value for a scholarship award amount is *$750.00*.

7 ▶ Switch to **Design** view. In the **Total** row, under **Amount**, click the **arrow**, and then click **Avg**. **Run** the query.

> The average scholarship award amount is *$358.33*.

8 ▶ Switch to **Design** view. In the **Total** row, under **Amount**, click the **arrow**, and then click **Sum**. **Run** the query.

> The values in the Amount field for all records are summed displaying a result of *$10,750.00*. The field name *SumOfAmount* is automatically created. The query answers the question, *What is the total dollar amount of all scholarships awarded?*

Activity 2.31 | Grouping Records in a Query

You can use aggregate functions and then group the records by the data in a field. For example, to group (summarize) the amount of scholarships awarded to each student, you include the Student ID field in addition to the Amount field. Using the Sum aggregate function, the records will be grouped by the Student ID so you can see the total amount of scholarships awarded to each student. Similarly, you can group the records by the Sport field so you can see the total amount of scholarships awarded for each sport.

1 ▶ Switch to **Design** view. From the field list, drag the **Student ID** field to the first column of the design grid—the **Amount** field moves to the second column. In the **Total** row, under **Student ID**, notice that *Group By* displays.

> This query will group—summarize—the records by Student ID and will calculate a total amount for each student.

2 ▶ **Run** the query, and then compare your screen with Figure 2.47.

> The query calculates the total amount of all scholarships for each student.

FIGURE 2.47

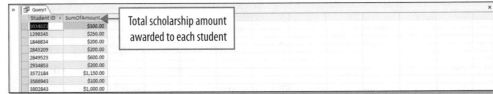

Total scholarship amount awarded to each student

3 ▶ Switch to **Design** view. In the design grid, above **Student ID**, point to the selection bar to display the ↓ pointer. Click to select the column, and then press Del to remove the **Student ID** field from the design grid.

4 ▶ From the field list, drag the **Sport** field to the first column in the design grid—the **Amount** field moves to the second column. Click in the **Sort** row under **Amount**, click the **arrow**, and then click **Descending**.

5 ▸ On the **DESIGN tab**, in the **Show/Hide group**, click **Property Sheet**. In the **Property Sheet**, set the **Decimal Places** property to **0**, and then **Close** ✗ the **Property Sheet**.

6 ▸ **Run** the query, and then compare your screen with Figure 2.48.

> Access groups—summarizes—the records by each sport and displays the groupings in descending order by the total amount of scholarships awarded for each sport. Basketball scholarships were awarded the largest total amount—*$3,500*—and Volleyball scholarships were awarded the smallest total amount—*$650*.

FIGURE 2.48

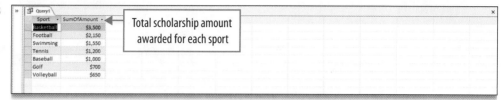

7 ▸ **Save** 🖫 the query as **Lastname Firstname 2B Total by Sport Query** and then display the query results in **Print Preview**. Create a paper or electronic printout as directed, click **Close Print Preview**, and then **Close** ✗ the query.

Objective 14 Create a Crosstab Query

Video A2-14

A **crosstab query** uses an aggregate function for data that can be grouped by two types of information, and then displays the data in a compact, spreadsheet-like format with column headings and row headings. A crosstab query always has at least one row heading, one column heading, and one summary field. Use a crosstab query to summarize a large amount of data in a compact space that is easy to read.

Activity 2.32 | Creating a Crosstab Query Using the Query Wizard

In this activity, you will create a crosstab query that displays the total amount of scholarships awarded for each sport and for each type of team—men's or women's.

1 ▸ On the ribbon, click the **CREATE tab**, and then in the **Queries group**, click **Query Wizard**.

2 ▸ In the **New Query** dialog box, click **Crosstab Query Wizard**, and then click **OK**.

3 ▸ In the **Crosstab Query Wizard**, click your **Table: 2B Scholarships Awarded**, and then click **Next**.

4 ▸ In the wizard under **Available Fields**, double-click **Sport** to move the field to the **Selected Fields** list and to group the scholarship amounts by the sports—the sports will display as row headings. Click **Next**, and then compare your screen with Figure 2.49.

> The sport names will be grouped and displayed as row headings, and you are prompted to select column headings.

FIGURE 2.49

5 In the wizard, in the field list, click **Team** to select the column headings. Click **Next**, and then compare your screen with Figure 2.50.

> The Team types—*Men's* and *Women's*—will display as column headings, and you are prompted to select a field to summarize.

FIGURE 2.50

6 In the wizard under **Fields**, click **Amount**. Under **Functions**, click **Sum**.

> The crosstab query will calculate the total scholarship amount for each sport and for each type of team.

7 Click **Next**. In the **What do you want to name your query?** box, select the existing text, type **Lastname Firstname 2B Sport and Team Crosstab Query** and then click **Finish**. Apply **Best Fit** to the datasheet, **Save** 🖫 the query, click in any field to cancel the selection, and then compare your screen with Figure 2.51.

> The field widths adjust to display fully the calculated field names.

FIGURE 2.51

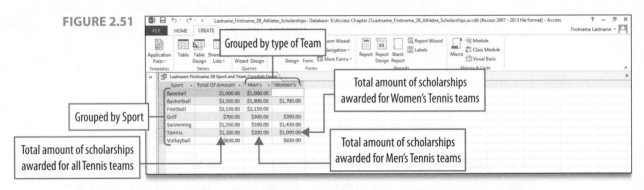

8 Display the query results in **Print Preview**. Create a paper or electronic printout as directed, click **Close Print Preview**, and then **Close** ☒ the query.

More Knowledge | **Creating a Crosstab Query Using Data from Two Related Tables**

To create a crosstab query using fields from more than one table, you must first create a select query with the fields from both tables, and then use the query as the data source for the crosstab query.

Video A2-15

A **parameter query** prompts you for criteria before running the query. For example, you might need to display the records for students who live in different cities serviced by Texas Lakes Community College. You can create a select query and enter the criteria for a city such as Austin, but when you open the query, only the records for those students who live in Austin will display. To find the students who live in Round Rock, you must open the query in Design view, change the criteria, and then run the query again.

A parameter query eliminates the need to change the design of a select query. You create a single query that prompts you to enter the city; the results are based upon the criteria you enter when prompted.

Activity 2.33 | Creating a Parameter Query with One Criteria

In this activity, you will create a parameter query that displays student athletes from a specified city in the areas serviced by Texas Lakes Community College.

1 On the **CREATE tab**, in the **Queries group**, click **Query Design**.

2 In the **Show Table** dialog box, double-click your **2B Athletes** table to add it to the table area, **Close** the **Show Table** dialog box, and then resize the field list.

3 Add the following fields to the design grid in the order given: **Last Name**, **First Name**, **Address**, **City**, **State**, and **Postal Code**.

4 Click in the **Sort** row under **Last Name**, click the **arrow**, and then click **Ascending**. Click in the **Sort** row under **First Name**, click the **arrow**, and then click **Ascending**.

5 In the **Criteria** row under **City**, type **[Enter a City]** and then press Enter. Compare your screen with Figure 2.52.

> The bracketed text indicates a *parameter*—a value that can be changed—rather than specific criteria.

FIGURE 2.52

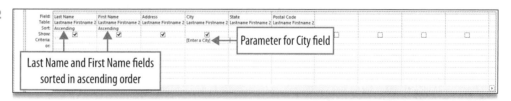

6 **Run** the query. In the **Enter Parameter Value** dialog box, type **austin** and then compare your screen with Figure 2.53.

> The Enter Parameter Value dialog box prompts you to *Enter a City*, which is the text enclosed in brackets that you entered in the Criteria row under City. The city you enter will be set as the criteria for the query. Because you are prompted for the criteria, you can reuse this query without having to edit the Criteria row in Design view. The value you enter is not case sensitive—you can enter *austin*, *Austin*, or *AUSTIN*.

FIGURE 2.53

Enter Parameter Value dialog box

Value entered—*austin*—will be used as criteria for City field

---

ALERT!   Did the Enter Parameter Value Dialog Box Not Display?

If the Enter Parameter Value dialog box does not display, you may have typed the parameter incorrectly in the design grid. Common errors include using parentheses or curly braces instead of brackets around the parameter text, which Access interprets as specific criteria, resulting in no records matching the criteria. If you type curly braces instead of brackets, the query will not run. To correct, display the query in Design view and correct the parameter entered in the Criteria row.

---

7 ▸ In the **Enter Parameter Value** dialog box, click **OK**.

Twenty-three students live in the city of Austin, and the records are sorted in alphabetical order by the Last Name field. If students have the same last name, those records will be sorted by the First Name field.

8 ▸ Save 🖫 the query as **Lastname Firstname 2B City Parameter Query** and then **Close** ✕ the query.

Recall that only the query design is saved; each time you open a query, it is run using the most up-to-date information from the data source.

9 ▸ Open ≫ the **Navigation Pane**. In the **Navigation Pane**, under your **2B Athletes** table, double-click your **2B City Parameter Query**. In the **Enter Parameter Value** dialog box, type **round rock** and then click **OK**. **Close** ≪ the **Navigation Pane**. Compare your screen with Figure 2.54.

Nine students live in the city of Round Rock. Every time you open a parameter query, you are prompted to enter criteria. You may have to apply Best Fit to the columns if all of the data in the fields does not display and you wish to print the query results—the length of the data in the fields changes as new records display depending upon the criteria entered.

FIGURE 2.54

Nine students live in Round Rock

10 ▸ Display the query results in **Print Preview**, and change the orientation to **Landscape**. Create a paper or electronic printout as directed, click **Close Print Preview**, and then **Close** ✕ the query.

11 ▶ **Open** » the **Navigation Pane**, and, if necessary increase the width of the pane so that all object names display fully. On the right side of the title bar, click **Close** ☒ to close the database and to exit Access. As directed by your instructor, submit your database and the paper or electronic printouts of the 11 objects—relationship report and 10 queries—that are the results of this project. Specifically, in this project, using your own name, you created the following database and printouts or electronic printouts:

1. Lastname_Firstname_2B_Athletes_Scholarships	Database file
2. Lastname Firstname 2B Relationships	Relationships Report (printout or electronic printout)
3. Lastname Firstname 2B $300 or More Query	Query (printout or electronic printout)
4. Lastname Firstname 2B Awards May-June Query	Query (printout or electronic printout)
5. Lastname Firstname 2B Football AND Over $500 Query	Query (printout or electronic printout)
6. Lastname Firstname 2B Volleyball OR Golf AND Over $200 Query	Query (printout or electronic printout)
7. Lastname Firstname 2B Tennis OR Swimming Query	Query (printout or electronic printout)
8. Lastname Firstname 2B Wildcard Query	Query (printout or electronic printout)
9. Lastname Firstname 2B Alumni Donations Query	Query (printout or electronic printout)
10. Lastname Firstname 2B Total by Sport Query	Query (printout or electronic printout)
11. Lastname Firstname 2B Sport and Team Crosstab Query	Query (printout or electronic printout)
12. Lastname Firstname 2B City Parameter Query	Query (printout or electronic printout - Round Rock)

More Knowledge   **Parameter Query Prompts**

Be sure that the parameter you enter in the Criteria row as a prompt is not the same as the field name. For example, do not use *[City]* as the parameter. Access interprets this as the field name of *City*. Recall that you entered a field name in brackets when creating a calculated field in a query. If you use a field name as the parameter, the Enter Parameter Value dialog box *will not* display, and all of the records *will* display.

The parameter should inform the individual running the query of the data required to display the correct results. If you want to use the field name by itself as the prompt, type a question mark at the end of the text; for example, *[City?]*. You cannot use a period, exclamation mark (!), curly braces ({ }), another set of brackets ([ ]), or the ampersand (&) as part of the parameter.

END | You have completed Project 2B

GO! with Office Web Apps

Objective	Export an Access Query to a PDF File, Save the PDF File to Google Drive, and Share the File

Access web apps are designed to work with Microsoft's SharePoint, a service for setting up websites to share and manage documents. Your college may not have SharePoint installed, so you will use other tools to share objects from your database so that you can work collaboratively with others. Recall that Google Docs is Google's free, web-based word processor, spreadsheet, slide show, form, and data storage service. Google Drive is Google's free file storage and sharing service. For Access, you can export a database object to an Excel worksheet, a PDF file, or a text file, and then save the file to Google Drive.

> **ALERT!** **Working with Web-Based Applications and Services**
>
> Computer programs and services on the web receive continuous updates and improvements. Thus, the steps to complete this web-based activity may differ from the ones shown. You can often look at the screens and the information presented to determine how to complete the activity.

Activity | **Exporting an Access Query to a PDF File, Saving the PDF file to Google Drive, and Sharing the File**

In this activity, you will export your 2B Sport and Team Crosstab Query object to a PDF file, upload your PDF file to Google Drive, and then share the file.

1 **Start** Access, navigate to your **Access Chapter 2** folder, and then **Open** your **2B_Athletes_Scholarships** database file. If necessary, on the Message Bar, click **Enable Content**. In the **Navigation Pane**, click your **2B Sport and Team Crosstab Query** object to select it—do not open it.

2 On the ribbon, click the **EXTERNAL DATA tab**, and then in the **Export group**, click **PDF or XPS**. In the **Publish as PDF or XPS** dialog box, navigate to your

Access Chapter 2 folder. Click in the **File name** box. Using your own name, type **Lastname_Firstname_AC_2B_Web** and then be sure that the **Open file after publishing** check box is selected, and the **Minimum size (publishing online)** option button is selected. Click **Publish**, and then compare your screen with Figure A.

The PDF file is created and opens in Windows 8 Reader, Adobe Reader, or Adobe Acrobat, depending on the software that is installed on your computer.

FIGURE A

Your 2B Sport and Team Crosstab Query exported as a PDF file and opened in Adobe Reader (yours may open in Windows Reader 8 or Adobe Acrobat)

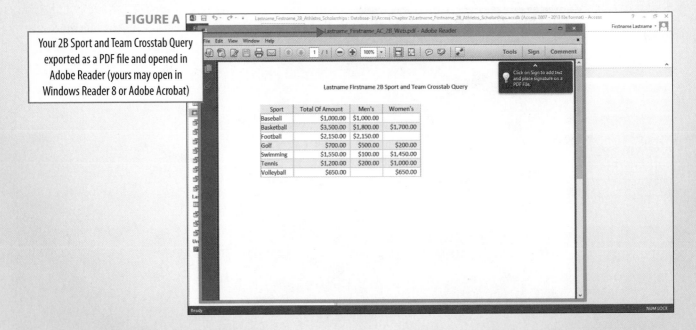

Lastname Firstname 2B Sport and Team Crosstab Query

Sport	Total Of Amount	Men's	Women's
Baseball	$1,000.00	$1,000.00	
Basketball	$3,500.00	$1,800.00	$1,700.00
Football	$2,150.00	$2,150.00	
Golf	$700.00	$500.00	$200.00
Swimming	$1,550.00	$100.00	$1,450.00
Tennis	$1,200.00	$200.00	$1,000.00
Volleyball	$650.00		$650.00

(GO! with Office Web Apps continues on the next page)

3 **Close** your **AC_2B_Web** file. In the **Export – PDF** dialog box, click **Close**, and then **Close** Access.

4 From the desktop, start Internet Explorer, navigate to **http://drive.google.com**, and sign in to your Google account, or create one.

5 Open your **GO! Web Projects** folder—or create and open this folder if necessary. Under **Drive**, to the right of **Create**, click **Upload** , and then click **Files**. In the **Choose File to Upload** dialog box, navigate to your **Access Chapter 2** folder, and then double-click your **AC_2B_Web** file to upload it to Google Drive. When the title bar of the message box indicates *Upload complete*, **Close** the message box.

6 Click your **AC_2B_Web** file to open the file in Google Drive. Notice that it displays as a PDF file on a separate tab in the browser window.

7 In the browser window, locate the tab for the PDF file, and then **Close** the tab to display your folder in Google Drive.

8 Right-click your **AC_2B_Web** file, point to **Share**, and then click **Share**.

9 In the **Sharing settings** dialog box, click in the **Add people** box, and then type your own email address that you use at your college. Click the **Can edit arrow**, and click **Can comment**. Click **Add message**, type **Please share your comments about the results of this crosstab query.** and then compare your screen with Figure B.

10 On your keyboard, press the ⊞ key, type **snip** and then click **Snipping Tool**. In the **Snipping Tool** dialog box, click the **New arrow**, and then click **Full-screen snip**.

11 On the **Snipping Tool** toolbar, click **Save Snip** 🖫. In the **Save As** dialog box, navigate to your **Access Chapter 2** folder. Click in the **File name** box, type **Lastname_Firstname_AC_2B_Web_Snip** and then be sure that the **Save as type** box displays **JPEG file**. Click **Save**, and then **Close** ☒ the **Snipping Tool** window.

12 In the **Sharing settings** dialog box, click **Share & save**. In the **Sharing settings** dialog box, click **Done**.

You can change who has access to the file in the Sharing settings dialog box. By default, the file is private and is shared only with specific people you have designated. You can grant access to anyone on the web or to anyone who has the link to this file.

13 In Google Drive, click your Google Drive name, and then click **Sign out**. **Close** your browser window.

14 If directed to submit a paper printout of your pdf and snip file, follow the directions given in the Note. As directed by your instructor, submit your pdf file and your snip file that are the results of this project. Your instructor may also request that you submit a copy of the email that was sent to you notifying you of the shared file.

NOTE | **Printing Your PDF and Snip .jpeg File**

Use File Explorer to navigate to your Access Chapter 2 folder. Locate and double-click your AC_2B_Web file. On the toolbar, click the Print file button. Then Close the Windows 8 Reader, Adobe Reader, or Adobe Acrobat window. In your Access Chapter 2 folder, locate and double-click your AC_2B_Web_Snip file. If this is the first time you have tried to open a .jpeg file, you will be asked to identify a program. If you are not sure which program to use, select Windows Photo Viewer. From the ribbon, menu bar, or toolbar, click the Print command, and then Close the program window.

FIGURE B

Andrew Rodriguez / Fotolia; FotolEdhar/ Fotolia; apops/ Fotolia; Yuri Arcurs/ Fotolia

Sharing Your Calendar in Office 365: With Office 365, you set up your Calendar in Outlook—either in Outlook Web App or on the desktop app—and then you can share your calendar, add appointments and meetings, and see your calendar from anywhere that you have Internet access. Recall that Outlook Web App and the Outlook desktop app work seamlessly together. When you use the desktop app, you have some additional features that are not available in Outlook Web App, but any information you add is available in either app. You will be able to view your calendar—and use email—from your smartphone or from anywhere you have an Internet connection.

In an Office 365 environment, the most important thing to do with your calendar is to share it with others. Recall that Office 365 is specifically designed to help teams work together, and the first step to working together successfully is to share as much information as possible to facilitate good communication.

When you create an appointment in your calendar, Outlook displays one of four indicators associated with your availability for that date and time: Busy, Free, Tentative, or Out of Office. This is referred to as your *free/busy information*. Outlook's default setting for all appointments is Busy. The free/busy indicators also display when others view your calendar on the Office 365 shared Exchange server. Recall that Exchange Server is Microsoft's system for sharing Outlook information among members on a network. Your free/busy schedule is shared automatically with all other users.

In an Exchange Online environment, you can share your calendar with other Exchange Online users in your organization. Additionally, you can publish your calendar to the Internet and other people so they can access it. You could even share your calendar with a customer or client.

Activity | Sharing Calendars

This group project relates to the **Bell Orchid Hotels**. If your instructor assigns this project to your class, you can expect to use your **Outlook Calendar** in **Office 365 Exchange Online** to set meeting times for the following tasks for this chapter:

- If you are in the **Accounting Group**, you and your teammates will set meeting times to sort, filter, and create queries for the Stockholders database you created in Chapter 1.

- If you are in the **Engineering Group**, you and your teammates will set meeting times to sort, filter, and create queries for the Subcontractors database you created in Chapter 1.

- If you are in the **Food and Beverage Group**, you and your teammates will set meeting times to sort, filter, and create queries for the Banquet Clients database you created in Chapter 1.

- If you are in the **Human Resources Group**, you and your teammates will set meeting times to sort, filter, and create queries for the Employee database you created in Chapter 1.

- If you are in the **Operations Group**, you and your teammates will set meeting times to sort, filter, and create queries for the Guests database you created in Chapter 1.

- If you are in the **Sales and Marketing Group**, you and your teammates will set meeting times to sort, filter, and create queries for the Associations database you created in Chapter 1.

FIGURE A

END OF CHAPTER

SUMMARY

Table relationships are created by joining the common fields in tables and provide a means for you to extract information from multiple tables when you create queries, forms, and reports.

Queries are created to answer questions and to extract information from your database tables; saving a query with your database saves you time when you need to answer the question many times.

Queries range from simple queries where you ask a single question to complex queries where you use compound criteria, wildcard characters, logical operators, and create calculated fields.

A crosstab query displays information grouped by two fields that is an easy way to display complex data, and a parameter query prompts you to enter the criteria when you open or run the query.

GO! LEARN IT ONLINE

Review the concepts and key terms in this chapter by completing these online challenges, which you can find at **www.pearsonhighered.com/go**.

Matching and Multiple Choice:
Answer matching and multiple choice questions to test what you learned in this chapter. MyITLab®

Crossword Puzzle:
Spell out the words that match the numbered clues, and put them in the puzzle squares.

Flipboard:
Flip through the definitions of the key terms in this chapter and match them with the correct term.

GO! FOR JOB SUCCESS

Video: Making Ethical Choices

Your instructor may assign this video to your class, and then ask you to think about, or discuss with your classmates, these questions:

FotolEdhar / Fotolia

Which behaviors in this video do you think were unethical?

Is it unethical to "borrow" things from your employer? Why? What would you do if you saw this behavior going on?

What do you think an employer could do to prevent unethical behavior?

Your instructor may assign one or more of these projects to help you review the chapter and assess your mastery and understanding of the chapter.

	Review and Assessment Guide for Access Chapter 2		
Project	**Apply Skills from These Chapter Objectives**	**Project Type**	**Project Location**
2C	Objectives 1-7 from Project 2A	**2C Skills Review** A guided review of the skills from Project 2A.	On the following pages
2D	Objectives 8-15 from Project 2B	**2D Skills Review** A guided review of the skills from Project 2B.	On the following pages
2E	Objectives 1-7 from Project 2A	**2E Mastery (Grader Project)** A demonstration of your mastery of the skills in Project 2A with extensive decision making.	In MyITLab and on the following pages
2F	Objectives 8-15 from Project 2B	**2F Mastery (Grader Project)** A demonstration of your mastery of the skills in Project 2B with extensive decision making.	In MyITLab and on the following pages
2G	Objectives 1-15 from Projects 2A and 2B	**2G Mastery (Grader Project)** A demonstration of your mastery of the skills in Projects 2A and 2B with extensive decision making.	In MyITLab and on the following pages
2H	Combination of Objectives from Projects 2A and 2B	**2H GO! Fix It** A demonstration of your mastery of the skills in Projects 2A and 2B by creating a correct result from a document that contains errors you must find.	Online
2I	Combination of Objectives from Projects 2A and 2B	**2I GO! Make It** A demonstration of your mastery of the skills in Projects 2A and 2B by creating a result from a supplied picture.	Online
2J	Combination of Objectives from Projects 2A and 2B	**2J GO! Solve It** A demonstration of your mastery of the skills in Projects 2A and 2B, your decision-making skills, and your critical thinking skills. A task-specific rubric helps you self-assess your result.	Online
2K	Combination of Objectives from Projects 2A and 2B	**2K GO! Solve It** A demonstration of your mastery of the skills in Projects 2A and 2B, your decision-making skills, and your critical thinking skills. A task-specific rubric helps you self-assess your result.	On the following pages
2L	Combination of Objectives from Projects 2A and 2B	**2L GO! Think** A demonstration of your understanding of the chapter concepts applied in a manner that you would outside of college. An analytic rubric helps you and your instructor grade the quality of your work by comparing it to the work an expert in the discipline would create.	On the following pages
2M	Combination of Objectives from Projects 2A and 2B	**2M GO! Think** A demonstration of your understanding of the chapter concepts applied in a manner that you would outside of college. An analytic rubric helps you and your instructor grade the quality of your work by comparing it to the work an expert in the discipline would create.	Online
2N	Combination of Objectives from Projects 2A and 2B	**2N You and GO!** A demonstration of your understanding of the chapter concepts applied in a manner that you would in a personal situation. An analytic rubric helps you and your instructor grade the quality of your work.	Online
2O	Combination of Objectives from Projects 2A and 2B	**2O Cumulative Group Project for Access Chapter 2** A demonstration of your understanding of concepts and your ability to work collaboratively in a group role-playing assessment, requiring both collaboration and self-management.	Online

GLOSSARY

GLOSSARY OF CHAPTER KEY TERMS

Aggregate functions Calculations such as Min, Max, Avg, and Sum that are performed on a group of records.

AND condition A compound criteria used to display records that match all parts of the specified criteria.

Ascending order A sorting order that arranges text alphabetically (A to Z) and numbers from the lowest number to the highest number.

Between … And operator A comparison operator that looks for values within a range.

Calculated field A field that stores the value of a mathematical operation.

Cascade Delete Related Records A cascade option that enables you to delete a record in a table on the *one* side of the relationship and also delete all of the related records in related tables.

Cascade options Relationship options that enable you to update records in related tables when referential integrity is enforced.

Cascade Update Related Fields A cascade option that enables you to change the data in the primary key field in the table on the *one* side of the relationship and update that change to any fields storing that same data in related tables.

Comparison operators Symbols that are used to evaluate data in the field to determine if it is the same (=), greater than (>), less than (<), or in between a range of values as specified by the criteria.

Compound criteria Multiple conditions in a query or filter.

Criteria Conditions in a query that identify the specific records you are looking for.

Crosstab query A query that uses an aggregate function for data that can be grouped by two types of information and displays the data in a compact, spreadsheet-like format with column headings and row headings.

Data source The table or tables from which a form, query, or report retrieves its data.

Descending order A sorting order that arranges text in reverse alphabetical order (Z to A) and numbers from the highest number to the lowest number.

Design grid The lower area of the query window that displays the design of the query.

Expression A formula.

Field list A list of field names in a table.

Foreign key The field that is included in the related table so the field can be joined with the primary key in another table for the purpose of creating a relationship.

Free/Busy information In the Outlook calendar, one of four indicators—Busy, Free, Tentative, or Out of Office—associated with your availability for a specific date and time.

Innermost sort field When sorting on multiple fields in Datasheet view, the field that is used for the second level of sorting.

Is Not Null A criteria that searches for fields that are not empty.

Is Null A criteria that searches for fields that are empty.

Join line In the Relationships window, the line joining two tables that visually indicates the common fields and the type of relationship.

Logical operators Operators that are used to evaluate data to determine if a condition is met (true) or not met (false). With two criteria, AND requires that both conditions be met and OR requires that either condition be met for a record to display in the query results.

Message Bar The area directly below the ribbon that displays information such as security alerts when there is potentially unsafe, active content in an Office document that you open.

One-to-many relationship A relationship between two tables where one record in the first table corresponds to many records in the second table—the most common type of relationship in Access.

OR condition A compound criteria used to display records that match at least one of the specified criteria.

Outermost sort field When sorting on multiple fields in Datasheet view, the field that is used for the first level of sorting.

Parameter A value that can be changed.

Parameter query A query that prompts you for criteria before running the query.

Referential integrity A set of rules that Access uses to ensure that the data between related tables is valid.

Relationship An association that you establish between two tables based on common fields.

Run The process in which Access looks at the records in the table(s) included in the query design, finds the records that match the specified criteria, and then displays the records in a datasheet; only the fields included in the query design display.

Sorting The process of arranging data in a specific order based on the value in a field.

Subdatasheet A format for displaying related records when you click ⊞ next to a record in a table on the *one* side of the relationship.

Subset A portion of the total records available.

Table area The upper area of the query window that displays field lists for the tables that are used in a query.

Text string A sequence of characters.

Trust Center An area of Access where you can view the security and privacy settings for your Access installation.

Wildcard character In a query, a character that serves as a placeholder for one or more unknown characters in criteria; an asterisk (*) represents one or more unknown characters, and a question mark (?) represents a single unknown character.

CHAPTER REVIEW

Apply 2A skills from these Objectives:

1 Open and Save an Existing Database
2 Create Table Relationships
3 Sort Records in a Table
4 Create a Query in Design View
5 Create a New Query from an Existing Query
6 Sort Query Results
7 Specify Criteria in a Query

Skills Review | Project 2C Freshman Orientation

In the following Skills Review, you will assist Dr. Wendy Bowie, the director of counseling at the Southwest Campus, in using her database to answer several questions about the freshman orientation sessions that will be held prior to class registration. Your completed database objects will look similar to Figure 2.55.

PROJECT FILES

For Project 2C, you will need the following file:

a02C_Freshman_Orientation

You will save your database as:

Lastname_Firstname_2C_Freshman_Orientation

PROJECT RESULTS

FIGURE 2.55

(Project 2C Freshman Orientation continues on the next page)

1 **Start** Access. In the Access opening screen, click **Open Other Files**. Under **Open**, click **Computer**. Under **Recent Folders**, if displayed, click the location where your student data files are stored; otherwise, click **Browse** and then navigate to the location where your student data files are stored. Double-click **a02C_Freshman_Orientation** to open the database.

a. On the ribbon, click the **FILE tab**, and then click **Save As**. Under **File Types**, be sure **Save Database As** is selected. On the right, under **Database File Types**, be sure **Access Database** is selected, and then click **Save As**.

b. In the **Save As** dialog box, navigate to your **Access Chapter 2** folder. Click in the **File name** box, type **Lastname_Firstname_2C_Freshman_Orientation** and then press [Enter]. On the **Message Bar**, click **Enable Content**.

c. In the **Navigation Pane**, right-click **2C New Students**, and then click **Rename**. With the table name selected and using your own name, type **Lastname Firstname 2C New Students** and then press [Enter]. **Rename** the 2C Orientation Sessions table to **Lastname Firstname 2C Orientation Sessions** and then point to the right edge of the **Navigation Pane** to display the [↔] pointer. Drag to the right to increase the width of the pane until both tables names display fully.

2 In the **Navigation Pane**, double-click your 2C New Students table to open it in the object window, and examine the fields in the table. Double-click your 2C Orientation Sessions table, and examine the fields in the table. In the object window, right-click either **object tab**, and then click **Close All** to close both tables. **Close** the **Navigation Pane**.

a. On the ribbon, click the **DATABASE TOOLS tab**, and then in the **Relationships group**, click **Relationships**. Point to the title bar of the **Show Table** dialog box, and then drag downward and slightly to the right to move the dialog box away from the top of the **Relationships** window.

b. In the **Show Table** dialog box, click your 2C Orientation Sessions table, and then click **Add**. In the **Show Table** dialog box, double-click your **2C New Students** table to add it to the **Relationships** window. In the **Show Table** dialog box, click **Close**.

c. In the **2C New Students** field list—the field list on the right—point to the title bar to display the [⬚] pointer, and then drag the field list to the right until there are approximately three inches of space between the field lists. In the **2C New Students** field list, point to the lower right corner of the field list to display the [⬚] pointer, and then drag downward and to the right to resize the field list and display all of the field names and the entire table name. Use the same technique to resize the **2C Orientation Sessions** field list—the field list on the left—so that the table name displays fully.

d. In the **2C Orientation Sessions** field list, point to **Orientation ID**, and then drag the field name downward and to the right into the **2C New Students** field list until the [⬚] pointer's arrow is on top of **Orientation ID**. Release the mouse button to display the **Edit Relationships** dialog box. Drag the **Edit Relationships** dialog box downward below the two field lists.

e. In the **Edit Relationships** dialog box, click to select the **Enforce Referential Integrity** check box, the **Cascade Update Related Fields** check box, and the **Cascade Delete Related Records** check box. In the **Edit Relationships** dialog box, click **Create** to create a one-to-many relationship—*one* orientation session can be scheduled for *many* new students.

f. Under **RELATIONSHIP TOOLS**, on the **DESIGN tab**, in the **Tools group**, click **Relationship Report**. On the **PRINT PREVIEW tab**, in the **Page Size group**, click **Margins**, and then click **Normal**. Create a paper or electronic printout as directed. On the **Quick Access Toolbar**, click **Save**. In the **Save As** dialog box, click **OK** to accept the default report name. In the object window, **Close** the report, and then **Close** the **Relationships** window.

g. **Open** the **Navigation Pane**, double-click your 2C Orientation Sessions table to open it in the object window, and then **Close** the **Navigation Pane**. On the left side of the last record—*Orientation ID* of *O-1*—click [⊞] to display the subdatasheet, and notice that 13 new students are scheduled to attend this orientation session. Click [⊟] to collapse the subdatasheet.

(Project 2C Freshman Orientation continues on the next page)

CHAPTER REVIEW

h. In the last record, in the **Orientation ID** field, select the existing data—*O-1*—and then type **O-001**—the first character is the letter *O* followed by a hyphen, two zeros, and the number *1*— to make the data consistent with the Orientation IDs of the other sessions. The 13 related records in your 2C New Students table are updated with the new Orientation ID because you selected **Cascade Update Related Fields** in the **Edit Relationships** dialog box.

i. Display the subdatasheet for the record with an **Orientation ID** of **O-010**, and notice that one student—*Student ID* of *8273485*—is scheduled for this orientation session. Collapse the subdatasheet. To the left of the record, point to the record selector box to display the ➡ pointer, and then click to select the record. On the **HOME tab**, in the **Records group**, click **Delete**. In the message box, click **Yes** to delete this record and the related student record in the **2C New Students** table.

3 In the **Date** field, click in any record. On the **HOME tab**, in the **Sort & Filter group**, click **Ascending** to sort the records by the date. In the field names row, click the **Room arrow**, and then click **Sort Z to A** to sort the rooms from Room 203 to Room 201. The records are sorted first by the **Room** field and then by the **Date** field. On the **FILE tab**, click **Print**, and then click **Print Preview**. Create a paper or electronic printout as directed, and then click **Close Print Preview**. On the **HOME tab**, in the **Sort & Filter group**, click **Remove Sort**. **Close** the table, and in the message box, click **No;** you do not need to save any design changes to the table.

4 On the ribbon, click the **CREATE tab**, and then in the **Queries group**, click **Query Design**. In the **Show Table** dialog box, double-click your **2C Orientation Sessions** table, and then **Close** the **Show Table** dialog box. Point to the lower right corner of the field list to display the ⬂ pointer, and then drag downward and to the right to resize the field list, displaying all of the field names and the entire table name.

a. In the field list, double-click **Orientation ID** to add the field to the first column in the design grid. In the field list, point to **Date**, and then drag the field name down into the design grid until the ⬂ pointer displays in the **Field** row in the second

column, and then release the mouse button. In the design grid, in the **Field** row, click in the third column, click the **arrow**, and then click **Day of Week** to add the field to the design grid. Using one of the three techniques you just practiced, add the **Time** field to the fourth column and the **Room** field to the fifth column in the design grid.

b. Under **QUERY TOOLS**, on the **DESIGN tab**, in the **Results group**, click **Run**. This query answers the question, *What is the Orientation ID, date, day of week, time, and room for all of the orientation sessions in the 2C Orientation Sessions table?*

c. On the **Quick Access Toolbar**, click **Save**. In the **Save As** dialog box, type **Lastname Firstname 2C All Sessions Query** and then click **OK**. On the ribbon, click the **FILE tab**, click **Print**, and then click **Print Preview**. Create a paper or electronic printout as directed, and then click **Close Print Preview**. **Close** your **2C All Sessions Query**, and then **Open** the **Navigation Pane**.

5 In the **Navigation Pane**, right-click your **2C All Sessions Query** object, and then click **Copy**. In the **Navigation Pane**, point to a blank area, right-click, and then click **Paste**. In the **Paste As** dialog box, type **Lastname Firstname 2C Day of Week Query** and then click **OK** to create a new query based on an existing query.

a. In the **Navigation Pane**, right click your **2C Day of Week Query** object, and then click **Design View**. **Close** the **Navigation Pane**. In the design grid, point to the thin gray selection bar above the **Orientation ID** field name to display the ⬇ pointer, click to select the column, and then press [Del].

b. Point to the selection bar above the **Day of Week** field name to display the ⬋ pointer, and then drag to the left until a dark vertical line displays on the left side of the **Date** column. Release the mouse button to position the **Day of Week** field in the first column.

c. **Run** the query. The query results display four fields. This query answers the question, *What is the day of week, date, time, and room for every orientation session in the 2C Orientation Sessions table?*

(Project 2C Freshman Orientation continues on the next page)

CHAPTER REVIEW

d. On the **FILE tab**, click **Print**, and then click **Print Preview**. Create a paper or electronic printout as directed, and then click **Close Print Preview**. **Close** the query, and in the message box, click **Yes** to save the changes to the design—you deleted one field and moved another field. **Open** the **Navigation Pane**.

6 In the **Navigation Pane**, right-click your **2C Day of Week Query** object, and then click **Copy**. In the **Navigation Pane**, point to a blank area, right-click, and then click **Paste**. In the **Paste As** dialog box, type **Lastname Firstname 2C Sessions Sort Query** and then click **OK** to create a new query based on an existing query. Increase the width of the **Navigation Pane** so that the names of all of the objects display fully.

a. In the **Navigation Pane**, right-click your **2C Sessions Sort Query** click **Design View**, and then **Close** the **Navigation Pane**. In the design grid, drag the **Room** field to the left of the **Day of Week** field to position it in the first column. In the design grid, click in the **Sort** row under **Room**, click the **arrow**, and then click **Descending**. Click in the **Sort** row under **Date**, click the **arrow**, and then click **Ascending**.

b. **Run** the query. This query answers the question, *For every session, within each room (with the Room field sorted in descending order), what is the day of week, date (with the Date field sorted in ascending order), and time?*

c. Display the query results in **Print Preview**, create a paper or electronic printout as directed, and then click **Close Print Preview**. **Close** the query, and in the message box, click **Yes** to save the changes to the query design.

7 On the ribbon, click the **CREATE tab**, and then in the **Queries group**, click **Query Design**. In the **Show Table** dialog box, double-click your **2C New Students** table to add it to the table area, and then **Close** the **Show Table** dialog box. Resize the field list to display all of the field names and the entire table name. Add the following fields to the design grid in the order given: **Student ID**, **Last Name**, **First Name**, and **Orientation ID**.

a. In the design grid, click in the **Criteria** row under **Orientation ID**, type **O-001**—the first character is the letter *O* followed by a hyphen, two zeros, and the number *1*—and then press [Enter].

b. **Run** the query to display 13 records that meet the specified criteria—records that have *O-001* in the *Orientation ID* field. **Save** the query as **Lastname Firstname 2C First Session Query** and then display the query results in **Print Preview**. Create a paper or electronic printout as directed, click **Close Print Preview**, and then **Close** the query.

c. On the ribbon, click the **CREATE tab**, and then in the **Queries group**, click **Query Design**. In the **Show Table** dialog box, double-click your **2C New Students** table to add it to the table area, and then **Close** the **Show Table** dialog box. Resize the field list, and then add the following fields to the design grid in the order given: **Student ID**, **First Name**, **Last Name**, **Phone Number**, **Email Address**, and **City**. Click in the **Criteria** row under **City**, type **dripping springs** and then press [Enter].

d. **Run** the query to display the five new students who live in *Dripping Springs*. Switch to **Design** view. In the design grid, in the **Show** row under **City**, click to clear the check box. Recall that if all of the results use the same criteria, such as *dripping springs*, it is not necessary to display that field in the query results. **Run** the query again. **Save** the query as **Lastname Firstname 2C Dripping Springs Query** and then display the query results in **Print Preview**. Create a paper or electronic printout as directed, click **Close Print Preview**, and then **Close** the query.

e. On the ribbon, click the **CREATE tab**, and then in the **Queries group**, click **Query Design**. In the **Show Table** dialog box, double-click your **2C New Students** table to add it to the table area, and then **Close** the **Show Table** dialog box. Resize the field list, and then add the following fields to the design grid in the order given: **Student ID**, **Last Name**, **First Name**, **Email Address**, **Phone Number**, and **Orientation ID**. Click in the **Sort** row under **Last Name**, click the **arrow**, and then click **Ascending**. Click in the **Sort** row under **First Name**, click the **arrow**, and then click **Ascending**. Click in the **Criteria** row under **Orientation ID**, type **is null** and then press [Enter].

(Project 2C Freshman Orientation continues on the next page)

CHAPTER REVIEW

f. **Run** the query to display the three new students who have not signed up for an orientation session. **Save** the query as **Lastname Firstname 2C Missing Orientation ID Query** and then display the query results in **Print Preview**. On the **PRINT PREVIEW** tab, in the **Page Size group**, click **Margins**, and then click **Normal**. Create a paper or electronic printout as directed, click **Close Print Preview**, and then **Close** the query.

g. **Open** the **Navigation Pane**. If necessary, increase the width of the pane so that all object names display fully. On the right side of the title bar, click **Close** to close the database and to exit Access. As directed by your instructor, submit your database and the paper or electronic printouts of the eight objects—relationship report, sorted table, and six queries—that are the results of this project. Specifically, in this project, using your own name, you created the following database and printouts or electronic printouts:

1. Lastname_Firstname_2C_Freshman_Orientation	Database file
2. Relationships for Lastname_Firstname_2C_Freshman_Orientation	Relationships Report (printout or electronic printout)
3. Lastname Firstname 2C Orientation Sessions table sorted (not saved)	Table sorted (printout or electronic printout)
4. Lastname Firstname 2C All Sessions Query	Query (printout or electronic printout)
5. Lastname Firstname 2C Day of Week Query	Query (printout or electronic printout)
6. Lastname Firstname 2C Sessions Sort Query	Query (printout or electronic printout)
7. Lastname Firstname 2C First Session Query	Query (printout or electronic printout)
8. Lastname Firstname 2C Dripping Springs Query	Query (printout or electronic printout)
9. Lastname Firstname 2C Missing Orientation ID Query	Query (printout or electronic printout)

END | You have completed Project 2C

CHAPTER REVIEW

Apply 2B skills from these Objectives:

8 Specify Numeric Criteria in a Query

9 Use Compound Criteria in a Query

10 Create a Query Based on More Than One Table

11 Use Wildcards in a Query

12 Create Calculated Fields in a Query

13 Calculate Statistics and Group Data in a Query

14 Create a Crosstab Query

15 Create a Parameter Query

Skills Review | Project 2D Club Fundraisers

In the following Skills Review, you will assist Dr. Michael Bransford, the student activities director for Texas Lakes Community College, in answering his questions about fundraisers, clubs, donations, dates of fundraiser events, and fundraiser locations. Your completed database objects will look similar to Figure 2.56.

PROJECT FILES

For Project 2D, you will need the following files:

a02D_Club_Fundraisers

a02D_Clubs (Excel workbook)

You will save your database as:

Lastname_Firstname_2D_Club_Fundraisers

PROJECT RESULTS

FIGURE 2.56

(Project 2D Club Fundraisers continues on the next page)

CHAPTER REVIEW

1 ▶ **Start** Access. In the Access opening screen, click **Open Other Files**. Under **Open**, click **Computer**. Under **Recent Folders**, if displayed, click the location where your student data files are stored; otherwise, click **Browse** and then navigate to the location where your student data files are stored. Double-click **a02D_Club_Fundraisers** to open the database.

a. On the ribbon, click the **FILE tab**, and then click **Save As**. Under **File Types**, be sure **Save Database As** is selected. On the right, under **Database File Types**, be sure **Access Database** is selected, and then at the bottom of the screen, click **Save As**. In the **Save As** dialog box, navigate to your **Access Chapter 2** folder. Click in the **File name** box, type **Lastname_ Firstname_2D_Club_Fundraisers** and then press Enter. On the **Message Bar**, click **Enable Content**.

b. In the **Navigation Pane**, right-click **2D Fundraisers**, click **Rename**, type **Lastname Firstname 2D Fundraisers** and then press Enter. Increase the width of the **Navigation Pane** to display the entire table name. Double-click the table name to open it, examine the fields in the table, and then **Close** the table.

c. On the ribbon, click the **EXTERNAL DATA tab**, and then in the **Import & Link group**, click **Excel**. In the **Get External Data – Excel Spreadsheet** dialog box, to the right of the **File name** box, click **Browse**. In the **File Open** dialog box, navigate to your student data files, and then double-click **a02D_Clubs**. Be sure that the **Import the source data into a new table in the current database** option button is selected, and then click **OK**.

d. In the upper left area of the wizard, select the **First Row Contains Column Headings** check box, click **Next**, and then click **Next** again. In the wizard, click the **Choose my own primary key** option button, be sure that **Club ID** displays, and then click **Next**. With the text selected in the **Import to Table** box and using your own name, type **Lastname Firstname 2D Clubs**, and then click **Finish**. In the **Get External Data – Excel Spreadsheet** dialog box, click **Close**.

e. In the **Navigation Pane**, right-click your **2D Clubs** table, and then click **Design View**. **Close** the **Navigation Pane**. In the **Field Name** column, click

Club ID. In the **Field Properties** area, click **Field Size**, type **8** and then press Enter. Under **TABLE TOOLS**, on the **DESIGN tab**, in the **Views group**, click the upper portion of the **View** button to switch to **Datasheet** view. In the message box, click **Yes** to save the design changes. In the second message box, click **Yes**—no data will be lost. Examine the fields and data in the table. To the left of the **Club ID** field name, click **Select All**. On the **HOME tab**, in the **Records group**, click **More**, and then click **Field Width**. In the **Column Width** dialog box, click **Best Fit**. **Save** the table, click in any record to cancel the selection, and then **Close** the table.

f. On the ribbon, click the **DATABASE TOOLS tab**, and then in the **Relationships group**, click **Relationships**. In the **Show Table** dialog box, double-click your **2D Clubs** table, and then double-click your **2D Fundraisers** table to add both tables to the **Relationships** window. **Close** the **Show Table** dialog box. Point to the title bar of the field list on the right, and drag the field list to the right until there are approximately two inches of space between the field lists. By dragging the lower right corner of the field list, resize each field list to display all of the field names and the entire table name.

g. In the **2D Clubs** field list, point to **Club ID**, drag the field name into the **2D Fundraisers** table on top of **Club ID**, and then release the mouse button. Point to the title bar of the **Edit Relationships** dialog box, and then drag it downward below the two field lists. In the **Edit Relationships** dialog box, select the **Enforce Referential Integrity** check box, the **Cascade Update Related Fields** check box, the **Cascade Delete Related Records** check box, and then click **Create**. A *one-to-many* relationship is established; *one* student club can raise money for *many* fundraising events.

h. Under **RELATIONSHIP TOOLS**, on the **DESIGN tab**, in the **Tools group**, click **Relationship Report**. On the **PRINT PREVIEW tab**, in the **Page Size group**, click **Margins**, and then click **Normal**. **Save** the report as **Lastname Firstname 2D Relationships** and then create a paper or electronic printout as directed. In the object window, right-click either **object tab**, and then click **Close All**.

(Project 2D Club Fundraisers continues on the next page)

2 On the ribbon, click the **CREATE tab**. In the **Queries group**, click **Query Design**. In the **Show Table** dialog box, double-click your **2D Fundraisers** table to add it to the table area, and then **Close** the **Show Table** dialog box. Resize the field list. Add the following fields to the design grid in the order given: **Fundraiser Name**, **Donation**, and **Fundraiser Location**.

a. Click in the **Sort** row under **Fundraiser Name**, click the **arrow**, and then click **Ascending**. Click in the **Criteria** row under **Donation**, type **>=1000** and then press [Enter]. **Run** the query, and notice that seven records match the criteria. This query answers the question, *Where was each fundraiser held (in alphabetical order by the Fundraiser Name field) for fundraisers with a donation greater than or equal to $1,000?*

b. **Save** the query as **Lastname Firstname 2D $1000 or More Donation Query** and then display the query results in **Print Preview**. Create a paper or electronic printout as directed, click **Close Print preview**, and then **Close** your query object. **Open** the **Navigation Pane**.

c. In the **Navigation Pane**, right-click your **2D $1000 or More Donation Query** object, and then click **Copy**. In the **Navigation Pane**, point to a blank area, right-click, and then click **Paste**. In the **Paste As** dialog box, type **Lastname Firstname 2D Fundraisers June-July Query** and then click **OK**. In the **Navigation Pane**, right-click your **2D Fundraisers June-July Query** object, and then click **Design View**. **Close** the **Navigation Pane**.

d. In the **2D Fundraisers** field list, double-click **Date** to add it to the fourth column in the design grid. Click in the **Sort** row under **Fundraiser Name**, click the **arrow**, and then click (**not sorted**). Click in the **Sort** row under **Date**, click the **arrow**, and then click **Ascending**.

e. In the **Criteria** row under **Donation**, select the existing criteria of *>=1000*, and then press [Del] so that the query results are not restricted by a monetary value. Click in the **Criteria** row under **Date**, type **between 6/1/18 and 7/31/18** and then press [Enter]. **Run** the query, and notice that four records match the criteria. This query answers the question, *What is the fundraiser name, donation, fundraiser location, and date (in chronological order) for events held between June 1, 2018 and July 31, 2018?*

f. Display the query results in **Print Preview**, create a paper or electronic printout as directed, and then click **Close Print Preview**. **Close** the query, and in the message box, click **Yes** to save the changes to the query design.

3 On the ribbon, click the **CREATE tab**, and in the **Queries group**, click **Query Design**. In the **Show Table** dialog box, double-click your **2D Fundraisers** table to add it to the table area, and then **Close** the **Show Table** dialog box. Resize the field list. Add the following fields to the design grid in the order given: **Fundraiser Name**, **Fundraiser Location**, **Donation**, and **Club ID**.

a. Click in the **Sort** row under **Fundraiser Name**, click the **arrow**, and then click **Ascending**. Click in the **Criteria** row under **Club ID**, type **club-109** and then press [Enter]. Click in the **Criteria** row under **Donation**, type **<=1000** and then press [Enter]. **Run** the query, and notice that two records match the criteria. Switch back to **Design** view, and in the **Show** row under **Club ID**, clear the check box. **Run** the query again. This query answers the question, *Which fundraiser events with their locations listed had donations raised by CLUB-109 of $1,000 or less?*

b. **Save** the query as **Lastname Firstname 2D CLUB-109 Low Donations Query** and then display the query results in **Print Preview**. Create a paper or electronic printout as directed, click **Close Print Preview**, and then **Close** the query.

c. On the ribbon, click the **CREATE tab**, and then in the **Queries group**, click **Query Design**. In the **Show Table** dialog box, double-click your **2D Fundraisers** table to add it to the table area, and then **Close** the **Show Table** dialog box. Resize the field list. Add the following fields to the design grid in the order given: **Club ID**, **Fundraiser Name**, **Date**, and **Donation**.

d. Click in the **Sort** row under **Date**, click the **arrow**, and then click **Ascending**. Click in the **Criteria** row under **Club ID**, type **club-107 or club-115** and then press [Enter]. Click in the **Criteria** row under **Donation**, type **>1000** and then press [Enter]. **Run** the query, and notice that two records match the criteria. This query answers the questions, *Which fundraiser events received donations over $1,000 from either CLUB-107 or CLUB-115, and on what dates (in chronological order) were the fundraiser events held?*

(Project 2D Club Fundraisers continues on the next page)

CHAPTER REVIEW

e. **Save** the query as **Lastname Firstname 2D CLUB 107 OR 115 Over $1000 Query** and then display the query results in **Print Preview**. Create a paper or electronic printout as directed, click **Close Print Preview**, and then **Close** the query.

4 On the ribbon, click the **CREATE tab**, and then in the **Queries group**, click **Query Design**. In the **Show Table** dialog box, double-click your **2D Clubs** table, and then double-click your **2D Fundraisers** table to add both tables to the table area. **Close** the **Show Table** dialog box. Drag the field list on the right side to the right until there are approximately two inches of space between the field lists, and then resize each field list.

a. From the **2D Clubs** field list, add the following fields to the design grid in the order given: **Club Name**, **Campus**, and **Club Email**. From the **2D Fundraisers** field list, add the following fields to the design grid in the order given: **Fundraiser Name**, **Date**, and **Donation**. In the design grid, drag the **Donation** field to the left to position it as the first column.

b. Click in the **Sort** row under **Donation**, click the **arrow**, and then click **Descending**. Click in the **Criteria** row under **Campus**, type **southeast** and then press Enter. Click in the **or** row under **Campus**, type **northeast** and then press Enter. **Run** the query, and notice that 10 records match the criteria. This query answers the question, *For the Southeast and Northeast campuses, what is the donation (in descending order), club name, campus name, club email address, fundraiser name, and date of all fundraising events?*

c. **Save** the query as **Lastname Firstname 2D SE OR NE Donations Query** and then display the query results in **Print Preview**. On the **PRINT PREVIEW tab**, in the **Page Layout group**, click **Landscape**. In the **Page Size group**, click **Margins**, and then click **Normal**. Create a paper or electronic printout as directed, click **Close Print Preview**, and then **Close** the query.

5 On the ribbon, click the **CREATE tab**, and then in the **Queries group**, click **Query Design**. In the **Show Table** dialog box, double-click your **2D Clubs** table, and then double-click your **2D Fundraisers** table to add both tables to the table area. **Close** the **Show Table** dialog box. Drag the field list on the right side to the right until there are approximately two inches of space between the field lists, and then resize each field list. From the **2D Clubs** field

list, add the **Club Name** field to the design grid. From the **2D Fundraisers** field list, add the **Fundraiser Name** field to the design grid.

a. Click in the **Sort** row under **Club Name**, click the **arrow**, and then click **Ascending**. Click in the **Criteria** row under **Club Name**, type **phi*** and then press Enter. In the **Criteria** row under **Fundraiser Name**, type ***walk*** and then press Enter. **Run** the query, and notice that two records match the criteria—Club Name begins with *Phi* and Fundraiser Name has *Walk* anywhere in its name. This query answers the question, *Which clubs (in alphabetical order) that have names starting with Phi have raised money for fundraisers that involve walking?*

b. **Save** the query as **Lastname Firstname 2D Phi Walk Query** and then display the query results in **Print Preview**. Create a paper or electronic printout as directed, click **Close Print Preview**, and then **Close** the query.

6 On the ribbon, click the **CREATE tab**, and then in the **Queries group**, click **Query Design**. In the **Show Table** dialog box, double-click your **2D Clubs** table, and then double-click your **2D Fundraisers** table to add both tables to the table area. **Close** the **Show Table** dialog box. Drag the field list on the right side to the right until there are approximately two inches of space between the field lists, and then resize each field list. From the field lists, add the following fields to the design grid in the order given: **Fundraiser ID**, **Club Name**, and **Donation**.

a. Click in the **Sort** row under **Fundraiser ID**, click the **arrow**, and then click **Ascending**. Alumni will donate an additional 25 percent based on the value in the **Donation** field. In the **Field** row, right-click in the fourth column, and then click **Zoom**. In the **Zoom** dialog box, type **Alumni Donation:[Donation]*0.25** and then click **OK**. **Run** the query to be sure the new field—*Alumni Donation*—displays. In the first record, the *Alumni Donation* displays as *156.25*.

b. Switch to **Design** view. In the **Field** row, right-click in the first empty column, and then click **Zoom**. In the **Zoom** dialog box, type **Total Donation:[Donation]+[Alumni Donation]** and then click **OK**. **Run** the query to be sure that the new field—*Total Donation*—displays. In the first record, the *Total Donation* displays as *$781.25*.

(Project 2D Club Fundraisers continues on the next page)

CHAPTER REVIEW

c. Switch to **Design** view. In the **Field** row, click in the **Alumni Donation** field name box. Under **QUERY TOOLS**, on the **DESIGN tab**, in the **Show/Hide group**, click **Property Sheet**. In the **Property Sheet**, click **Format**. In the property setting box, click the **arrow**, and then click **Currency**. In the **Property Sheet**, click **Decimal Places**. In the property setting box, click the **arrow**, and then click **2**. **Close** the **Property Sheet**, and then **Run** the query. This query answers the question, *In ascending order by Fundraiser ID, what is the club name, donation, alumni donation, and total donation for each fundraising event if the alumni donate an additional 25 percent based on the value in the Donation field?*

d. To the left of the **Fundraiser ID** field name, click **Select All**. On the **HOME tab**, in the **Records group**, click **More**, and then click **Field Width**. In the **Column Width** dialog box, click **Best Fit**. Save the query as **Lastname Firstname 2D Alumni Donation Query** and then click in any field to cancel the selection. Display the query results in **Print Preview**. On the **PRINT PREVIEW tab**, in the **Page Layout group**, click **Landscape**. Create a paper or electronic printout as directed, click **Close Print Preview**, and then **Close** the query.

7 On the ribbon, click the **CREATE tab**, and then in the **Queries group**, click **Query Design**. In the **Show Table** dialog box, double-click your **2D Fundraisers** table to add the table to the table area. **Close** the **Show Table** dialog box. Resize the field list, and then add the **Donation** field to the design grid.

a. Under **QUERY TOOLS**, on the **DESIGN tab**, in the **Show/Hide group**, click **Totals** to add a **Total** row as the third row in the design grid. In the **Total** row under **Donation**, click in the box that displays *Group By*, click the **arrow**, and then click **Sum**. In the **Show/Hide group**, click **Property Sheet**. In the **Property Sheet**, set **Decimal Places** to **0**, and then **Close** the **Property Sheet**. **Run** the query. Point to the right edge of the first column to display the ⊹ pointer, and then double-click to apply Best Fit to the field. The sum of the Donation fields is *$20,259*.

b. Switch to **Design** view. From the field list, drag the **Club ID** field to the first column in the design grid—the **Donation** field moves to the second column. **Run** the query. This query answers the question, *For each club ID, what are the total donations?*

c. **Save** the query as **Lastname Firstname 2D Total Donations by Club Query** and then display the query results in **Print Preview**. Create a paper or electronic printout as directed, click **Close Print Preview**, and then **Close** the query.

8 On the ribbon, click the **CREATE tab**, and then in the **Queries group**, click **Query Wizard**. In the **New Query** dialog box, click **Crosstab Query Wizard**, and then click **OK**. In the **Crosstab Query Wizard**, click your **Table: 2D Fundraisers**, and then click **Next**. In the wizard under **Available Fields**, double-click **Fundraiser ID** to group the records by this field and display the Fundraiser IDs as row headings. Click **Next**.

a. In the wizard, in the field list, click **Club ID** to select the column headings, and then click **Next**. Under **Fields**, click **Donation**. Under **Functions**, click **Sum**, and then click **Next**. In the **What do you want to name your query?** box, select the existing text, type **Lastname Firstname 2D Fundraisers and Clubs Crosstab Query** and then click **Finish**.

b. On the ribbon, click the **HOME** tab, and then switch to **Design** view. In the design grid, click in the [**Donation**] column. Under **QUERY TOOLS**, on the **DESIGN tab**, in the **Show/Hide group**, click **Property Sheet**. In the **Property Sheet**, click **Decimal Places**. In the property settings box, click the **arrow**, and then click **0**. In the design grid, click in the **Total Of Donation** column, set the **Decimal Places** to **0**, and then **Close** the **Property Sheet**. **Run** the query. Select all of the columns, apply **Best Fit**, and then **Save** the query. This query answers the question, *Grouped by Fundraiser ID and Club ID, what are the total donations?*

c. Display the query results in **Print Preview**. On the **PRINT PREVIEW tab**, in the **Page Layout group**, click **Landscape**. Create a paper or electronic printout as directed—two pages result. Click **Close Print Preview**, and then **Close** the query.

9 On the ribbon, click the **CREATE tab**, and then in the **Queries group**, click **Query Design**. In the **Show Table** dialog box, double-click your **2D Fundraisers** table to add the table to the table area. **Close** the **Show Table** dialog box, and then resize the field list. Add the following fields to the design grid in the order given: **Club ID**, **Fundraiser Location**, and **Date**.

(Project 2D Club Fundraisers continues on the next page)

CHAPTER REVIEW

a. Click in the **Sort** row under **Date**, click the **arrow**, and then click **Ascending**. In the **Criteria** row under **Club ID**, right-click, and then click **Zoom**. In the **Zoom** dialog box, type **[Enter a Club ID in the format club-###]** and then click **OK**. **Run** the query. In the **Enter Parameter Value** dialog box, type **club-109** and then click **OK**. Three records match the criteria.

b. **Save** the query as **Lastname Firstname 2D Club ID Parameter Query** and then display the query results in **Print Preview**. Create a paper or electronic printout as directed, click **Close Print Preview**, and then **Close** the query.

c. **Open** the **Navigation Pane**, and increase the width of the pane so that all object names display fully. On the right side of the title bar, click **Close** to close the database and to exit Access. As directed by your instructor, submit your database and the paper or electronic printouts of the 11 objects—relationship report and 10 queries, one of which printed on two pages—that are the results of this project. Specifically, in this project, using your own name, you created the following database and printouts or electronic printouts:

1. Lastname_Firstname_2D_Clubs_Fundraisers	Database file
2. Lastname Firstname 2D Relationships	Relationships Report (printout or electronic printout)
3. Lastname Firstname 2D $1000 or More Donation Query	Query (printout or electronic printout)
4. Lastname Firstname 2D Fundraisers June-July Query	Query (printout or electronic printout)
5. Lastname Firstname 2D CLUB-109 Low Donations Query	Query (printout or electronic printout)
6. Lastname Firstname 2D CLUB-107 OR 115 Over $1000 Query	Query (printout or electronic printout)
7. Lastname Firstname 2D SE OR NE Donations Query	Query (printout or electronic printout)
8. Lastname Firstname 2D Phi Walk Query	Query (printout or electronic printout)
9. Lastname Firstname 2D Alumni Donation Query	Query (printout or electronic printout)
10. Lastname Firstname 2D Total Donations by Club Query	Query (printout or electronic printout)
11. Lastname Firstname 2D Fundraisers and Clubs Crosstab Query	Query (printout or electronic printout - two pages)
12. Lastname Firstname 2D Club ID Parameter Query	Query (printout or electronic printout - CLUB-109)

END | You have completed Project 2D

CONTENT-BASED ASSESSMENTS

| Mastering Access | Project 2E Biology Supplies |

In the following Mastering Access project, you will assist Greg Franklin, chair of the Biology Department at the Southwest Campus, in using his database to answer questions about biology laboratory supplies. Your completed database objects will look similar to Figure 2.57.

Apply 2A skills from these Objectives:

1 Open and Save an Existing Database

2 Create Table Relationships

3 Sort Records in a Table

4 Create a Query in Design View

5 Create a New Query from an Existing Query

6 Sort Query Results

7 Specify Criteria in a Query

PROJECT FILES

For Project 2E, you will need the following file:

a02E_Biology_Supplies

You will save your database as:

Lastname_Firstname_2E_Biology_Supplies

PROJECT RESULTS

FIGURE 2.57

(Project 2E Biology Supplies continues on the next page)

CONTENT-BASED ASSESSMENTS

1 **Start** Access. From your student data files, open **a02E_Biology_Supplies**. Save the database in your **Access Chapter 2** folder as **Lastname_Firstname_2E_Biology_Supplies** and then enable the content. In the **Navigation Pane**, **Rename** each table by adding **Lastname Firstname** to the beginning of the table name. Increase the width of the **Navigation Pane** so that all object names display fully.

2 Open both tables to examine the fields and data, and then **Close** both tables. Create a *one-to-many* relationship between your **2E Vendors** table and your **2E Biology Lab Supplies** table using the common field **Vendor ID**. **Enforce Referential Integrity**, and enable both cascade options. *One* vendor can be the provider of *many* supplies. Create a **Relationship Report** with **Normal Margins**, saving it with the default name. Create a paper or electronic printout as directed, and then **Close All** open objects. Open your **2E Vendors** table. In the last record, in the **Vendor ID** field, select **V-100**, type **V-001** and then press ↓ to save the record. **Close** the table.

3 Open your **2E Biology Lab Supplies** table. Sort the records first in **Descending** order by **Price Per Item** and then in **Ascending** order by **Category**. Using **Landscape** orientation, create a paper or electronic printout as directed. **Close** the table, and do *not* save changes to the table.

4 Create a query in **Query Design** view using your **2E Biology Lab Supplies** table to answer the question, *What is the item ID, item name, room, location, and quantity in stock for all of the items, sorted in ascending order by the Room field and the Location field?* Display the fields in the order listed in the question. **Save** the query as **Lastname Firstname 2E Items by Room Query** and then create a paper or electronic printout as directed. **Close** the query.

5 From the **Navigation Pane**, copy your **2E Items by Room Query** object to create a new query object named **Lastname Firstname 2E Item Categories Query** and then redesign the query to answer the question, *What is the item ID, item name, category, vendor ID, and quantity*

in stock for all items, sorted in ascending order by the Category field and in ascending order by the Vendor ID field? Display only the fields necessary to answer the question and in the order listed in the question. Create a paper or electronic printout as directed. **Close** the query, saving the design changes.

6 From the **Navigation Pane**, copy your **2E Items by Room Query** object to create a new query object named **Lastname Firstname 2E Supplies Sort Query** and then redesign the query to answer the question, *What is the item name, category, price per item, and quantity in stock for all supplies, sorted in ascending order by the Category field and then in descending order by the Price Per Item field?* Display only the fields necessary to answer the question and in the order listed in the question. Create a paper or electronic printout as directed. **Close** the query, saving the design changes.

7 From the **Navigation Pane**, copy your **2E Supplies Sort Query** object to create a new query object named **Lastname Firstname 2E Kits Query** and then redesign the query to answer the question, *What is the item name, category, price per item, quantity in stock, and vendor ID for all items that have a category of kits, sorted in ascending order only by the Item Name field?* Do not display the **Category** field in the query results, and display the rest of the fields in the order listed in the question. Six records match the criteria. Create a paper or electronic printout as directed. **Close** the query, saving the design changes.

8 Create a query in **Query Design** view using your **2E Vendors** table to answer the question, *What is the vendor ID and vendor name where the phone number is missing from the table, sorted in ascending order by the Vendor Name field?* Display the fields in the order listed in the question. Two records match the criteria. **Save** the query as **Lastname Firstname 2E Missing Phone Query** and then create a paper or electronic printout as directed. **Close** the query.

(Project 2E Biology Supplies continues on the next page)

CONTENT-BASED ASSESSMENTS

9 Be sure all objects are closed. **Open** the **Navigation Pane**, be sure that all object names display fully, and then **Close** Access. As directed by your instructor, submit your database and the paper or electronic printouts of the

seven objects—relationship report, sorted table, and five queries—that are the results of this project. Specifically, in this project, using your own name, you created the following database and printouts or electronic printouts:

1. Lastname_Firstname_2E_Biology_Supplies	Database file
2. Relationships for Lastname_Firstname_2E_Biology_Supplies	Relationships Report (printout or electronic printout)
3. Lastname Firstname 2E Biology Lab Supplies table sorted (not saved)	Table sorted (printout or electronic printout - one page)
4. Lastname Firstname 2E Items by Room Query	Query (printout or electronic printout)
5. Lastname Firstname 2E Item Categories Query	Query (printout or electronic printout)
6. Lastname Firstname 2E Supplies Sort Query	Query (printout or electronic printout)
7. Lastname Firstname 2E Kits Query	Query (printout or electronic printout)
8. Lastname Firstname 2E Missing Phone Query	Query (printout or electronic printout)

END | You have completed Project 2E

CONTENT-BASED ASSESSMENTS

In the following Mastering Access project, you will assist Siobhan Reiss, the English Writing Lab coordinator, in using her database to answer questions about student publications. Your completed database objects will look similar to Figure 2.58.

Apply 2B skills from these Objectives:

8 Specify Numeric Criteria in a Query

9 Use Compound Criteria in a Query

10 Create a Query Based on More Than One Table

11 Use Wildcards in a Query

12 Create Calculated Fields in a Query

13 Calculate Statistics and Group Data in a Query

14 Create a Crosstab Query

15 Create a Parameter Query

PROJECT FILES

For Project 2F, you will need the following files:

a02F_Student_Publications

a02F_Student_Papers (Excel workbook)

You will save your database as:

Lastname_Firstname_2F_Student_Publications

PROJECT RESULTS

FIGURE 2.58

(Project 2F Student Publications continues on the next page)

CONTENT-BASED ASSESSMENTS

1 **Start** Access. From your student data files, open **a02F_Student_Publications**. Save the database in your **Access Chapter 2** folder as **Lastname_Firstname_2F_ Student_Publications** and then enable the content. In the **Navigation Pane**, **Rename** the **2F Publishers** table by adding **Lastname Firstname** to the beginning of the table name. From your student data files, import the **a02F_Student_Papers** Excel file as a new table in the database. Designate the first row of the spreadsheet as column headings, and designate **Paper ID** as the primary key. Name the new table **Lastname Firstname 2F Student Papers** and then increase the width of the **Navigation Pane** so that all object names display fully.

Open your **2F Student Papers** table in **Design** view. For the **Student ID** field, change the **Data Type** to **Short Text**. Switch to **Datasheet** view, saving the change, apply **Best Fit** to all of the columns, and then **Save** the table. Examine the fields and data in this table. Open your **2F Publishers** table, examine the fields and data, and then **Close All** open objects.

Create a *one-to-many* relationship between your **2F Publishers** table and your **2F Student Papers** table using the common field **Publisher ID**. **Enforce Referential Integrity**, and enable both cascade options. *One* publisher can publish *many* student papers. Create a **Relationship Report** with **Normal Margins**, saving it as **Lastname Firstname 2F Relationships** and then create a paper or electronic printout as directed. **Close All** open objects.

2 Create a query in **Query Design** view using your **2F Student Papers** table to answer the question, *What is the student ID, home campus, award paid, and publisher ID for awards greater than or equal to $50, sorted in ascending order by the Student ID field?* Display the fields in the order listed in the question. Five records match the criteria. **Save** the query as **Lastname Firstname 2F Awards $50 or More Query** and then create a paper or electronic printout as directed. **Close** the query.

3 From the **Navigation Pane**, copy your **2F Awards $50 or More Query** object to create a new query object named **Lastname Firstname 2F 2nd Qtr NW Students Query** and then redesign the query to answer the questions, *Which students (Student ID) from the Northwest campus had papers published between 4/1/18 and 6/30/18, and what was the paper name, the award paid, and the category, sorted in ascending order only by the Publication Date field?* Do not restrict the results by **Award Paid**. Do not display the **Home Campus** field in

the query results, and display the rest of the fields in the order listed in the question. Three records match the criteria. Using **Landscape** orientation, create a paper or electronic printout as directed. **Close** the query, saving the design changes.

4 Create a query in **Query Design** view using your **2F Student Papers** table to answer the question, *Which paper IDs, paper names, and category for students from the Southeast or Northeast campuses were published that had an award paid greater than $25, sorted in descending order by the Award Paid field?* Display the fields in the order listed in the question. Six records match the criteria. **Save** the query as **Lastname Firstname 2F SE OR NE Over $25 Query** and then using **Normal Margins**, create a paper or electronic printout as directed. **Close** the query.

5 Create a query in **Query Design** view using both tables to answer the questions, *Which paper names were published with a publisher name that has Texas as part of its name, what is the contact name and contact phone number, and what was the award paid, sorted in descending order by the Award Paid field?* (Hint: Use a wildcard character in the **Criteria** row.) Display the fields in the order listed in the question. Eight records match the criteria. **Save** the query as **Lastname Firstname 2F Texas Publishers Query** and then using **Landscape** orientation, create a paper or electronic printout as directed. **Close** the query.

6 The college's Federation of English Faculty will donate money to the English Writing Lab based on 50 percent of the awards paid to the students. Create a query in **Query Design** view using your **2F Student Papers** table to answer the question, *In ascending order by the Paper ID field, what will be the total of each donation to the Writing Lab if the Federation donates an additional 50 percent of each award paid to students?* (Hint: First calculate the amount of the donation, naming the new field **Federation Donation**, and then run the query to be sure the correct results display. Then calculate the total donation, naming the new field **Total Donation**.) Change the property settings of the **Federation Donation** field to display with a **Format** of **Currency** and with **Decimal Places** set to **2**. For the **Publisher ID** of **P-20**, the *Federation Donation* is *$22.50*, and the *Total Donation* is *$67.50*. Apply **Best Fit** to all of the columns, **Save** the query as **Lastname Firstname 2F Federation Donation Query** and then create a paper or electronic printout as directed. **Close** the query.

(Project 2F Student Publications continues on the next page)

CONTENT-BASED ASSESSMENTS

7 Create a query in **Query Design** view using your **2F Student Papers** table and the **Sum** aggregate function to answer the question, *What are the total awards paid for each category, sorted in descending order by the Award Paid field?* Display the fields in the order listed in the question. Change the property settings of the **Award Paid** field to display with **Decimal Places** set to **0**. For the **Category** of **Student Life**, total awards paid are *$265*. Apply **Best Fit** to the **SumOfAward Paid** column. **Save** the query as **Lastname Firstname 2F Awards by Category Query** and then create a paper or electronic printout as directed. **Close** the query.

8 Use the **Query Wizard** to create a crosstab query based on your **2F Student Papers** table. Select **Home Campus** as the row headings and **Category** as the column headings. **Sum** the **Award Paid** field. Name the query **Lastname Firstname 2F Campus and Category Crosstab Query** In **Design** view, change the property settings of the last two fields to display with **Decimal Places** set to **0**. This query answers the question, *What are the total awards paid for student publications by each home campus and by each category?* Apply **Best Fit** to all of the columns, and then **Save** the query. Using **Landscape** orientation and **Normal Margins**, create a paper or electronic printout as directed. **Close** the query.

9 Create a query in **Query Design** view using your **2F Student Papers** table that prompts you to enter the **Home Campus**, and then answers the question, *What is the home campus, student ID, paper name, category, and publication date for student publications, sorted in ascending order by the Publication Date field?* Display the fields in the order listed in the question. **Run** the query, entering **southwest** when prompted for criteria. Seven records match the criteria. **Save** the query as **Lastname Firstname 2F Campus Parameter Query** and then using **Normal Margins**, create a paper or electronic printout as directed. **Close** the query.

10 Open the **Navigation Pane**, and be sure that all object names display fully. **Close** Access. As directed by your instructor, submit your database and the paper or electronic printouts of the nine objects—relationship report and eight queries—that are the results of this project. Specifically, in this project, using your own name, you created the following database and printouts or electronic printouts:

1. Lastname_Firstname_2F_Student_Publications	Database file
2. Lastname Firstname 2F Relationships	Relationships Report (printout or electronic printout)
3. Lastname Firstname 2F Awards $50 or More Query	Query (printout or electronic printout)
4. Lastname Firstname 2F 2nd Qtr NW Students Query	Query (printout or electronic printout)
5. Lastname Firstname 2F SE OR NE Over $25 Query	Query (printout or electronic printout)
6. Lastname Firstname 2F Texas Publishers Query	Query (printout or electronic printout)
7. Lastname Firstname 2F Federation Donation Query	Query (printout or electronic printout)
8. Lastname Firstname 2F Awards by Category Query	Query (printout or electronic printout)
9. Lastname Firstname 2F Campus and Category Crosstab Query	Query (printout or electronic printout)
10. Lastname Firstname 2F Campus Parameter Query	Query (printout or electronic printout - Southwest)

END | You have completed Project 2F

CONTENT-BASED ASSESSMENTS

In the following Mastering Access project, you will assist Kim Ngo, director of Academic Scholarships, in using her database to answer questions about scholarships awarded to students. Your completed database objects will look similar to Figure 2.59.

PROJECT FILES

For Project 2G, you will need the following file:

a02G_Student_Scholarships

You will save your database as:

Lastname_Firstname_2G_Student_Scholarships

PROJECT RESULTS

FIGURE 2.59

(Project 2G Student Scholarships continues on the next page)

CONTENT-BASED ASSESSMENTS

1 ▶ **Start** Access. From your student data files, open **a02G_Student_Scholarships**. Save the database in your **Access Chapter 2** folder as **Lastname_Firstname_2G_Student_Scholarships** and then enable the content. In the Navigation Pane, **Rename** each table by adding **Lastname Firstname** to the beginning of the table name. Increase the width of the **Navigation Pane** so that all object names display fully.

2 ▶ Open both tables to examine the fields and data, and then **Close** both tables. Create a *one-to-many* relationship between your **2G Students** table and your **2G Scholarships Awarded** table using the common field **Student ID**. **Enforce Referential Integrity**, and enable both cascade options. *One* student can have *many* scholarships. Create a **Relationship Report** with **Normal Margins**, saving it with the default name. Create a paper or electronic printout as directed, and then **Close All** open objects. Open your **2G Students** table. In the last record, in the **Student ID** field, select **9999999**, type **2839403** and then press ↓ to save the record. **Close** the table.

3 ▶ Create a query in **Query Design** view using your **2G Scholarships Awarded** table to answer the question, *What is the scholarship name, amount, and major for scholarships greater than or equal to $500, sorted in ascending order by the Scholarship Name field?* Display the fields in the order listed in the question. Eight records match the criteria. **Save** the query as **Lastname Firstname 2G Amount $500 or More Query** and then create a paper or electronic printout as directed. **Close** the query.

4 ▶ From the **Navigation Pane**, copy your **2G Amount $500 or More Query** object to create a new query object named **Lastname Firstname 2G Awards 4th Qtr Query** and then redesign the query to answer the question, *Which scholarships (Scholarship Name) were awarded between 10/1/18 and 12/31/18, for what amount, and for which student (Student ID), sorted in ascending order only by the Award Date field?* Display only the fields necessary to answer the question and in the order listed in the question. Do not restrict the results by amount. Five records match the criteria. Create a paper or electronic printout as directed. **Close** the query, saving the design changes.

5 ▶ Create a query in **Query Design** view using your **2G Scholarships Awarded** table to answer the question, *Which scholarships (Scholarship Name) were awarded for either Math or Business majors for amounts of more than $200, sorted in descending order by the Amount field?*

Display the fields in the order listed in the question. Four records match the criteria. (Hint: If six records display, switch to **Design** view and combine the majors on one criteria line using OR.) **Save** the query as **Lastname Firstname 2G Math OR Business Over $200 Query** and then create a paper or electronic printout as directed. **Close** the query.

6 ▶ Create a query in **Query Design** view using your **2G Students** table and a wildcard character to answer the question, *What is the city, student ID, last name, and first name of students from cities that begin with the letter L, sorted in ascending order by the City field, in ascending order by the Last Name field, and ascending order by the First Name field?* Display the fields in the order listed in the question. Five records match the criteria. **Save** the query as **Lastname Firstname 2G L Cities Query** and then create a paper or electronic printout as directed. **Close** the query.

7 ▶ Create a query in **Query Design** view using your **2G Students** table and all of the fields in the same order that they display in the field list to answer the question, *For which students is the Postal Code missing?* Three records match the criteria. **Save** the query as **Lastname Firstname 2G Missing Postal Code Query** and then using **Normal Margins**, create a paper or electronic printout as directed. **Close** the query.

8 ▶ The Board of Trustees for the college will donate an amount equal to 50 percent of each scholarship amount. Create a query in **Query Design** view using both tables to answer the question, *In ascending order by the Scholarship Name field, and including the first name and last name of the scholarship recipient, what will be the total value of each scholarship if the Board of Trustees donates an additional 50 percent of each award paid to students?* (Hint: First calculate the amount of the donation, naming the new field **Board Donation**, and then run the query to be sure the correct results display. Then calculate the total donation, naming the new field **Total Donation**.) Change the property settings of the appropriate fields to display with a **Format** of **Currency** and with **Decimal Places** set to **0**. For the **Scholarship Name** of **Amanda Snyder Foundation Scholarship**, the *Board Donation* is *$125*, and the *Total Donation* is *$375*. Apply **Best Fit** to all of the columns, **Save** the query as **Lastname Firstname 2G Board Donation Query** and then using **Landscape** orientation, create a paper or electronic printout as directed. **Close** the query.

(Project 2G Student Scholarships continues on the next page)

CONTENT-BASED ASSESSMENTS

9 Create a query in **Query Design** view using your **2G Scholarships Awarded** table and the **Sum** aggregate function to answer the question, *For each major, what is the total scholarship amount, sorted in descending order by the Amount field?* Display the fields in the order listed in the question. Change the property settings of the **Amount** field to display with **Decimal Places** set to **0**. For the **Major** of **History**, the total scholarship amount is *$1,850.* Apply **Best Fit** to all of the columns. **Save** the query as **Lastname Firstname 2G Amount by Major Query** and then create a paper or electronic printout as directed. **Close** the query.

10 Use the **Query Wizard** to create a crosstab query based on your **2G Scholarships Awarded** table. Select **Student ID** as the row headings and **Major** as the column headings. **Sum** the **Amount** field. Name the query **Lastname Firstname 2G Student ID and Major Crosstab Query** In **Design** view, change the property settings of the last two fields to display with **Decimal Places** set to **0**. This query answers the question, *What are the total scholarship amounts paid by each student ID and by each major?* Apply **Best Fit** to all of the columns, and then **Save** the query. Using **Landscape** orientation, create a paper or electronic printout as directed—two pages result. **Close** the query.

11 Create a query in **Query Design** view using your **2G Scholarships Awarded** table that prompts you to enter the **Major**, and then answers the question, *What is the scholarship name and amount for a major, sorted in ascending order by the Scholarship Name field?* Display the fields in the order listed in the question. **Run** the query, entering **history** when prompted for criteria. Four records match the criteria. **Save** the query as **Lastname Firstname 2G Major Parameter Query** and then create a paper or electronic printout as directed. **Close** the query.

12 Open the **Navigation Pane**, and be sure that all object names display fully. **Close** Access. As directed by your instructor, submit your database and the paper or electronic printouts of the 10 objects—relationship report and nine queries, one of which prints on two pages—that are the results of this project. Specifically, in this project, using your own name, you created the following database and printouts or electronic printouts:

1. Lastname_Firstname_2G_Student_Scholarships	Database file
2. Relationships for Lastname_Firstname_2G_Student_Scholarships	Relationships Report (printout or electronic printout)
3. Lastname Firstname 2G Amount $500 or More Query	Query (printout or electronic printout)
4. Lastname Firstname 2G Awards 4th Qtr Query	Query (printout or electronic printout)
5. Lastname Firstname 2G Math OR Business Over $200 Query	Query (printout or electronic printout)
6. Lastname Firstname 2G L Cities Query	Query (printout or electronic printout)
7. Lastname Firstname 2G Missing Postal Code Query	Query (printout or electronic printout)
8. Lastname Firstname 2G Board Donation Query	Query (printout or electronic printout)
9. Lastname Firstname 2G Amount by Major Query	Query (printout or electronic printout)
10. Lastname Firstname 2G Student ID and Major Crosstab Query	Query (printout or electronic printout - two pages)
11. Lastname Firstname 2G Major Parameter Query (using History)	Query (printout or electronic printout)

END | You have completed Project 2G

CONTENT-BASED ASSESSMENTS

Apply a combination of the 2A and 2B skills.

GO! Fix It	Project 2H Social Sciences	Online
GO! Make It	Project 2I Faculty Awards	Online
GO! Solve It	Project 2J Student Refunds	Online
GO! Solve It	Project 2K Leave	

PROJECT FILES

For Project 2K, you will need the following file:

a02K_Leave

You will save your database as:

Lastname_Firstname_2K_Leave

Start Access, navigate to your student data files, open a02K_Leave, and then save the database in your Access Chapter 2 folder as **Lastname_Firstname_2K_Leave** Add **Lastname Firstname** to the beginning of both table names, create a one-to-many relationship with cascade options between the two tables—*one* employee can have *many* leave transactions—and then create a relationship report saving it as **Lastname Firstname 2K Relationships**

Create and save four queries to answer the following questions:

- What is the last name and first name of employees who have used personal leave, sorted in ascending order by the Last Name and First Name fields? Do not display the Leave field in the query results.
- What is the last name, first name, and email address of employees who have no phone number listed, sorted in ascending order by the Last Name and First Name fields?
- Grouped by the Leave Classification field, what is the total of each type of leave used? (Hint: Use the aggregate function Count.)
- What is the total number of leave transactions grouped in rows by the Employee# field and grouped in columns by the Leave Classification field?

As directed, create paper or electronic printouts of the relationship report and the four queries. Be sure that each object prints on one page, and that the object names display fully in the Navigation Pane. As directed, submit your database and the paper or electronic printouts of the five objects that are the results of this project.

(Project 2K Leave continues on the next page)

CONTENT-BASED ASSESSMENTS

Performance Level

Performance Criteria		Exemplary	Proficient	Developing
	Create relationship and relationship report	Relationship and relationship report created correctly.	Relationship and relationship report created with one error.	Relationship and relationship report created with two or more errors, or missing entirely.
	Create Personal Leave query	Query created with correct name, fields, sorting, and criteria.	Query created with one element incorrect.	Query created with two or more elements incorrect, or missing entirely.
	Create Missing Phone query	Query created with correct name, fields, sorting, and criteria.	Query created with one element incorrect.	Query created with two or more elements incorrect, or missing entirely.
	Create Type of Leave query	Query created with correct name, fields, and aggregate function.	Query created with one element incorrect.	Query created with two or more elements incorrect, or missing entirely.
	Create Crosstab query	Query created with correct name, row headings, column headings, and aggregate function.	Query created with one element incorrect.	Query created with two or more elements incorrect, or missing entirely.

END | You have completed Project 2K

OUTCOMES-BASED ASSESSMENTS

RUBRIC

The following outcomes-based assessments are *open-ended assessments*. That is, there is no specific correct result; your result will depend on your approach to the information provided. Make *Professional Quality* your goal. Use the following scoring rubric to guide you in *how* to approach the problem and then to evaluate *how well* your approach solves the problem.

The *criteria*—Software Mastery, Content, Format & Layout, and Process—represent the knowledge and skills you have gained that you can apply to solving the problem. The *levels of performance*—Professional Quality, Approaching Professional Quality, or Needs Quality Improvements—help you and your instructor evaluate your result.

	Your completed project is of Professional Quality if you:	Your completed project is Approaching Professional Quality if you:	Your completed project Needs Quality Improvements if you:
1-Software Mastery	Choose and apply the most appropriate skills, tools, and features and identify efficient methods to solve the problem.	Choose and apply some appropriate skills, tools, and features, but not in the most efficient manner.	Choose inappropriate skills, tools, or features, or are inefficient in solving the problem.
2-Content	Construct a solution that is clear and well organized, contains content that is accurate, appropriate to the audience and purpose, and is complete. Provide a solution that contains no errors in spelling, grammar, or style.	Construct a solution in which some components are unclear, poorly organized, inconsistent, or incomplete. Misjudge the needs of the audience. Have some errors in spelling, grammar, or style, but the errors do not detract from comprehension.	Construct a solution that is unclear, incomplete, or poorly organized; contains some inaccurate or inappropriate content; and contains many errors in spelling, grammar, or style. Do not solve the problem.
3-Format & Layout	Format and arrange all elements to communicate information and ideas, clarify function, illustrate relationships, and indicate relative importance.	Apply appropriate format and layout features to some elements, but not others. Overuse features, causing minor distraction.	Apply format and layout that does not communicate information or ideas clearly. Do not use format and layout features to clarify function, illustrate relationships, or indicate relative importance. Use available features excessively, causing distraction.
4-Process	Use an organized approach that integrates planning, development, self-assessment, revision, and reflection.	Demonstrate an organized approach in some areas, but not others; or, use an insufficient process of organization throughout.	Do not use an organized approach to solve the problem.

OUTCOMES-BASED ASSESSMENTS

Apply a combination of the 2A and 2B skills.

GO! Think   Project 2L Coaches

PROJECT FILES

For Project 2L, you will need the following file:

a02L_Coaches

You will save your database as

Lastname_Firstname_2L_Coaches

Start Access, navigate to your student data files, open a02L_Coaches, and then save the database in your Access Chapter 2 folder as **Lastname_Firstname_2L_Coaches** Add **Lastname Firstname** to the beginning of both table names, create a one-to-many relationship with cascade options between the two tables—*one* coach can participate in *many* activities—and then create a relationship report saving it as **Lastname Firstname 2L Relationships**

Create queries to assist Randy Garza, the athletic director, in answering the following questions about the coaches at Texas Lakes Community College:

- What is the last name and first name of every coach involved in *Dive* activities, sorted in ascending order by the Last Name field and First Name fields?
- What is the last name and first name of every coach involved in basketball or football activities, sorted in ascending order first by the Activity Name field and then by the Last Name and First Name fields?
- Grouped by division, what is the total number of activity names, sorted in descending order by the total number? (Hint: Use the Count aggregate function.)
- What is the skill specialty, last name, first name, and phone number for coaches in a specified position that is entered when prompted for the Position, sorted in ascending order first by the Skill Specialty field and then by the Last Name and First Name fields? (When prompted, enter the position of *director* for your paper or electronic printout.)

As directed, create paper or electronic printouts of the relationship report and the four queries. Be sure that each object prints on one page, and that the object names display fully in the Navigation Pane. As directed, submit your database and the paper or electronic printouts of the five objects that are the results of this project.

END | You have completed Project 2L

GO! Think   Project 2M Club Donations   Online

Build from Scratch

You and GO!   Project 2N Personal Inventory   Online

Build from Scratch

GO! Cumulative Group Project   Project 2O Bell Orchid Hotels
Online

Forms, Filters, and Reports

PROJECT 3A	OUTCOMES
	Create forms to enter and delete records and to display data in a database.

OBJECTIVES

1. Create and Use a Form to Add and Delete Records
2. Filter Records
3. Create a Form by Using the Form Wizard
4. Modify a Form in Layout View and in Design View

PROJECT 3B	OUTCOMES
	Create reports to display database information.

OBJECTIVES

5. Create a Report by Using the Report Tool and Modify the Report in Layout View
6. Create a Report by Using the Report Wizard
7. Modify the Design of a Report
8. Keep Grouped Data Together in a Printed Report

Riccardo Piccinini/Fotolia

In This Chapter

In this chapter, you will create forms to enter and delete data and to view data in database tables. Forms can display one record at a time with fields placed in the same order to match a paper source document. Records in a form or table can be filtered to display a subset of the records based on matching specific values. You will modify forms by adding fields, changing field widths, and adding labels to the forms. You will create professional-looking reports that summarize the data stored in a query or table. You will modify the reports by changing the fields in the report, by changing the layout of the report, by grouping data, and by making sure that groupings of data stay together on the printed page.

The projects in this chapter relate to **Texas Lakes Community College**, which is located in the Austin, Texas, area. Its four campuses serve over 30,000 students and offer more than 140 certificate programs and degrees. The college has a highly acclaimed Distance Education program and an extensive Workforce Development program. The college makes positive contributions to the community through cultural and athletic programs and has significant partnerships with businesses and nonprofit organizations. Popular fields of study include nursing and health care, solar technology, computer technology, and graphic design.

Students and Majors Database

PROJECT

3A

MyITLab®
Project 3A Training

PROJECT ACTIVITIES

In Activities 3.01 through 3.15, you will assist Sean Fitchette, director of Enrollment Services at Texas Lakes Community College, in using his Access database to track new students and their major fields of study. Your completed forms will look similar to Figure 3.1.

PROJECT FILES

For Project 3A, you will need the following file:

a03A_Students_Majors

You will save your database as:

Lastname_Firstname_3A_Students_Majors

PROJECT RESULTS

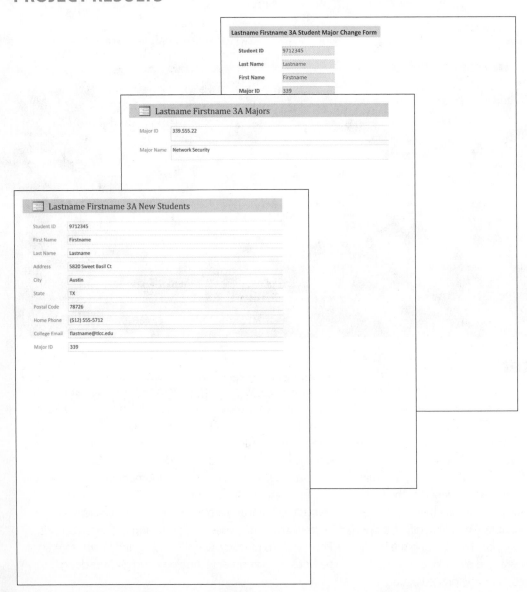

FIGURE 3.1 Project 3A Students and Majors

<table>
<tr><td colspan="2">N O T E</td><td>If You Are Using a Touchscreen</td></tr>
</table>

- Tap an item to click it.
- Press and hold for a few seconds to right-click; release when the information or command displays.
- Touch the screen with two or more fingers and then pinch together to zoom in or stretch your fingers apart to zoom out.
- Slide your finger on the screen to scroll—slide left to scroll right and slide right to scroll left.
- Slide to rearrange—similar to dragging with a mouse.
- Swipe from edge: from right to display charms; from left to expose open apps, snap apps, or close apps; from top or bottom to show commands or close an app.
- Swipe to select—slide an item a short distance with a quick movement—to select an item and bring up commands, if any.

Objective 1 Create and Use a Form to Add and Delete Records

Video A3-1

A *form* is a database object that you can use to enter new records into a table, or to edit, delete, or display existing records in a table. A form is useful to control access to the data. For example, you can design a form for college registration assistants so that they can see and enter the courses scheduled and fees paid by an individual student. However, they cannot see or enter grades for a student.

Some forms display only one record at a time; other forms display multiple records at the same time. A form that displays only one record at a time is useful not only to the individual who performs the *data entry*—entering the actual records—but also to anyone who has the job of viewing information in a database. For example, when you request a transcript from your college, someone displays your record on the screen. For the individual viewing your transcript, it is much easier to look at one record at a time, using a form, than to look at all of the student transcripts in the database.

Activity 3.01 | Opening and Saving an Existing Database, Renaming Tables, and Viewing a Table Relationship

1 Start Access. In the Access opening screen, click **Open Other Files**. Under **Open**, click **Computer**, and then on the right, click **Browse**. In the **Open** dialog box, navigate to the location where your student data files for this chapter are stored, and then double-click **a03A_Students_Majors** to open the database.

2 On the ribbon, click the **FILE tab**, and then click **Save As**. Under **File Types**, be sure **Save Database As** is selected. On the right, under **Database File Types**, be sure **Access Database** is selected, and then at the bottom of the screen, click **Save As**.

3 In the **Save As** dialog box, navigate to the location where you are saving your databases. Create a **New folder** named **Access Chapter 3**, and then **Open** the folder. In the **File name** box and using your own name, replace the existing text with **Lastname_Firstname_3A_Students_ Majors** and then click **Save** or press Enter.

4 On the **Message Bar**, click **Enable Content**. In the **Navigation Pane**, right-click the **3A Majors** table, and then click **Rename**. With the table name selected and using your own name, type **Lastname Firstname 3A Majors** and then press Enter to rename the table. Use the same technique to **Rename** the **3A New Students** table to **Lastname Firstname 3A New Students**

5 Point to the right edge of the **Navigation Pane** to display the ↔ pointer. Drag to the right to increase the width of the pane until both table names display fully.

6 On the ribbon, click the **DATABASE TOOLS tab**. In the **Relationships group**, click **Relationships**. On the **DESIGN tab**, in the **Relationships group**, click **All Relationships**. If necessary, resize and move the field lists so that the entire table name and fields display for each field list.

Because you renamed the tables, the field lists do not automatically display in the Relationships window.

7 In the **Relationships** window, click the **join line** between the two field lists. In the **Tools group**, click **Edit Relationships**. Point to the title bar of the **Edit Relationships** dialog box, and drag the dialog box downward below the two field lists. Compare your screen with Figure 3.2.

One major is associated with *many* students. A one-to-many relationship is established between your 3A Majors table and your 3A New Students table using the Major ID field as the common field. Recall that Cascade Update Related Fields enables you to change the primary key in the 3A Majors table, and then the data in the foreign key field in the 3A New Students field is automatically updated. Recall that Cascade Delete Related Records enables you to delete a record in the 3A Majors table, and then all related records in the 3A New Students table are automatically deleted.

ANOTHER WAY   In the Relationships window, double-click the join line to display the Edit Relationships dialog box.

FIGURE 3.2

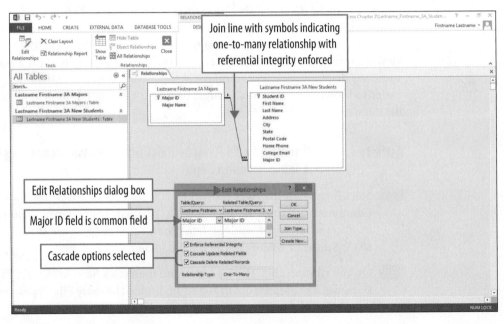

ALERT!   **Is Your Edit Relationships Dialog Box Empty?**

The Edit Relationships dialog box does not display any information if you do not first click the join line. If this happens, close the Edit Relationships dialog box, and then be sure that you click the join line—when selected, the join line is darker.

---

8 **Close** ☒ the **Edit Relationships** dialog box, and then **Close** ☒ the **Relationships** window. In the message box, click **Yes** to save changes to the layout of the relationships.

Activity 3.02 | Creating a Form and Viewing Records

There are several ways to create a form in Access, but the fastest and easiest way is to use the *Form tool*. With a single mouse click, all fields from the data source are placed on the form. You can use the new form immediately, or you can modify the form in Layout view or in Design view.

The Form tool uses all of the field names and all of the records from an existing table or query. Records that you create or edit using a form are automatically updated in the underlying table or tables. In this activity, you will create a form and then view records from the underlying table—the data source.

1 In the **Navigation Pane**, double-click your **3A New Students** table to open it. Scroll as needed to view all 10 fields—*Student ID*, *First Name*, *Last Name*, *Address*, *City*, *State*, *Postal Code*, *Home Phone*, *College Email*, and *Major ID*. **Close** ✕ the table.

2 In the **Navigation Pane**, be sure your **3A New Students** table is selected. On the ribbon, click the **CREATE tab**, and then in the **Forms group**, click **Form**. **Close** « the **Navigation Pane**, and then compare your screen with Figure 3.3.

The form is created based on the currently selected object—your 3A New Students table—and displays in *Layout view*. In Layout view, you can modify the form with the data displayed in the fields. For example, you can adjust the size of the text boxes to fit the data.

The form is created in a simple top-to-bottom layout, with all 10 fields from your 3A New Students table lined up in a single column. The data for the first record in the data source displays.

FIGURE 3.3

3 In the navigation area, click **Next record** ▶ four times to display the fifth record—*Student ID 1298345*. In the navigation area, select the text in the Current record box, type **62** and then press Enter to display the record for *Student ID 5720358*. In the navigation area, click **Last record** ▶| to display the record for *Student ID 9583924*, and then click **First record** |◀ to display the record for *Student ID 1034823*.

Use the navigation buttons to scroll among the records or the Current record box to display any single record.

4 **Save** 🖫 the form as **Lastname Firstname 3A New Student Form** and then **Close** ✕ the form object.

5 **Open** » the **Navigation Pane**. Notice that your new form displays under the table with which it is related—your **3A New Students** table.

Activity 3.03 | Creating a Second Form

In this activity, you will use the Form tool to create a form for your 3A Majors table.

1 In the **Navigation Pane**, click your **3A Majors** table to select it. On the ribbon, click the **CREATE tab**, and then in the **Forms group**, click **Form. Close** ⊠ the **Navigation Pane**, and then compare your screen with Figure 3.4.

Because a one-to-many relationship is established, the form displays related records in the 3A New Students table for each record in the 3A Majors table. Five new students have selected a major of *Diagnostic Medical Sonography—Major ID 105*.

FIGURE 3.4

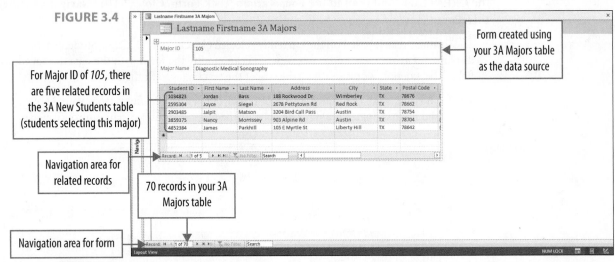

For Major ID of *105*, there are five related records in the 3A New Students table (students selecting this major)

Navigation area for related records

70 records in your 3A Majors table

Navigation area for form

Form created using your 3A Majors table as the data source

2 **Close** ⊠ your **3A Majors** form. In the message box, click **Yes**. In the **Save As** dialog box, in the **Form Name** box, type **Lastname Firstname 3A Major Form** and then click **OK**.

Recall that if you do not save an object, you are prompted to do so when you close the object.

3 **Open** ⊠ the **Navigation Pane**. Notice that your new form displays under the table with which it is related—your **3A Majors** table.

Activity 3.04 | Adding Records to a Table by Using a Form

By using a single-record form to add, modify, and delete records, you can reduce the number of data entry errors, because the individual performing the data entry is looking at only one record at a time. Recall that your database is useful only if the information is accurate—just like your contact list is useful only if it contains accurate phone numbers and email addresses.

Forms are based on—also referred to as ***bound*** to—the table where the records are stored. When a record is entered in a form, the new record is added to the underlying table. The reverse is also true—when a record is added to the table, the new record can be viewed in the related form.

In this activity, you will add a new record to both tables by using the forms that you just created.

1 In the **Navigation Pane**, double-click your **3A New Student Form** object to open it, and then **Close** ⊠ the **Navigation Pane**. In the navigation area, click **New (blank) record** ⊠ to display a new blank form.

When you open a form, the first record in the underlying table displays in ***Form view***, which is used to view, add, modify, and delete records stored in the table.

2 In the **Student ID** field, type **9712345** and then press Tab.

Use the Tab key to move from field to field in a form. ***Tab order*** is the order in which the insertion point moves from one field to the next when you press the Tab key. As you start typing, the pencil icon displays in the ***record selector bar*** at the left—the bar used to select an entire record. The pencil icon displays when a record is being created or edited.

ANOTHER WAY   Press the Enter key, provided there are no special links on the form, such as a link to create a new form or a link to print the form.

> 3 ▸ Using your own first name and last name and using the first initial of your first name and your last name for the *College Email* field, continue entering the data shown in the following table, and then compare your screen with Figure 3.5.

Student ID	First Name	Last Name	Address	City	State	Postal Code	Home Phone	College Email	Major ID
9712345	**First Name**	**Last Name**	**5820 Sweet Basil Ct**	**Austin**	**TX**	**78726**	**(512) 555-5712**	**flastname@ tlcc.edu**	**339**

FIGURE 3.5

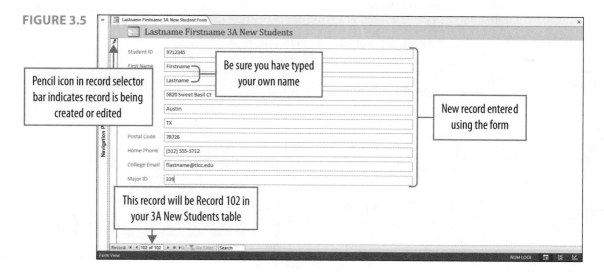

> 4 ▸ With the insertion point positioned in the last field, press Tab to save the record and display a new blank record. **Close** ☒ your **3A New Student Form** object.

> 5 ▸ **Open** ⟩⟩ the **Navigation Pane**, and then double-click your **3A New Students** table to open it. In the navigation area, click **Last record** ▶⎮ to verify that the record you entered in the form is stored in the underlying table. **Close** ☒ your **3A New Students** table.

> 6 ▸ In the **Navigation Pane**, double-click your **3A Major Form** object to open it. At the bottom of the screen, in the navigation area for the form—*not* the navigation area for the subdatasheet—click **New (blank) record** ▶⧉. In the blank form enter the data shown in the following table:

Major ID	Major Name
339.555.22	**Network Security**

> 7 ▸ **Close** ☒ your **3A Major Form** object. In the **Navigation Pane**, double-click your **3A Majors** table, and then scroll to verify that the record for *Major ID 339.555.22 Network Security* displays in the table—records are sorted by the *Major ID* field. **Close** ☒ the table.

Activity 3.05 | Deleting Records from a Table by Using a Form

You can delete records from a database table by using a form. In this activity, you will delete the record for *Major ID 800.03* because the program has been discontinued.

1 In the **Navigation Pane**, double-click your **3A Major Form** object to open it, and then **Close** « the **Navigation Pane**. On the **HOME tab**, in the **Find group**, click **Find** to open the **Find and Replace** dialog box.

↻ **ANOTHER WAY**   Press Ctrl + F to open the Find and Replace dialog box.

2 In the **Look In** box, notice that *Current field* displays. In the **Find What** box, type **800.03** and then click **Find Next**. Compare your screen with Figure 3.6, and verify that the record for *Major ID 800.03* displays.

Because the insertion point was positioned in the *Major ID* field before opening the dialog box, Access will search for data in this field—the *Current field*.

FIGURE 3.6

3 Close ⊠ the **Find and Replace** dialog box. On the **HOME tab**, in the **Records group**, click the **Delete arrow**, and then click **Delete Record**.

The record is removed from the screen, and a message displays alerting you that you are about to delete *1 record(s)*. Once you click *Yes*, you cannot click Undo to reverse this action. If you delete a record by mistake, you must re-create the record by reentering the data. Because no students are associated with this major and the program is being discontinued, you can delete it from the table.

4 In the message box, click **Yes** to delete the record. In the navigation area for the form, notice that the total number of records in the table is *70*. **Close** ⊠ your **3A Major Form** object.

5 **Open** » the **Navigation Pane**, and then double-click your **3A Majors** table to open it. Examine the table to verify that the *Major ID 800.03* record has been deleted from the table, and then **Close** ⊠ the table.

Adding and deleting records in a form updates the records stored in the underlying table.

Activity 3.06 | Printing a Form

When a form is displayed, clicking Print causes *all* of the records to print in the form layout. In this activity, you will print only *one* record.

1 In the **Navigation Pane**, double-click your **3A New Student Form** object to open it, and then **Close** « the **Navigation Pane**. Press Ctrl + F to open the **Find and Replace** dialog box. In the **Find What** box, type **9712345** and then click **Find Next** to display the record with your name. **Close** ⊠ the **Find and Replace** dialog box.

2 ▶ On the ribbon, click the **FILE tab**, click **Print**, and then on the right, click **Print**. In the **Print** dialog box, under **Print Range**, click the **Selected Record(s)** option button. In the lower left corner of the dialog box, click **Setup**.

3 ▶ In the **Page Setup** dialog box, click the **Columns tab**. Under **Column Size**, double-click in the **Width** box to select the existing value, type **7.5** and then compare your screen with Figure 3.7.

Change the width of the column in this manner so that the form prints on one page. Forms are not typically printed, so the width of the column in a form might be greater than the width of the paper on which you are printing. The maximum column width that you can enter is dependent upon the printer that is installed on your system. This setting is saved when you save or close the form.

FIGURE 3.7

Record with your name

Page Setup dialog box

Column Size Width set to 7.5 so that form will print on one page

4 ▶ In the **Page Setup** dialog box, click **OK**. To create a paper printout, in the **Print** dialog box click **OK**. To create an electronic printout of this single form, click **Cancel** and then follow the instructions in the Note below.

NOTE **Printing a Single Form in PDF**

To create an electronic printout of a single form in PDF, change the column width to 7.5 as described in Step 3 above, and then in the Print dialog box, click Cancel. On the left side of the form, click the Record Selector bar so that it is black—selected. On the ribbon, click the EXTERNAL DATA tab. In the Export group, click PDF or XPS.

In the Publish as PDF or XPS dialog box, navigate to your chapter folder. In the File name box, the form has the same name as the form. Be sure that the Open file after publishing check box is selected, and that the Minimum size (publishing online) option button is selected. In the Publish as PDF or XPS dialog box, Click Options. In the Options dialog box, under Range, click the Selected records option button, click OK, and then click Publish. Close the Windows 8 Reader, Adobe Reader or Adobe Acrobat window, and then submit the file as directed by your instructor.

---

5 ▶ Close ⌧ your **3A New Student Form** object, **Open** ⟩⟩ the **Navigation Pane**, and then double-click your **3A Major Form** object to open it. **Close** ⟨⟨ the **Navigation Pane**.

6 ▶ Use the techniques you just practiced to **Find** the record for the **Major ID** of **339.555.22**, and then create a paper or electronic printout as directed by your instructor of that record only on one page. After printing, **Close** ⌧ your **3A Major Form** object.

If there are no related records in the subdatasheet, the empty subdatasheet does not display in the printed form.

Objective 2   Filter Records

Video A3-2

Filtering records in a form displays only a portion of the total records—a *subset*—based on matching specific values. Filters are commonly used to provide a quick answer, and the result is not generally saved for future use. For example, by filtering records in a form, you can quickly display a subset of records for students majoring in Information Systems Technology, which is identified by the Major ID of 339.

A form provides an interface for the database. For example, because of security reasons, the registration assistants at your college may not have access to the entire student database. Rather, by using a form, they can access and edit only some information—the information necessary for them to do their jobs. Filtering records within a form provides individuals who do not have access to the entire database a way to ask questions of the database without constructing a query. You can save the filter with the form if you are going to use the filter frequently.

Activity 3.07 | Filtering Data by Selection of One Field

In this activity, you will assist a counselor at the college who wants to see records for students majoring in Information Systems Technology. In a form, you can use the *Filter By Selection* command to display only the records that contain the value in the selected field and to hide the records that do *not* contain the value in the selected field.

1 **Open** ` » ` the **Navigation Pane**, double-click your **3A New Student Form** object to open it in **Form** view, and then **Close** ` « ` the **Navigation Pane**.

2 In the first record, click the **Major ID** field name—or you can click in the field box. Press `Ctrl` + `F` to display the **Find and Replace** dialog box. In the **Find What** box, type **339** If necessary, in the Match box, click the arrow, and then click Whole Field. Click **Find Next**, and then compare your screen with Figure 3.8.

This action finds and displays a record with a *Major ID* of *339*—the major of *Information Systems Technology*. You will use this action to filter the records using the value of *339*.

FIGURE 3.8

3 **Close** ` X ` the **Find and Replace** dialog box. On the **HOME tab**, in the **Sort & Filter group**, click **Selection**, and then click **Equals "339"**. Compare your screen with Figure 3.9.

Seven records match the contents of the selected Major ID field—*339*—the Major ID for the Information Systems Technology major. In the navigation area, *Filtered* with a funnel icon displays next to the number of records. *Filtered* also displays on the right side of the status bar to indicate that a filter is applied. On the HOME tab, in the Sort & Filter group, Toggle Filter is active.

ANOTHER WAY   With the data selected in the field, right-click the selection, and then click Equals "339".

FIGURE 3.9

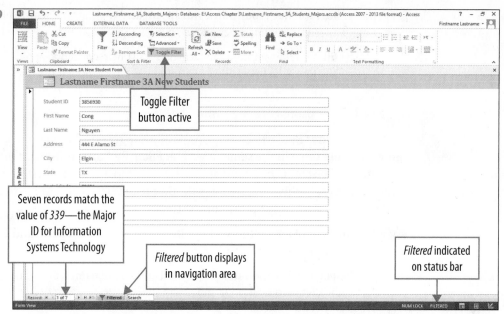

4 ▶ On the **HOME tab**, in the **Sort & Filter group**, click **Toggle Filter** to remove the filter and display all 102 records. Notice *Unfiltered* in the navigation area, which indicates a filter is created but is not active.

🔄 **ANOTHER WAY**　　　Click Filtered in the navigation area to remove the filter.

NOTE　　**The Toggle Filter Button**

On the HOME tab, in the Sort & Filter group, the Toggle Filter button is used to apply or remove a filter. If no filter is created, the button is not available. After a filter is created, the button becomes available. Because it is a toggle button used to apply or remove a filter, the ScreenTip that displays for this button alternates between Apply Filter—when a filter is created but is not currently applied—and Remove Filter—when a filter is applied.

---

5 ▶ Be sure that the first record—for *Jordan Bass*—displays. On the **HOME tab**, in the **Sort & Filter group**, click **Toggle Filter** to reapply the filter. In the navigation area, click **Last record** ⏭ to display the last of the seven records that match a Major ID of *339*.

The record for *Student ID 9712345* displays—the record with your name. Use Toggle Filter to apply or remove filters as needed.

6 ▶ In the navigation area, click **Filtered** to remove the filter and display all of the records.

In the navigation area, *Filtered* changes to *Unfiltered*.

7 ▶ In the first record for *Jordan Bass*, in the **Last Name** field, select the first letter—**B**—in *Bass*. In the **Sort & Filter group**, click **Selection**, and then click **Begins with "B"**.

A new filter is applied that displays eight records in which the *Last Name* begins with the letter *B*.

🔄 **ANOTHER WAY**　　　With the letter *B* selected, right-click the selection, and then click Begins with "B".

8 ▶ Use either **Toggle Filter** in the **Sort & Filter group** or **Filtered** in the navigation area to remove the filter and display all of the records.

9 In the **Sort & Filter group**, click **Advanced**, and then click **Clear All Filters**. Notice, that in the navigation area, *Unfiltered* changed to *No Filter*.

> The filter is removed from the form and must be recreated to apply it. If you toggle the filter off and save the form, the filter is saved with the form even though the filter is not currently applied.

Activity 3.08 | Using Filter By Form

Use the ***Filter By Form*** command to filter the records based on one or more fields, or based on more than one value in the same field. The Filter By Form command offers greater flexibility than the Filter By Selection command and can be used to answer a question that requires matching multiple values. In this activity, you will filter records to help Mr. Fitchette determine how many students live in Dripping Springs or Austin.

1 On the **HOME tab**, in the **Sort & Filter group**, click **Advanced**, and then click **Filter By Form**. Compare your screen with Figure 3.10.

> The Filter by Form window displays all of the field names, but without any data. In the empty text box for each field, you can type a value or select a value from a list. The *Look for* and *Or* tabs display at the bottom.

FIGURE 3.10

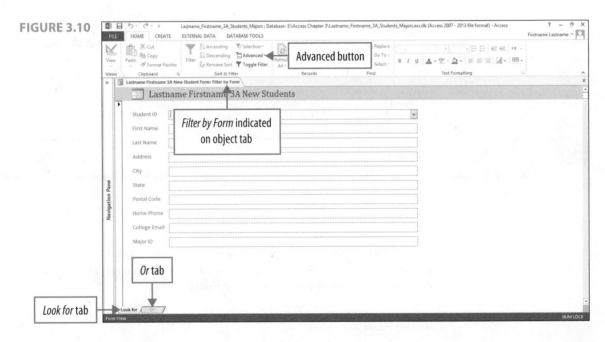

2 In the form, click the **City** field name to position the insertion point in the **City** field box. At the right edge of the **City** field box, click the **arrow**, and then click **Dripping Springs**. In the **Sort & Filter group**, click **Toggle Filter**.

> As displayed in the navigation area, four student records have *Dripping Springs* stored in the City field.

3 In the **Sort & Filter group**, click **Advanced**, and then click **Filter By Form**. In the lower left corner of the form, click the **Or tab**. Click the **City** field box **arrow**, and then click **Austin**. In the **Sort & Filter group**, click **Toggle Filter**, and then compare your screen with Figure 3.11.

> As displayed in the navigation area, 28 student records have either *Dripping Springs* OR *Austin* stored in the City field. You have created an ***OR condition***; that is, records display where, in this instance, either of two values—Dripping Springs *or* Austin—is present in the selected field.

 ANOTHER WAY   Click in the field box, and type the criteria separated by the word *or*. For example, in the City field box, type *Dripping Springs or Austin*.

FIGURE 3.11

28 students live in either *Dripping Springs* or *Austin*

Indicates filter is applied

4 In the **Sort & Filter group**, click **Advanced**, and then click **Clear All Filters** to display all 102 records.

Activity 3.09 | Using Advanced Filter/Sort

In this activity, you will use the Advanced Filter/Sort command to filter records to locate students who live in Austin with a Major ID of *339*—Information Systems Technology.

1 In the **Sort & Filter group**, click **Advanced**, and then click **Advanced Filter/Sort**.

The Advanced Filter design grid displays, which is similar to the query design grid. A field list for the underlying table of the form displays.

2 In the table area, resize the field list so that the entire table name and all of the field names display.

3 In the **3A New Students** field list, double-click **City**, and then double-click **Major ID** to add both fields to the design grid. In the **Criteria** row under **City**, type **Austin** and then press Enter. In the **Criteria** row under **Major ID**, type **339** and then press Enter. Compare your screen with Figure 3.12.

FIGURE 3.12

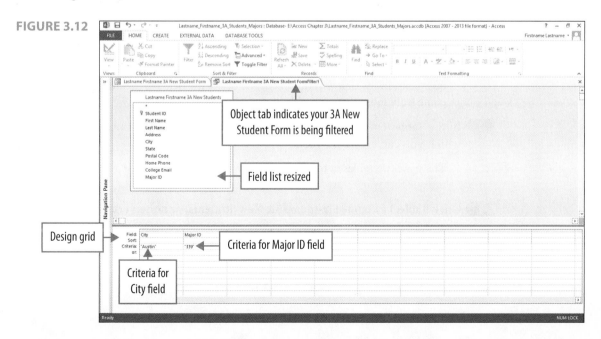

Object tab indicates your 3A New Student Form is being filtered

Field list resized

Design grid

Criteria for Major ID field

Criteria for City field

4 In the **Sort & Filter group**, click **Toggle Filter** to display the filtered records.

Three records match the criteria. You have created an *AND condition*; that is, only records where both values—Austin *and* 339—are present in the selected fields display. There are three students who live in Austin who have declared a major of Information Systems Technology.

5 In the **Sort & Filter group**, click **Toggle Filter** to remove the filter and to display all of the records.

In the navigation area, *Unfiltered* displays, which indicates that a filter has been created for this form. Unless you click Clear All Filters, the filter is saved with the form when the form is closed. When you reopen the form, you can click Toggle Filter or Unfiltered to reapply the filter.

6 **Close** ☒ your **3A New Student Form** object, and notice that the Advanced Filter grid also closes.

More Knowledge | **Using the Filter Button**

You can filter a form in a manner similar to the way you filter records in a table. Click in the field you wish to use for the filter. On the HOME tab, in the Sort & Filter group, click Filter to display a shortcut menu. Select the (Select All) check box to clear the option, and then select the data by which you want to filter your records by clicking the check boxes preceding the data. To remove the filter, redisplay the menu, and then select the (Select All) check box.

Objective 3 | Create a Form by Using the Form Wizard

Video A3-3

The ***Form Wizard*** walks you step by step through the creation of a form and gives you more flexibility in the design, layout, and number of fields in a form than the Form tool. Design a form for the individuals who use the form—either for entering new records or viewing records. For example, when your college counselor displays student information, it may be easier for the counselor to view the information if the fields are arranged in a layout that more closely matches a paper form.

Activity 3.10 | Creating a Form by Using the Form Wizard

In this activity, you will create a form to match the layout of a paper form that a student at Texas Lakes Community College completes when that student changes his or her major. This will make it easier for the individual who changes the data in the database.

1 On the ribbon, click the **CREATE tab**, and then in the **Forms group**, click **Form Wizard**.

The Form Wizard walks you step by step through the process of creating a form by asking questions. In the first wizard screen, you select the fields to include on the form. The fields can come from more than one table or query.

2 In the **Tables/Queries** box, click the **arrow** to display a list of available tables and queries from which you can create the form.

There are two tables in the database from which you can create a new form. The selected table is the one that you last worked with.

3 Click **Table: Lastname Firstname 3A New Students**, and then compare your screen with Figure 3.13.

In the Available Fields list, the field names from your 3A New Students table display.

FIGURE 3.13

Form Wizard button

Your 3A New Students table selected

Available Fields list displays field names in your 3A New Students table

Selected Fields list box

4 In the **Available Fields** list, double-click the following field names in the order given to move them to the **Selected Fields** list: **First Name**, **Last Name**, and **Major ID**. Compare your screen with Figure 3.14.

Three field names from your 3A New Students table display in the Selected Fields list.

ANOTHER WAY Click the field name, and then click One Field > to move a field from the Available Fields list to the Selected Fields list.

FIGURE 3.14

Three fields that will display in the form

5 Click **Next**. In the wizard, be sure **Columnar** is selected as the layout, and then click **Next**. In the **What title do you want for your form?** box, select the existing text, type **Lastname Firstname 3A Student Major Change Form** and then click **Finish** to close the wizard and create the form.

The three fields and the data from the first record in your 3A New Students table display in Form view.

6 Open » the **Navigation Pane**. If necessary, increase the width of the Navigation Pane so that all object names display fully. Compare your screen with Figure 3.15.

In the Navigation Pane, the form displays under its data source—your 3A New Students table.

FIGURE 3.15

Form created using the Form Wizard

Lastname Firstname 3A Student Major Change Form

New form displays under its data source

Data from first record in your 3A New Students table displays in form

Video A3-4

After you create a form, you can make changes to it. For example, you can group the fields, resize the fields, add more fields to the form, and change the style of the form. Layout view enables you to see the data in the form as you modify the form. Most changes to a form can be made in Layout view.

Activity 3.11 | Grouping Controls in Layout View

In this activity, you will group *controls* in the form so that you can work with them as one unit. Controls are objects on a form that display data or text, perform actions, and let you view and work with information.

1 **Close** « the **Navigation Pane**, and be sure that your **3A Student Major Change Form** object displays in the object window. On the **HOME tab**, in the **Views group**, click the top portion of the **View** button to switch to **Layout** view. If the Field List pane displays on the right side of your screen, click Close ✕ to close the pane. Compare your screen with Figure 3.16.

The field names and data for the first record in your 3A New Students record display in controls. The data for the first record displays in *text box controls*. The most commonly used control is the text box control, which typically displays data from a field in the underlying table. A text box control is a *bound control*—its data comes from a field in a table or query.

The field names—*First Name*, *Last Name*, and *Major ID*—display in *label controls*. A label control displays to the left of a text box control and contains descriptive information that displays on the form, usually the field name. A control that does not have a data source is an *unbound control*. Another example of an unbound control is a label control that displays the title of a form.

 ANOTHER WAY On the right side of the status bar, click Layout View ▣ to switch from Form view to Layout view.

FIGURE 3.16

2 Click the **First Name label control**. Hold down Shift, and then click the **Last Name label control**, the **Major ID label control**, and the three **text box controls** to select all of the label and text box controls on the form.

ALERT! **Do Your Controls Change Order When Selecting?**

If, when selecting multiple controls, the controls change order, click Undo, and then select the controls again. Be careful not to drag the mouse when you are selecting multiple controls.

---

3 ▸ With all six controls selected—surrounded by a colored border—on the ribbon, under **FORM LAYOUT TOOLS**, click the **ARRANGE tab**. In the **Table group**, click **Stacked**. Click the **First Name label control** to cancel the selection of all of the controls and to surround the **First Name label control** with a colored border. Compare your screen with Figure 3.17.

This action groups the controls together in the *Stacked layout* format—a layout similar to a paper form, with labels to the left of each field. Because the controls are grouped, you can move and edit the controls more easily as you redesign your form.

A dotted line forms a border around the controls, which indicates that the controls are grouped together. Above and to the left of the first label control that displays *First Name*, the *layout selector* displays. The layout selector is used to select and move or format the entire group of controls.

FIGURE 3.17

Activity 3.12 | **Applying a Theme and Formatting a Form in Layout View**

In this activity, you will apply a *theme* to the form in Layout view. A theme is a predesigned set of colors, fonts, lines, and fill effects that look good together and that can be applied to all of the objects in the database or to individual objects in the database.

1 ▸ On the ribbon, under **FORM LAYOUT TOOLS**, click the **DESIGN tab**. In the **Themes group**, click **Themes**. In the **Themes** gallery, using the ScreenTips, point to the **Retrospect** theme, right-click, and then click **Apply Theme to This Object Only**.

Right-click a theme so that you can apply the theme to an individual object within the database. Apply a theme before formatting any other controls in your form.

NOTE **Applying a Theme to an Object and Determining the Applied Theme**

If you click a theme rather than right-clicking it and selecting an option, the theme is applied to all objects in the database. You cannot click Undo to cancel the application of the theme to all objects. To determine the applied theme, in the Themes group, point to Themes. The ScreenTip displays the name of the current theme.

---

2 ▸ Click anywhere in the title of the form—*Lastname Firstname 3A Student Major Change Form*—to select the title. On the ribbon, under **FORM LAYOUT TOOLS**, click the **FORMAT tab**. In the **Font group**, click the **Font Size arrow**, and then click **14**. In the **Font group**, click **Bold B**. Click the **Font Color arrow**, and then under **Theme Colors**, in the fourth column, click the last color—**Olive Green, Text 2, Darker 50%**.

Activity 3.13 | Adding, Resizing, and Moving Controls in Layout View

In Layout view, you can change the form's *control layout*—the grouped arrangement of controls.

1 Be sure that your **3A Student Major Change Form** object displays in **Layout** view. On the ribbon, click the **DESIGN tab**, and in the **Tools group**, click **Add Existing Fields**. Compare your screen with Figure 3.18.

The Field List pane displays, which lists the fields in the underlying table—your 3A New Students table.

FIGURE 3.18

2 In the **Field List** pane, click **Student ID**, and then drag the field name to the left until the pointer displays above the **First Name label control** and a colored line displays above the control. Release the mouse button, and then compare your screen with Figure 3.19. If you are not satisfied with the result, click Undo, and begin again.

This action adds the Student ID label control and text box control to the form above the First Name controls.

FIGURE 3.19

3 **Close** [×] the **Field List** pane. Click the **Student ID text box control**, which displays *1034823*, to surround it with a border and to remove the border from the label control.

4 On the **DESIGN tab**, in the **Tools group**, click **Property Sheet**.

The Property Sheet for the Student ID text box control displays. Recall that each control has an associated Property Sheet where precise changes to the properties—characteristics—of selected controls can be made. At the top of the Property Sheet, to the right of *Selection type:*, *Text Box* displays because you selected the Student ID text box control.

5 In the **Property Sheet**, click the **Format tab**. Click **Width** to select the property setting, type **1.5** and then press Enter to decrease the width of the text box controls. Compare your screen with Figure 3.20.

All four text box controls are resized simultaneously. Because the controls are grouped together in a stacked layout, you can adjust the width of all of the text box controls at one time without having to select all of the controls. By decreasing the width of the text box controls, you have more space in which to rearrange the form controls. Because you can see the data in Layout view, you can determine visually that the space you have allotted is adequate to display all of the data in every field for every record.

🔄 ANOTHER WAY   With the text box control selected, point to the right edge of the text box control until the ↔ pointer displays, and then drag left to the desired location.

FIGURE 3.20

6 **Close** ✕ the **Property Sheet**. Click the **Last Name text box control**, which displays *Bass*. On the ribbon, under **FORM LAYOUT TOOLS**, click the **ARRANGE tab**. In the **Rows & Columns group**, click **Select Row** to select the text box control and its associated label control.

7 In the **Move group**, click **Move Up** to move both controls above the **First Name** controls, and then compare your screen with Figure 3.21.

🔄 ANOTHER WAY   Drag the selected controls to the desired location and then release the mouse button.

FIGURE 3.21

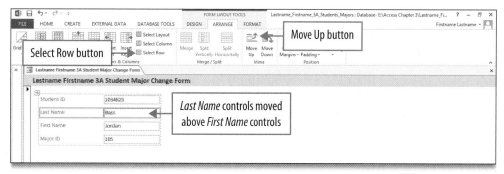

ALERT!   **Did the Last Name Label Control Not Move with the Last Name Text Box Control?**

Be sure to select both the text box control and the label control before moving the controls; otherwise, only one of the controls will move. If this happens, click Undo, select both controls, and try again. Controls are stacked from top to bottom, not right to left.

---

8 **Save** 🖫 the changes you have made to the design of your form.

Activity 3.14 | Formatting Controls in Layout View

In this activity, you will format and change the property settings for multiple controls.

1 With the form displayed in **Layout** view, click the **Student ID text box control**, which displays *1034823*. On the **ARRANGE tab**, in the **Rows & Columns group**, click **Select Column** to select all four text box controls.

ANOTHER WAY   Click the first text box control, hold down ⇧Shift, and then click the last text box control to select all four text box controls.

2 With all four text box controls selected, on the ribbon, click the **FORMAT tab**. In the **Font group**, click the **Background Color arrow** 🎨 ▾. Under **Theme Colors**, in the last column, click the second color—**Green, Accent 6, Lighter 80%**.

All of the text box controls display a background color of light green. This formatting is not applied to the label controls on the left.

3 Click the **Student ID label control**. On the ribbon, click the **ARRANGE tab**, and then in the **Rows & Columns group**, click **Select Column**. On the ribbon, click the **FORMAT tab**, and then click the **Font Color arrow**—*not* the **Background Color arrow**. Under **Theme Colors**, in the fourth column, click the first color—**Olive Green, Text 2**. Click **Bold** **B**. Click in a blank area of the form to cancel the selection, and then compare your screen with Figure 3.22.

FIGURE 3.22

Font color and bold applied to label controls

Background color changed for text box controls

4 Click any **label control** to display the **layout selector** ⊞, and then click the **layout selector** ⊞ to select all of the grouped controls.

Recall that the layout selector, which displays to the left and above the Student ID label control, enables you to select and move the entire group of controls in Layout view.

ANOTHER WAY   Click any control, and then on the ARRANGE tab, in the Rows & Columns group, click Select Layout.

5 On the **FORMAT tab**, in the **Font group**, click the **Font Size arrow**, and then click **12** to change the font size of all of the text in all of the controls.

6 With all of the controls still selected, on the ribbon, click the **DESIGN tab**. In the **Tools group**, click **Property Sheet**, and then compare your screen with Figure 3.23.

The Property Sheet for the selected controls displays. At the top of the Property Sheet, to the right of *Selection type:*, *Multiple selection* displays because you have more than one control selected.

FIGURE 3.23

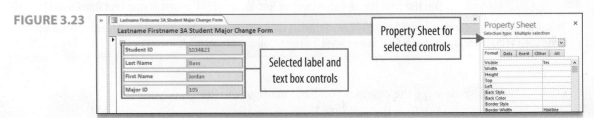

Property Sheet for selected controls

Selected label and text box controls

7 In the **Property Sheet**, click **Height**, type **0.25** and then press Enter to change the height of each selected control.

8 Click the **Student ID label control** to cancel the selection of all of the controls and to select only this label control. In the **Property Sheet**, click **Width**, type **1.25** and then press Enter.

The width of every label control changed to 1.25 inches. Recall that because the label controls are arranged in a stacked layout, you can change the width of all controls by selecting only one control. This is one of the few properties that can be changed without first selecting the column.

9 Close ☒ the **Property Sheet**, and then Save 🖫 the design changes to your form.

Activity 3.15 | Modifying a Form in Design View

Design view presents a detailed view of the structure of your form. Because the form is not actually running when displayed in Design view, the data does not display in the text box controls. However, some tasks, such as resizing sections, must be completed in Design view.

1 On the status bar, click **Design View** 🖳, and then compare your screen with Figure 3.24.

The form in Design view displays three sections, each designated by a *section bar* at the top of each section. The *Form Header* contains information, such as the form title, that displays at the top of the screen in Form view or Layout view and is printed at the top of the first page when records are printed as forms. The *Detail section* displays the records from the underlying table, and the *Form Footer* displays at the bottom of the screen in Form view or Layout view and is printed after the last detail section on the last page of a printout.

⟳ ANOTHER WAY   On the HOME tab, in the Views group, click the View arrow, and then click Design view; or right-click the object tab, and then click Design View.

FIGURE 3.24

2 At the bottom of the form, click the **Form Footer section bar** to select it. On the ribbon, click the **DESIGN tab**, and in the **Tools group**, click **Property Sheet**. In the **Property Sheet**, on the **Format tab**, click **Height**, type **0.5** and then press Enter. Compare your screen with Figure 3.25.

In addition to properties for controls, you can make precise changes to sections of the form. Because you selected the Form Footer section bar, the Property Sheet displays a *Selection type* of *Section*, and the section is identified as *Form Footer*.

⟳ ANOTHER WAY   At the bottom of the form, point to the lower edge of the Form Footer section bar to display the ⊞ pointer, and then drag downward approximately 0.5 inch to increase the height of the section.

FIGURE 3.25

Property Sheet for Form Footer section

Height changed to 0.5"

Form Footer section bar selected

Form Footer section height increased to 0.5"

3 ▶ On the **DESIGN tab**, in the **Controls group**, click **Label** $\boxed{Aa}$. Move the $^{+}\!A$ pointer into the **Form Footer** section and then position the plus sign of the $^{+}\!A$ pointer at approximately **0.25 inch on the horizontal ruler** and even with the lower edge of the **Form Footer section bar**—the position does not need to be precise. Compare your screen with Figure 3.26.

FIGURE 3.26

0.25 inch on horizontal ruler

Label control button

Label control pointer

4 ▶ Click one time. Type **Texas Lakes Community College** and then press Enter. With the **label control** selected, on the ribbon, click the **FORMAT tab**. In the **Font group**, click **Bold** $\boxed{B}$. Click the **Font Color arrow**, and then under **Theme Colors**, in the fourth column, click the first color—**Olive Green, Text 2**.

5 ▶ With the **label control** still selected, in the **Property Sheet**, click **Top**, type **0.1** and then press Enter. In the **Property Sheet**, in the **Left** property setting, type **0.6** and then press Enter. **Close** $\boxed{X}$ the **Property Sheet**, and then **Save** $\boxed{\blacksquare}$ the design changes to your form.

The top edge of the label control in the Form Footer section displays 0.1 inch from the lower edge of the Form Footer Section bar. The left edge of the label control aligns at 0.6 inch from the left margin of the form. In this manner, you can place a control in a specific location on the form.

6 ▶ On the right side of the status bar, click **Form View** $\boxed{\blacksquare}$, and then compare your screen with Figure 3.27.

Form Footer text displays on the screen at the bottom of the form and prints only on the last page if all of the forms are printed. Recall, that in Form view, you can add, modify, or delete records stored in the underlying table.

ANOTHER WAY On the HOME tab, in the Views group, click the View arrow, and then click Form View; or right-click the object tab, and then click Form View.

FIGURE 3.27

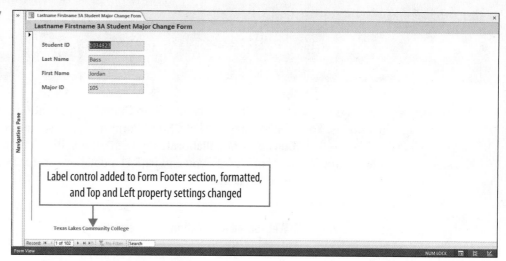

7 In the navigation area, click **Last record** to display the record containing your name.

8 On the ribbon, click the **FILE tab**, click **Print**, and then on the right, click **Print**. In the **Print** dialog box, under **Print Range**, click the **Selected Records(s)** option button. Create a paper or electronic printout as directed by your instructor. To create an electronic printout, follow the directions given in the Note in Activity 3.06.

Because you decreased the width of the text box controls, you do *not* have to adjust the Column size Width in the Page Setup dialog box as you did with the form you created by using the Form tool.

9 **Close** all open objects, and then **Open** the **Navigation Pane**. On the right side of the title bar, click **Close** to close the database and to exit Access. As directed by your instructor, submit your database and the paper or electronic printouts of the three forms that are the results of this project. Specifically, in this project, using your own name, you created the following database and printouts or electronic printouts:

1. Lastname_Firstname_3A_Students_Majors	Database file
2. Lastname Firstname 3A New Student Form	Form (printout or electronic printout - Record 102)
3. Lastname Firstname 3A Major Form	Form (printout or electronic printout - Record 33)
4. Lastname Firstname 3A Student Major Change Form	Form (printout or electronic printout - Record 102)

END | You have completed Project 3A

Objective | Export an Access Form to an Excel Spreadsheet, Save to SkyDrive, Edit a Record, and Save to Your Computer

Access web apps are designed to work with Microsoft's SharePoint, an application for setting up websites to share and manage documents. Your college may not have SharePoint installed, so you will use other tools to share objects from your database so that you can work collaboratively with others. Recall that Window's SkyDrive is a free file storage and file sharing service. For Access, you can export a database object to an Excel worksheet, a PDF file, or a text file, and then save the file to SkyDrive.

ALERT! **Working with Web-Based Applications and Services**

Computer programs and services on the web receive continuous updates and improvements. Thus, the steps to complete this web-based activity may differ from the ones shown. You can often look at the screens and the information presented to determine how to complete the activity.

Activity | **Exporting an Access Form to an Excel Spreadsheet, Saving the Spreadsheet to SkyDrive, Editing a Record in SkyDrive, and Saving to Your Computer**

In this activity, you will export your 3A Student Major Change Form object to an Excel spreadsheet, upload your Excel file to SkyDrive, edit a record in SkyDrive, and then download a copy of the edited spreadsheet to your computer.

1 Start Access, navigate to your **Access Chapter 3** folder, and then **Open** your **3A_Students_Majors** database file. If necessary, on the Message Bar, click Enable Content. In the **Navigation Pane**, click your **3A Student Major Change Form** object to select it.

2 On the ribbon, click the **EXTERNAL DATA tab**, and in the **Export group**, click **Excel**. In the **Export – Excel Spreadsheet** dialog box, click **Browse**, and then navigate to your **Access Chapter 3** folder. In the **File Save** dialog box, click in the **File name** box, type **Lastname_Firstname_AC_3A_Web** and then click **Save**.

3 In the **Export – Excel Spreadsheet** dialog box, under **Specify export options**, select the second check box—**Open the destination file after the export operation is complete**—and then click **OK**.

The records from the underlying table of the form display in Excel. When you export a form to Excel, the formatting and layout are automatically saved. For example, notice the olive green background color of the cells, which was the color that was applied to the text box controls in the form.

4 In the **Microsoft Excel** window, in the column headings row, to the left of column **A**, click **Select All**. On the **HOME tab**, in the **Cells group**, click **Format**, and then click **AutoFit Column Width**. Click in cell **A1** to cancel the selection, and then compare your screen with Figure A.

FIGURE A

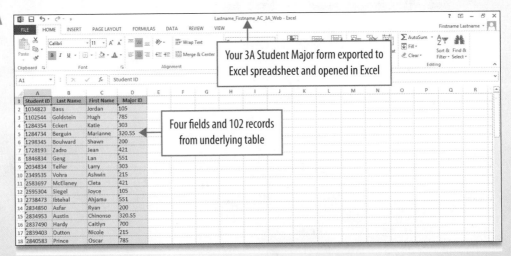

Your 3A Student Major form exported to Excel spreadsheet and opened in Excel

Four fields and 102 records from underlying table

(GO! with Office Web Apps continues on the next page)

5 Save the spreadsheet, and then Close Excel. In the **Export – Excel Spreadsheet** dialog box, click **Close**, and then **Close** Access.

6 From the desktop, start Internet Explorer, navigate to **http://skydrive.com**, and then sign in to your Microsoft account. Open your **GO! Web Projects** folder—or create and then open this folder if necessary.

7 On the menu bar, click **Upload**. In the **Choose File to Upload** dialog box, navigate to your **Access Chapter 3** folder, and then double-click your **AC_3A_Web** file to upload it to SkyDrive.

8 In your **GO! Web Projects** folder, click your **AC_3A_Web** file to open it in Microsoft Excel Web App.

On the ribbon, notice that you can open this worksheet in Excel instead of using the web app. If you are working on a computer that does not have Microsoft Excel installed, you can still create and modify workbooks in your web browser by using the Microsoft Excel Web App.

9 In the second record, click in the **Last Name** field, using your own last name, type **Lastname** and then press Tab. In the **First Name** field, using your own first name, type **Firstname** and then press ↓ to save the record. Compare your screen with Figure B.

10 On the ribbon, click the **FILE tab**, click **Save As**, and then click **Download**. In the message box—which usually displays at the bottom of your screen—click the **Save arrow**, and then click **Save as**. In the **Save As** dialog box, navigate to your **Access Chapter 3** folder, click in the **File name** box, and then type **Lastname_Firstname_A3A_Web_Download** and then click **Save**. **Close** the message box.

11 In SkyDrive, on the title bar, click **SkyDrive** to return to your home page. At the top right corner of your screen, click your SkyDrive name, and then click **Sign out**. **Close** your browser window.

12 Start Excel. In the Excel opening screen, click **Open Other Workbooks**. Under **Open**, click **Computer**, and then on the right, click **Browse**. Navigate to your **Access Chapter 3** folder, and then double-click your **A3A_Web** file. Notice that this file is the original file—the second record is not changed. If you are required to print your documents, use one of the methods in the Note box below. **Close** your Excel file, saving the changes to your worksheet, and then **Open** and print your **A3A_Web_Download** file following one of the methods in the Note box below. **Close** Excel, saving the changes to your worksheet. As directed by your instructor, submit your two workbooks and the two paper or electronic printouts that are the results of this project.

NOTE **Adding the File Name to the Footer and Printing or Creating an Electronic Printout of an Excel Spreadsheet of Only One Page**

Click the FILE tab, click Print, and then click Page Setup. In the Page Setup dialog box, click the Header/Footer tab, and then click Custom Footer. With the insertion point blinking in the Left section box, click the Insert File Name button, and then click OK. In the Page Setup dialog box, click OK. Under Settings, click the *Pages* spin box up arrow to display *1* in the box. Click the *to* spin box up arrow to display *1* in the box.

To print on paper, click Print. To create an electronic file of your printout, on the left side of your screen, click Export. Under Export, be sure Create PDF/XPS Document is selected, and then click Create PDF/XPS. In the Publish as PDF or XPS dialog box, click Options. In the Options dialog box, under Page range, click Pages, and be sure the From box displays *1* and the To box displays *1*; then click OK. Navigate to your Access Chapter 3 folder, and then click Publish to save the file with the default name and an extension of pdf.

FIGURE B

Job Openings Database

PROJECT ACTIVITIES

In Activities 3.16 through 3.24, you will assist Jack Woods, director of the Career Center for Texas Lakes Community College, in using his Access database to track the employees and job openings advertised for the annual job fair. Your completed reports will look similar to Figure 3.28.

PROJECT FILES

For Project 3B, you will need the following file:

a03B_Job_Openings

You will save your database as:

Lastname_Firstname_3B_Job_Openings

PROJECT RESULTS

Position	Employer Name	# Openings	Annual Salary
Senior Web Designer	Hi-Tech Solutions	1	$65,000
SQL/Unix Programmer	Hi-Tech Solutions	5	$78,000
		100	

Industry	Employer Name	Fee Paid
Hotel and Food Service		
	Robyn Rostamo Associates	$300
	Sweeney Catering	$500
	Van Etten Consulting	$500
Total Booth Fees by Industry		$1,300
		$800
		$200
		$1,000
		$300
		$300
		$600
		$300
		$300
		$20,400

Lastname Firstname 3B Salary $40,000 or More Report   Saturday, December 1, 2012
2:14:10 PM

Position	Employer Name	# Openings	Annual Salary
Actuary, Entry Level	Capital Insurance Brokers	5	$43,000
Actuary, Senior	Capital Insurance Brokers	3	$98,000
Actuary, Senior	Elgin Business Corporation	2	$83,450
Assistant Director of Pharmacy	Georgetown Medical Center	3	$95,000
ATM Operations Manager	Capital Eastern Bank	1	$60,000
Biostatistician, Entry Level	Buda Corporation	5	$50,225
Branch Manager	Capital Eastern Bank	2	$45,000
Catering Manager	Van Etten Consulting	3	$50,200
Civil Engineering Supervisor	Woodward Brothers Construction	5	$80,000
Clinical Studies Manager	Austin Medical Technologies Corp	1	$57,000
Clinical Studies Manager	Manor Pharmaceuticals	2	$59,800
Compensation Administrator	Smithville Management Association	2	$65,000
Construction Site Manager	Snyder Industrial	2	$78,450
Cruise Manager	Roberta Cool Travel	1	$55,000
Electrical Engineer	Freedom Data Storage	2	$105,000
Emergency Room Supervisor	Georgetown Medical Center	2	$82,000
Estimating Manager	Monroe Heating & Air Conditioning	6	$60,000
Executive Assistant	Greene Global Energy	1	$61,000
Executive Assistant	Van Etten Consulting	5	$40,000
Geologist	Texas Lakes Energy	3	$45,000
Human Resources Technician	Van Etten Consulting	5	$42,000
Internal Auditor	Dale Accounting Partners	3	$54,000
Management Consultant	Synergy Consulting	2	$75,000
Network Engineer	Pinewood Wireless	1	$42,000
Network Engineer	Freedom Data Storage	3	$66,000
Nuclear Medicine Director	Austin Medical Technologies Corp	1	$75,000
Nursing Supervisor	Georgetown Medical Center	10	$62,000
Petroleum Engineer, Mid Level	Texas Lakes Energy	5	$70,000
Physician Assistant	Underwood Medical Systems	4	$65,000
Quality Assurance Manager	Austin Medical Technologies Corp	1	$85,500
Senior Accountant	Buda Corporation	3	$65,000

Page 1 of 2

Lastname Firstname 3B Booth Fees by Industry Report

Industry	Employer Name	Fee Paid
Banking and Finance		
	Capital Eastern Bank	$300
	Dale Accounting Partners	$800
	Southwest Bank	$1,000
	Wimberley Bank and Trust Co	$2,300
Total Booth Fees by Industry		$4,400
Computer Hardware		
	Freedom Data Storage	$1,200
	Hart Computing	$300
	Pinewood Wireless	$1,000
Total Booth Fees by Industry		$2,500
Computer Software		
	Hi-Tech Solutions	$1,000
Total Booth Fees by Industry		$1,000
Construction		
	Monroe Heating & Air Conditioning	$900
	Snyder Industrial	$800
	Woodward Brothers Construction	$200
Total Booth Fees by Industry		$1,900
Environmental Technology		
	Greene Global Energy	$1,000
	Texas Lakes Energy	$1,500
Total Booth Fees by Industry		$2,500
General Administrative		
	Round Rock Business Systems	$500
	Smithville Management Association	$900
	Synergy Consulting	$700
Total Booth Fees by Industry		$2,100
Health Care		
	Austin Medical Technologies Corp	$1,000
	Georgetown Medical Center	$1,200
	Underwood Medical Systems	$600
Total Booth Fees by Industry		$2,800

Saturday, December 1, 2012   Page 1 of 2

Page 2 of 2

FIGURE 3.28 Project 3B Job Openings

Video A3-5

A *report* is a database object that summarizes the fields and records from a query or from a table in an easy-to-read format suitable for printing. A report consists of information extracted from queries or tables and report design controls, such as labels, headings, and graphics. The queries or tables that provide the underlying data for a report are referred to as the report's *record source*.

Activity 3.16   Opening and Saving an Existing Database, Renaming Objects, and Viewing a Table Relationship

1 Start Access. In the Access opening screen, click **Open Other Files**. Under **Open**, click **Computer**. Under **Recent Folders**, if displayed, click the location where your student data files are stored; otherwise, click **Browse** and then navigate to the location where your student data files are stored. Double-click **a03B_Job_Openings** to open the database.

2 On the **FILE tab**, click **Save As**. Under **File Types**, be sure **Save Database As** is selected. On the right, under **Database File Types**, be sure **Access Database** is selected, and then click **Save As**. In the **Save As** dialog box, navigate to your **Access Chapter 3** folder. In the **File name** box, replace the existing text with **Lastname_Firstname_3B_Job_Openings** and then press Enter.

3 On the **Message Bar**, click **Enable Content**. In the **Navigation Pane**, right-click the **3B Employers** table, and then click **Rename**. With the table name selected and using your own name, type **Lastname Firstname 3B Employers** and then press Enter to rename the table. Use the same technique to **Rename** the **3B Job Openings** table to **Lastname Firstname 3B Job Openings** and then **Rename** the first **3B Salary $40,000 or More Query** object to **Lastname Firstname 3B Salary $40,000 or More Query**

> Recall that a query that selects data from more than one table displays under both table names in the Navigation Pane. When you rename one of the query objects, the name of the second occurrence automatically changes.

4 Point to the right edge of the **Navigation Pane** to display the ⟷ pointer. Drag to the right to increase the width of the pane until all object names display fully.

5 On the ribbon, click the **DATABASE TOOLS tab**. In the **Relationships group**, click **Relationships**. Under **RELATIONSHIP TOOLS**, on the **DESIGN tab**, in the **Relationships group**, click **All Relationships**. Resize and move the field lists so that the entire table name and fields display for each field list.

> Because you renamed the tables, the field lists do not automatically display in the Relationships window.

6 In the **Relationships** window, click the **join line** between the two field lists. In the **Tools group**, click **Edit Relationships**. Point to the title bar of the **Edit Relationships** dialog box, and drag the dialog box downward below the **3B Job Openings** field list. Compare your screen with Figure 3.29.

> *One* employer is associated with *many* job openings. Thus, a one-to-many relationship is established between the 3B Employers table and the 3B Job Openings table by using Employee ID as the common field. Referential integrity is enforced, and cascade options are selected.

FIGURE 3.29

Join line with symbols indicating one-to-many relationships with referential integrity enforced

All objects renamed

Width of Navigation Pane increased

Employer ID is the common field

Edit Relationships dialog box

Cascade options selected

7 Close ⊠ the **Edit Relationships** dialog box, and then **Close** ✕ the **Relationships** window. In the message box, click **Yes** to save changes to the layout of the relationships.

8 In the **Navigation Pane**, double-click each table, and then examine the fields and data in each table. Double-click the query object to run the query and examine the query results, apply **Best Fit** to the query results, and then **Save** the query. Switch to **Design** view to examine the design grid.

> Because you renamed the tables that are the underlying source of data for the query, you have to reapply Best Fit to the query results. The query answers the question, *What is the Job ID, position, employer name, number of job openings, and annual salary for job openings that have an annual salary of $40,000 or more, in ascending order by the Employer Name field within the Position field?*

9 In the object window, right-click any **object tab**, and then click **Close All**.

Activity 3.17 | Creating a Report by Using the Report Tool and Applying a Theme to the Report

The ***Report tool*** is the fastest way to create a report. This tool displays all of the fields and records from the record source that you select. You can use the Report tool to look at the underlying data quickly in an easy-to-read format, after which you can save the report and modify it in Layout view or in Design view.

In this activity, you will use the Report tool to create a report from a query that lists all of the job openings with an annual salary of at least $40,000 and apply a theme to the report.

1 In the **Navigation Pane**, if necessary, click to select your **3B Salary $40,000 or More Query** object. On the ribbon, click the **CREATE tab**, and in the **Reports group**, click **Report**. **Close** ≪ the **Navigation Pane**, and then compare your screen with Figure 3.30.

> The report is created using the query as the record source and displays in Layout view. The report includes all of the fields and all of the records from the query and the title of the query. In Layout view, the broken lines indicate the page margins in the report.

FIGURE 3.30

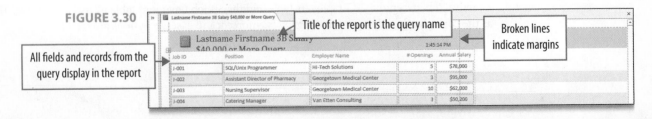

Title of the report is the query name

Broken lines indicate margins

All fields and records from the query display in the report

2 Under **REPORT LAYOUT TOOLS**, on the **DESIGN tab**, in the **Themes group**, click **Themes**. In the **Themes** gallery, use the ScreenTips to locate the **Integral** theme, right-click the **Integral** theme, and then click **Apply Theme to This Object Only**.

Recall that right-clicking a theme enables you to apply a predefined format to the active object only, which is a quick way to apply a professional look to a report. Apply a theme before formatting any other controls on the report.

Activity 3.18 | Modifying a Report in Layout View

After you create a report, you can make changes to it. For example, you can add or delete fields, resize the fields, and change the style of the report. Layout view enables you to see the data in the report as you modify the report. Most changes to a report can be made in Layout view.

1 Click the **Job ID** field name. On the ribbon, under **REPORT LAYOUT TOOLS**, click the **ARRANGE tab**. In the **Rows & Columns group**, click **Select Column** to select the field name and all of the data for each record in the field. Press Del to remove the field from the report.

The Job ID field is deleted, and the remaining fields move to the left. No fields extend beyond the right margin of the report.

ANOTHER WAY   With the column selected, on the HOME tab, in the Records group, click Delete; or right-click the selected column, and then click Delete or Delete Column.

2 Scroll down, and notice that for the position of *Estimating Manager*, there is an extra blank line in the fields for this record. In the **Employer Name** field, click in the **text box control** that displays *Monroe Heating & Air Conditioning* to select all of the text box controls in this field.

3 On the ribbon, under **REPORT LAYOUT TOOLS**, click the **DESIGN tab**. In the **Tools group**, click **Property Sheet**. In the **Property Sheet**, on the **Format tab**, click **Width**, type **2.5** and then press Enter. Compare your screen with Figure 3.31.

Recall that you can use the Property Sheet to make precise changes to control properties.

ANOTHER WAY   Point to the right edge of the text box control to display the ↔ pointer. Drag to the right slightly until the data in the text box control displays on one line.

FIGURE 3.31

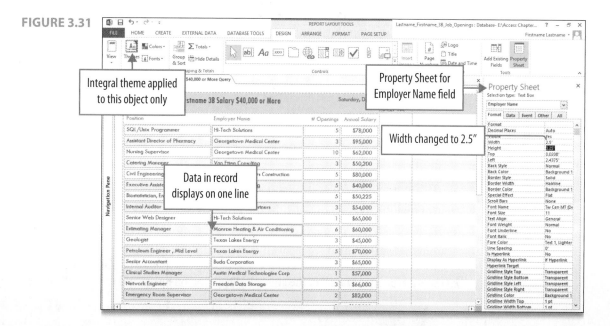

4 Close ☒ the **Property Sheet**. Click the **Position** field name, and then on the ribbon, click the **HOME tab**. In the **Sort & Filter group**, click **Ascending** to sort the records in ascending order by the Position field.

⟳ ANOTHER WAY   Right-click the selected field name and then click Sort A to Z.

5 Scroll to the bottom of the report, and then click the **calculated control** that displays *$2,157,625*, which is truncated at the bottom. Press Del to remove this control.

In a report created by using the Report tool, a *calculated control* is automatically created to sum any field that is formatted as currency. A calculated control contains an expression, often a formula or a function. Here, the total is not a useful number and thus can be deleted.

6 Scroll to the bottom of the report again, and then under the last column, click the horizontal line that is the border between the last record and the calculated control that you deleted. Press Del to remove this line, and then scroll to the bottom of the report to verify that the line has been deleted.

7 Scroll to the top of the report, and then click the **# Openings** field name. On the ribbon, click the **DESIGN tab**. In the **Grouping & Totals group**, click **Totals**, and then click **Sum**.

8 Scroll to the bottom of the report, and then click the **calculated control** that displays *100*. On the **DESIGN tab**, in the **Tools group**, click **Property Sheet**. In the **Property Sheet**, on the **Format tab**, click **Height**, type **0.25** and then press Enter. Compare your screen with Figure 3.32.

The total number of job openings for positions with a salary of $40,000 or more is 100.

⟳ ANOTHER WAY   Point to the lower edge of the text box control to display the ↕ pointer, and then double-click to resize the control, or drag downward to increase the height of the control.

FIGURE 3.32

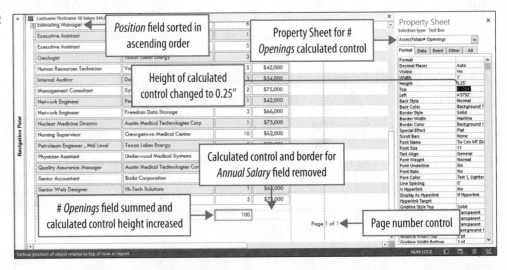

9 At the bottom of the report to the right of the calculated control, notice that the control that displays the page number does not fit entirely within the margins of the report. Click the **control** that displays *Page 1 of 1*. In the **Property Sheet**, click **Left**, type **2.5** and then press Enter.

The control moves within the margins of the report with the left edge of the control 2.5 inches in from the left margin of the report. When you click on different controls in a report or form, the Property Sheet changes to match the selected control. Before printing, always scroll through the report to be sure that all of the controls display on one page and not outside of the margins.

10 Scroll to the top of the report, and then click the **label control** that displays the title of the report—*Lastname Firstname 3B Salary $40,000 or More Query*. On the ribbon, under **REPORT LAYOUT TOOLS**, click the **FORMAT tab**. In the **Font group**, click the **Font Size arrow**, and then click **14**.

11 With the **label control** for the title still selected, double-click **Query** to select the word, type **Report** and then press Enter to change the name of the report to *Lastname Firstname 3B Salary $40,000 or More Report*.

12 Click the **Position** field name. In the **Property Sheet**, click **Left**, type **0.5** and then press Enter to move this field 0.5 inch in from the left margin of the report. Compare your screen with Figure 3.33.

The other fields adjust by moving to the right. The fields are centered approximately within the margins of the report.

FIGURE 3.33

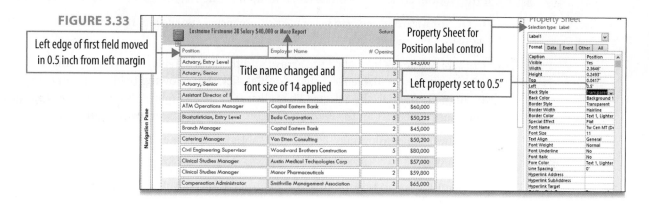

13 **Close** ![X] the **Property Sheet**, and then **Save** ![save] the report as **Lastname Firstname 3B Salary $40,000 or More Report**

Activity 3.19 | Printing a Report

In this activity, you will view your report in Print Preview and display the two pages of the report.

1 On the right side of the status bar, click **Print Preview** ![icon].

2 On the **PRINT PREVIEW tab**, in the **Zoom group**, click **Two Pages** to view the two pages of your report. Notice that the page number displays at the bottom of each page.

3 Create a paper or electronic printout as directed—two pages result, and then click **Close Print Preview**. **Close** ☒ the report, and then **Open** ☒ the **Navigation Pane**.

> The report displays under both tables from which the query was created. The report object name displays with a small green notebook icon.

4 **Close** ☒ the **Navigation Pane**.

Objective 6   Create a Report by Using the Report Wizard

Video A3-6

Use the ***Report Wizard*** when you need more flexibility in the design of your report. You can group and sort data by using the wizard and use fields from more than one table or query if you have created the relationships between tables. The Report Wizard is similar to the Form Wizard; the wizard walks you step by step through the process of creating the report by asking you questions and then designs the report based on your answers.

Activity 3.20   Creating a Report by Using the Report Wizard

In this activity, you will prepare a report for Mr. Woods that displays the employers, grouped by industry, and the total fees paid by employers for renting a booth at the Job Fair.

1 On the ribbon, click the **CREATE tab**, and then in the **Reports group**, click **Report Wizard**.

> In the first wizard screen, you select the fields to include on the report. The fields can come from more than one table or query.

2 In the **Tables/Queries** box, click the **arrow**, and then click **Table: Lastname Firstname 3B Employers**. In the **Available Fields** list, double-click the following field names in the order given to move them to the **Selected Fields** list: **Industry**, **Employer Name**, and **Fee Paid** (scroll as necessary to locate the *Fee Paid* field). Compare your screen with Figure 3.34.

> Three field names from your 3B Employers table display in the Selected Fields list.

 ANOTHER WAY   Click the field name, and then click One Field ⟩ to move a field from the Available Fields list to the Selected Fields list.

FIGURE 3.34

---

3 Click **Next**. In the wizard, notice that you can add grouping levels and that a preview of the grouping level displays on the right.

> Grouping data helps to organize and summarize the data in your report.

4 On the left, double-click **Industry**, and then compare your screen with Figure 3.35.

> The preview displays how the data will be grouped in the report. Grouping data in a report places all of the records that have the same data in a field together as a group—in this instance, the records will be grouped by *Industry*. Within each Industry name, the Employer Name and Fee Paid will display.

FIGURE 3.35

5 Click **Next**. Click the **1** box **arrow**, click **Employer Name**, and then compare your screen with Figure 3.36.

> In this step of the wizard, you indicate how you want to sort the records and summarize the information. You can sort up to four fields. The Summary Options button displays because the data is grouped, and at least one of the fields—*Fee Paid*—contains numerical or currency data. Within each Industry grouping, the records will be sorted alphabetically by the Employer Name. Sorting records in a report presents a more organized view of the records.

FIGURE 3.36

6 In the wizard, click **Summary Options**, and then compare your screen with Figure 3.37.

> The Summary Options dialog box displays. The *Fee Paid* field can be summarized by selecting one of the four check boxes for Sum, Avg, Min, or Max. You can also display only summary information or display both the details—each record—and the summary information. The default setting is to display *Detail and Summary*.

FIGURE 3.37

7 In the **Summary Options** dialog box, click to select the **Sum** check box. Under **Show**, be sure that **Detail and Summary** is selected, and then click **OK**. In the wizard, click **Next**.

> In this step of the wizard, you select the layout and page orientation. A preview of the layout displays on the left.

8 Click each **Layout** option button, noticing the changes in the preview, and then click **Stepped** to select it as the layout for your report. Under **Orientation**, be sure that **Portrait** is selected. At the bottom of the wizard, be sure that the **Adjust the field width so all fields fit on a page** check box is selected, and then click **Next**.

9 In the **What title do you want for your report?** box, select the existing text, type **Lastname Firstname 3B Booth Fees by Industry Report** and then click **Finish**. Compare your screen with Figure 3.38.

> The report is saved and displays in Print Preview using the specifications you defined in the Report Wizard. The records are grouped by Industry. Within each Industry, the records display in ascending order by the Employer Name. Within each Industry grouping, the Fee paid is summed or totaled—the word *Sum* displays at the end of each grouping.

FIGURE 3.38

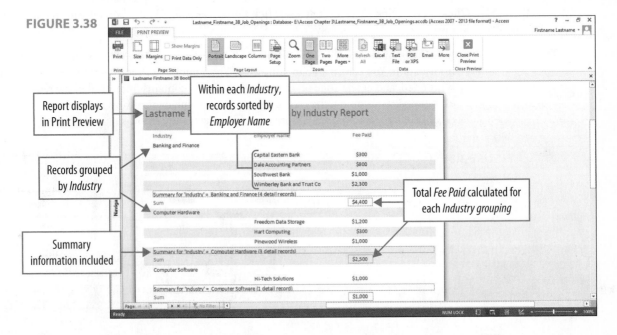

10 In the object window, right-click the **object tab** for the report, and then click **Layout View**.

 ANOTHER WAY   On the status bar, click Layout View 🔲; or click Close Print Preview, and then on the HOME tab or the DESIGN tab, click the View arrow, and then click Layout View.

Objective 7   Modify the Design of a Report

Video A3-7

You can modify the design of a report that is created using the Report Wizard by using the same techniques and tools that you use to modify a report created with the Report tool. Recall that most report modifications can be made in Layout view.

Activity 3.21 | Formatting and Deleting Controls in Layout View

In this activity, you will apply a theme to the report, format the title of the report, and delete the summary information controls.

1 Be sure that your **3B Booth Fees by Industry Report** object is displayed in **Layout** view. Under **REPORT LAYOUT TOOLS**, on the **DESIGN tab**, in the **Themes group**, click **Themes**. In the **Themes** gallery, use the ScreenTips to locate the **Ion Boardroom** theme, right-click the **Ion Boardroom** theme, and then click **Apply Theme to This Object Only**.

Recall that you should apply a theme before applying any other formatting changes. Also, recall that if you click a theme—instead of right-clicking—the theme is applied to all of the objects in the database.

2 At the top of the report, click the title—*Lastname Firstname 3B Booth Fees by Industry*—to display a border around the label control. On the ribbon, under **REPORT LAYOUT TOOLS**, click the **FORMAT tab**. In the **Font group**, click the **Font Size arrow**, and then click **14**. In the **Font group**, click **Bold** $\boxed{\text{B}}$.

By changing the font size, the report name is no longer truncated and includes the word *Report*.

3 Within each *Industry* grouping, notice the **Summary for 'Industry'** information.

Because you selected Summary Options, a summary line is included at the end of each grouping that details what is being summarized—in this case, summed—and the number of records that are included in the summary total. Now that Mr. Woods has viewed the report, he has decided that this information is not necessary and can be removed.

4 Click any one of the controls that begins with **Summary for 'Industry'**.

The control that you clicked is surrounded by a border, and all of the other summary information controls are surrounded by paler borders to indicate that all controls are selected.

5 Press $\boxed{\text{Del}}$ to remove the controls from the report, and then compare your screen with Figure 3.39.

ANOTHER WAY Right-click any of the selected controls, and then click Delete to remove the controls from the report.

FIGURE 3.39

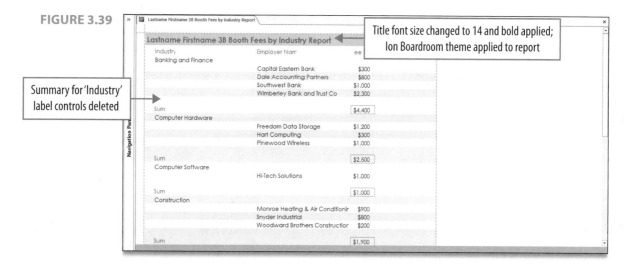

Summary for 'Industry' label controls deleted

Title font size changed to 14 and bold applied; Ion Boardroom theme applied to report

6 Save $\boxed{\text{H}}$ the changes you have made to the design of the report.

Activity 3.22 | Modifying Controls in Layout View

In this activity, you will modify the text in controls, move controls, resize controls, and add a control to the report in Layout view.

1 On the left side of the report, click a **Sum label control**, which selects all of the related controls. Double-click the control to select the text—*Sum*. Type **Total Booth Fees by Industry** and then press Enter. Compare your screen with Figure 3.40.

This text states more clearly what is being summed.

FIGURE 3.40

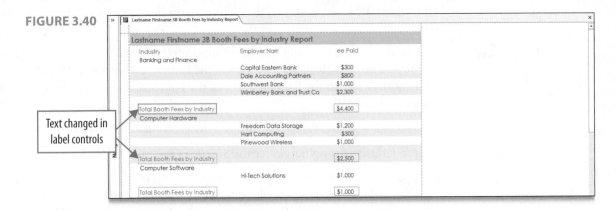

2 At the top of the report, click the **Industry label control** to select it. Hold down Shift, click the **Employer Name label control**, and then click the **Fee Paid label control** to select all three field names. On the **FORMAT tab**, in the **Font group**, click **Bold** B.

Clicking Bold also increases the size of the controls so that the text is no longer truncated.

3 At the top of the report, under the **Fee Paid label control**, click the **text box control** that displays *$300* to select the text box controls for all of the records for this field. On the ribbon, click the **DESIGN tab**. In the **Tools group**, click **Property Sheet**. In the **Property Sheet**, on the **Format tab**, click **Left**, type **7** and then press Enter. Compare your screen with Figure 3.41.

All of the Fee Paid text box controls move to the right—7" in from the left margin. Do not be concerned that the summary total and the field name are not aligned with the data; you will correct this in the next activity. The field is moved to the right so that you can increase the width of the Employer Name text box controls so that all of the data for every record displays.

FIGURE 3.41

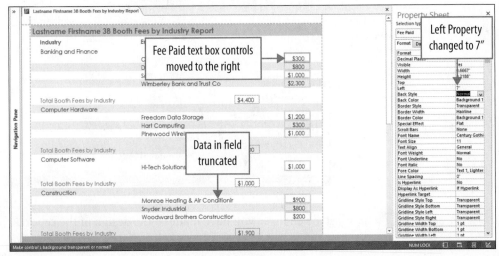

4 Scroll to view the bottom of the report. Click to select the **calculated control** for the **Grand Total,** which displays *20,400* and part of the dollar symbol. In the **Property Sheet**, click **Width**, type **0.8** and then press Enter.

> The width of the calculated control increases to display the dollar symbol. Do not be concerned that the right edge of the control no longer aligns with the control above it; you will correct this in the next activity. Recall that a calculated control contains an expression—a formula or function—that displays the result of the expression when the report is displayed in Report view, Print Preview, or Layout view.

↻ ANOTHER WAY Point to the left edge of the control to display the ↔ pointer. Drag to the left slightly to increase the width of the calculated control.

5 At the bottom of the report, on the left side, click the **Grand Total label control**. In the **Property Sheet**, click **Width**, type **1** and then press Enter. Compare your screen with Figure 3.42.

> The width of the label control is increased so that all of the text displays.

↻ ANOTHER WAY Point to the right edge of the control to display the ↔ pointer, and then double-click to resize the control.

FIGURE 3.42

6 Scroll to the top to display the Industry grouping of **Construction**, and notice that the first and third records have truncated data in the **Employer Name** field. In the **Construction** grouping, click, the **Employer Name text box control** that starts with *Monroe Heating* to select all of the text box controls for this field.

7 In the **Property Sheet**, click **Width**, type **3** and then press Enter. **Save** 🖫 the design changes to your report, and then compare your screen with Figure 3.43.

> The width of the Employer Name text box controls is increased so that all of the data in this field for every record displays. Recall that you moved the Fee Paid text box controls to the right to make room for the increased width of these controls.

FIGURE 3.43

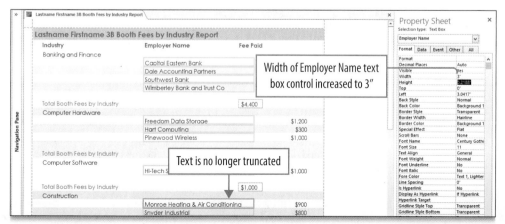

Activity 3.23 | Aligning Controls in Design View

Design view gives you a more detailed view of the structure of your report. You can see the header and footer sections for the report, for the page, and for groups. In Design view, your report is not running, so you cannot see the data from the table in the controls. In the same manner as forms, you can add labels to the Page Footer section or increase the height of sections. Some tasks, such as aligning controls, must be completed in Design view.

1 **Close** ✖ the **Property Sheet**. On the status bar, click **Design View** ✎, and then compare your screen with Figure 3.44.

Design view for a report is similar to Design view for a form. You can modify the layout of the report in this view, and use the dotted grid pattern to align controls. This report has several sections. The **Report Header** displays information at the top of the *first page* of a report. The **Page Header** displays information at the top of *every page* of a report. The **Group Header** displays the name of data in the field by which the records are grouped; in this case, the *Industry* name. The **Detail** section displays the data for each record. The **Group Footer** displays the summary information for each grouping; in this case, the Industry name. The **Page Footer** displays information at the bottom of *every page* of the report. The **Report Footer** displays information at the bottom of the *last page* of the report.

If you do not group data in a report, the Group Header section and Group Footer section will not display. If you do not summarize the data, the Group Footer section will not display.

FIGURE 3.44

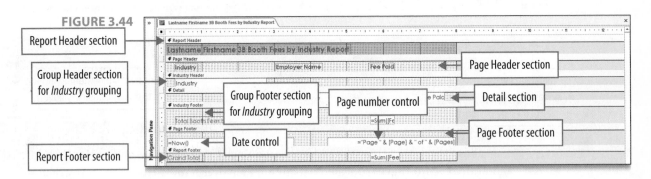

2 In the **Page Footer** section of the report, examine the two controls in this section. Recall that information in the Page Footer section displays at the bottom of every page in the report.

On the left side, the **date control** displays *=Now( )*, which inserts the current date each time the report is opened. On the right side, the **page number control** displays *="Page " & [Page] & " of " & [Pages]*, which inserts the page number, for example *Page 1 of 2*, when the report is displayed in Print Preview or when printed. Both of these controls contain examples of functions that are used by Access to create controls in a report.

3 In the **Industry Footer** section, click the **Total Booth Fees by Industry label control**. Hold down Shift, and in the **Report Footer** section, click the **Grand Total label control** to select both label controls.

4 On the ribbon, under **REPORT DESIGN TOOLS**, click the **ARRANGE tab**. In the **Sizing & Ordering group**, click **Align**, and then click **Left**.

The left edge of the *Grand Total label control* is aligned with the left edge of the *Total Booth Fees by Industry label control*. When using the Align Left command, the left edges of the selected controls are aligned with the control that is the farthest to the left in the report.

5 In the **Page Header** section, click the **Fee Paid label control**. Hold down ⇧Shift while you click the following: in the **Detail** section, click the **Fee Paid text box control**; in the **Industry Footer** section, click the **calculated control** that begins with =*Sum*; and in the **Report Footer** section, click the **calculated control** that begins with =*Sum*.

> Four controls are selected.

6 On the **ARRANGE tab**, in the **Sizing & Ordering group**, click **Align**, and then click **Right**. **Save** 🖫 the design changes to your report, and then compare your screen with Figure 3.45.

> The right edges of the four selected controls are aligned with the right edge of the *Fee Paid text box control*. When using the Align Right command, the right edges of the selected controls are aligned with the control that is the farthest to the right in the report.

FIGURE 3.45

7 On the status bar, click **Layout View** 🗉 to display the underlying data in the controls. Scroll to view the bottom of the report. On the left side, notice that the **Total Booth Fees by Industry label control** and the **Grand Total label control** are left aligned. Also, notice the right alignment of the controls in the **Fee Paid** column.

Objective 8 Keep Grouped Data Together in a Printed Report

Video A3-8

Before you print a report, examine the report in Print Preview to be sure that all of the labels and data display fully and to be sure that all of the data is properly grouped. Sometimes a page break occurs in the middle of a group of data, leaving the labels on one page and the data or summary information on another page.

Activity 3.24 | Keeping Grouped Data Together in a Printed Report

In this activity, you will preview the document and then will keep the data in each group together so a grouping is not split between two pages of the report. This is possible if the data in a grouping does not exceed the length of a page.

1 On the status bar, click **Print Preview** 🔍. On the **PRINT PREVIEW tab**, in the **Zoom group**, click **Two Pages**, and then compare your screen with Figure 3.46.

> The report will print on two pages. For the Industry grouping of *Hotel and Food Service*, one record and the summary data display at the top of Page 2 and is separated from the rest of the grouping that displays at the bottom of page 1. Your display may differ depending upon your printer configuration.

> In Print Preview, the One Page or Two Pages Zoom view causes the records to be compressed slightly and might display with the bottoms of records truncated. The records, however, will print correctly.

FIGURE 3.46

Bottom of first page—*Industry* grouping name and two records

Top of second page—one record and summary data for *Hotel and Food Service* grouping

2 On the ribbon, click **Close Print Preview** to return to **Layout** view. On the **DESIGN tab**, in the **Grouping & Totals group**, click **Group & Sort**.

At the bottom of the screen, the *Group, Sort, and Total pane* displays. This pane is used to control how information is grouped, sorted, or totaled. Layout view is the preferred view in which to accomplish these tasks because you can see how the changes affect the display of the data in the report.

3 In the **Group, Sort, and Total** pane, on the **Group on Industry** bar, click **More**. To the right of **do not keep group together on one page**, click the **arrow**, and then compare your screen with Figure 3.47.

The *keep whole group together on one page* command keeps each industry group together, from the name in the Group Header section through the summary information in the Group Footer section. The default setting is *do not keep group together on one page*. Next to *Group on Industry*, with *A on top* indicates that the industry names are sorted in ascending order.

FIGURE 3.47

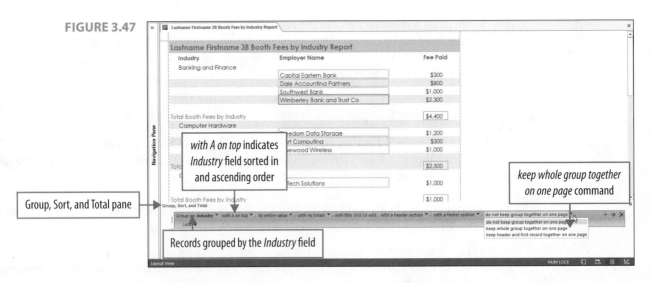

Group, Sort, and Total pane

with A on top indicates *Industry* field sorted in and ascending order

Records grouped by the *Industry* field

keep whole group together on one page command

4 Click **keep whole group together on one page**. On the **DESIGN tab**, in the **Grouping & Totals group**, click **Group & Sort** to close the **Group, Sort, and Total** pane.

5 On the status bar, click **Print Preview** 🔍. If necessary, in the Zoom group, click Two Pages. Compare your screen with Figure 3.48.

> The entire grouping for the Industry of *Hotel and Food Service* displays at the top of page 2. The grouping no longer breaks between page 1 and page 2. Recall that even though the bottoms of records display truncated because of the compressed Print Preview setting of Two Pages, the records will print correctly.

FIGURE 3.48

Entire *Hotel and Food Service* grouping kept together at top of second page

6 **Save** 💾 the design changes to your report, and then create a paper or electronic printout of the report as directed—two pages result.

7 **Close** ❎ the report, and then **Open** » the **Navigation Pane**. If necessary, increase the width of the Navigation Pane so that all object names display fully.

8 On the right side of the title bar, click **Close** ❎ to close the database and to exit Access. As directed by your instructor, submit your database and the paper or electronic printouts of the two reports—each report is two pages—that are the results of this project. Specifically, in this project, using your own name you created the following database and printouts or electronic printouts:

1. Lastname_Firstname_3B_Job_Openings	Database file
2. Lastname Firstname 3B Salary $40,000 or More Report	Report (printout or electronic printout - two pages)
3. Lastname Firstname 3B Booth Fees by Industry Report	Report (printout or electronic printout - two pages)

END | You have completed Project 3B

GO! with Office Web Apps

Objective Export an Access Report to a Word File, Save to SkyDrive, and Add a Description to the Word File

Access web apps are designed to work with Microsoft's SharePoint, an application for setting up websites to share and manage documents. Your college may not have SharePoint installed, so you will use other tools to share objects from your database so that you can work collaboratively with others. When you have information that you want to share with others, you can upload files to SkyDrive. Some files can be opened in SkyDrive; some can only be downloaded. Because database files are typically large in size, and free storage space on SkyDrive is limited, you can export database objects to different formats and then upload those files to SkyDrive.

> **ALERT!**   Working with Web-Based Applications and Services
>
> Computer programs and services on the web receive continuous updates and improvements. Thus, the steps to complete this web-based activity may differ from the ones shown. You can often look at the screens and the information presented to determine how to complete the activity.

Activity | Exporting an Access Report to a Word File, Uploading the Word File to SkyDrive, and Adding a Description to the Word File

In this activity, you will export your 3B Salary $40,000 or More Report object to a Word file, upload your Word file to SkyDrive, and then add a description to the Word file. The report will be available for individuals with whom you have shared your SkyDrive files or folders.

1 Start Access, navigate to your **Access Chapter 3** folder, and then **Open** your **3B_Job_Openings** database file. If necessary, on the Message Bar, click Enable Content. In the **Navigation Pane**, click your **3B Salary $40,000 or More Report** object to select it.

2 On the ribbon, click the **EXTERNAL DATA tab**, and in the **Export group**, click **More**, and then click **Word**.

The report will be exported as a *Rich Text Format (RTF)*—a standard file format that contains text and some formatting such as underline, bold, italic, font sizes, and colors. RTF documents can be opened in many word processing programs and text editors.

3 In the **Export – RTF File** dialog box, navigate to your **Access Chapter 3** folder. In the **File Save** dialog box, click in the **File name** box to select the existing text. Type **Lastname_Firstname_AC_3B_Web** and then click **Save**. In the **Export – RTF File** dialog box, select the **Open the destination file after the export operation is complete** check box, and then click **OK**. Compare your screen with Figure A.

The RTF file is created and opens in Word.

4 **Close** ☒ Word. In the **Export – RTF File** dialog box, click **Close**, and then **Close** ☒ Access.

FIGURE A

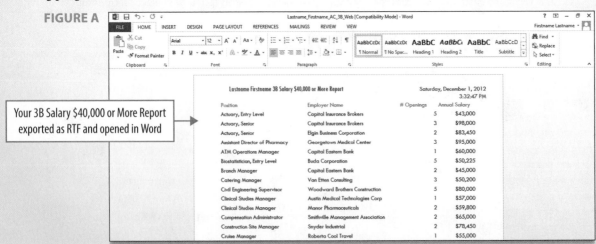

Your 3B Salary $40,000 or More Report exported as RTF and opened in Word

(GO! with Office Web Apps continues on the next page)

5 From the desktop, start Internet Explorer, navigate to **http://skydrive.com**, and then sign in to your Microsoft account. Open your **GO! Web Projects** folder—or create and then open this folder if necessary.

6 On the menu bar, click **Upload**. In the **Choose File to Upload** dialog box, navigate to your **Access Chapter 3** folder, and then double-click your **AC_3B_Web** file to upload it to SkyDrive.

7 After the file is uploaded, in your **GO! Web Projects** folder, right-click your **AC_3B_Web** file, and then click **Properties**.

A Properties panel displays on the right side of your screen.

8 In the **Properties** panel, click **Add a description**. In the box, type **This report displays job openings in our area that have a salary of $40,000 or more for which our students can apply.** Press Enter, and then compare your screen with Figure B.

9 On your keyboard, press the ⊞ key, type **snip**, and then click **Snipping Tool**. In the **Snipping Tool** dialog box, click the **New arrow**, and then click **Full-screen Snip**.

10 On the **Snipping Tool** toolbar, click **Save Snip** 🖫. In the **Save As** dialog box, navigate to your **Access Chapter 3** folder. Click in the **File name** box to select the existing text. Type **Lastname_Firstname_AC_3B_Web_Snip** and then, if necessary, click the **Save as type arrow**, and click **JPEG file**. In the **Save As** dialog box, click **Save**, and then **Close** ⊠ the **Snipping Tool** window.

11 In SkyDrive, on the title bar, click **SkyDrive** to return to your home page. At the top right corner of your screen, click your SkyDrive name, and then click **Sign out**. **Close** your browser window.

12 If directed to submit a paper printout of your RTF document and snip file, follow the directions given in the Note below. As directed by your instructor, submit your RTF document, which is two pages, and your snip file that are the results of this project.

N O T E   **Printing your RTF Document and Your Snip .JPEG File**

Using Windows Explorer, navigate to your Access Chapter 3 folder. Locate and double-click your AC_3B_Web file—it will open in Word. On the ribbon, click the FILE tab, and then click Print. To print on paper, on the right, click Print. To create an electronic file of your printout, on the left side of your screen, click Export. Under Export, be sure Create PDF/XPS Document is selected, and then click Create PDF/XPS. Navigate to your Access Chapter 3 folder, and then click Publish to save the file with the default name and an extension of pdf.

In your Access Chapter 3 folder, locate and double-click your AC_3B_Web_Snip file. If this is the first time you have tried to open a .jpeg file, you will be asked to identify a program. If you are not sure which program to use, select Windows Photo Viewer. From the ribbon, menu bar, or toolbar, click the Print command, and then Close the program window.

FIGURE B

Andrew Rodriguez / Fotolia; FotolEdhar/ Fotolia; apops/ Fotolia; Yuri Arcurs/ Fotolia

The advantage of using Office 365 is that your organization does not have to purchase and install server hardware and software for sophisticated business applications and does not need a full-time IT person or staff just to manage the technology your teams need.

By using Office 365, you are able to have business-class services for your employees without investing in expensive hardware, software, and personnel. However, at least one person in an organization must be designated as the *Office 365 Administrator*—the person who creates and manages the account, adds new users, sets up the services your organization wants to use, sets permission levels, and manages the SharePoint team sites. You can have more than one administrator if you want to share these tasks with others.

Microsoft provides easy-to-use instructions and videos to get you started, and you might also have contact with a Microsoft representative. You will probably find, however, that subscribing to and setting up the account, adding users, and activating services is a straightforward process that requires little or no assistance.

After purchasing the required number of licenses, you will add each team member as a user that includes his or her email address. The Admin Overview page, as shown in Figure A, assists the Office 365 Administrator. On the left, there are links to manage the users and domains in your Office 365 account. This is where you can add new users, delete users, set permission levels, enter and change passwords, and update the user properties and the licenses.

On this page, you can see the various services available to you in Office 365. In the site shown in Figure A, Outlook, Lync, SharePoint (team sites), and a public-facing website are all part of the services.

Activity | Using a Team Site to Collaborate

This group project relates to the **Bell Orchid Hotels**. If your instructor assigns this project to your class, you will use a SharePoint team site in **Office 365** to collaborate on the following tasks for this chapter:

- If you are in the **Accounting Group**, you and your teammates will finalize the Stockholders database and post it on the SharePoint team site.

- If you are in the **Engineering Group**, you and your teammates will finalize the Subcontractors database and post it on the SharePoint team site.

- If you are in the **Food and Beverage Group**, you and your teammates will finalize Banquet Clients database and post it on the SharePoint team site.

- If you are in the **Human Resources Group**, you and your teammates will finalize the Employees database and post it on the SharePoint team site.

- If you are in the **Operations Group**, you and your teammates will finalize the Guests Database and post it on the SharePoint team site.

- If you are in the **Sales and Marketing Group**, you and your teammates will finalize the Associations database and post it on the SharePoint team site.

FIGURE A

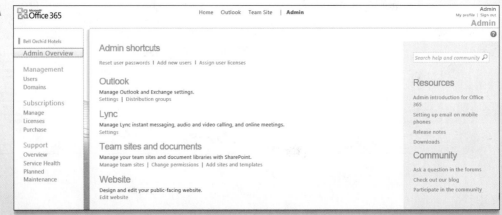

END OF CHAPTER

SUMMARY

A form is a database object that you can use to enter new records into a table, or to edit, delete, or display existing records in a table and can be used to control access to the data in a database.

Filter records in a form to display only a subset of the total records based on matching specific values to provide a quick answer to a question. Filters are generally not saved with a form.

A report is a database object that summarizes the fields and records from a query or from a table, in an easy-to-read format suitable for printing. You can group records and summarize the data in a report.

Most changes to forms and reports can be done in Layout view where the underlying data displays in the controls; however, some modifications, such as aligning controls, must be done in Design view.

GO! LEARN IT ONLINE

Review the concepts and key terms in this chapter by completing these online challenges, which you can find at **www.pearsonhighered.com/go**.

Matching and Multiple Choice:
Answer matching and multiple choice questions to test what you learned in this chapter. MyITLab®

Crossword Puzzle:
Spell out the words that match the numbered clues, and put them in the puzzle squares.

Flipboard:
Flip through the definitions of the key terms in this chapter and match them with the correct term.

GO! FOR JOB SUCCESS

Video: Performance Evaluations

Your instructor may assign this video to your class, and then ask you to think about, or discuss with your classmates, these questions:

FotolEdhar / Fotolia

What kind of message is Sara sending by forgetting to do the self-assessment review she was assigned for her evaluation? Why is it important to do a self-assessment for a review?

How should Sara react to her supervisor's criticisms in her review?

How important is it to follow a company's dress code policy? Do you think Sara's response to not following the dress code is appropriate? Why or why not?

END OF CHAPTER

REVIEW AND ASSESSMENT GUIDE FOR ACCESS CHAPTER 3

Your instructor may assign one or more of these projects to help you review the chapter and assess your mastery and understanding of the chapter.

	Review and Assessment Guide for Access Chapter 3		
Project	**Apply Skills from These Chapter Objectives**	**Project Type**	**Project Location**
3C	Objectives 1-4 from Project 3A	**3C Skills Review** A guided review of the skills from Project 3A.	On the following pages
3D	Objectives 5-8 from Project 3B	**3D Skills Review** A guided review of the skills from Project 3B.	On the following pages
3E	Objectives 1-4 from Project 3A	**3E Mastery (Grader Project)** A demonstration of your mastery of the skills in Project 3A with extensive decision making.	In MyITLab and on the following pages
3F	Objectives 5-8 from Project 3B	**3F Mastery (Grader Project)** A demonstration of your mastery of the skills in Project 3B with extensive decision making.	In MyITLab and on the following pages
3G	Objectives 1-8 from Projects 3A and 3B	**3G Mastery (Grader Project)** A demonstration of your mastery of the skills in Projects 3A and 3B with extensive decision making.	In MyITLab and on the following pages
3H	Combination of Objectives from Projects 3A and 3B	**3H GO! Fix It** A demonstration of your mastery of the skills in Projects 3A and 3B by creating a correct result from a document that contains errors you must find.	Online
3I	Combination of Objectives from Projects 3A and 3B	**3I GO! Make It** A demonstration of your mastery of the skills in Projects 3A and 3B by creating a result from a supplied picture.	Online
3J	Combination of Objectives from Projects 3A and 3B	**3J GO! Solve It** A demonstration of your mastery of the skills in Projects 3A and 3B, your decision-making skills, and your critical thinking skills. A task-specific rubric helps you self-assess your result.	Online
3K	Combination of Objectives from Projects 3A and 3B	**3K GO! Solve It** A demonstration of your mastery of the skills in Projects 3A and 3B, your decision-making skills, and your critical thinking skills. A task-specific rubric helps you self-assess your result.	On the following pages
3L	Combination of Objectives from Projects 3A and 3B	**3L GO! Think** A demonstration of your understanding of the chapter concepts applied in a manner that you would outside of college. An analytic rubric helps you and your instructor grade the quality of your work by comparing it to the work an expert in the discipline would create.	On the following pages
3M	Combination of Objectives from Projects 3A and 3B	**3M GO! Think** A demonstration of your understanding of the chapter concepts applied in a manner that you would outside of college. An analytic rubric helps you and your instructor grade the quality of your work by comparing it to the work an expert in the discipline would create.	Online
3N	Combination of Objectives from Projects 3A and 3B	**3N You and GO!** A demonstration of your understanding of the chapter concepts applied in a manner that you would in a personal situation. An analytic rubric helps you and your instructor grade the quality of your work.	Online
3O	Combination of Objectives from Projects 3A and 3B	**3O Cumulative Group Project for Access Chapter 3** A demonstration of your understanding of concepts and your ability to work collaboratively in a group role-playing assessment, requiring both collaboration and self-management.	Online
Capstone Project for Access Chapters 1-3	Combination of Objectives from Projects 1A, 1B, 2A, 2B, 3A, and 3B	A demonstration of your mastery of the skills in Chapters 1-3 with extensive decision making. **(Grader Project)**	In MyITLab and online

GLOSSARY

GLOSSARY OF CHAPTER KEY TERMS

AND condition A condition in which records display only when all of the values are present in the selected fields.

Bound A term used to describe objects and controls that are based on data that is stored in tables.

Bound control A control that retrieves its data from an underlying table or query; a text box control is an example of a bound control.

Calculated control A control that contains an expression, often a formula or function, that most often summarizes a field that contains numerical data.

Control An object on a form or report that displays data or text, performs actions, and lets you view and work with information.

Control layout The grouped arrangement of controls on a form or report; for example, the Stacked layout.

Data entry The action of entering the data into a record in a database table or form.

Date control A control on a form or report that inserts the current date each time the form or report is opened.

Design view The Access view that displays the detailed structure of a query, form, or report; for forms and reports, may be the view in which some tasks must be performed, and only the controls, and not the data, display.

Detail section The section of a form or report that displays the records from the underlying table or query.

Filter by Form An Access command that filters the records in a form based on one or more fields, or based on more than one value in the field.

Filter by Selection An Access command that displays only the records that contain the value in the selected field and hides the records that do not contain the value.

Filtering The process of displaying only a portion of the total records (a subset) based on matching specific values to provide a quick answer to a question.

Form A database object that you can use to enter new records into a table, or to edit, delete, and display existing records in a table.

Form Footer Information at the bottom of the screen in Form view or Layout view that is printed after the last detail section on the last page of a printout.

Form Header Information such as a form's title that displays at the top of the screen in Form view or Layout view and is printed at the top of the first page when records are printed as forms.

Form tool An Access tool that creates a form with a single mouse click, which includes all of the fields from the underlying data source (table or query).

Form view The Access view in which you can view, modify, delete, or add records in a table; but you cannot change the layout or design of the form.

Form Wizard An Access tool that walks you step by step through the creation of a form and that gives you more flexibility in the design, layout, and number of fields in a form.

Group Footer Information printed at the end of each group of records; used to display summary information for the group.

Group Header Information printed at the beginning of each new group of records; for example, the group name.

Group, Sort, and Total pane A pane that displays at the bottom of the screen in which you can control how information is sorted and grouped in a report; provides the most flexibility for adding or modifying groups, sort orders, or totals options on a report.

Label control A control on a form or report that contains descriptive information, usually a field name or title.

Layout selector A small symbol that displays in the upper left corner of a selected control layout in a form or report that is displayed in Layout view or Design view; used to move or format an entire group of controls.

Layout view The Access view in which you can make changes to a form or report while the object is running—the data from the underlying data source displays.

Office 365 Administrator In Office 365, the person who creates and manages the account, adds new users, sets up the services your organization wants to use, sets permission levels, and manages the SharePoint team sites.

OR condition A condition in which records display that match at least one of the specified values.

Page Footer Information printed at the bottom of every page in a report; most often includes the page number.

Page Header Information printed at the top of every page in a report.

Page number control A control on a form or report that inserts the page numbers when displayed in Print Preview or when printed.

Record selector bar The vertical bar at the left edge of a record when it is displayed in a form that is used to select an entire record.

Record source The tables or queries that provide the underlying data for a form or report.

Report A database object that summarizes the fields and records from a query or table in an easy-to-read format suitable for printing.

Report Footer Information printed at the bottom of the last page of a report.

Report Header Information printed on the first page of a report; used for logos, titles, and dates.

Report tool An Access tool that creates a report with one mouse click and displays all of the fields and records from the record source that you select.

Report Wizard An Access tool that walks you step by step through the creation of a report and that gives you more flexibility in the design, layout, and number of fields in a report.

Rich Text Format (RTF) A standard file format that contains text and some formatting such as underline, bold, italic, font sizes, and colors; RTF documents can be opened in many word processing programs and text editors.

Section bar In Design view, a gray bar in a form or report that identifies and separates one section from another; used to select the section and to change the size of the section.

Stacked layout A control layout format that is similar to a paper form, with label controls placed to the left of each text box control; the controls are grouped together for easy editing.

Subset A portion of the total records available.

Tab order The order in which the insertion point moves from one field to another in a form when you press the Tab key.

Text box control A bound control on a form or report that displays the data from the underlying table or query.

Theme A predesigned set of colors, fonts, lines, and fill effects that look good together and that can be applied to all of the objects in the database or to individual objects in the database.

Unbound control A control that does not have a source of data, such as the title in a form or report.

CHAPTER REVIEW

Apply **3A** skills from these Objectives:
1 Create and Use a Form to Add and Delete Records
2 Filter Records
3 Create a Form by Using the Form Wizard
4 Modify a Form in Layout View and in Design View

Skills Review Project 3C Student Internships

In the following Skills Review, you will assist Erinique Jerlin, the dean of Business at the Northwest Campus, in using her database to track business students and their internship placements for the current semester. Your completed forms will look similar to Figure 3.49.

PROJECT FILES

For Project 3C, you will need the following file:

a03C_Student_Internships

You will save your database as:

Lastname_Firstname_3C_Student_Internships

PROJECT RESULTS

FIGURE 3.49

(Project 3C Student Internships continues on the next page)

CHAPTER REVIEW

1 Start Access. In the Access opening screen, click **Open Other Files**. Under **Open**, click **Computer**. Under **Recent Folders**, if displayed, click the location where your student data files are stored; otherwise, click **Browse** and then navigate to the location where your student data files are stored. Double-click **a03C_Student_Internships** to open the database.

a. On the ribbon, click the **FILE tab**, and then click **Save As**. Under **File Types**, be sure **Save Database As** is selected. On the right, under **Database File Types**, be sure **Access Database** is selected, and then click **Save As**.

b. In the **Save As** dialog box, navigate to your **Access Chapter 3** folder. In the **File name** box, replace the existing text with **Lastname_Firstname_3C_Student_Internships** and then press `Enter`. On the **Message Bar**, click **Enable Content**.

c. In the **Navigation Pane**, right-click **3C Students**, and then click **Rename**. With the table name selected and using your own name, type **Lastname Firstname 3C Students** and then press `Enter`. **Rename** the 3C Internships table to **Lastname Firstname 3C Internships** and then point to the right edge of the **Navigation Pane** to display the ⟺ pointer. Drag to the right to increase the width of the pane until both tables names display fully.

d. On the ribbon, click the **DATABASE TOOLS tab**, and then in the **Relationships group**, click **Relationships**. Under **RELATIONSHIP TOOLS**, on the **DESIGN tab**, in the **Relationships group**, click **All Relationships**. Resize and move the field lists so that the entire table name and fields display for each field list. In the **Relationships** window, click the **join line** between the two field lists. In the **Tools group**, click **Edit Relationships**. Point to the title bar of the **Edit Relationships** dialog box, and drag the dialog box downward below the two field lists. Notice that a *one-to-many* relationship is established between

the two tables by using *Internship ID* as the common field. **Close** the **Edit Relationships** dialog box, and then **Close** the **Relationships** window. In the message box, click **Yes** to save changes to the layout of the relationships.

e. In the **Navigation Pane**, click your **3C Students** table to select it. On the ribbon, click the **CREATE tab**, and then in the **Forms group**, click **Form**. **Save** the form as **Lastname Firstname 3C Student Form** and then **Close** the form object.

f. In the **Navigation Pane**, click your **3C Internships** table to select it. On the ribbon, click the **CREATE tab**, and then in the **Forms group**, click **Form**. Notice that for the first record—*Internship ID INTERN-1000* for *Lakes Realty Inc*—there are two student records in the subdatasheet—two students have been assigned internships for this employer. **Close** the form, and in the message box, click **Yes** to save the form. In the **Save As** dialog box, type **Lastname Firstname 3C Internship Company Form** and then press `Enter`. If necessary, increase the width of the Navigation Pane so that all object names display fully.

g. In the **Navigation Pane**, double-click your **3C Student Form** object to open it, and then **Close** the **Navigation Pane**. In the navigation area, click **New (blank) record** to display a new blank form. In the **Student ID** field, type **3120045** and then press `Tab`. Using your own last name and first name, continue entering the data as shown in **Table 1**.

h. With the insertion point positioned in the last field, press `Tab` to save the record and display a new blank record. **Close** your **3C Student Form** object, and then **Open** the **Navigation Pane**. Double-click your **3C Internship Company Form** object to open it, and then **Close** the **Navigation Pane**. Notice that for the first record, in the subdatasheet, the record you just entered displays. Scroll to view the bottom of

TABLE 1

Student ID	Last Name	First Name	Phone Number	Email	Internship ID
3120045	**Lastname**	**Firstname**	**(512) 555-3263**	**ns3120@tlcc.edu**	**INTERN-1000**

`- - - - ▶` Return to Step 1-h

(Project 3C Student Internships continues on the next page)

the form. In the navigation area for the form—*not the navigation area for the subdatasheet*—click **New (blank) record**. In the blank form, using your own first name and last name, enter the data as shown in **Table 2**.

i. In the navigation area for the form, click **First record**. Click in the **Employer Name** field, and then on the **HOME tab**, in the **Find group**, click **Find**. In the **Find and Replace** dialog box, in the **Find What** box, type **Jones Consulting** and then click **Find Next**. **Close** the **Find and Replace** dialog box. On the **HOME tab**, in the **Records group**, click the **Delete arrow**, and then click **Delete Record**. In the message box, click **Yes** to delete the record. In the navigation area for the form, notice that the total number of records is *27*.

j. Use the technique you just practiced to **Find** the form for the **Internship ID** of INTERN-1027, and then **Close** the **Find and Replace** dialog box. On the ribbon, click the **FILE tab**, click **Print**, and then on the right, click **Print**. In the **Print** dialog box, under **Print Range**, click the **Selected Record(s)** option button. In the lower left corner of the dialog box, click **Setup**. In the **Page Setup** dialog box, click the **Columns tab**. Under **Column Size**, double-click in the **Width** box to select the existing value, type **7.5** and then click **OK**. If directed to print the form, in the **Print** dialog box, click **OK**. If directed to submit an electronic printout of the form, click **Cancel**, and then follow the directions given in the Note in Activity 3.06.

k. **Close** your **3C Internship Company Form** object, and then **Open** the **Navigation Pane**. In the **Navigation Pane**, double-click your **3C Student Form** object to open it, and then **Close** the **Navigation Pane**. Use the **Find** command to display the record where the **Last Name** field contains your last name, and then create a paper or electronic printout of only

that record, being sure to change the **Column Size Width** to **7.5**.

2 With your **3C Student Form** object displayed in **Form** view, in the navigation area, click **First record**, and then click the **Internship ID** field name to select the text in the field box. Press Ctrl + F to display the **Find and Replace** dialog box. In the **Find What** box, type **INTERN-1009** and then click **Find Next** to find and display the record for *Michael Fresch*. **Close** the **Find and Replace** dialog box. On the **HOME tab**, in the **Sort & Filter group**, click **Selection**, and then click **Equals "INTERN-1009"**. In the navigation area, notice that two students are assigned internships with the company identified as INTERN-1009.

a. In the **Sort & Filter group**, click **Toggle Filter** to remove the filter and display all 52 records. **Close** the form. If prompted, click **Yes** to save the form.

b. **Open** the **Navigation Pane**, double-click your **3C Internship Company Form** object to open it, and then **Close** the **Navigation Pane**. On the **HOME tab**, in the **Sort & Filter group**, click **Advanced**, and then click **Filter By Form**. In the form, click the **City** field name to position the insertion point in the **City** field box, click the **arrow**, and then click **Georgetown**. In the **Sort & Filter group**, click **Toggle Filter** to display the filtered records. In the navigation area for the form, notice that three internships are located in the *City* of *Georgetown*.

c. In the **Sort & Filter group**, click **Advanced**, and then click **Filter By Form**. In the lower left corner of the form, click the **Or tab**. Click the **City** field box **arrow**, and then click **Elgin**. In the **Sort & Filter group**, click **Toggle Filter**. In the navigation area for the form, notice that five internships are located in either *Georgetown* or *Elgin*. In the **Sort & Filter group**, click **Advanced**, and then click **Clear All Filters** to display all 27 records.

TABLE 2

Internship ID	Employer Name	Contact First Name	Contact Last Name	Address	City	State	Postal Code	Phone	Hrs Per Week
INTERN-1027	**College Suppliers**	**Firstname**	**Lastname**	**1700 College Cres**	**Austin**	**TX**	**78755**	**(512) 555-3133**	**10**

(Return to Step 1-i)

(Project 3C Student Internships continues on the next page)

d. In the **Sort & Filter group**, click **Advanced**, and then click **Advanced Filter/Sort**. Resize the field list. In the **3C Internships** field list, double-click **City**, and then double-click **Hrs Per Week** to add both fields to the design grid. Click in the **Criteria** row under **City**, type **Austin** and then press ⏎. In the **Criteria** row under **Hrs Per Week**, type **>10** and then press ⏎. In the **Sort & Filter group**, click **Toggle Filter** to display the filtered records, and notice that that there are five internships in the *City* of *Austin* offering *more than 10* hours per week of work. In the **Sort & Filter group**, click **Toggle Filter** to remove the filter and display all 27 records. **Save** and then **Close** your **3C Internship Company Form** object, which also closes the Advanced Filter grid.

3 On the ribbon, click the **CREATE tab**, and then in the **Forms group**, click **Form Wizard**. In the **Tables/Queries** box, click the **arrow**, and then click **Table: Lastname Firstname 3C Students**. In the **Available Fields** list, double-click the following field names in the order given to move them to the **Selected Fields** list: **First Name**, **Last Name**, and **Internship ID**. Click **Next**. In the wizard, be sure **Columnar** is selected as the layout, and then click **Next**. In the **What title do you want for your form?** box, select the existing text, type **Lastname Firstname 3C Student Internship Form** and then click **Finish** to close the wizard and create the form.

4 On the **HOME tab**, in the **Views group**, click the top portion of the **View** button to switch to **Layout** view. If the **Field List** pane displays on the right side of your screen, close the pane. Click the **First Name label control**. Hold down ⇧, and then click the **Last Name label control**, the **Internship ID label control**, and the three **text box controls** to select all of the controls. On the ribbon, under **FORM LAYOUT TOOLS**, click the **ARRANGE tab**. In the **Table group**, click **Stacked** to group all of the controls. Click the **First Name label control** to cancel the selection of all of the controls.

a. On the ribbon, under **FORM LAYOUT TOOLS**, click the **DESIGN tab**. In the **Themes group** click **Themes**. In the **Themes** gallery, using the ScreenTips, point to the **Wisp** theme, right-click, and then click **Apply Theme to This Object Only**. Click anywhere in the title—*Lastname Firstname 3C Student Internship*

Form—to select the title. On the ribbon, under **FORM LAYOUT TOOLS**, click the **FORMAT tab**. In the **Font group**, click the **Font Size arrow**, and then click **14**. In the **Font group**, click **Bold**. Click the **Font Color arrow**, and then under **Theme Colors**, in the sixth column, click the last color—**Orange, Accent 2, Darker 50%**.

b. On the ribbon, click the **DESIGN tab**. In the **Tools group**, click **Add Existing Fields**. In the **Field List** pane, click **Student ID**, and then drag the field name to the left until the 🔲 pointer displays above the **First Name label control** and a colored line displays above the control. Release the mouse button to add the *Student ID* controls to the form, and then **Close** the **Field List** pane.

c. Click the **First Name text box control**, which displays *Jordan*, to select it. On the **DESIGN tab**, in the **Tools group**, click **Property Sheet**. In the **Property Sheet**, on the **Format tab**, click **Width**, type **1.75** and then press ⏎ to decrease the width of the text box controls. **Close** the **Property Sheet**. Be sure that the **First Name text box control** is still selected. On the ribbon, click the **ARRANGE tab**, and in the **Rows & Columns group**, click **Select Row**. In the **Move group**, click **Move Down** to move both controls below the **Last Name** controls. **Save** the changes you have made to the design of your form.

d. Click the **Student ID text box control**, which displays *1010101*. On the **ARRANGE tab**, in the **Rows & Columns group**, click **Select Column** to select all four text box controls. On the ribbon, click the **FORMAT tab**, and in the **Font group**, click the **Background Color arrow**. Under **Theme Colors**, in the fourth column, click the second color—**Brown, Text 2, Lighter 80%**.

e. Click the **Student ID label control**, and then on the ribbon, click the **ARRANGE tab**. In the **Rows & Columns group**, click **Select Column** to select all four label controls. On the ribbon, click the **FORMAT tab**, and then click the **Font Color arrow**—*not* the **Background Color arrow**. Under **Theme Colors**, in the fourth column, click the first color—**Brown, Text 2**. In the **Font group**, click **Bold**.

(Project 3C Student Internships continues on the next page)

CHAPTER REVIEW

f. Click the **layout selector** ⊞ to select all of the controls. In the **Font group**, click the **Font Size arrow**, and then click **12**. With all of the controls still selected, on the ribbon, click the **DESIGN tab**, and in the **Tools group**, click **Property Sheet**. In the **Property Sheet**, on the **Format tab**, click **Height**, type **0.25** and then press Enter to change the height of each selected control.

g. Click the **Student ID label control** to select only that control. In the **Property Sheet**, click **Width**, type **1.75** and then press Enter to change the width of all of the label controls. **Save** the design changes to your form.

h. On the status bar, click **Design View**. At the bottom of the form, click the **Form Footer section bar** to select it. In the **Property Sheet**, click **Height**, type **0.5** and then press Enter to increase the height of the **Form Footer** section.

i. On the ribbon, under **FORM DESIGN TOOLS**, click the **DESIGN tab**. In the **Controls group**, click **Label**. Move the pointer into the **Form Footer** section and then position the plus sign of the pointer at approximately **0.25 inch on the horizontal ruler** and even with the lower edge of the **Form Footer section bar**—the placement does not need to be precise. Click one time, type **Texas Lakes Community College** and then press Enter.

j. With the **label control** selected, on the ribbon, click the **FORMAT tab**. In the **Font group**, click **Bold**. Click the **Font Color arrow**, and then under **Theme Colors**, in the fourth column, click the first

color—**Brown, Text 2**. If necessary, double-click the right edge of the label control to resize the control so that all of the data displays.

k. With the **label control** still selected, in the **Property Sheet**, click **Top**, type **0.1** and then press Enter. In the **Property Sheet**, in the **Left** property setting box, type **0.9** and then press Enter. **Close** the **Property Sheet**, and then **Save** the design changes to your form.

l. On the right side of the status bar, click **Form View**. In the navigation area, click **Last record** to display the record containing your name. On the ribbon, click the **FILE tab**, and then click **Print**. In the **Print** dialog box, under **Print Range**, click the **Selected Records(s)** option button. Because you changed the field widths, you do not need to change the Column Size Width in the **Print** dialog box. Create a paper or electronic printout as directed by your instructor. To create an electronic printout, follow the directions given in the Note in Activity 3.06.

m. **Close** all open objects, and then **Open** the **Navigation Pane**. If necessary, increase the width of the pane so that all object names display fully. On the right side of the title bar, click **Close** to close the database and to exit Access. As directed by your instructor, submit your database and the paper or electronic printouts of the three forms that are the results of this project. Specifically, in this project, using your own name, you created the following database and printouts or electronic printouts:

1. Lastname_Firstname_3C_Student_Internships	Database file
2. Lastname Firstname 3C Student Form	Form (printout or electronic printout - Record 52)
3. Lastname Firstname 3C Internship Company Form	Form (printout or electronic printout - Record 27)
4. Lastname Firstname 3C Student Internship Form	Form (printout or electronic printout - Record 52)

END | You have completed Project 3C

CHAPTER REVIEW

Skills Review | Project 3D Student Parking

Apply **3B** skills from these Objectives:

5 Create a Report by Using the Report Tool and Modify the Report in Layout View

6 Create a Report by Using the Report Wizard

7 Modify the Design of a Report

8 Keep Grouped Data Together in a Printed Report

In the following Skills Review, you will assist Carlos Medina, the chief of security, in using his Access database to track the details about students who have paid for parking in designated lots at the Southeast Campus of Texas Lakes Community College. Your completed reports will look similar to Figure 3.50.

PROJECT FILES

For Project 3D, you will need the following file:

a03D_Student_Parking

You will save your database as:

Lastname_Firstname_3D_Student_Parking

PROJECT RESULTS

FIGURE 3.50

(Project 3D Student Parking continues on the next page)

CHAPTER REVIEW

1 Start Access. In the Access opening screen, click **Open Other Files**. Under **Open**, click **Computer**. Under **Recent Folders**, if displayed, click the location where your student data files are stored; otherwise, click **Browse** and then navigate to the location where your student data files are stored. Double-click **a03D_Student_Parking** to open the database.

a. On the ribbon, click the **FILE tab**, and then click **Save As**. Under **File Types**, be sure **Save Database As** is selected. On the right, under **Database File Types**, be sure **Access Database** is selected, and then at the bottom of the screen, click **Save As**. In the **Save As** dialog box, navigate to your **Access Chapter 3** folder. In the **File name** box, replace the existing text with **Lastname_Firstname_3D_Student_Parking** and then press Enter. On the **Message Bar**, click **Enable Content**.

b. In the **Navigation Pane**, right-click the **3D Parking Lots** table, and then click **Rename**. Using your own name, type **Lastname Firstname 3D Parking Lots** and then press Enter. Use this same technique to add your last name and first name to the beginning of the names of the two queries and the **3D Students** table. Increase the width of the **Navigation Pane** so that all object names display fully.

c. On the ribbon, click the **DATABASE TOOLS tab**, and then in the **Relationships group**, click **Relationships**. On the **DESIGN tab**, in the **Relationships group**, click **All Relationships**. Resize and move the field lists so that the entire table name and fields display for each field list. In the **Relationships** window, click the **join line** between the two field lists. In the **Tools group**, click **Edit Relationships**. Point to the title bar of the **Edit Relationships** dialog box, and drag the dialog box downward below the two field lists. Notice that a *one-to-many* relationship is established between the two tables by using *Lot ID* as the common field. **Close** the **Edit Relationships** dialog box, and then **Close** the **Relationships** window. In the message box, click **Yes** to save changes to the layout of the relationships.

d. In the **Navigation Pane**, double-click each table to open them, and then examine the fields and data in each table. In the **Navigation Pane**, double-click

your **3D Building G Student Parking Query** object to run the query and view the results. Apply **Best Fit** to the query results, and then **Save** the query. Switch to **Design** view to examine the design grid. This query answers the question, *What is the lot ID, lot location, student ID, student last name, student first name, license plate, and semester fee for students who have paid for parking in front of Building G, in ascending order by the Last Name field?* In the **Navigation Pane**, double-click your **3D Student Parking by Lots Query** object, apply **Best Fit** to the query results, **Save** the query, and then switch to **Design** view to examine the design grid. This query answers the question, *What is the lot ID, student ID, student last name, student first name, license plate, state, and semester fee for all students?* In the object window, right-click any **object tab**, and then click **Close All**.

e. In the **Navigation Pane**, click to select your **3D Building G Student Parking Query** object. On the ribbon, click the **CREATE tab**, and in the **Reports group**, click **Report**. **Close** the **Navigation Pane**. Under **REPORT LAYOUT TOOLS**, on the **DESIGN tab**, in the **Themes group**, click **Themes**. In the **Themes** gallery, use the ScreenTips to locate the **Retrospect** theme, right-click the **Retrospect** theme, and then click **Apply Theme to This Object Only**.

f. Click the **Lot Location** field name. On the ribbon, under **REPORT LAYOUT TOOLS**, click the **ARRANGE tab**. In the **Rows & Columns group**, click **Select Column** to select the field name and all of the data for each record in the field. Press Del to remove the field from the report.

g. Click the **Last Name** field name, hold down Shift, and then click the **First Name** field name. On the ribbon, click the **DESIGN tab**, and in the **Tools group**, click **Property Sheet**. In the **Property Sheet**, on the **Format tab**, click **Width**, type **1.25** and then press Enter to decrease the width of the two fields. **Close** the **Property Sheet**.

h. Click the **Last Name** field name to cancel the selection of both fields and to select only this field. On the ribbon, click the **HOME tab**, and in the **Sort & Filter group**, click **Ascending** to sort the records in ascending order by the Last Name field.

(Project 3D Student Parking continues on the next page)

i. If necessary, scroll to the bottom of the report, and notice that the *Semester Fee* column is automatically totaled. At the top of the report, click the **Student ID** field name. On the ribbon, click the **DESIGN tab**. In the **Grouping & Totals group**, click **Totals**, and then click **Count Records**. If necessary, scroll to the bottom of the report, and notice that *14* students have paid for parking in front of Building G.

j. At the bottom of the report, under **Student ID**, click the **calculated control** that displays *14*. Hold down Ctrl, and then under **Semester Fee**, click the **calculated control** that displays *$1,075*—the two calculated controls are selected. On the **DESIGN tab**, in the **Tools group**, click **Property Sheet**. In the **Property Sheet**, click **Height**, type **0.25** and then press Enter to increase the height of both controls. At the bottom of the report, to the right of the **calculated control** that displays *$1,075*, click the **control** that displays *Page 1 of 1*. In the **Property Sheet**, click **Left**, type **2.5** and then press Enter to move the page number within the margins of the report.

k. At the top of the report, click the **label control** that displays the title of the report—*Lastname Firstname 3D Building G Student Parking Query*. On the ribbon, under **REPORT LAYOUT TOOLS**, click the **FORMAT tab**. In the **Font group**, click the **Font Size arrow**, and then click **14**. With the **label control** still selected, double-click **Query** to select the word, type **Report** and then press Enter to change the title of the report to *Lastname Firstname 3D Building G Student Parking Report*.

l. Click the **Lot ID** field name. In the **Property Sheet**, click **Left**, type **0.25** and then press Enter to move all of the fields slightly to the right from the left margin. **Close** the **Property Sheet**, and then **Save** the report as **Lastname Firstname 3D Building G Student Parking Report**

m. On the right side of the status bar, click **Print Preview**. On the **PRINT PREVIEW tab**, in the **Zoom group**, click **Two Pages**, and notice that the report will print on one page. Create a paper or electronic printout as directed, click **Close Print Preview**, and then **Close** the report.

2 On the ribbon, click the **CREATE tab**, and then in the **Reports group**, click **Report Wizard**. In the **Tables/Queries box**, click the **arrow**, and then click

Query: Lastname Firstname 3D Student Parking by Lots Query. In the **Available Fields** list, double-click the following field names in the order given to move them to the **Selected Fields** list: **Lot ID**, **Last Name**, **First Name**, **Student ID**, and **Semester Fee**.

a. Click **Next**. In the **How do you want to view your data?** box, click **by Lastname Firstname 3D Students**, and then click **Next**. In the list on the left, double-click **Lot ID** to group the records by this field, and then click **Next**. Click the **1 box arrow**, and then click **Last Name** to sort the records by the student's last name within each Lot ID.

b. In the wizard, click **Summary Options**. In the **Summary Options** dialog box, to the right of **Semester Fee**, click to select the **Sum** check box. Under **Show**, be sure that **Detail and Summary** is selected, and then click **OK**. In the wizard, click **Next**.

c. In the wizard, under **Layout**, be sure that **Stepped** is selected. Under **Orientation**, click **Landscape**. At the bottom of the wizard, be sure that the **Adjust the field width so all fields fit on a page** check box is selected, and then click **Next**. In the **What title do you want for your report?** box, select the existing text, type **Lastname Firstname 3D Fees by Parking Lot Report** and then click **Finish**. In the object window, right-click the **object tab** for the report, and then click **Layout View**.

3 Under **REPORT LAYOUT TOOLS**, on the **DESIGN tab**, in the **Themes group**, click **Themes**. In the **Themes** gallery, use the ScreenTips to locate the **Ion Boardroom** theme, right-click the **Ion Boardroom** theme, and then click **Apply Theme to This Object Only**. In the report, click the title—*Lastname Firstname 3D Fees by Parking Lot*—to display a border around the label control. On the ribbon, under **REPORT LAYOUT TOOLS**, click the **FORMAT tab**. In the **Font group**, click the **Font Size arrow**, and then click **14**. In the **Font group**, click **Bold**. In the body of the report, click any one of the controls that begins with **Summary for 'Lot ID'**, and then press Del. **Save** the design changes to your report.

a. On the left side of the report, click a **Sum label control**, which will select all of the related controls. Double-click the control to select the text—*Sum*. Type **Total Fees by Parking Lot** and then press Enter.

(Project 3D Student Parking continues on the next page)

CHAPTER REVIEW

b. At the top of the report, click the **Lot ID label control** to select it. Hold down Shift, and then click each one of the four other label controls that display the field names to select all five label controls. On the **FORMAT tab**, in the **Font group**, click **Bold**.

c. In the report, under **Last Name**, click the **text box control** that displays *Dolensky*. Hold down Shift, and then under **First Name**, click the **text box control** that displays *Adam*. On the ribbon, click the **DESIGN tab**. In the **Tools group**, click **Property Sheet**. In the **Property Sheet**, click **Width**, type **1.5** and then press Enter.

d. In the report, click the **Student ID label control**. In the **Property Sheet**, click **Left**, type **7.25** and then press Enter. Do not be concerned that the data in the field is not aligned with the field name; you will adjust this later in this project. Scroll to the bottom of the report, and then click the **Grand Total label control**. In the **Property Sheet**, click **Width**, type **1** and then press Enter. **Close** the **Property Sheet**, and then **Save** the design changes to your report.

e. On the status bar, click **Design View**. In the **Lot ID Footer** section, click the **Total Fees by Parking Lot label control**. Hold down Shift, and in the **Report Footer** section, click the **Grand Total label control** to select both controls. On the ribbon, under **REPORT DESIGN TOOLS**, click the **ARRANGE tab**. In the **Sizing & Ordering group**, click **Align**, and then click **Left**.

f. In the report, in the **Page Header** section, click the **Student ID label control**. Hold down Shift, and in the **Detail** section, click the **Student ID text box control**. On the **ARRANGE tab**, in the **Sizing & Ordering group**, click **Align**, and then click **Left**. On the status bar, click **Layout View** and notice the left alignment of the two sets of controls.

4 On the status bar, click **Print Preview**. On the **PRINT PREVIEW tab**, in the **Zoom group**, click **More Pages**, and then click **Four Pages** to view how your report is currently laid out. In the **Zoom group**, click the **Zoom arrow**, and then click **50%**. Notice at the bottom of Page 1 and the top of Page 2, that the grouping for **LOT-2B** breaks across these two pages. Notice at the bottom of Page 2 and the top of Page 3, that the grouping for **LOT-6A** breaks across these two pages. Your pages may display differently depending upon the printer that is installed on your system.

a. On the ribbon, click **Close Print Preview** to return to **Layout** view. On the **DESIGN tab**, in the **Grouping & Totals group**, click **Group & Sort**. In the **Group, Sort, and Total** pane, on the **Group on Lot ID** bar, click **More**. Click the **do not keep group together on one page arrow**, and then click **keep whole group together on one page**. On the **DESIGN tab**, in the **Grouping & Totals group**, click **Group & Sort** to close the **Group, Sort, and Total** pane. **Save** the design changes to your report.

b. On the status bar, click **Print Preview**. Notice that the entire grouping for **LOT-2B** displays at the top of Page 2. Keeping this group together forced the groupings for **LOT-5C** and **LOT-6A** to move to the top of Page 3—your groupings may display differently depending upon the printer that is installed on your system. Create a paper or electronic printout as directed—three pages result.

c. **Close** the report, and then **Open** the **Navigation Pane**. If necessary, increase the width of the pane so that all object names display fully. On the right side of the title bar, click **Close** to close the database and to exit Access. As directed by your instructor, submit your database and the paper or electronic printouts of the two reports—one report is three pages—that are the results of this project. Specifically, in this project, using your own name, you created the following database and printouts or electronic printouts:

1. Lastname_Firstname_3D_Student_Parking	Database file
2. Lastname Firstname 3D Building G Student Parking Report	Report (printout or electronic printout)
3. Lastname Firstname 3D Fees by Parking Lot Report	Report (printout or electronic printout - three pages)

END | You have completed Project 3D

CONTENT-BASED ASSESSMENTS

Mastering Access Project 3E Textbook Publishers

In the following Mastering Access project, you will assist Donna Rider, manager of the bookstore, in using her database to track textbooks and publishers for courses being offered by the Science Department at the Northeast Campus of Texas Lakes Community College. Your completed forms will look similar to Figure 3.51.

Apply 3A skills from these Objectives:

1 Create and Use a Form to Add and Delete Records

2 Filter Records

3 Create a Form by Using the Form Wizard

4 Modify a Form in Layout View and in Design View

PROJECT FILES

For Project 3E, you will need the following file:

a03E_Textbook_Publishers

You will save your database as:

Lastname_Firstname_3E_Textbook_Publishers

PROJECT RESULTS

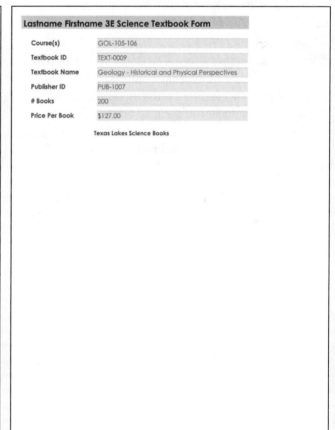

FIGURE 3.51

(Project 3E Textbook Publishers continues on the next page)

CONTENT-BASED ASSESSMENTS

1 Start Access. From your student data files, open a03E_Textbook_Publishers. Save the database in your **Access Chapter 3** folder as **Lastname_Firstname_3E_Textbook_Publishers** and then enable the content. In the **Navigation Pane**, **Rename** each table by adding **Lastname Firstname** to the beginning of the table name. Increase the width of the **Navigation Pane** so that all object names display fully. View the relationship between the *3E Publishers* table and the *3E Science Textbooks* table; *one* publisher can provide *many* textbooks for the science courses. Save the changes to the layout of the relationships.

2 Based on your **3E Publishers** table, use the **Form** tool to create a form. **Save** the form as **Lastname Firstname 3E Publisher Form** and then switch to **Form** view. Using the form, add a new record to the underlying table as shown in **Table 1**.

3 Display the first record, and click in the **Publisher ID** field. **Find** the record for the **Publisher ID** of **PUB-1006**, and then **Delete** the record. Display the record you entered for **PUB-1008**, and then, as directed, create a paper or electronic printout of only that record, changing the **Column Size Width** in the **Print** dialog box to **7.5 Save** the design changes to your form.

4 Use the **Filter By Form** tool in your **3E Publisher Form** object to create a filter that displays records with a **State** of **CA** or **TX**. After verifying that three records match this criteria, click **Toggle Filter** to display all seven records. **Save** your form, and then **Close** your form.

5 Use the **Form Wizard** to create a form based on your **3E Science Textbooks** table that includes the following fields in the order given: **Course(s)**, **Textbook Name**, **Publisher ID**, **Price Per Book**, and **# Books**. Apply a **Columnar** layout, and name the form **Lastname Firstname 3E Science Textbook Form.**

6 In **Layout** view, apply the **Stacked** layout to all of the controls, and then apply the **Ion Boardroom** theme to this form only. For the title of the form, change the **Font Size** to **16**, apply **Bold**, and then change the **Font Color** to **Dark Purple, Text 2**—under **Theme Colors**, in the fourth column, the first color. **Save** the design changes to the form.

7 From the **Field List** pane, add the **Textbook ID** field to the form directly above the **Textbook Name** field. Move the **# Books** controls directly above the **Price Per Book** controls. **Close** the **Field List** pane. Display Record 9—this record's textbook name is the longest entry of all records. Click the **Textbook Name text box control**, set the **Width** property to **4** and then **Save** the design changes to your form.

8 Select all six **text box controls**, and change the **Background Color** to **Orange, Accent 4, Lighter 80%**—under **Theme Colors**, in the eighth column, the second color. Select all six **label controls**, and change the **Font Color** to **Orange, Accent 4, Darker 50%**—under **Theme Colors**, in the eighth column, the last color. Apply **Bold** to the **label controls**. With the **label controls** still selected, set the **Width** property to **1.75** and then select all of the **label controls** and all of the **text box controls**. Change the **Font Size** to **12**, set the **Height** property to **0.25** and then **Save** the design changes to your form.

9 In **Design** view, set the **Form Footer** section **Height** property to **0.5** Add a **Label control** to the **Form Footer** section that displays **Texas Lakes Science Books** For this **label control**, change the **Font Color** to **Orange, Accent 4, Darker 50%**—under **Theme Colors**, in the eighth column, the last color—and then apply **Bold**. For this **label control**, set the **Width** property to **2.2** Set the **Top** property to **0.1** and then set the **Left** property to **1.95**

TABLE 1

Publisher ID	Publisher Name	Address	City	State	Postal Code	Phone Number	Publisher Web Site
PUB-1008	**Hidden Hills Publishing Co**	**5100 Live Oak St**	**Dallas**	**TX**	**75201**	**(214) 555-0857**	**http://www. hhpubco.pub**

(Return to Step 3)

(Project 3E Textbook Publishers continues on the next page)

CONTENT-BASED ASSESSMENTS

10 **Close** the **Property Sheet**, **Save** your form, and then switch to **Form** view. **Find** the record for the **Textbook ID** of **TEXT-0009**, and then, as directed, create a paper or electronic printout of only this record. Because you changed the field widths, you do not need to change the Column Size Width in the **Print** dialog box.

11 **Close** all open objects, and then **Open** the **Navigation Pane**. If necessary, increase the width of the pane so that all object names display fully. **Close** Access. As directed by your instructor, submit your database and the paper or electronic printouts of the two forms that are the results of this project. Specifically, in this project, using your own name, you created the following database and printouts or electronic printouts:

1. Lastname_Firstname_3E_Textbook_Publishers	Database file
2. Lastname Firstname 3E Publisher Form	Form (printout or electronic printout - Record 7)
3. Lastname Firstname 3E Science Textbook Form	Form (printout or electronic printout - Record 9)

END | You have completed Project 3E

CONTENT-BASED ASSESSMENTS

In the following Mastering Access project, you will assist Tom Catogrides, the registrar, in using his database to track degrees and grade point averages for honor students in the health professions program in preparation for graduation. Your completed database objects will look similar to Figure 3.52.

PROJECT FILES

For Project 3F, you will need the following file:

a03F_Degrees_Students

You will save your database as:

Lastname_Firstname_3F_Degrees_Students

PROJECT RESULTS

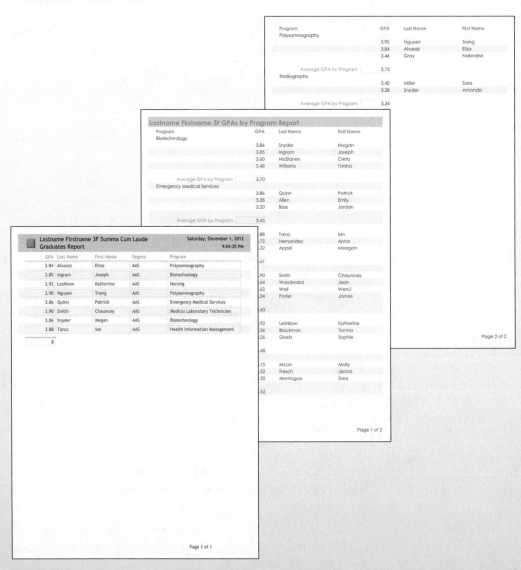

FIGURE 3.52

(Project 3F Degrees and Students continues on the next page)

CONTENT-BASED ASSESSMENTS

1 Start Access. From your student data files, open **a03F_Degrees_Students**. **Save** the database in your **Access Chapter 3** folder as **Lastname_Firstname_3F_Degrees_ Students** and then enable the content. In the **Navigation Pane**, **Rename** the two tables and two queries by adding **Lastname Firstname** to the beginning of each object name, and then increase the width of the **Navigation Pane** so that all object names display fully. View the relationship that is established between the *3F Degrees* tables and the *3F Students* table—*one* type of degree can be awarded to *many* students. Save the changes to the layout of the relationships. **Run** each query to display the query results, apply **Best Fit**, and then **Save** each query.

Open each query in **Design** view to examine the design grid. The *3F Summa Cum Laude Graduates Query* answers the question, *What is the GPA, student ID, last name, first name, degree, and program for students graduating with a grade point average of 3.8 or higher, in descending order by GPA?* The *3F GPAs by Degree Program Query* answers the question, *What is the program, last name, first name, and GPA for all students, in ascending order by the Last Name field within the Program field?* **Close All** objects.

Based on your **3F Summa Cum Laude Graduates Query** object, use the **Report** tool to create a report. Apply the **Facet** theme to only this report. Delete the **Student ID** field from the report. For the **Last Name, First Name**, and **Degree text box controls**, set the **Width** property to **1.25** and then **Sort** the **Last Name** field in **Ascending** order. For the **Program text box controls**, set the **Width** property to **2.5**

At the bottom of the report, for the **calculated control**, which displays *8*, set the **Height** to **0.25** and then for the **page number control**, set the **Left** property to **5** For the title of the report, set the **Font Size** to **14** and change the word *Query* to **Report** For the **GPA** field, set the **Left** property to **0.25** to approximately center the fields within the margins of the report. **Save** the report as **Lastname Firstname 3F Summa Cum Laude Graduates Report** and then create a paper or electronic printout as directed. **Close Print Preview, Close** the **Property Sheet**, and then **Close** the report.

2 Use the **Report Wizard** to create a report based on your **3F GPAs by Degree Program Query** object that includes the following fields in the order given: **Program, GPA, Last Name**, and **First Name**. View your data **by 3F Degrees** and do not add any other grouping to the report. Sort first in **Descending** order by **GPA**, and second in **Ascending** order by **Last Name**. Summarize the report by averaging the **GPA** field. Be sure the layout is **Stepped** and the orientation is **Portrait**. For the report title, type **Lastname Firstname 3F GPAs by Program Report** and then switch to **Layout** view.

3 Apply the **Wisp** theme to only this report. For the report title, change the **Font Size** to **16**, and then apply **Bold**. Delete the controls that begin with **Summary for 'Program'**. Under **Program**, for the **text box controls**, set the **Width** property to **2.75** Change the text in the **Avg label control** to **Average GPA by Program** At the top of the report, select the four **label controls** that display the field names, and then apply **Bold**. Select the **GPA label control**, the **GPA text box controls**, and the **calculated controls** for the average GPA, and then set the **Width** property to **1** and the **Left** property to **3 Close** the **Property Sheet**. Display the report in **Design** view. Under **Program Header**, click the **Program text box control**, hold down Shift, and under **Program Footer**, click the **Average GPA by Program label control**. **Align** the controls on the **Right**, and then **Save** the design changes to your report.

4 Switch to **Print Preview, Zoom** to display **Two Pages** of the report, and examine how the groupings break across the pages. Switch to **Layout** view, display the **Group, Sort, and Total** pane, select **keep whole group together on one page**, and then close the **Group, Sort, and Total** pane. Switch to **Print Preview**, and notice that the groupings are not split between pages. **Save** the report, and then create a paper or electronic printout as directed—two pages result.

(Project 3F Degrees and Students continues on the next page)

5 **Close Print Preview**, and then **Close** the report. **Open** the **Navigation Pane**, and, if necessary, increase the width of the pane so that all object names display fully. On the right side of the title bar, click **Close** to close the database and to exit Access. As directed by your instructor, submit your database and the paper or electronic printouts of the two reports—one report is two pages—that are the results of this project. Specifically, in this project, using your own name, you created the following database and printouts or electronic printouts:

1. Lastname_Firstname_3F_Degrees_Students	Database file
2. Lastname Firstname 3F Summa Cum Laude Graduates Report	Report (printout or electronic printout)
3. Lastname Firstname 3F GPAs by Program Report	Report (printout or electronic printout - two pages)

END | You have completed Project 3F

CONTENT-BASED ASSESSMENTS

MyITLab®
grader

Mastering Access Project 3G Career Books

Apply 3A and 3B skills from these Objectives:

1 Create and Use a Form to Add and Delete Records
2 Filter Records
3 Create a Form by Using the Form Wizard
4 Modify a Form in Layout View and in Design View
5 Create a Report by Using the Report Tool and Modify the Report in Layout View
6 Create a Report by Using the Report Wizard
7 Modify the Design of a Report
8 Keep Grouped Data Together in a Printed Report

In the following Mastering Access project, you will assist Rebecca Hennelly, head librarian at the Southwest Campus of Texas Lakes Community College, in using her database to track publishers and book titles that assist students in finding employment. Your completed forms and report will look similar to Figure 3.53.

PROJECT FILES

For Project 3G, you will need the following file:

a03G_Career_Books

You will save your database as:

Lastname_Firstname_3G_Career_Books

PROJECT RESULTS

FIGURE 3.53

(Project 3G Career Books continues on the next page)

Project 3G: Career Books | Access **269**

CONTENT-BASED ASSESSMENTS

1 Start Access. From your student data files, open **a03G_Career_Books**. Save the database in your **Access Chapter 3** folder as **Lastname_Firstname_3G_Career_Books** and then enable the content. In the **Navigation Pane**, **Rename** the two tables and one query by adding **Lastname Firstname** to the beginning of each object name. Increase the width of the **Navigation Pane** so that all object names display fully. View the relationship that is established between the *3G Publishers* tables and the *3G Career Books* table—*one* publisher can publish *many* career books. Save the changes to the layout of the relationships.

Open the **3G Resume or Interview Books Query**, apply **Best Fit**, and then **Save** the query. Switch the query to **Design** view, examine the design of the query, and then **Close** the query object.

2 Based on your **3G Career Books** table, use the **Form** tool to create a form. **Save** the form as **Lastname Firstname 3G Career Book Form** and then switch to **Form** view. Using the form, add a new record to the underlying table as shown in **Table 1**.

3 Display the first record, and click in the **Title ID** field. **Find** the record for the **Title ID** of **T-19**, and then **Delete** the record. Display the record you entered for **T-25**, and then, as directed, create a paper or electronic printout of only that record, changing the **Column Size Width** in the **Print** dialog box to **7.5 Save** the design changes to your form.

4 Use the **Filter By Form** tool in your **3G Career Book Form** object to create a filter that displays records with a **Category** of **Interviewing Strategies** or **Resumes**. After verifying that 10 records match this criteria, click **Toggle Filter** to display all 24 records. **Save** the form, and then **Close** the form.

5 Use the **Form Wizard** to create a form based on your **3G Publishers** table that includes the following fields in the order given: **Company Name**, **Rep Last Name**, **Rep First Name**, **Job Title**, and **Phone Number**. Apply a **Columnar** layout, and name the form **Lastname Firstname 3G Publisher Form**

6 In **Layout** view, apply the **Stacked** layout to all of the controls, and then apply the **Integral** theme to this form only. For the title of the form, change the **Font Size** to **16**, apply **Bold**, and then change the **Font Color** to **Dark Teal, Text 2, Darker 50%**—under **Theme Colors**, in the fourth column, the last color. **Save** the design changes to the form.

7 From the **Field List** pane, add the **Publisher ID** field to the form directly above the **Company Name** field. **Close** the **Field List** pane. Move the **Rep First Name** controls directly above the **Rep Last Name** controls. Click the **Job Title text box control**, set the **Width** property to **2.5** and then **Save** the design changes to your form.

8 Select all six **text box controls**, and change the **Background Color** to **Turquoise, Accent 1, Lighter 80%**—under **Theme Colors**, in the fifth column, the second color. Select all six **label controls**, and change the **Font Color** to **Dark Teal, Text 2, Darker 50%**—under **Theme Colors**, in the fourth column, the last color. Apply **Bold** to the **label controls**. With the **label controls** still selected, set the **Width** property to **1.75** and then select all of the **label controls** and all of the **text box controls**. Change the **Font Size** to **12**, set the **Height** property to **0.25** and then **Save** the design changes to your form.

TABLE 1

Title ID	Title	Author Last Name	Author First Name	Publisher ID	Category	Copies On Hand	Value of Books
T-25	Effective Networking	Nunez	Charlene	PUB-109	Job Search	6	180

(Return to Step 3)

(Project 3G Career Books continues on the next page)

CONTENT-BASED ASSESSMENTS

9 In **Design** view, set the **Form Footer** section **Height** property to **0.5** Add a **Label** control to the **Form Footer** section that displays **Texas Lakes Southwest Campus** For this **label control**, change the **Font Color** to **Dark Teal, Text 2, Darker 50%**—under **Theme Colors**, in the fourth column, the last color —and then apply **Bold**. For this **label control**, set the **Width** property to **2.2** Set the **Top** property to **0.1** and then set the **Left** property to **1** **Close** the **Property Sheet**, **Save** your form, and then switch to **Form** view. Using the form, add a new record to the underlying table as shown in **Table 2**.

10 Display the record that you just created, and then, as directed, create a paper or electronic printout of only this record. Because you changed the field widths, you do not need to change the Column Size Width in the **Print** dialog box. **Close** the form.

11 Based on your **3G Resume or Interview Books Query** object, use the **Report** tool to create a report. Apply the **Retrospect** theme to only this report. Delete the following fields from the report: **Publisher ID**, **Category**, and **Company Name**. For the **Title text box controls**, set the **Width** property to **3** and then **Sort** the **Title** field in **Ascending** order. For the **Author Last Name text box controls** and the **Author First Name text box controls**, set the **Width** property to **1.5**

12 Click the **Title** field name, and then add a calculated control that counts the number of records. At the bottom of the report, for the **calculated control**, which displays *10*, set the **Height** to **0.25** and then for the **page number control**, set the **Left** property to **5** For the title of the report, set the **Font Size** to **14** and change the word *Query* to **Report** Click the **Title** field name, and then set the **Left** property to **0.75** to move all of the controls to the right. **Save** the report as **Lastname Firstname 3G Resume or Interview Books Report** and then create a paper or electronic printout as directed. **Close Print Preview**, **Close** the **Property Sheet**, and then **Close** the report.

13 Use the **Report Wizard** to create a report based on your **3G Career Books** table that includes the following fields in the order given: **Category**, **Title**, and **Value of Books**. Group your data by **Category**, sort in **Ascending** order by **Title**, and then summarize the report by summing the **Value of Books** field. Be sure the layout is **Stepped** and the orientation is **Portrait**. For the report title, type **Lastname Firstname 3G Book Values by Category Report** and then switch to **Layout** view.

14 Apply the **Ion Boardroom** theme to only this report. For the report title, change the **Font Size** to **14**, and then apply **Bold**. Delete the controls that begin with **Summary for 'Category'**. Select the **Category**, **Title**, and **Value of Books label controls**, and then apply **Bold**. Under **Title**, for the **text box controls**, set the **Width** property to **3.5** For the **Value of Books label control**, set the **Left** property to **6** and then **Save** the design changes to your report.

15 At the bottom of the report in the last column, select the following three controls: **text box control** that displays *$420*, **calculated control** that displays *$945*, and the **calculated control** that displays *7,730*. Set the **Width** property to **1.25** and the **Left** property to **6** For the **Grand Total label control**, set the **Width** property to **1** and then change the text in the **Sum label control** to **Total Value of Books by Category** Click any **Title text box control**, set the **Height** property to **0.35** and then **Save** your report.

16 **Close** the **Property Sheet**, and then display your report in **Design** view. Under **Category Footer**, click the **label control** that displays *Total Value of Books by Category*, hold down (Shift), and then under **Report Footer**, click the **Grand Total label control**. **Align** the controls on the **Left**, and then **Save** the design changes to your report.

TABLE 2

Publisher ID	Company Name	Rep First Name	Rep Last Name	Job Title	Phone Number
PUB-111	Associated Publishers	Marquis	Sullivan	Sales Associate	(512) 555-7373

(Return to Step 10)

(Project 3G Career Books continues on the next page)

CONTENT-BASED ASSESSMENTS

17 Switch to **Print Preview**, **Zoom** to display **Two Pages** of the report, and examine how the groupings break across the pages. Switch to **Layout** view, display the **Group, Sort, and Total** pane, select **keep whole group together on one page**, and then close the **Group, Sort, and Total** pane. Switch to **Print Preview**, and notice that the groupings are no longer split between pages. **Save** the report, and then create a paper or electronic printout as directed—two pages result.

18 **Close Print Preview**, and then **Close** the report. **Open** the **Navigation Pane**, and, if necessary, increase the width of the pane so that all object names display fully. On the right side of the title bar, click **Close** to close the database and to exit Access. As directed by your instructor, submit your database and the paper or electronic printouts of the two forms and two reports—one report is two pages—that are the results of this project. Specifically, in this project, using your own name, you created the following database and printouts or electronic printouts:

1. Lastname_Firstname_3G_Career_Books	Database file
2. Lastname Firstname 3G Career Book Form	Form (printout or electronic printout - Record 24)
3. Lastname Firstname 3G Publisher Form	Form (printout or electronic printout - Record 12)
4. Lastname Firstname 3G Resume or Interview Books Report	Report (printout or electronic printout)
5. Lastname Firstname 3G Book Values by Category Report	Report (printout or electronic printout - two pages)

END | You have completed Project 3G

CONTENT-BASED ASSESSMENTS

Apply a combination of the 3A and 3B skills.

| GO! Fix It | Project 3H Resume Workshops | Online |

| GO! Make It | Project 3I Study Abroad | Online |

| GO! Solve It | Project 3J Job Offers | Online |

| GO! Solve It | Project 3K Financial Aid | |

PROJECT FILES

For Project 3K, you will need the following file:

a03K_Financial_Aid

You will save your database as:

Lastname_Firstname_3K_Financial_Aid

Start Access, navigate to your student data files, open a03K_Financial_Aid, and then save the database in your **Access Chapter 3** folder as **Lastname_Firstname_3K_Financial_Aid** Using your own name, add **Lastname Firstname** to the beginning of both table names and the query name. Sivia Long, the financial aid director, would like you to create an attractive form and a report for this database, using the following guidelines:

- The form will be used to update student records in the 3K FA Students table. Be sure that the Last Name field displays above the First Name field. After the form is created, enter a new record using your own information with a Student ID of **9091246** and Financial Aid ID of **FA-07** and a Home Phone of **(512) 555-9876** and a College Email of **ns246@tlcc.edu** Create a filter that when toggled on displays the records for those students whose last names begin with the letter *S*. Add a footer to the form that displays **Texas Lakes Community College Financial Aid** Save the form as **Lastname Firstname 3K FA Student Update Form** and then create a paper or electronic printout of your record only.

- The report should use the query and list the Award Name, the Student ID, and the Award Amount for financial aid offered to students, grouped by the Award Name field, and sorted in ascending order by the Student ID field. Include a total for the Award Amount field, save the report as **Lastname Firstname 3K FA Amount by Award Report** and be sure the groupings do not break across pages when the report is printed. Create a paper or electronic printout as directed—multiple pages result.

Open the Navigation Pane, be sure that all object names display fully, and then close Access. As directed, submit your database and the paper or electronic printout of the form and report—the report is multiple pages—that are the results of this project. Specifically, in this project, using your own name, you created the following database and printouts or electronic printouts:

1. Lastname_Firstname_3K_Financial_Aid	Database file
2. Lastname Firstname 3K FA Student Update Form	Form (printout or electronic printout - Record 35)
3. Lastname Firstname 3K FA Amount by Award Report	Report (printout or electronic printout - multiple pages)

(Project 3K Financial Aid continues on the next page)

CONTENT-BASED ASSESSMENTS

Performance Level

		Exemplary	Proficient	Developing
Performance Criteria	**Create 3K FA Student Update Form**	Form created with correct fields, new record, footer, and filter in an attractive format.	Form created with no more than two missing elements.	Form created with more than two missing elements.
	Create 3K FA Amount by Award Report	Report created with correct fields, grouped, sorted, and summarized correctly, with groupings kept together in an attractive format.	Report created with no more than two missing elements.	Report created with more than two missing elements.

END | You have completed Project 3K

OUTCOMES-BASED ASSESSMENTS

RUBRIC

The following outcomes-based assessments are *open-ended assessments*. That is, there is no specific correct result; your result will depend on your approach to the information provided. Make *Professional Quality* your goal. Use the following scoring rubric to guide you in *how* to approach the problem and then to evaluate *how well* your approach solves the problem.

The *criteria*—Software Mastery, Content, Format & Layout, and Process—represent the knowledge and skills you have gained that you can apply to solving the problem. The *levels of performance*—Professional Quality, Approaching Professional Quality, or Needs Quality Improvements—help you and your instructor evaluate your result.

	Your completed project is of Professional Quality if you:	Your completed project is Approaching Professional Quality if you:	Your completed project Needs Quality Improvements if you:
1-Software Mastery	Choose and apply the most appropriate skills, tools, and features and identify efficient methods to solve the problem.	Choose and apply some appropriate skills, tools, and features, but not in the most efficient manner.	Choose inappropriate skills, tools, or features, or are inefficient in solving the problem.
2-Content	Construct a solution that is clear and well organized, contains content that is accurate, appropriate to the audience and purpose, and is complete. Provide a solution that contains no errors in spelling, grammar, or style.	Construct a solution in which some components are unclear, poorly organized, inconsistent, or incomplete. Misjudge the needs of the audience. Have some errors in spelling, grammar, or style, but the errors do not detract from comprehension.	Construct a solution that is unclear, incomplete, or poorly organized; contains some inaccurate or inappropriate content; and contains many errors in spelling, grammar, or style. Do not solve the problem.
3-Format & Layout	Format and arrange all elements to communicate information and ideas, clarify function, illustrate relationships, and indicate relative importance.	Apply appropriate format and layout features to some elements, but not others. Overuse features, causing minor distraction.	Apply format and layout that does not communicate information or ideas clearly. Do not use format and layout features to clarify function, illustrate relationships, or indicate relative importance. Use available features excessively, causing distraction.
4-Process	Use an organized approach that integrates planning, development, self-assessment, revision, and reflection.	Demonstrate an organized approach in some areas, but not others; or, use an insufficient process of organization throughout.	Do not use an organized approach to solve the problem.

OUTCOMES-BASED ASSESSMENTS

Apply a combination of the 3A and 3B skills.

GO! Think Project 3L Food Services

PROJECT FILES

For Project 3L, you will need the following file:

a03L_Food_Services

You will save your database as:

Lastname_Firstname_3L_Food_Services

Start Access, navigate to your student data files, open a03L_Food_Services, save the database in your **Access Chapter 3** folder as **Lastname_Firstname_3L_Food_Services** and then enable the content. Using your own name, add **Lastname Firstname** to the beginning of both table names. Luciano Gonzalez, the hospitality director, would like you to create to create an attractive form and a report to assist him with the staff scheduling of food services for a two-day student orientation workshop using the following guidelines:

- The form will be used to update records in the 3L Staff table. Be sure that the Last Name field displays above the First Name field. After the form is created, enter a new record using your own last name and first name with a Staff ID of **STAFF-1119** and a Phone Number of **(512) 555-0845** and a Title of **Server** Create a filter that when toggled on displays the records for staff with a Title of *Server*. Add a footer to the form that displays **Texas Lakes Community College Hospitality Services** Save the form as **Lastname Firstname 3L Staff Update Form** and then create a paper or electronic printout of your record only.

- The report will be used by Mr. Gonzalez to call staff members when the schedule changes. Add a report footer that displays **Texas Lakes Community College Hospitality Services** and then save the report as **Lastname Firstname 3L Staff Phone List** Create a paper or electronic printout as directed.

Open the Navigation Pane, be sure that all object names display fully, and then close Access. As directed, submit your database and the paper or electronic printout of the form and report that are the results of this project. Specifically, in this project, using your own name, you created the following database and printouts or electronic printouts:

1. Lastname_Firstname_3L_Food_Services	Database file
2. Lastname Firstname 3L Staff Update Form	Form (printout or electronic printout - Record 19)
3. Lastname Firstname 3L Staff Phone List	Report (printout or electronic printout)

END | You have completed Project 3L

GO! Think   Project 3M Donor Gifts   Online

Build from Scratch

You and GO!   Project 3N Personal Inventory   Online

Build from Scratch

GO! Cumulative Group Project   Project 3O Bell Orchid Hotels
Online

Glossary

Address bar (Internet Explorer) The area at the top of the Internet Explorer window that displays, and where you can type, a URL—Uniform Resource Locator—which is an address that uniquely identifies a location on the Internet.

Address bar (Windows) The bar at the top of a folder window with which you can navigate to a different folder or library, or to go back to a previous one.

Aggregate functions Calculations such as Min, Max, Avg, and Sum that are performed on a group of records.

Alignment The placement of text or objects relative to the left and right margins.

Alignment guides Green lines that display when you move an object to assist in alignment.

AND condition A compound criteria used to display records that match all parts of the specified criteria.

App The term that commonly refers to computer programs that run from the device software on a smartphone or a tablet computer—for example, iOS, Android, or Windows Phone—or computer programs that run from the browser software on a desktop PC or laptop PC—for example Internet Explorer, Safari, Firefox, or Chrome.

App for Office A webpage that works within one of the Office applications, such as Excel, and that you download from the Office Store.

Append To add on to the end of an object; for example, to add records to the end of an existing table.

Apps for Office 2013 and SharePoint 2013 A collection of downloadable apps that enables you to create and view information within your familiar Office programs.

Ascending order A sorting order that arranges text alphabetically (A to Z) and numbers from the lowest number to the highest number.

AutoNumber data type A data type that describes a unique sequential or random number assigned by Access as each record is entered and that is useful for data that has no distinct field that can be considered unique.

Backstage tabs The area along the left side of Backstage view with tabs to display screens with related groups of commands.

Backstage view A centralized space for file management tasks; for example, opening, saving, printing, publishing, or sharing a file. A navigation pane displays along the left side with tabs that group file-related tasks together.

Best Fit An Access command that adjusts the width of a column to accommodate the column's longest entry.

Between ... And operator A comparison operator that looks for values within a range.

Blank desktop database A database that has no data and has no database tools—you must create the data and tools as you need them; the database is stored on your computer or other storage device.

Bound A term used to describe objects and controls that are based on data that is stored in tables.

Bound control A control that retrieves its data from an underlying table or query; a text box control is an example of a bound control.

Calculated control A control that contains an expression, often a formula or function, that most often summarizes a field that contains numerical data.

Calculated field A field that stores the value of a mathematical operation.

Caption A property setting that displays a name for a field in a table, query, form, or report other than that listed as the field name.

Cascade Delete Related Records A cascade option that enables you to delete a record in a table on the *one* side of the relationship and also delete all of the related records in related tables.

Cascade options Relationship options that enable you to update records in related tables when referential integrity is enforced.

Cascade Update Related Fields A cascade option that enables you to change the data in the primary key field in the table on the *one* side of the relationship and update that change to any fields storing that same data in related tables.

Center alignment The alignment of text or objects that is centered horizontally between the left and right margins.

Click The action of pressing and releasing the left button on a mouse pointing device one time.

Clip art Downloadable predefined graphics available online from Office.com and other sites.

Clipboard A temporary storage area that holds text or graphics that you select and then cut or copy.

Cloud computing Refers to applications and services that are accessed over the Internet, rather than to applications that are installed on your local computer.

Cloud storage Online storage of data so that you can access your data from different places and devices.

Collaborate To work with others as a team in an intellectual endeavor to complete a shared task or to achieve a shared goal.

Commands An instruction to a computer program that causes an action to be carried out.

Common dialog boxes The set of dialog boxes that includes Open, Save, and Save As, which are provided by the Windows programming interface, and which display and operate in all of the Office programs in the same manner.

Common field A field in two or more tables that stores the same data.

Comparison operators Symbols that are used to evaluate data in the field to determine if it is the same (=), greater than (>), less than (<), or in between a range of values as specified by the criteria.

Compound criteria Multiple conditions in a query or filter.

Compressed file A file that has been reduced in size and thus takes up less storage space and can be transferred to other computers quickly.

Compressed folder A folder that has been reduced in size and thus takes up less storage space and can be transferred to other computers quickly; also called a *zipped* folder.

Context menus Menus that display commands and options relevant to the selected text or object; also called *shortcut menus*.

Context-sensitive commands Commands that display on a shortcut menu that relate to the object or text that you right-clicked.

Contextual tabs Tabs that are added to the ribbon automatically when a specific object, such as a picture, is selected, and that contain commands relevant to the selected object.

Control An object on a form or report that displays data or text, performs actions, and lets you view and work with information.

Control layout The grouped arrangement of controls on a form or report; for example, the Stacked layout.

Copy A command that duplicates a selection and places it on the Clipboard.

Criteria Conditions in a query that identify the specific records you are looking for.

Crosstab query A query that uses an aggregate function for data that can be grouped by two types of information and displays the data in a compact, spreadsheet-like format with column headings and row headings.

Currency data type An Access data type that describes monetary values and numeric data that can be used in mathematical calculations involving values with one to four decimal places.

Custom web app A database that you can publish and share with others over the Internet.

Cut A command that removes a selection and places it on the Clipboard.

Data Facts about people, events, things, or ideas.

Data entry The action of entering the data into a record in a database table or form.

Data source The table or tables from which a form, query, or report retrieves its data.

Data type The characteristic that defines the kind of data that can be stored in a field, such as numbers, text, or dates.

Database An organized collection of facts about people, events, things, or ideas related to a specific topic or purpose.

Database management system (DBMS) Database software that controls how related collections of data are stored, organized, retrieved, and secured; also known as a DBMS.

Database template A preformatted database that contains prebuilt tables, queries, forms, and reports that perform a specific task, such as tracking events.

Datasheet view The Access view that displays data organized in columns and rows similar to an Excel worksheet.

Date control A control on a form or report that inserts the current date each time the form or report is opened.

DBMS An acronym for database management system.

Default The term that refers to the current selection or setting that is automatically used by a computer program unless you specify otherwise.

Descending order A sorting order that arranges text in reverse alphabetical order (Z to A) and numbers from the highest number to the lowest number.

Deselect The action of canceling the selection of an object or block of text by clicking outside of the selection.

Design grid The lower area of the query window that displays the design of the query.

Design view The Access view that displays the detailed structure of a query, form, or report; for forms and reports, may be the view in which some tasks must be performed, and only the controls, and not the data, display.

Desktop In Windows, the screen that simulates your work area.

Desktop app The term that commonly refers to a computer program that is installed on your computer and requires a computer operating system like Microsoft Windows or Apple OS to run.

Destination table The table to which you import or append data.

Detail section The section of a form or report that displays the records from the underlying table or query.

Dialog box A small window that contains options for completing a task.

Dialog Box Launcher A small icon that displays to the right of some group names on the ribbon, and which opens a related dialog box or pane providing additional options and commands related to that group.

Document properties Details about a file that describe or identify it, including the title, author name, subject, and keywords that identify the document's topic or contents; also known as *metadata*.

Drag The action of holding down the left mouse button while moving your mouse.

Edit The process of making changes to text or graphics in an Office file.

Ellipsis A set of three dots indicating incompleteness; an ellipsis following a command name indicates that a dialog box will display if you click the command.

Enhanced ScreenTip A ScreenTip that displays more descriptive text than a normal ScreenTip.

Export The process of copying data from one file into another file, such as an Access table into an Excel spreadsheet.

Expression A formula.

Extract To decompress, or pull out, files from a compressed form.

Field A single piece of information that is stored in every record; represented by a column in a database table.

Field list A list of field names in a table.

Field properties Characteristics of a field that control how the field displays and how data can be entered in the field.

File A collection of information stored on a computer under a single name, for example, a Word document or a PowerPoint presentation.

File Explorer The program that displays the files and folders on your computer, and which is at work anytime you are viewing the contents of files and folders in a window.

Fill The inside color of an object.

Filter by Form An Access command that filters the records in a form based on one or more fields, or based on more than one value in the field.

Filter by Selection An Access command that displays only the records that contain the value in the selected field and hides the records that do not contain the value.

Filtering The process of displaying only a portion of the total records (a subset) based on matching specific values to provide a quick answer to a question.

First principle of good database design A principle of good database design stating that data is organized in tables so that there is no redundant data.

Flat database A simple database file that is not related or linked to any other collection of data.

Folder A container in which you store files.

Folder window In Windows, a window that displays the contents of the current folder, library, or device, and contains helpful parts so that you can navigate the Windows file structure.

Font A set of characters with the same design and shape.

Font styles Formatting emphasis such as bold, italic, and underline.

Footer A reserved area for text or graphics that displays at the bottom of each page in a document.

Foreign key The field that is included in the related table so the field can be joined with the primary key in another table for the purpose of creating a relationship.

Form A database object that you can use to enter new records into a table, or to edit, delete, and display existing records in a table.

Form Footer Information at the bottom of the screen in Form view or Layout view that is printed after the last detail section on the last page of a printout.

Form Header Information such as a form's title that displays at the top of the screen in Form view or Layout view and is printed at the top of the first page when records are printed as forms.

Form tool An Access tool that creates a form with a single mouse click, which includes all of the fields from the underlying data source (table or query).

Form view The Access view in which you can view, modify, delete, or add records in a table; but you cannot change the layout or design of the form.

Form Wizard An Access tool that walks you step by step through the creation of a form and that gives you more flexibility in the design, layout, and number of fields in a form.

Formatting The process of establishing the overall appearance of text, graphics, and pages in an Office file—for example, in a Word document.

Formatting marks Characters that display on the screen, but do not print, indicating where the Enter key, the Spacebar, and the Tab key were pressed; also called *nonprinting characters*.

Free/Busy information In the Outlook calendar, one of four indicators—Busy, Free, Tentative, or Out of Office—associated with your availability for a specific date and time.

Gallery An Office feature that displays a list of potential results instead of just the command name.

Gradient fill A fill effect in which one color fades into another.

Group Footer Information printed at the end of each group of records; used to display summary information for the group.

Group Header Information printed at the beginning of each new group of records; for example, the group name.

Group, Sort, and Total pane A pane that displays at the bottom of the screen in which you can control how information is sorted and grouped in a report; provides the most flexibility for adding or modifying groups, sort orders, or totals options on a report.

Groups On the Office ribbon, the sets of related commands that you might need for a specific type of task.

Header A reserved area for text or graphics that displays at the top of each page in a document.

Import The process of copying data from another file, such as a Word table or an Excel workbook, into a separate file, such as an Access database.

Info tab The tab in Backstage view that displays information about the current file.

Information Data that is organized in a useful manner.

Innermost sort field When sorting on multiple fields in Datasheet view, the field that is used for the second level of sorting.

Insertion point A blinking vertical line that indicates where text or graphics will be inserted.

Is Not Null A criteria that searches for fields that are not empty.

Is Null A criteria that searches for fields that are empty.

Join line In the Relationships window, the line joining two tables that visually indicates the common fields and the type of relationship.

Keyboard shortcut A combination of two or more keyboard keys, used to perform a task that would otherwise require a mouse.

KeyTip The letter that displays on a command in the ribbon and that indicates the key you can press to activate the command when keyboard control of the ribbon is activated.

Keywords Custom file properties in the form of words that you associate with a document to give an indication of the document's content; used to help find and organize files. Also called *tags*.

Label control A control on a form or report that contains descriptive information, usually a field name or title.

Landscape orientation A page orientation in which the paper is wider than it is tall.

Layout Options A button that displays when an object is selected and that has commands to choose how the object interacts with surrounding text.

Layout selector A small symbol that displays in the upper left corner of a selected control layout in a form or report that is displayed in Layout view or Design view; used to move or format an entire group of controls.

Layout view The Access view in which you can make changes to a form or report while the object is running—the data from the underlying data source displays.

Link A connection to data in another file.

Live Preview A technology that shows the result of applying an editing or formatting change as you point to possible results—*before* you actually apply it.

Location Any disk drive, folder, or other place in which you can store files and folders.

Logical operators Operators that are used to evaluate data to determine if a condition is met (true) or not met (false). With two criteria, AND requires that both conditions be met and OR requires that either condition be met for a record to display in the query results.

Message Bar The area directly below the ribbon that displays information such as security alerts when there is potentially unsafe, active content in an Office document that you open.

Metadata Details about a file that describe or identify it, including the title, author name, subject, and keywords that identify the document's topic or contents; also known as *document properties*.

Mini toolbar A small toolbar containing frequently used formatting commands that displays as a result of selecting text or objects.

MRU Acronym for *most recently used*, which refers to the state of some commands that retain the characteristic most recently applied; for example, the Font Color button retains the most recently used color until a new color is chosen.

Multiple-items form A form that enables you to display or enter multiple records in a table.

Navigate The process of exploring within the organizing structure of Windows.

Navigation area An area at the bottom of the Access window that indicates the number of records in the table and contains controls in the form of arrows that you click to navigate among the records.

Navigation Pane An area of the Access window that displays and organizes the names of the objects in a database; from here, you open objects for use.

Nonprinting characters Characters that display on the screen, but do not print, indicating where the Enter key, the Spacebar, and the Tab key were pressed; also called *formatting marks*.

Normalization The process of applying design rules and principles to ensure that your database performs as expected.

Notification bar An area at the bottom of an Internet Explorer window that displays information about pending downloads, security issues, add-ons, and other issues related to the operation of your computer.

Number data type An Access data type that describes numbers that might be used in calculations.

Objects The basic parts of a database that you create to store your data and to work with your data; for example, tables, queries, forms, and reports.

Object tab In the object window, a tab that identifies the object and which enables you to make the open object active.

Object window An area of the Access window that displays open objects, such as tables, queries, forms, or reports; by default, each object displays on its own tab.

Office 365 Administrator In Office 365, the person who creates and manages the account, adds new users, sets up the services your organization wants to use, sets permission levels, and manages the SharePoint team sites.

Office Web Apps The free online companions to Microsoft Word, Excel, PowerPoint, Access, and OneNote.

One-to-many relationship A relationship between two tables where one record in the first table corresponds to many records in the second table—the most common type of relationship in Access.

Open dialog box A dialog box from which you can navigate to, and then open on your screen, an existing file that was created in that same program.

Option button In a dialog box, a round button that enables you to make one choice among two or more options.

Options dialog box A dialog box within each Office application where you can select program settings and other options and preferences.

OR condition A compound criteria used to display records that match at least one of the specified criteria.

Outermost sort field When sorting on multiple fields in Datasheet view, the field that is used for the first level of sorting.

Page Footer Information printed at the bottom of every page in a report; most often includes the page number.

Page Header Information printed at the top of every page in a report.

Page number control A control on a form or report that inserts the page numbers when displayed in Print Preview or when printed.

Pane A separate area of a window.

Parameter A value that can be changed.

Paragraph symbol The symbol (¶) that represents the end of a paragraph.

Parameter query A query that prompts you for criteria before running the query.

Paste The action of placing text or objects that have been copied or cut from one location to another location.

Paste Options gallery A gallery of buttons that provides a Live Preview of all the Paste options available in the current context.

Path A sequence of folders that leads to a specific file or folder.

PDF The acronym for Portable Document Format, which is a file format that creates an image that preserves the look of your file; this is a popular format for sending documents electronically because the document will display on most computers.

Point The action of moving your mouse pointer over something on your screen.

Pointer Any symbol that displays on your screen in response to moving your mouse.

Populate The action of filling a database table with records.

Portable Document Format A file format that creates an image that preserves the look of your file, but that cannot be easily changed; a popular format for sending documents electronically, because the document will display on most computers.

Portrait orientation A page orientation in which the paper is taller than it is wide.

Primary key The field in a table that uniquely identifies a record; for example, a Student ID number at a college.

Print Preview A view of a document as it will appear when you print it.

Progress bar In a dialog box or taskbar button, a bar that indicates visually the progress of a task such as a download or file transfer.

Property Sheet A list of characteristics—properties—for fields or controls on a form or report in which you can make precise changes to each property associated with the field or control.

Protected View A security feature in Office 2013 that protects your computer from malicious files by opening them in a restricted environment until you enable them; you might encounter this feature if you open a file from an email or download files from the Internet.

pt The abbreviation for *point*; for example, when referring to a font size.

Query A database object that retrieves specific data from one or more database objects—either tables or other queries—and then, in a single datasheet, displays only the data you specify.

Quick Access Toolbar In an Office program window, the small row of buttons in the upper left corner of the screen from which you can perform frequently used commands.

Read-Only A property assigned to a file that prevents the file from being modified or deleted; it indicates that you cannot save any changes to the displayed document unless you first save it with a new name.

Record All of the categories of data pertaining to one person, place, event, thing, or idea; represented by a row in a database table.

Record selector bar The vertical bar at the left edge of a record when it is displayed in a form that is used to select an entire record.

Record selector box The small box at the left of a record in Datasheet view that, when clicked, selects the entire record.

Record source The tables or queries that provide the underlying data for a form or report.

Redundant In a database, information that is duplicated in a manner that indicates poor database design.

Referential integrity A set of rules that Access uses to ensure that the data between related tables is valid.

Relational database A sophisticated type of database that has multiple collections of data within the file that are related to one another.

Relationship An association that you establish between two tables based on common fields.

Report A database object that summarizes the fields and records from a query or table in an easy-to-read format suitable for printing.

Report Footer Information printed at the bottom of the last page of a report.

Report Header Information printed on the first page of a report; used for logos, titles, and dates.

Report tool An Access tool that creates a report with one mouse click and displays all of the fields and records from the record source that you select.

Report Wizard An Access tool that walks you step by step through the creation of a report and that gives you more flexibility in the design, layout, and number of fields in a report.

Ribbon A user interface in both Office 2013 and File Explorer that groups the commands for performing related tasks on tabs across the upper portion of the program window.

Rich Text Format (RTF) A standard file format that contains text and some formatting such as underline, bold, italic, font sizes, and colors; RTF documents can be opened in many word processing programs and text editors.

Right-click The action of clicking the right mouse button one time.

Run The process in which Access searches the records in the table(s) included in the query design, finds the records that match the specified criteria, and then displays the records in a datasheet; only the fields that have been included in the query design display.

Sans serif font A font design with no lines or extensions on the ends of characters.

ScreenTip A small box that displays useful information when you perform various mouse actions such as pointing to screen elements or dragging.

Scroll bar A vertical or horizontal bar in a window or a pane to assist in bringing an area into view, and which contains a scroll box and scroll arrows.

Scroll box The box in the vertical and horizontal scroll bars that can be dragged to reposition the contents of a window or pane on the screen.

Second principle of good database design A principle stating that appropriate database techniques are used to ensure the accuracy and consistency of data as it is entered into the table.

Section bar In Design view, a gray bar in a form or report that identifies and separates one section from another; used to select the section and to change the size of the section.

Secure environment A system that uses controlled servers to ensure the security and privacy of email, to control the storage and use of information and to protect against the loss of confidential data.

Select query A type of Access query that retrieves (selects) data from one or more tables or queries, displaying the selected data in a datasheet; also known as a simple select query.

Selecting Highlighting, by dragging with your mouse, areas of text or data or graphics, so that the selection can be edited, formatted, copied, or moved.

Serif font A font design that includes small line extensions on the ends of the letters to guide the eye in reading from left to right.

Server A computer that provides services on a network such as an email server or a file server.

SharePoint Collaboration software with which people in an organization can set up team sites to share information, manage documents, and publish reports for others to see.

Short Text data type An Access data type that describes text, a combination of text and numbers, or numbers that are not used in calculations, such as a Postal Code.

Shortcut menu A menu that displays commands and options relevant to the selected text or object; also called a *context menu*.

Simple select query Another name for a select query.

Single-record form A form that enables you to display or enter one record at a time in a table.

Sizing handles Small squares that indicate a picture or object is selected.

SkyDrive Microsoft's free cloud storage for anyone with a free Microsoft account.

Sorting The process of arranging data in a specific order based on the value in a field.

Source file When importing a file, refers to the file being imported.

Split button A button divided into two parts and in which clicking the main part of the button performs a command and clicking the arrow opens a menu with choices.

Stacked layout A control layout format that is similar to a paper form, with label controls placed to the left of each text box control; the controls are grouped together for easy editing.

Start search The search feature in Windows 8 in which, from the Start screen, you can begin to type and by default, Windows 8 searches for apps; you can adjust the search to search for files or settings.

Status bar The area along the lower edge of an Office program window that displays file information on the left and buttons to control how the window looks on the right.

Structure In Access, the underlying design of a table, including field names, data types, descriptions, and field properties.

Style A group of formatting commands, such as font, font size, font color, paragraph alignment, and line spacing that can be applied to a paragraph with one command.

Subdatasheet A format for displaying related records when you click ⊞ next to a record in a table on the *one* side of the relationship.

Subfolder A folder within a folder.

Subset A portion of the total records available.

Synchronization The process of updating computer files that are in two or more locations according to specific rules—also called *syncing*.

Syncing The process of updating computer files that are in two or more locations according to specific rules—also called *synchronization*.

Tab order The order in which the insertion point moves from one field to another in a form when you press the Tab key.

Table A format for information that organizes and presents text and data in columns and rows; the foundation of a database.

Table area The upper area of the query window that displays field lists for the tables that are used in a query.

Tables and Related Views An arrangement in the Navigation Pane that groups objects by the table to which they are related.

Tabs (ribbon) On the Office ribbon, the name of each activity area.

Tags Custom file properties in the form of words that you associate with a document to give an indication of the document's content; used to help find and organize files; also called *keywords*.

Taskbar The area along the lower edge of the desktop that displays buttons representing programs.

Template A preformatted document that you can use as a starting point and then change to suit your needs.

Text box control A bound control on a form or report that displays the data from the underlying table or query.

Text string A sequence of characters.

Theme A predesigned set of colors, fonts, lines, and fill effects that look good together and that can be applied to all of the objects in the database or to individual objects in the database.

Title bar The bar at the top edge of the program window that indicates the name of the current file and the program name.

Toggle button A button that can be turned on by clicking it once, and then turned off by clicking it again.

Toolbar In a folder window, a row of buttons with which you can perform common tasks, such as changing the view of your files and folders or burning files to a CD.

Triple-click The action of clicking the left mouse button three times in rapid succession.

Truncated Refers to data that is cut off or shortened because the field or column is not wide enough to display all of the data or the field size is too small to contain all of the data.

Trust Center An area of Access where you can view the security and privacy settings for your Access installation.

Trusted Documents A security feature in Office that remembers which files you have already enabled; you might encounter this feature if you open a file from an email or download files from the Internet.

Unbound control A control that does not have a source of data, such as the title in a form or report.

Uniform Resource Locator An address that uniquely identifies a location on the Internet.

URL The acronym for Uniform Resource Locator, which is an address that uniquely identifies a location on the Internet.

USB flash drive A small data storage device that plugs into a computer USB port.

Wildcard character In a query, a character that serves as a placeholder for one or more unknown characters in criteria; an asterisk (*) represents one or more unknown characters, and a question mark (?) represents a single unknown character.

Window A rectangular area on a computer screen in which programs and content appear, and which can be moved, resized, minimized, or closed.

Wizard A feature in Microsoft Office that walks you step by step through a process.

XML Paper Specification A Microsoft file format that creates an image of your document and that opens in the XPS viewer.

XPS The acronym for XML Paper Specification—a Microsoft file format that creates an image of your document and that opens in the XPS viewer.

Zipped folder A folder that has been reduced in size and thus takes up less storage space and can be transferred to other computers quickly; also called a *compressed* folder.

Zoom The action of increasing or decreasing the size of the viewing area on the screen.

Index